D0875266

On Innovative Art(ist)s

Also by Richard Kostelanetz

BOOKS AUTHORED

The Theatre of Mixed Means (1968)
Master Minds (1969)
Visual Language (1970)
In the Beginning (1971)
The End of Intelligent Writing (1974)
I Articulations/Short Fictions (1974)
Recyclings, Volume One (1974)
Openings & Closings (1975)
Portraits from Memory (1975)
Constructs (1975)
Numbers: Poems & Stories (1975)
Illuminations (1977)
One Night Stood (1977)
Extrapolate (1975)
Modulations (1975)
Tabula Rasa (1978)
Inexistences (1978)
Wordsand (1978)
Constructs Two (1978)
"The End" Appendix/"The End" Essen-
   tials (1979)
Twenties in the Sixties (1979)
And So Forth (1979)
More Short Fictions (1980)
Metamorphosis in the Arts (1980)
The Old Poetries and the New (1981)
Reincarnations (1981)
Autobiographies (1981)
Arenas/Fields/Pitches/Turfs (1982)
Epiphanies (1983)
American Imaginations (1983)
Recyclings (1984)
Autobiographien New York Berlin (1986)
The Old Fictions and the New (1987)
Prose Pieces/Aftertexts (1987)
The Grants-Fix (1987)
Conversing with Cage (1988)
On Innovative Music(ian)s (1989)
The New Poetries and Some Old (1991)
Politics in the African-American Novel
   (1991)
Solos, Duets, Trios, & Choruses (1991)

BOOKS COAUTHORED & EDITED

The New American Arts (1965)

PORTFOLIOS OF PRINTS

Numbers One (1974)
Word Prints (1975)

VIDEOTAPES

Three Prose Pieces (1975)
Openings & Closings (1975)
Declaration of Independence (1979)
Epiphanies (1980)
Partitions (1986)
Video Writing (1987)
Home Movies Reconsidered (1987)
Two Erotic Videotapes (1988)
Invocations (1988)
Americas' Game (1988)
The Gospels Abridged (1988)
Turfs/Arenas/Fields/Pitches
   (1989)
Kinetic Writings (1989)
Video Strings (1989)
Two Sacred Texts (1989)
Die Evengelien (1989)
Stringsieben (1989)
String Two (1990)
Onomatopoeia (1990)
Kaddish (1991)

HOLOGRAMS

On Holography (1978)
Antitheses (1985)
Hidden Meanings (1987)

FILMS PRODUCED & DIRECTED

Epiphanies (in German, 1983)
   (in English, 1981–92)

FILMS COPRODUCED & CODIRECTED

Constructivist Fictions (1978)
Ein Verlorenes Berlin (1983)
Ett Forlorat Berlin (1984)
A Berlin Lost (1985)
Berlin Perdu (1986)
El Berlin Perdido (1987)
Berlin Sche-Einena Jother (1988)

RETROSPECTIVE EXHIBITIONS

Wordsand (1978)

On Innovative Art(ist)s

Recollections of an Expanding Field

by

Richard Kostelanetz

McFarland & Company, Inc., Publishers

Jefferson, North Carolina, and London

Acknowledgments: The following are original sources for chapters from *On Innovative Art(ist)s*, some of which first appeared in different form: *American Book Review*: "Art/Literature: Wholesale/Retail" (1988), "*Artforum*: Looking 'Critically'" (1988), "Books by 'Artists'" (1983), "Moholy-Nagy Reconsidered" (1986), "The Perils of Preaching to the Converted" (1991), "The Truest Polyartist" (1986); *American Poetry*: parts of "Art Autobiography" (1985); Association of Artist-Run Galleries & Marilyn Belford: "Time & Space Concepts" (1977); *Art & Artists*: "The Opiate of the Intellectuals" (1979); *Art-Rite*: "'Artists' Books'" (1975); *Arts in Society*: parts of "Precursors of Polyartistry" (1968), "The New Arts' Scenes (1970)"; *Ballet Review*: "Artists' Self-Books" (1969); *Bennington Review*: "American Architecture, 1945–65" (1978); *The Book of Predictions*: "The Artistic Explosion" (1980); *Books, U.S.A.* (London): "On the New Arts in America" (1965); *Chronicles*: "Kenneth Clark: Truth in Titling?" (1985); *Commonweal*: "Architectural Criticism?" (1967); *Confrontation*: "My Nonsync, Two-Person Films" (1988); *Contemporary Masterworks* (St. James Press): "James Turrell" (1990), "To End in a Book" (1991); *Denver Quarterly*: "The Cast of American Painting" (1969); Granary Books: "Paul Zelevansky's Trilogy" (1991); *Harper's Bazaar*: "USCO" (copyright © 1967 the Hearst Corporation, reprinted courtesy of *Harper's Bazaar*); Illinois State Museum: parts of "Two Ways of Polyartistry" (1990); *Journal of Art*: parts of "Our Continuing Discovery of Soviet Art" (1990), "Technological Art Reconsidered" (1990), "Two Ways of Polyartistry" (1990), "Waiting for Revisionism" (1991); *Kenyon Review*: "Printout on the New Art" (1968); *Leonardo*: parts of "Art Autobiography" (1985), reprinted by permission of the publisher, copyright © 1986 by I.S.A.S.T.; Lyons, Joan, ed., *Artists' Books: A Critical Anthology and Sourcebook* (Layton, UT: Gibbs Smith, 1985): "Book Art" (1985); *Michigan Quarterly Review*, Fall 1975: "Merce Cunningham" (1973); *New Art Examiner*: "Andy Warhol" (1988), "Donald Kuspit" (1989); *New York Arts Journal*: "Don Celender" (1980); *New York Magazine*: "The End of Art" (1969); *Partisan Review*: "Robert Rauschenberg Conversation" (1968); *Reader's Digest Almanac*: "The New Arts in 1968, 1969, 1971, 1972" (1969–73); *Salmagundi*: "The Risk and Necessity of Artistic Adventurism" (1969); *Span*: "Visionaries in American Painting" (1978); *The Structurist*: parts of "Precursors of Polyartistry" (1969–75), "Protoholographer" (1987); *Sun & Moon*: "Contempoary American Esthetics" (1970); Visual Studies Workshop: "Book Art" (1985); *The World & I* (a publication of the Washington Times Corporation): "Tsaibernetics" (1990); *Z Miscellaneous*: "Autochronology."

British Library Cataloguing-in-Publication data are available

Library of Congress Cataloguing-in-Publication Data

Kostelanetz, Richard.
    On innovative art(ist)s : recollections of an expanding field / by Richard Kostelanetz.
    p.   cm.
    Includes index.
    ISBN 0-89950-641-0 (lib. bdg. : 50# alk. paper) ∞
    1. Art, American.   2. Avant-garde (Aesthetics)—United States—History—20th century.   3. Avant-garde (Aesthetics)—History—20th century.   I. Title.   II. Title: On innovative art.
    N6512.K68   1992
    700'.973'09045—dc20   91-52756
                                                                              CIP

Manufactured in the United States of America

McFarland & Company, Inc., Publishers
Box 611, Jefferson, North Carolina 28640

For Kathy Antrim

Contents

Part III: Positions

Preface

The most important move I ever made in my cultural life was to downtown Manhattan. After graduating from college in 1962, I lived for four years near Columbia University, where I was a graduate student in American history. When I got my M.A., I took leave not only of the academic world but of a wife who stayed behind. I went to live in the East Village, as it was then called, down the street from the Bowery, in an apartment on Fifth Street, both geographically and symbolically very much between avant-garde poetry a few blocks to the northeast and avant-garde visual art a few blocks to the southwest. That was a different land from Columbia's world, with a culture scarcely understood by the people who lived uptown. The rewards of my new residence included not only a different set of friends (and lovers) but a new education. Having written critically about literature, I began to write about visual art, now from a different perspective, with a fresh intimacy and assurance.

Looking back, I see that I have remained loyal to the esthetic of high modernism, with its values of innovation, abstraction, intelligence, and complexity. I am still devoted to the principles of intermedia and the concomitant expansion of the territory of art, all of which are still continuing. The first commitment accounts for why I've resisted "postmodernism" and related fads, which I've come to regard as retrograde, as well as such aberrations as, say, superrealism or expressionism in visual art. The second commitment accounts for why the subjects of my criticism lie often on the edge of the visual arts, as traditionally defined, as well as why they are so different from those featured in the art magazines or in other collections of criticism of recent art. It should not be forgotten that critical ethics include not just taking an opinion different from the common run but selecting different subjects.

What separates critics predisposed to the avant-garde from conservatives is that we prefer art different from what we know, while they prefer art that fulfills convention. A second difference is that the former eventually get around to producing their own creative work, which at its best reflects principles articulated in their criticism. And so just as my poetry and fiction came after my criticism of fiction and poetry, in the wake of my art criticism came visual art, initially with words and then with numbers and lines, first for printed media and later for audio, video, film, and holography. (And it can be observed that my 1985 "Art Autobiography" echoes in several ways my 1968 appreciation of Moholy-Nagy.) The further I moved into creative work, the less interested I became in writing the kinds of disinterested arts history I did in the 1960s; I began instead to write theoretical essays, polemical position papers, often in an autobiographical mode.

By 1974, I moved to a loft farther downtown, in SoHo, an industrially zoned district where, at the time, one needed to be a visual or performing artist to get the variance requisite to living there legally. (When guests would flatter the generous space available for my books, I would necessarily remind them of my visual art also on the walls. As people who did writing only could never pass the accrediting commission, few of them have ever lived here.) I find that much of what I have written about art since then reflects my location as a writer who lives among artists, rather than other literati or, worse, academics. (Indeed, one could do a revelatory essay distinguishing American visual art critics who live among artists — say, Lucy Lippard, Barbara Rose, Harold Rosenberg, Doré Ashton — from those who don't — Hilton Kramer, Donald Kuspit, Selden Rodman, Arthur Danto, among others. And then another essay explaining why this residential distinction is not so relevant in discussing critics of literature or music.)

Had I not moved downtown, I would have been a different person and *On Innovative Art(ist)s*, I'm sure, would have never been written.

As I had recently collected two decades of my critical essays on music, in the wake of earlier collections of essays on poetry (1981), fiction (1987), and poetry again (1991), it seemed appropriate to put together a companion volume of my criticism of visual art. As one theme of these essays (and of my understanding of the recent period of art history) is the expansion of the number of activities accepted within the "art world," it is not surprising that while some of these essays discuss painting and architecture, a few deal with avant-garde performance, others with kinetic sculptures that could also be classified as machines, and yet others with books and literature that reflect the world of visual art. It can also be observed that I have avoided genre categories in organizing the essays, preferring instead the general rubrics of Histories, Individuals, and Positions.

The first practical rule was that this new book would not include any essays reprinted in those earlier collections; it would as well eschew reprinting from previous books of mine wholly about the arts described here — *The Theatre of Mixed Means* (1968; reprinted 1980) and *Metamorphosis in the Arts* (1980).

The acknowledgments show that few of these essays appeared in the familiar art magazines, which I've come to regard as dubious cultural terrain, limited (or should I say riddled) by faddism in their choice of subjects and obfuscations and or flaccidity in their prose. When I began writing criticism, my heroes were those who wrote notices that were substantial enough to be collected into books without any fear of betraying confusion or, worse, transient journalistic opportunism.

Another commitment made at the beginning was to Anglo-American standards of verifiable critical discourse, which is to say a refusal, or reluctance, to write anything that skeptical readers might find blatantly obscure or, heaven forbid, untrue. I would like to think that the variety of original sources for these essays reflects a certain integrity, to use a word that is not so often heard in critical discussion anymore.

I am grateful to many colleagues for supporting my work in an area I was not trained to do; to publishers for letting me reprint work initially done for them; to Laurie Weeks for editing the manuscript; to the dedicatee for keeping me on track; and to McFarland for contracting and producing it.

Richard Kostelanetz, SoHo, New York, 14 May 1991

Part I: Histories

Opposing the older philosophers and scientists who regarded knowledge as a simple, faithful picture of an immediately given reality, they observed in scientific law a considerable part of arbitrary design or convention, and even aesthetic choices — the immense role of hypothesis. A radical empiricism, criticizing a deductive, contemplative approach, gave to the experimental a programmatic value in all fields. — Meyer Schapiro, "The Introduction of Modern Art in America" (1952)

Young artists always move around a lot, but today they are exploring horizontally, their identity comes from their manner of working, not from the look of the work itself. — Max Kozloff, quoted in *Newsweek* (July 20, 1968)

What varies enormously in works of art is the quality of intellectual vision. No amount of technical skill can compensate for the intellectual poverty of artists like.... On the other hand, the unitary vision of a Blake or a Cézanne will go a long way to make up for defects of technique. — Herbert Read, *The Philosophy of Modern Art* (1952)

On the New Arts
in America (1965)
I

The famous "modern break with tradition" has lasted long enough to have produced its own tradition. — Harold Rosenberg, *The Tradition of the New (1959)*

Contemporary art demonstrates that the desire to create new forms and embody new themes, an ethos that has motivated Western artists particularly since the time of Baudelaire, has been and continues to be a prime force influencing artists, critics and audience alike. What prompts modern artists to create works that are distinctly new is, first, a dissatisfaction with what other artists are doing and, second, their truly felt need to engage the evolving spirit of their times. Thus, in the past hundred years, all the important painters, filmmakers, dancers, composers and writers, in Europe and America, have created works that were decisively and propitiously original; in turn, their new styles and/or themes have influenced their artistic successors and, of course, also provided the young with an "old" against which to rebel.

Moreover, history itself seems to be an accomplice of the impulse to create new styles; for with each great historical change in the twentieth century, in America as well as Europe — World War I, the Depression, World War II — an era of art came to an end only to be followed in all arts by styles appreciably different. In this respect, the twentieth century epitomizes art's entire history in which, as the cultural historian Meyer Schapiro has observed, "Important economic and political shifts . . . are often accompanied or followed by shifts in the centers of art and their styles."

In recent years, the twofold processes of social and esthetic change have, I believe, accelerated considerably — instead of passing through an overhauling alteration every fifty or twenty years, the world now seems to be transformed every ten; and contemporary art, with each year, departs more rapidly and radically from the past. This acceleration is a key reason why newness as such has, in recent years, become a more important value in our understanding of art and in art's understanding of itself. Given the influx into art of new ideas and new compositional materials, given a contemporary historical predicament rapidly distinguishing itself from those of the far- and near-past, given the widespread esthetic cross-fertilization that the tradition of the

new produces, one must say that no artist today or tomorrow will be considered significant unless his work either offers an expansion of formal range,
an original reordering of materials within the spectrum of possibility, or a new
perception of the changing esthetic and/or human situation of our time. Thus,
when hypothetically confronted with two recent artworks of equal substance,
most modern artists and critics will usually consider an achieved newness to
be the crucial criterion that distinguishes the competent from the imaginative,
the enjoyable from the invaluable, the acceptable from the brilliant.

For several reasons, then, to understand the overall direction of today's
art and to appreciate the best recent works in Europe and America, an on-
looker cannot depend upon modes of perception and criteria of judgment
based on the past — he will surely wallow in misapprehension and confusion.
Rather, he must slough off esthetic commitments to prior work to gain the
open-minded attitude that initiates a rapport with new art.

II

*What I would describe as realism — the humble subordination of the artist before the
natural phenomenon — is very rare in America.* — Sir Herbert Read, "Some Observations on Art in America."

After many years of cultural isolation, American artists are no longer ex-
empt from the dynamics of European art; for although Americans until 1920
seemed unaffected by European modernist developments (and vice versa),
since that date American culture, in becoming a major contributor to world
art, has assumed many of the characteristics and values of the international
scene, among them a commitment to the tradition of the new. Despite the recent proclamations of conservative and theory-haunted native critics that the
age of revolt has exhausted itself or is stalled in esthetic dead ends, American
artists continue to produce works of dance and literature, cinema and music
that have no precedent in our culture or, sometimes, that of the world. In
sum, they enliven and extend America's participation in the modernist tradition. Moreover, the continuing receptiveness to true originality is affirmed,
on one hand, in statements by the artists themselves — John Barth's and Saul
Bellow's on the recent novel, Edward Albee's on the development of
American theatre, and Merce Cunningham's on the dance — and, on the
other, by the impact that the work of these and other original artists has upon
knowledgeable segments of the American art public.

Though the idea of the tradition of the new spread from its European
origins to America, avant-garde arts in America assume a cast quite different
from those abroad, largely because the isolated working environment of the
experimental American artist both defines his condition and influences the
character of his work. Just as the individual pitted against an indomitable
Nature was a frequent protagonist in nineteenth-century painting and

literature, so, in fact, this same aloof, eccentric, impatient, perhaps Faustian spirit, wrestling with art's limits, inhabits the major American artists. If nearly all European avant-garde artists gravitate toward the culture centers — usually Paris, but often one of several German cities — and develop their originality in an atmosphere of camaraderie and criticism, American artists start their careers as rather isolated figures scattered around the country, out of touch with the centers of established modern art, unapprenticed to recognized masters. Often in their later success they reaffirm the isolation of their youth, as William Faulkner clung to Mississippi, Charles Ives to northwest Connecticut, Robinson Jeffers to his California cliff, and William Carlos Williams to his New Jersey medical practice.

Today, although nearly all the leading figures in the non-literary arts and theatre live in New York, which is the gravitational center of the cultural mainstream that runs from Boston to Philadelphia, only a few were born or educated there (while, in contrast, most of the important critics are A-to-Z New Yorkers). The prime activity in creative literature is widely scattered — John Barth writes about his native eastern shore Maryland from a western Pennsylvania university town; James Wright and Robert Bly live in Minnesota; William Stafford, in Washington; Thomas Pynchon, as a recluse reportedly in Mexico; John Ashbery, in Paris; Vladimir Nabokov and William Burroughs, in Europe and North Africa; and Sylvia Plath, until her death, had been living in England. Also, largely because culture in New York is so diffuse, young artists achieve a kind of isolation there, apart from universities, cliques, alliances of sympathy and promotional establishments. For its first ten years in Manhattan, The Living Theatre was hardly noticed, and Merce Cunningham, who has lived there for twenty years, still suffers the indignity of infrequent New York recitals. In short, the alienation that European artists of the twentieth century "discovered" had, from the start, defined the American cultural condition.

This isolation, in turn, influences the character of our advanced arts; for our archetypal creative artist is the "pathfinder" who leaves, often with naïve motives, the confines of "civilization," a metaphor for conventional, largely European notions of artistic possibility, to explore the uncharted frontier, sometimes achieving a "breakthrough" into esthetic country that Europe has never seen before. America becomes Europe's artistic virgin land, for so many of the compositional ideas that have strongly influenced the organized European avant-gardes, from Edgar Allan Poe's symbolist poetic theory, through Henry James' and Faulkner's fictional techniques to John Cage's notions of aleatory music, have been American in origin. This tradition accounts for why America's greatest representational arts, fiction as well as painting, tend to be more visionary and mythic (penetrating to the hidden essences of life), rather than concrete and realistic (encompassing a wealth of verifiable experience).

In an age when the quest for and response to the new moves artists every-where, what particularly characterizes American explorations is a willingness to pursue esthetic ideas literally, wholeheartedly and unselfconsciously to ulti-mate and unprecedented ends. In a culture where politics at its best is very much the art of the possible, art exemplifies the politics of the impossible. Thus, not until The Living Theatre's production of Kenneth H. Brown's *The Brig* (1963) were the influential, semi-mad ideas of the Frenchman Antonin Artaud's *The Theatre and Its Double* fully realized — ideas which Europeans had pondered over, discussed, reinterpreted and faintly reproduced in the nearly quarter-century since the book's publication. It is similarly appropriate that the most radical experiments at both extremes of the compositional spectrum in music, consciously arbitrary and totally planned, should be attempted by American composers — respectively, Morton Feldman and Milton Babbitt; that the notion of using the products of mass-production for artistic purposes which had remained dormant since constructivism and the prime of Marcel Duchamp should blossom again in the American Pop artists; that the literary tradition of irony should be so inclusively utilized in cinema by Stanley Kubrick in *Dr. Strangelove*; that John Cage should provide a rationale for "composing" a piece consisting of four minutes and thirty-three seconds of sheer silence (though no one has yet claimed its visual analogue, an unadorned sheet of cellophane, as "art"); and that the French idea of absurd literature, which has permeated European theatre, should father a school of fiction unlike any other, anywhere — the absurd novels of Joseph Heller, Thomas Pynchon and John Barth.

Of course, this passion to follow a suggestive idea to its extreme conclu-sion reflects, in general, a certain innocence about fixed ideas — the naïve belief that they can be true and ultimate — but out of this obsession has sprung that peculiarly American tradition of works of art whose originality and imag-inative strength exceed and eventually transform the going notions of artistic appropriateness and possibility. Walt Whitman, Herman Melville, Albert P. Ryder, Charles Ives, William Faulkner, Jackson Pollock, John Cage, D. W. Griffith, and Isadora Duncan all pushed their art into new realms, single-handedly initiating changes that influenced scores of younger artists in America and (but for Ives) Europe.

What the Europeans find so appealing in American art is its seemingly untutored, law-defying, concentrated (rather than broad), somewhat violent imaginative energy. As the American critic Kenneth Rexroth once tellingly characterized the enthusiastic French response to American action painting, "[They] got hold of the wrong catalogue and were under the impression the pictures were painted by Wyatt Earp and Al Capone and Bix Beiderbecke." But Wyatt Earp is an apt metaphor of the American artist, for the optimistic spirit of the frontier lawman — performing old tasks in new ways by taking the laws of form into one's own hands, with little awareness of the tragedy of *hubris* —

still dominates avant-garde American art. Once Europeans can understand and reproduce the Americans' rule-defying, innovations, these techniques often show up, in more secondhand forms, in their own works. Out of Faulkner, for instance, come the cerebral novels of Claude Simon; out of Cage, the systematized chance and indeterminacy of Karlheinz Stockhausen. For another example, the tone-cluster (the sounding of whole blocks of notes simultaneously) was invented by Charles Ives and independently reinvented by Henry Cowell, only to be more shrewdly used by Béla Bartók. (Perhaps this trick, along with John Cage's prepared piano, belongs in the great American tradition of inspired gimmickry.) Indeed, some American artists, such as John Cage and Barnett Newman and, perhaps, Henry Cowell and Ezra Pound, are more important for the original esthetic ideas they propagate than for any single realized work they create.

The origins of this risk-taking individualism probably lie in the singularities of the American experience — in the exploitation of the frontier; in our pervasive belief that man is superior to natural materials and can therefore freely and successfully impose his will upon them; in our basic assumption that in America everything is very possible; in an educational system that encourages from an early age the child's individual initiative; in our related commitment to the obsolescence of parental authority; and, more deeply, in the self-help capitalist ethos that atomizes rather than syndicates a society, coupled with the Protestant inclination for individual revelation that produces so many religious sects and which contrasts with the European Catholic tradition of communal revelation. In America, most of the very important artists, moguls, salvationists, scientists and intellectuals are, particularly early in their careers, inspired independent operators, each stamping his achievement with a highly individualized mark.

Just as capitalism and Protestantism are responsible for both the achievements and disasters of American life, the pioneering stance is paradoxically the source of the key achievements and most disappointing deficiencies in the American artistic experience. On one hand, the American art scene as a whole or the scene in each of the arts is generally not as broadly sophisticated or significant as that in European countries — surely, for instance, neither American theatre nor cinema is one-half as rich as the French. On the other hand, in each American art are works which in crucial respects completely transcend anything in the European arts today — the paintings of Jasper Johns, Robert Rauschenberg and Frank Stella, Jack Smith's *Flaming Creatures*, the fiction of John Barth, the productions of The Living Theatre, the poetry of John Berryman, the dance of Merce Cunningham and the Judson Church movement, the great static spatial conceptions of Stepan Wolpe, Ralph Shapey (particularly *Evocations*) and Earle Brown.

Similarly, the careers of nearly all the greatest American artists are uneven, characterized by sporadic achievements amidst masses of debris, loss or severe diminution of creative talent, sometimes a lack or slowness of recognition, and early decline or death. So many of our most significant novels from *Moby Dick* to *The Sound and the Fury*, from *The Great Gatsby* to *The Sun Also Rises* are written by men about 30 who never do as well again. Charles Ives did little composing after he turned 45; after publishing at 30 his great novel *Call It Sleep*, Henry Roth finished little else. Jackson Pollock, Isadora Duncan, Stephen Crane and Nathanael West all died much too young. H. L. Mencken, much-quoted and perceptive at 45, was unread and irrelevant at 55. In no other major culture did so many major artists voluntarily expatriate themselves, their work usually suffering a falling off; and nowhere else do so many great imaginations, from Griffith to Melville, spend their last years in undeserved obscurity. In an essay on the jazz guitarist Charlie Christian, who died at 23, Ralph Ellison, himself the author of one and only one great novel, noted perceptively, "Jazz, like the country which gave it birth, is fecund in its inventiveness, swift and traumatic in its development, and terribly wasteful of its resources."

Similarly, just as American art reflects the virtues of unsophistication (an originality stemming from a certain kind of innocence), it also embodies the perils of naïveté — a general inability to fashion neat wholes and an obsession in even the best artists with pursuing ideas to ridiculously unsuccessful ends. Charles Ives spent nearly forty-five years thinking about, and many of his last years working on, an unfinished *Universe Symphony* in which, write his biographers Henry and Sidney Cowell, "Several orchestras, with huge conclaves of singing men and women, were to be placed about in valleys, along hillsides, and on mountain tops." Who else but The Living Theatre, for example, would attempt with utter failure a theatrical work constructed on principles of chance. Who else but an American, Kenneth Koch, would produce an interminable poem of such arbitrary meaninglessness as *When the Sun Tries To Go On* (1953). Where else could a composer like La Monte Young claim that his burning of a violin was a piece of music (because it made a noise?) and, like the most backwoods/eccentric preacher, attract a small but vociferous following.

III

For all the inventive arts maintain, as it were, a sympathetic connection between each other, being no more than various expressions of one internal power, modified by different circumstances. — Percy Bysshe Shelley

Along with their commitment to the tradition of the new, most of the new American artists continue the modernist development of noncausal and spatial, rather than syllogistic and narrative-linear, relations — the artwork's basic connections coalesce across space, rather than in immediate, chronological succession — and, thus, of the unhindered exploration of abstract relational possibilities. As the structure of plays and films has become flat, as opposed to the pyramid of classical five-act drama, so painting in recent years, from the color fields of Morris Louis to the geometric designs of Frank Stella, discounts visual depth in favor of flatter, "planar" tensions and interests. Likewise, the best recent literature, from Edward Albee's *Who's Afraid of Virginia Woolf?* to John Berryman's *Dream Songs*, achieves its coherence and makes its points less through sequences of time, as a story in which one thing follows after another, than through space — by repeating images, attitudes, incidents, comments, rituals, fragmented feelings, aspects of character — so that we comprehend the whole by grasping the resonant details spatially, at once. That is, in Kenneth Burke's terms, our developed systems of formal comprehension, of expectations and fulfillments honed on architectonic structures, must be superseded by response systems that are attuned to formal coherence achieved by similarities, if not repetition — spatial systems of expectation and fulfillment. This change is exemplified in the history of dance — contrast ballet with Merce Cunningham — as well as music, where most advanced contemporary composers deemphasize the propulsive movement of harmony, polyphony, melody and accompaniment, concentrating instead upon the possibilities of sound in space, creating complex multilayered spatial forms built on juxtapositions of events and gestures, often abetted by some form of structural repetition.

This shift towards spatial form generally accompanies, but does not determine, other esthetic trends, such as the tendency towards visionary, non-naturalistic styles which focus upon hidden phenomena and metaphysical themes — the function of the artist is rendering the invisible visible — rather than the documenting of social and factual experience. (Thus, much of the greatest nineteeth-century American art is "modern" before its time.) Precisely because these artists reject any commitment to the realities of external subjects to concentrate on purifying the techniques of their art and using "facts" solely for esthetic purposes, esthetic form in some works, particularly in music, becomes by itself the major "content" and the esthetic line distinguishing form from subject is blurred. Just as Merce Cunningham's dances are primarily about the techniques and possibilities of non-referential dance and *The Brig's* subject is as much Artaud's theories of the theatre as it is the violence of contemporary life, so *Dr. Strangelove* is more about the resources of irony in film than the absurdity of contemporary nuclear politics. In a rather convincing explanation of this widespread shift, the brilliant American critic Joseph Frank, in drawing historical trends, perceptively relates it to man's changing attitude towards life around him. When mankind confidently understands his universe, he feels able to present it in depth — seeing experience in various planes — and in time. In contrast, two dimensional form arises, Frank believes, "when the relationship between man and the cosmos is one of disharmony and disequilibrium," and, as in our time, man loses "control over the meaning and purpose of life [especially] amidst the continuing triumphs of science and technics." Another theorist, Marshall McLuhan, in his *Understanding Media*, attributes the rise of discontinuous spatial form to technological development: as the printing press shaped an era of narrative form, so electronic instruments of communication create the age of spatial form. "Electricity," he writes, "ended sequence by making things instant," adding that "the movie medium [represents] a transition from lineal connections to configurations." The physical sciences, too, in the Quantum theory, insist that traditional concepts of linear causality are undemonstrable and irrelevant. In sum, Frank's and McLuhan's analyses complement each other; for both suggest that, although much recent art may not explicitly describe the contemporary world, it cannot help but reflect it.

At the same time that they embody extensions of the modernist tradition, each of the new American arts has rebelled against entrenched hierarchies dominant, in most cases, in the early and middle fifties; for as the era of Universal Threat replaced that of the Cold War, new artists, keyed to a new sensibility, sought to overthrow their artistic stepfathers, often pursuing to unprecedented lengths the impulse to rebel. In cinema, the enemy was that complex of clichés we call Hollywood; in painting, out of the lull that fell over art about 1955 with the decline of what Clement Greenberg christened Painterly Abstraction, arose the new styles of Jasper Johns, Pop Art and others. In theatre, Albee, The Living Theatre's playwrights and others have reacted against the psychology of Tennessee Williams and the sociology of Arthur Miller, while the new novelists conspicuously avoid creating a hero for our time or conducting a search for one. The best contemporary composers, such as Elliott Carter, Stepan Wolpe, Salvatore Martirano and the very young Charles Wuorinen, reject at one extreme the dogmatic chance and formlessness of Cage and his followers and, on the other, European total serialism and American neo-classical developmental styles (of Samuel Barber and the like) for a music that intelligently exploits the entire range of musical possibility. Similarly, the new dance discards conventions of movement and dependence upon an extrinsic subject for a dance of pure form and total possibility of movement. When Merce Cunningham says he wants "to make a space in which anything can happen," the dancer James Waring echoes him with, "I try to get rid of ideas and the Self. I don't like metaphor, or symbolism."

In the same spirit, some artists have endeavored to dismiss the categories of art (and thus of art criticism as well) as irrelevant by fusing two or more arts into a single whole — Rauschenberg's "combines" link painting and sculpture, "happenings" are theatre, music, dance and sometimes painting, *The Connection* and *The Brig* produce an original synthesis of drama and music. Sometimes, the artist's motives in creating combinations are ironic — Max Kozloff likens some happenings to "the Wagnerian dream of synthesis of the art upon which has been superimposed junk culture." Reflecting, more modestly, the same impulse toward cross-fertilization, some artists have taken esthetic ideas from other arts and applied them to their own, producing abstract poetry, chance dance, a serially organized novel, and the like.

As the revolutions got under way, in most of the arts there was a moment of conflict as the old challenged the new — when the new was condemned as "anti-art" and, in turn, the old as decadent and irrelevant; but as soon as the issues were drawn, the younger audience championed the new. Indicatively, all the major young American drama critics were enthusiastic about *The Brig* and, in unison, severely criticized Arthur Miller's *After the Fall*; and the new works in other arts received parallel critical responses. Thus, there is good reason to believe that the audience which enthusiastically supports new works today is comprised of a following considerably different from that which admired the new works of, say, fifteen years ago. All too often, one encounters a devotee of Arthur Miller who detests Albee and The Living Theatre, a fan of Martha Graham who walks out on Merce Cunningham, an aficionado of Hemingway who "can't read" *The Moviegoer* or *Catch-22*, or, even more tellingly, an admirer of the thirties' and forties' Aaron Copland who is put off by his recent, more complex serial works, *Piano Fantasy* (1957) and *Connotations for Orchestra* (1962); for the new works initiate not only a shift in style but also a change in the audience.

Not only do the young seem to comprehend the formal revolutions embodied in Pynchon's *V.* and *The Connection* with an ease that often baffles their elders, they also appear to have a strong sympathy for the content of new art. For instance, the totally negative sensibility — so thoroughly dissentient it finds nothing but the act of truth-telling worthy of loyalty or admiration — which some older critics and, more typically, parents find objectionable, is precisely the quality that the younger generation finds so attractive in *Who's Afraid of Virginia Woolf?* and *Dr. Strangelove*, in Nathanael West (revived in the late fifties to gain popularity in the sixties), the novels of John Barth and Joseph Heller and even the fadnihilism of Terry Southern and Mason Hoffenbergs' *Candy* and knee-jerk-No literary critics such as Dwight Macdonald.

To the young audience, so many of whom since early youth guffawed at the sentimentalities of Hollywood and whose sensibilities were honed on *Mad*, an acute, truly felt nay-saying offers the most immediately satisfactory explanation of their experience.

Coupled to this critical, negative attitude toward life today is an irreverence toward tradition expressed by contemporary artists. Whereas writers and artists of forty years ago would use the technique of quotation, as did T. S. Eliot in *The Waste Land* and Charles Ives in his Second Symphony, largely to weave resonant motifs into their work, almost all quotations in the best recent work function, often comically, as irony. From John Barth whose refer ences to history in *The Sot-Weed Factor* are inverted or ridiculously distorted, to Stanley Kubrick who juxtaposes the quoted Hollywood cliché of the cripple who learns to walk against a thermonuclear explosion, to Jack Smith who in *Flaming Creatures* has transvestites enact stock cinematic situations, to John Cage who indiscriminately mixes quoted noise (sometimes identifiable music) with nondescript sounds, to Kenneth Koch, Arthur L. Kopit, and the Pop artists, all of whom show an affinity with French 'pataphysics ("the science of imaginary [i.e., parody] solutions"), the art of the past, just like the external scene, is considered so ludicrously irrelevant that it is used, in the Eliotic sense, largely as fuel for irony.

As they are unable to speak through the past to the present, so the major recent artists (except for some of the filmmakers and poets, and William Burroughs in his early works) do not employ art as a vehicle for pure self-expression. They believe that art is a craftsman's product, to be put together consciously and critically, often to employ predetermined esthetic and thematic ideas; and that it reflects more upon itself than upon its author or external reality, evoking symbols rather than images of meaning. Therefore, because it resists immediate assimilation, art must be interpreted, often in a multiplicity of ways, before it is truly understood. As the English critic David Sylvester perceptively noted in an essay on Pop art, "Modern artists . . . use art as a form of meditation about art and its relation to reality." In muffling their own voice to speak wholly through the mask of artistic form, often with techniques of irony, these artists do not believe their work can have any extra-esthetic effect upon their audience, repudiating again and perhaps once and for all the heresy that swept over and nearly choked American arts in the 1930s. Quite consistently, then, those recent artists who find artistic examples in the American past, draw from pre-1930s culture—playwrights and poets from Cummings and Eliot, composers from Ives and early Varèse, and painters from Marcel Duchamp (who has lived here nearly fifty years)—thus making themselves heirs to the artistically most fruitful decade in American history, the 1920s.

Most of the revolutions described in these essays started around 1958, and many artists presented their crucial opening or transitional works in the years 1959 and 1960: Elliott Carter's Second String Quartet, Milton Babbitt's *Composition for Tenor and Six Instruments,* Robert Rauschenberg's *Monogram,* Ad Reinhardt's Black Paintings, Barth's *The Sot-Weed Factor,* Albee's *The Zoo Story,* Jack Gelber's *The Connection,* Kenneth Koch's *Ko,* Robert Lowell's *Life Studies* and the first dances of the Judson Church choreographers. Moreover, two of the liveliest and most influential quarterlies of the sixties, *Contact* and *Tulane Drama Review,* published their first issues in 1958. The explanation of this blossoming would seem to lie in two historical changes—one domestic, the other international—in the years just preceding 1959, which probably affected every sensitive American.

By the late fifties, the constrictive forces we call McCarthyism had weakened considerably, reducing the general nervousness over individualized expression and non-conformity that plagued creative Americans in the early fifties. The second event was the rise of Sputnik in October 1957, which, with a variety of other incidents, influenced the change in our attitudes to world politics from *we-they* (i.e., we and Russia), probably the dominant mode of political understanding since the rise of Hitler and the revelations of Nazi atrocities, to *it-us*, "it" being thermonuclear holocaust and "us" *all* the world's peoples. At this time, most of us became aware that the predicament of contemporary man was universal — since all of us could in a few swipes be erased from the earth, we-they distinctions, even in lesser social affairs, became less relevant. One recognized that in a world cemented to peace by a genuine balance of power — an equal capacity to threaten and retaliate — the two major powers are now ultimately more dependent upon a tacit trust in each other than upon faith in their allies. Just as Khrushchev became in 1959 the first Russian supreme leader to set foot in the United States, so in 1960 appeared Herman Kahn's *On Thermonuclear War* which, more than any other book, clarified the new world situation.

In this same vein, much narrative literature of the 1960s, from *Virginia Woolf* through Peter Kass and Ed Emshwiller's movie *Time of the Heathen* to *Catch-22*, refuses to suggest that one person's predicament is less critical than another's. (The exception is that strain of cinema which, in dealing with domestic issues of outsiders and civil rights, finds good reasons for seeing the world as we-they.) These historical forces which produced a shift in moral emphasis, coupled with lack of sympathy for the directions of art in the recent past, led artists, particularly younger ones, to work out new ways of dealing with the formal problems of art and of looking at the reality around them.

Just as world politics seem to be in fast flux in the mid-sixties, with the patterns of authority and loyalty being constantly realigned and an endless series of minor crises continually threatening precarious balances, so the world of American arts is permeated with varied and sprawling activity — energies extending in all directions, numerous schools (with a few members) forming and dissolving, practitioners gaining enthusiastic, but limited and often temporary, followings; so that the scene as a whole resembles, in contrast to the programmed production line around us, a primitive workshop where everyone is off in his own cubbyhole doing his own work. In art, times of flux are times of ferment; and although any final evaluations should be held in abeyance, I would say that the past six years of American art have witnessed an expansion of artistic possibility and of relations within that increased range, as well as numerous works of originality and substance. These years were considerably more fruitful than the preceding half dozen, and tentatively I would say we are passing through a period of a minor renaissance in our culture.

IV

It is hard to hear a new voice, as hard as it is to listen to an unknown language. —
D. H. Lawrence, *Studies in Classic American Literature* (1924)

What separates the practicing critic from the scholar is that while the scholar is the custodian of the defined tradition, the former, aware of the tradition, yet committed to his own intuition for judgments, focuses upon the present. The mark of the true critic becomes his eagerness to face the multiple problems posed by recent art and to understand them as well as he is able. "A critic worthy of the name," in Henri Peyre's words, "must also venture into the danger zone of new works as yet untried, apply on them his ingenious methods of text analysis, discover their relations with the traditional currents in which they will be inserted, but also perceive them in their newness and originality. To refuse this task or to fulfill it with too glaring inadequacy is, in our eyes, tantamount to confessing that the would-be critic is not equipped with the lucidity and the courage which are the primary requisites of his profession." Here Peyre prefigures the challenge that each of the following critics accepted and indicates the scope of understanding the reader may expect of their essays.

To modify Peyre, nonetheless, I would argue that, for many reasons, the task of dealing critically with new work is best handled by the younger critic who, less committed to certain old styles and ideas of how art should function and more attuned to the *Zeitgeist,* is more likely to recognize and explain perceptively the original form and content the new art manifests. In contrast, older critics often exhibit a reluctance to discuss the new. Edmund Wilson, who so shrewdly placed and illuminated the writing of the 1920s, has rarely written on the imaginative literature of the past twenty years; nor have the other major critics of his generation, or even those ten to fifteen years younger than he, rigorously confronted post–World War II writing. Many a younger critic hardly touches upon the very recent scene; for instance, Leslie A. Fiedler, whose essays so brilliantly defined the culture of the fifties, barely mentions the figures of the sixties in a recent book on the "contemporary" scene. And even when they do discuss important recent work, older writers often fail to grasp its distinctive character. Robert Brustein, surely an intelligent critic, in his review of *The Connection*, spoke of it as an extension of naturalistic theatre, using an academic label that only slightly fitted and hardly described the work at hand. A discerning newspaper reviewer, Walter Kerr, dismissed *The Brig* for lacking the dramatic form of conventional theatre, and not so long ago an art critic discussed Jackson Pollock's work as primarily "decorative." In other arts, too, one would not need to comb the sandy wastes too deeply to find critics who are unwilling, or unable, to discuss the present except in terms applicable only to the past.

For these reasons, our greatest books and essays on the recent revolutions in arts are written by men under forty, often thirty-five, and even under thirty. What Stanley Edgar Hyman did at twenty-nine in *The Armed Vision* towards defining the uncharted territory of the recent development of sophisticated criticism, Irving Howe did at thirty-two for *William Faulkner* (1952), Edmund Wilson did at thirty-six for the literature of the twenties in *Axel's Castle* (1931) and H. L. Mencken in his thirties did some fifteen years before Wilson for an earlier new literature. Likewise, some twenty years ago, Alfred Kazin, then in his twenties, defined the recent phase of American prose literature in *On Native Grounds* (1942), and Randall Jarrell, recent American poetry in "The End of the Line" (1942); while Joseph Frank, also in his twenties, wrote, in "Spatial Form in Modern Literature" (1944), one of the seminal essays on the modern sensibility. In the years following, each of these men did excellent work on precontemporary literature, for the coin of critical insight has its other side — the best books on classics and classical problems are written by men over forty.

To accomplish his task, the young critic must first rid himself of constricting prejudices which others, particularly older critics and some contemporary practitioners, will foist on him. These enemies of open-mindedness generally don one of three guises: the conservative, the revisionist, or the saint. The first insists that there are eternal rules for each art and that if an artwork is to be good and to be taken seriously it must conform to these rules. For example, an eminent musicologist, Leonard Meyer, recently complained that chance music is bad because it denies the artist the creative authority he always had in the past and that therefore, purely empirical criticism, which judges chance music solely by how well it sounds, is also wrongheaded because it fails to deal with what Meyer feels is the true issue, the hand of the author's control. Likewise, John Simon, in reviewing a recent collection of John Ashbery's poetry, ruled that since his lines did not read with the coherence of James Dickey's more conventional verse, that his work was not poetry. Again, Mary McCarthy, presaging her own conservative novel, recently wrote that fiction is defined by the interaction of character, that the good novel contains many full characters, and the best novelist is he who creates a wide variety of characters; in practice, these criteria are hardly applicable to the great literature of the twentieth century. Historically, art continues to change, leaving conservative critics behind, their hands clutching bags full of rules.

Distinguishing himself from the reactionary, the revisionist critic accepts the modernist revolutions; but he insists that since they lost their energy yesterday or the day before, now is the time for young artists to stop trying to be new and, instead, capitalize on the advances already made. "What we need now in literature and in the arts," Cecil Hemley wrote in *New World Writing* in 1957, "is a revolt against revolt." He continued, "Half a century of revolution has brought us to the limits of art, by which I mean the radical, ultimate technical limits." Only seven years later, we can say that artists have continued to undermine Mr. Hemley's sense of limits. The point is that there probably are no limits on artistic possibility, just as there are no limits upon the streams of the tradition or combinations of them from which the artist may draw; thus, neither the conservative nor the revisionist positions have any effect upon the working avant-garde artist.

The artists themselves, particularly the avant-garde ones, often propagate the apology of the saint — that holy motives place them above criticism. The creator of art so radically new, so much the vehicle of History, the "saint" claims that no critic for at least ten years, or until the artist's death, could possibly understand his work or, even more foolishly, try to discriminate between his successes and his failures. In suggesting that the final word about the new in art will not be uttered by a critic writing today, the saint has a point. No critic ever has the last word. Nonetheless, the saint's complaint should not discourage first remarks which, one hopes, will induce other critics to set down the second and the third.

Contemporary American
Esthetics (1970)

Aesthetics, or the science of art . . . is only the progressive systematization, always renewed and always renewing, of the problems arising from time to time out of reflection upon art.
— Benedetto Croce, "Aesthetics," *Encyclopaedia Britannica* (1929)

The questions of esthetics are unchanging — the definition of art (as distinct from non-art or sub-art), the function of art, the types of art, the genesis of art, the effects of art, the relation of art to society and history, the criteria of critical evaluation, the processes of perception, and the generic characteristics of superior work. As esthetic thinking deals with properties common yet peculiar to all things called "art," the philosophy of art, in contrast to "criticism," offers statements which are relevant to more than one art, if not fundamental to the arts in general — the presuppositions being, first, that the various arts are more interrelated than not and, second, that common artistic assumptions are more significant than differences in content and materials. Esthetics is, by definition, primarily concerned with "fine art," if not with only the very best art; and although the philosophy of art customarily depends upon the established hierarchies of critical reputation for its choice of individual examples, esthetics provides more foundation for critical practice than the latter offers the former. Concomitant esthetic concerns include the nature of badness and/or vulgarity in art, and the question of whether art is, or should be, primarily the imitation of nature, the expression of self, or wholly the creation of imagination; for these are issues that are most definitively considered with references to all of the arts.

Esthetics is more self-reflective than criticism, as well as more dispassionate about particular art forms or works; for it evinces not only a breadth of interest that is ideally all-encompassing but also an objective distance from individual artists, certain styles, internecine disputes and fluctuating hierarchies of reputation. Different esthetic philosophies emphasize different issues, as their basic choices often, on one hand, reflect prior metaphysical or epistemological assumptions (which may not always be explicit) and, on the other, determine their approach to remaining esthetic issues. Whereas the aim of science is systematic structure, the philosophy of art, even at its finest,

17

is a set of related propositions. Esthetic thinking also tends to be more prescriptive than other branches of philosophy, ethics of course excluded; the American philosopher Charles S. Pierce called esthetics "the basic normative science."

Esthetics has evolved as both a branch of philosophy (that currently has slight eminence within the American academic profession) and a collection of theoretical reflections by artists and critics, both making explicit those encompassing generalizations that are merely implicit in individual works, so that esthetic thought tends to come either from professional philosophers with an interest in art or from artists and critics with aspirations to philosophy. For these reasons, esthetics is not exclusively the domain of self-avowed estheticians, as the epithet is implicitly honorific, characterizing, first, a certain way of thinking about art and, then, a level of both perspective and generalization that distinguishes true esthetic ideas from mere art criticism. Since major theories of art emphasize not just different fundamental questions but different dimensions of artistic practice — the creation of art, say, rather than its perception; or evaluation, rather than generic forms — esthetic philosophies generally do not possess sufficient common touchstones to invite easy comparison with each other. A further presupposition holds that art is a particular kind of discourse, differing from both expository argument and verifiable demonstration; it is best regarded as a second nature, so to speak, which is distinct from primary nature.

The answers to classic esthetic questions change in time, particularly as the success of a persuasive new style in art renders many old answers dubious, if not ludicrous. Everyone familiar with current art would find obsolete the favorite nineteenth-century categories of the sublime, the tragic, the comic and the picturesque, all of which were derived from a theory of literary and artistic kinds. The reason is simply that those qualities, so conspicuous in nineteenth-century work, are just not particularly prominent in recent art. As Benedetto Croce wrote in 1929, "The chief problem of our time, to be overcome by esthetics, is connected with the [current] crisis in art and in judgments upon art produced by the romantic period"; and it is a modern truth that the same art which seemed incomprehensibly innovative to one generation is likely to strike succeeding generations as all too familiar. Indeed, a great change in art, as in our own time, challenges the old esthetic principles and raises a demand for new formulations that bring traditional preoccupations abreast of new experience; one result of every decisive revolution in art should be a comparable revolution in esthetic thinking.

American esthetics between the world wars was focused upon three large themes — the eternal characteristics of realized art, the nature of subjective processes in artistic creation and art's social relevance. The first concern unifies, in retrospective intellectual history, estheticians as otherwise contrary as the neo–Aristotelians, with their emphasis upon the resolution of linear forms, and the New Critics, who claimed to derive esthetic criteria (as well as critical methods) that were valid for all literature and, by implication, for all art too. A statement typical of the time (although its author's principal theory of art as wish fulfillment put him outside of these two schools) was DeWitt H. Parker's assertion, in *The Analysis of Art* (1924), that "the general characteristics of esthetic form" could be reduced to six simple principles: "The principle of organic unity, or unity in variety, as it has been called; the principle of the theme; the principle of thematic variation; balance; the principle of hierarchy; and evolution." Pursuing this concern with unifying structure, Parker followed Aristotle in defining "organic unity [as] the master principle of esthetic form; all the other principles serve it," so that, here and elsewhere, the quest for unifying esthetic principles inspired an emphasis upon internal artistic unities. Even an esthetician-critic as instinctively eccentric as Kenneth Burke made his major theme the insidiously unifying impact of realized artistic forms.

Another school of American esthetics, influenced by the Italian philosopher Benedetto Croce (and to a lesser extent by Henri Bergson), emphasized intuition, as opposed to intellect, in an expressionistic theory of art. This had much in common with yet another theory which was derived from the impact of Freudian psychology upon esthetic thinking — regarding all works as expressions (and, thus, symbolic revelations) of the submerged, nonrational psychic constitution of its creator. However, both the Crocean and the Freudian positions were ultimately neither objective nor systematic enough to forge philosophical statements with more profundity than obvious platitude. And although the Freudian position often informed illuminating literary criticism, its descriptions of creative processes remained too abstract and mechanical — too divorced from the real problems of artistic choice and construction. (The European origins and dissemination of these traditions perhaps explains why Jean-Paul Sartre's esthetics, say, or Theodor Adorno's, seem so similarly abstract and amorphous.) Moreover, the decidedly objectivist, self-effecting character of nearly all contemporary arts, especially since 1959, makes expressionist theories appear even more irrelevant.

It was characteristic of John Dewey, in contrast, to be less concerned with the creation of art, or even with George Santayana's earlier emphasis upon esthetic pleasure, than with the audience's experience of serious art. In his single most influential esthetic text, indicatively entitled *Art as Experience* (1934), Dewey first characterized the pattern of human experience and perception — intrinsically unending, yet full of short-term conclusions. He then defined art's function as the coherent organization of experience, which is to say the creation of conclusions. This definition leads Dewey to suggest that the materials available to art can include anything in the world, and then that any practical or intellectual activity, "provided that it is integrated and moved by its own urge to fulfillment, will have esthetic quality." It follows that all successful art is "clearly conceived and consistently ordered," no matter the quality of the medium's surface; for in true esthetic perception, "a beholder must *create* his own experience." (This emphasis upon the experience of art identified what became known as contextualist esthetics; its primary exponents have been Stephen C. Pepper and Irwin Edman.)

As persuasive as Dewey was in characterizing ideal esthetic experience, his book resembles much of his other philosophy (as well as Emerson's and Thoreau's before him) in casting essentially normative statements in a descriptive, matter-of-fact style. Second, the persuasiveness of his position is somewhat undermined by Dewey's evident ignorance of individual works of art and his equally evident insensitivity to issues of artistic quality. Finally, this emphasis upon the audience's experience becomes outright subjectivism in Curt John Ducasse's eccentric but influential *The Philosophy of Art* (1929), which holds that esthetic value depends upon individual experience and, thus, that works of art cannot be objectively compared to one another. It is scarcely surprising that those philosophers and critics who regard art as the diametric opposite of science should advocate a contrary intellectual methodology as more appropriate to esthetic discussion.

In the decade after the Second World War, no philosophy of art seemed more dominant in America than that expounded by Susanne K. Langer, first in *Philosophy in a New Key* (1942), and then in her most sustained esthetic exposition, *Feeling and Form* (1953). Her theory of art as symbolic representation is indebted to the German philosopher Ernest Cassirer, for symbolism became Langer's "new key" for generating philosophical answers. "The edifice of human knowledge," she wrote in the earlier book, "stands before us, not as a vast collection of sense reports, but as a structure of *facts that are symbols and laws that have their meanings* [italics hers]." The words of human language she regarded as one strain of symbolic activity; the nondiscursive material of the nonliterary arts became another. Both of them, she said, are devoted to "the creation of forms symbolic of human feeling," and a symbol is, in Langer's definition, "any device whereby we are enabled to make an abstraction." Thus, to answer the question of how artistic order is created, Langer suggests that the artist endeavors to create unique symbolic structures, that nonetheless present "semblances" of familiar feelings — a creative process that, as Langer describes it, scarcely draws upon unconscious materials. "The function of art," she writes, "is the symbolic expression not of the artist's actual emotions, but of his knowledge of emotions." If the symbolic presentation is true to the form of a certain feeling, then this formal abstraction will not only give esthetic pleasure by itself; it will also function to instigate that particular feeling in the spectator.

The intellectual achievement of Langer's esthetics is a richly supported theory of art-as-emotion which avoids traditional schemes of expression and individual personality on one hand, and explicit universal myth on the other.

One evident presupposition is that the ulterior meaning of nonlinguistic forms can be universally understood; in truth, however, cultural anthropology documents this last assumption as needlessly naïve — the color white, for instance, suggests to Eskimos feelings quite different from those it inspires in Bushmen. A more critical limitation of Langer's esthetics is the general sense that her ideas best characterize American art that was prominent in the 1930s and 1940s — the representational music of Aaron Copland, the programmatic dance of Martha Graham, the poetry of T. S. Eliot, and post-cubist abstract painting. The sensitive historian of esthetics, Thomas Munro, observed in 1950 that "symbols and symbolism" was then the dominant esthetic concept. (Similarly, one reason for the influence of gestalt psychology at that time was that it rationalized the perception of abstract painting.) Instead, the most significant art since 1960, in America and elsewhere, is by contrast so consciously constructivist and nonreferential that no symbolic translations are intended.

Indeed, a conspicuous lack of contemporary relevance continues to plague nearly all recent writing by American academic estheticians, most of whom appear more concerned with understanding and interpreting classic doctrines, and many of whom let their apparent ignorance of recent art slide into an unashamed hostility that fans the fires of philistinism. Even worse, as the British philosopher Richard Wollheim noted, "The great difficulty in any modern book of esthetics is to find anything to criticize. For by and large what is not unintelligible is truism." Anyone reading academic estheticians in bulk discovers that they rarely confront the major contemporary questions, and, if then, rarely decisively enough; and this general vagueness leads to further platitudinousness in their specific discussions. Perhaps one reason why they continually complain about being misunderstood, even by their professional peers, is that their initial expositions are so frequently unclear. Then too, they often make a point of emphasizing "value" or evaluation (as supposedly untemporal and, thus, a philosophical specialty); but this emphasis, like that upon "beauty," serves in practice to introduce precisely those archaic standards that modernist art tries to surpass. As values, both artistic and humane, do indeed change in time, evaluation remains among the less enlightening approaches to any new art (or to any unfamiliar experience, for that matter). New art, in contrast, customarily denies platitude and previous standards of excellence; it challenges accepted esthetic assumptions (particularly those separating art from non-art); it must be apprehended accurately before it is judged. Similarly, it is extreme works, rather than conventional ones, which prompt esthetic reawakening. With the acceptance of a radically different art comes the need to reinterpret, if not recreate, esthetic philosophy.

The truth is that just as so much consequential contemporary sociology comes from writers outside the official profession, so the esthetic philosophy more appropriate to our time has been forged largely by artists and critics.

This shift in origins comes not without shortcomings, of course. Whereas deductive estheticians tend to presume that their theories are relevant to all art, the artist or critic, customarily working inductively, makes no pretense of moving beyond his primary enthusiasms. Concomitantly, artists and even critics inevitably adopt an approach whose initial scope is much narrower than Langer's, say, or Dewey's; they do not feel the academic obligation to acknowledge prominent previous alternative theories before presenting their own. Indicatively, they find definition more essential than evaluation, and the qualities of "significance" or "interest" more laudatory than, say, "beauty." Thirdly, artists and critics tend to be more intimately familiar with the extreme artistic endeavors that pose the most radical challenges to a de facto philosophy of art. *These* up-to-date, inductive estheticians, at their best, forge generalizations relevant not just to one art but contemporary arts as a whole; and in the sum of their particular perspectives is perhaps a comprehensive esthetic philosophy that, except for minor divergences, would have fairly general contemporary relevance — at least to advanced American art since 1959.

One of the first American books to deal comprehensively, if not prophetically, with distinctively contemporary arts was L. Moholy-Nagy's *Vision in Motion* (1947). Its author, born in Hungary in 1895, became successively a painter and photographer in post–World War I Berlin, a teacher at the Weimar Bauhaus, a filmmaker, a designer, a sculptor, and much else. A refugee from Hitler's Germany, he emigrated first to London and then to Chicago in 1937 to head the New Bauhaus, which later became the Institute of Design (itself subsequently incorporated into the Illinois Institude of Technology). Published just after Moholy-Nagy's premature death in 1946, *Vision in Motion* draws upon its author's incomparably various artistic experience, in order to outline his innovative (and influential) program for artistic education. More importantly, as a participant-observer in the revolutions of modern art, Moholy-Nagy personally understood its radical break with past art; as an intellectual, he acknowledged the need for a new esthetics.

In the unprecedented activities of modern art, he found two encompassing tendencies: kinesis and arts-between-old-arts. The first revolutionary development — art that moves — he traced back to cubism and its innovation of systemic multiple perspective realized within a single plane; so that one change in the visual arts, for instance, was a decisive evolution from "fixed perspective to 'vision in motion' [of] seeing a constantly changing moving field of mutual relationship." This leads, of course, to mobile sculpture (in which Moholy-Nagy himself was a pioneer creator) and even to cinema, where the form of cinematic montage with multiple perspective represents a formally analogous extension of cubism. In all modern art, Moholy-Nagy finds "space-time" or "vision in motion," which he ultimately regards as "a new dynamic and kinetic existence free from the static, fixed framework of the past," and this art demands, in turn, unprecedented kinds of esthetic perception. Moholy-Nagy's generalization is, of course, as perspicacious for contemporary painterly arts as post-ballet modern dance; and the simultaneously multiple perspective of cubistic visual space has formal analogies with, among other phenomena, the aural experience of post–Schoenbergian serial music.

On the second point of arts-between-old-arts, Moholy-Nagy offers a discussion of sculpture, for instance, which acknowledges that an Alexander Calder mobile possessing negligible weight, kinetic form and virtual (imagined) volume is not sculpture in the traditional sense, but something else—a hybrid of sculpture and theater; and recognitions like this lead him to acknowledge an increased diversity of artistic types. A next step is his acceptance of the unprecedented perceptual experiences instigated by the new art forms. Indeed, precisely because his esthetic thinking is so free of a priori limitations (upon artistic forms, or systems of meaning), Moholy-Nagy can offer persuasive rationalizations for freedoms already forged in art. Underlying this acceptance is, nonetheless, a strong sense of the particular integrity and capabilities both of each traditional artistic medium and of each new intermedium as well; so that just as an artist would be ill-advised to do in one form what could better succeed in another, so a critic should not judge a painting or a Calder mobile with criteria more relevant to literature.

To explain the evolution of art, especially stylistic change (which remains the basic evolutionary unit), Moholy-Nagy introduces a theme previously unknown in American esthetics (which has tended to avoid the issues of artistic genesis and transformation). This new kind of sociological explanation, which can be called technological determinism, deals with the impact of crucial machinery upon the creative sensibility. The modern end of the Renaissance mode of representational space, where a scene is portrayed "from an *unchangeable*, fixed point following the rules of the vanishing-point perspective," is attributed to "speeding on the roads and circling in the skies. . . . The man at the wheel sees persons and objects in quick succession, in permanent motion." If technology transforms the sensibilities of both perceivers and creators, it follows that art created after the dissemination of radios and then television would differ from earlier art by reflecting those new technologies. (This theme was to be more prominently developed in the sixties by Marshall McLuhan.)

Moholy-Nagy also regards technology as crucially changing the sum of materials available to artists and thus, in turn, influencing stylistic development. For instance, the innovative design of even something as mundane as a chair reveals an indebtedness to "electricity, the gasoline and diesel engines, the airplanes, motion pictures, color photography, radio, metallurgy, new alloys, plastics, laminated materials. . . ." One obvious extension of this principle holds that electronic sound-generation not only creates an audibly different music but that the mere existence of electronically assisted sound would also affect musical works that are composed entirely by nonelectronic means. In addition, as technology continues to develop new forms, so will art, in turn, reflect new techniques. Extending this sense of history to politics, Moholy-Nagy suggests that changes in creativity and technology — in both mind and matter — must necessarily precede transformations in society.

No American has done more to forge an esthetics for post–World War II advanced art than John Cage, perhaps because no other avant-garde artist or critic has so persistently insisted that radical developments in his own initial specialty — in this case, the composition of music — are generatively relevant to other arts. Typically, those ideas suggesting esthetic respeculation have been scattered through Cage's numerous lectures and interviews, his innumerable conversations both private and public, and the essays and texts he collected into three books of miscellaneous writings — *Silence* (1961), *A Year from Monday* (1967), and *M.* (1973). His esthetic philosophy is also articulated, largely by resonant implication, in his musical works. Cage's purpose could be defined as opening all esthetic activity to creative processes and perceptual experience unknown before; so that he came to regard as most laudable those contemporary works that represent a purposeful violation of old artistic ideas. "Art, if you want a definition of it," he wrote, "is criminal action, because it conforms to no rules." In order to transcend ingrained convention Cage frequently exhibits a dialectical intelligence that asserts that art might be the opposite of everything it once was; yet by making diametrically contrary esthetic statements, Cage thus makes possible a range of intermediate syntheses. For example, if the aim of art was once the fabrication of a presentation that is as various and interesting as possible, Cage proposes creating something with minimal surface variety and little immediate interest, even espousing outright repetition and, thus, boredom as not only perceptually engrossing but fertilely inspiring ("The way to get ideas is to do something boring"):

> In Zen they say: If something is boring after two minutes, try it for four. If still boring, try it for eight, sixteen, thirty-two, and so on. Eventually one discovers that it's not boring but very interesting.

(This concern with repetition to cunning excess is also found in the works of Gertrude Stein, who was probably the most consequential precursor of radical American esthetics.) Cage's ideas have come to rationalize, for both better and worse, all in contemporary art that extends itself in time and space far more than was previously acceptable.

If past art aimed to display an artist's esthetic consciousness and the work's essential organization, Cage advocates the use of procedures that would both minimize the artist's taste and induce structural disorganization. In the case of music this principle informs Cage's invention of the prepared piano, where the strings' original pitches and timbres are radically changed. Cage then devised chance operations for "composing," or writing out a score, so that traditional structures would assuredly be avoided; and then came the use of live-time machines, such as a turned-on radio with spinning dials, so that the sounds emitted could not be predicted in advance. All these rejections of previous constraints also function, intentionally and intelligently, to free artistic creation from personal control and, therefore, the resulting work from both conventions and cliché. It follows that, in sharp contrast to previous composers, Cage intends to avoid giving his performer-collaborators a score that is too specific. He thereby allows them far more freedom of individual action than earlier musicians had. Indeed, he has followed his self-withdrawal logic to this radical esthetic definition: "Art instead of being an object made by one person is a process set in motion by a group of people." This esthetic theme of art as process, rather than product, also had immense influence upon painting and sculpture (even in different styles), as well as dance and intermedia, all through the sixties and seventies.

In the end, Cage favors not artistic improvisation, which depends too much upon acquired habits and, thus, conventions, but artistic indeterminacy — the creation of conditions or ground rules that force artists to work in unusual ways, which are in turn likely to produce unexpected, unpredictable results. Indeed, precisely in his preference for extreme originality and complex *acoherence*, coupled with his contempt for familiar objects and experiences, does Cage himself deny the absolute, indiscriminative license implied by his philosophy. His self-denying principles notwithstanding, Cage in practice usually retains some authority (invariably revealing ingenious and tasteful choices) over the frame of activity, thereby ensuring, paradoxically, an art of *purposeful purposelessness*, as distinct from purposeless purposelessness. Indeed, the key to his artistic intelligence is precisely the imposition of general constraints that allow, if not induce, a paradoxically circumscribed range of specified freedoms.

The artistic result of Cage's strategy of freedom within subtle constraints has usually been fields of disordered activities that are formally beyond collage, which is merely a juxtaposition of several dissimilars. Instead, Cage realizes a far more multiple mélange that is without symbolic references, without a formal center, without distinct beginnings or ends, thus suggesting unfinishedness. He regards such willful disorder as naturalistic — as an "imitation of nature in her manner of operation." More specifically, he initiates an ongoing event that is as formally nonclimactic and internally repetitive as nature herself usually is; and this conclusion explodes the art-life dichotomy, as well as the hierarchical structuring, that were both sacred to traditional esthetics.

Precisely because Cage's ideas rationalized works of art that a previous age (and archaic critics) would have found hopelessly chaotic (or in violation of old rules), he came to insist that audiences accept ordered disorder — in this case, atonal and astructual sound; so that in the course of reflecting the philosophic influence of Zen Buddhism, he asserts that not only must people perceive everything, but we must accept everything we perceive. However, this assertion too remains a dialectical antithesis in Cage's ironically systematic, ironically extreme but highly suggestive esthetics.

It should not be forgotten that the alarm over "disintegration of form" on the part of conservative critics such as Erich Kahler, expressed in his 1969 book of that title, actually indicates their own inability to grasp alternative formal structures (if not an experiential ignorance of what they condemn); for in fact, true formlessness in any created object or experience is impossible. Anything that can be characterized in one way rather than another, as resembling one thing rather than another thing, has, by that act of definition, a perceptible form. In the nonhierarchical evenness or pure formal diffuseness that is characteristic of Cage's own best art is a kind of definable unity that, needless to say, is not emphasized in his philosophy of art.

Another Cagean strategy has been the creation of artworks or events that, though superficially trivial, have great resonance as implied philosophical statements. In his *4'33"* (1952), for instance, an eminent pianist sits at his instrument and makes no audible pianistic sound for four minutes and thirty-three seconds. Nothing happens, in a superficial sense; yet by making no sound in a context where sound is expected, the piece implies that in the "silence" is the work's sound — or more precisely, in all the random, atonal and unstructured ambient noises audibly within the frame of *4'33"* is the "music." Thus, the esthetic point, by inference, is that art consists of all the sensory phenomena that one chooses to perceive. The next inference holds that normal life is rich in art or esthetic experiences that are continually available to the spectator who attunes or focuses his sensory equipment.

Cage's idea of art as anything that generates esthetic experience curiously carries John Dewey's thinking to a logical extreme, as Cage's notions of art as revealing experiential reality and of the beholder as necessarily creating his own experience. In addition, *4'33"* for all of its radicalness reveals a debt to Marcel Duchamp, whose great original idea consisted of imposing, by means of art rather than argument, esthetic value on things that were not initially, or previously, endowned with artistic status.

The radical gesture in Cage's esthetics lies in his justifying the creation and acceptance of perceptual disorder. Somewhat similar concerns inform Morse Peckham's highly original and provocative essay, *Man's Rage for Chaos* (1965), which is indicatively subtitled, *Biology, Behavior, and the Arts*. Drawing upon a scholarly background in English literature and culture history, its author suggests that, though man craves order in his life, esthetic experience "serves to break up orientations, to weaken and frustrate the tyrannous drive to order, to prepare the individual to observe what the orientation tells him is irrelevant, but what may well be highly relevant." In this emphasis upon the individual's experience of art, as well as the method of deducing artistic value from an idealization of perceptual processes, Peckham also resembles John Dewey (who likewise confessed to more interest in behavior than art); but quite contrary to Dewey, who wanted art to provide artistic order for the sake of common experience, Peckham takes the radical tack of advocating artistic disorder on humane grounds. "Art is the reinforcement of the capacity to endure disorientation," his book concludes, "so that man may endure exposing himself to the tensions and problems of the real world. . . . Art is rehearsal for the orientation which makes innovation possible." By implication, then, the new forms of "disordered" art better prepare our perceptual equipment to comprehend the unprecedented structures of contemporary life; but in philosophical contrast to Cage, Peckham advocates disorder with respect to previous art (or conventions), not in imitation of lifelike processes.

Peckham is by training a scholar-critic of literature; Cage, initially a creator of music, who has extended his talents to several arts. Another philosopher of the new art was, at his professional beginnings, a painter who also took degrees in philosophy and art history; so that Allan Kaprow's most important text, *Assemblage, Environments & Happenings* (1966, though first drafted and circulated several years before) exhibits a participant-observer's synthesis of both involvement and distance — and an intelligent awareness of both personal experience and esthetic issues. A sometime composition student of John Cage, Kaprow assimilated his teacher's passion for stretching both the creative imagination and the receptive sensibility. Indicatively, he first became known for advocating, in his essay "The Legacy of Jackson Pollock" (1958), the use of all possible materials and "unheard-of happenings and events" in the processes and preoccupations of painting — a position ultimately traceable to Marcel Duchamp, with a nod to Cage. Kaprow's book outlines an evolution, in part his own, from collaged paintings to assemblages (or three dimensional collage) to environments (or artistically enclosed spaces), and finally to a mixed means performance art that he characterized in retrospect as "a collage of events in certain spans of time and in certain spaces." In short, Kaprow follows Moholy-Nagy in advocating the rejection of conventional barriers between the arts; and like Cage, Kaprow challenges the traditional distinction between art and life. In Kaprow's thinking, the latter position demands, first of all, the strict elimination, in one's artistic practice, of the materials, actions, and themes indigenous to earlier arts:

> A picture, a piece of music, a poem, a drama, each confined within its respective frame, fixed number of measures, stanzas, and stages, however great they may be in their own right, simply will not allow for breaking the barrier between art and life. And this is what the objective is.

Indeed, the new art Kaprow invented, to which he gave the unfortunately catchy name of "a happening," is perhaps the closest that art has yet come to meshing with life (and reducing the psychic distance of traditional esthetic experience), while yet retaining a distinct artistic, nonlife identity. The crucial point for the philosophy of art lay in the fact that a true happening — a performance occurring outside a theatrical setting, completely open (or unfixed) in both time and space, and involving everyone who happens to be within its frame of activity — was by intention as unpredictable, as impermanent, and as changing as life itself. Nonetheless, the endeavor still satisfied an old definition of art as reflecting more or less deliberate operations — in this case, the scenario of roughly outlined activities that the happenings-artist provided in advance to his prospective collaborators.

"At present," Kaprow's book concludes, "any avant-garde is primarily a philosophical quest and a finding of truths, rather than purely an esthetic activity." Thus, whereas Cage offered an esthetic for unpredictability (and the acceptance of happenstance), Kaprow forged instead a philosophy advocating impermanence on one hand, and art independent of any objective forms on the other. "Once, the task of the artist was to make good art," he wrote in a manifesto first published in 1966, "now it is to avoid making art of any kind." What, then, is the "artist" to do? Kaprow's answer was *anything*, regardless of exhibited craftsmanship or permanence, yet with both the intention of uniqueness and the awareness that his or her doings would probably be recognized as artistic endeavor:

> The decision to be an artist thus assumes both the existence of a unique activity and an endless series of deeds which deny it. . . . Anything I say, do, notice, or think, is art — whether or not desired — because everyone else aware of what is occurring today will probably (not possibly) say it is, or think of it as art at some time or other.

Kaprow's ideas, along with such examples of inferential art as Cage's *4'33"*, forge an idealist philosophy of art, which bases significance primarily upon perception and contextual awareness rather than the art object. Several radical implications of this view were suggestively developed by another artist-critic, Michael Kirby, first in *Happenings* (1965), and then in essays, especially "The Aesthetics of the Avant-Garde," that he collected in *The Art of Time* (1969).

The contemporary impact of epistemological empiricism, as well as analytic philosophy, inspires the ideal of a rigorously empirical esthetics. Such a discipline would be capable of clearly distinguishing analytic elucidation from evaluation, and then of making precisely accurate statements which, as a prime criterion of acceptability, could be verified, in roughly similar form, by every equally knowledgeable observer. Of course, such empirical esthetics would become valuable only to the extent that the commentaries of its exponents moved beyond unarguable facts and superficial descriptions to more profound critical illuminations which would, nonetheless, exhibit a logical consistency, a linguistic precision and a verifiable accuracy that were previously unknown in discourse about art. In a retrospective summary, written in 1951, of a program first presented in his earlier essay "Scientific Method in Esthetics" (1928), Thomas Munro championed "a scientific, naturalistic approach to aesthetics: one which should be broadly experimental and empirical, but not limited to quantitative measurement; utilizing the insights of art criticism and philosophy as hypotheses, but deriving objective data from two main sources — the analysis and history of form in the arts, and psychological studies of the production, appreciation, and teaching of the arts." However, as Munro himself is a prodigiously thorough scholar and decisive theorist, his own major contributions have been not a philosophy of art but exhaustive and definitive studies of, first, the categories of artistic endeavor, *The Arts and Their Interrelations* (1949), and then historiographical theories of *Evolution and Art* (1963). (One result of analytic philosophy alone — especially Ludwig Wittgenstein's influence — has been an academic concern with the language of art and literary criticism.)

Among the more eccentrically suggestive, and yet patently unsuccessful American attempts at an empirical theory of artistic value were the foolishly simplistic algebraic formulas that the Harvard mathematician George Birkhoff proposed in his *Aesthetic Measure* (1933): $M = O/C$ where, "within each class of aesthetic objects," M equals esthetic measure, O is order, and C is complexity. However, one problem with this "quantitative index of [art objects'] comparative esthetic effectiveness" is that it offered no empirical methods for specifying the exact degree of each factor in the equation — for verifiably quantifying the components. A second problem with Birkhoff's formula is that it measures unity in variety, which is at best only one of several dimensions of artistic value. Such deductive theorizing, in contrast to the inductive generalizations more appropriate to science, prompted Thomas Munro himself to comment in 1946 that quantitative esthetics so far "has dealt less with works of art than with preferences for various arbitrary, simplified linear shapes, color combinations, and tone-combinations."

Beyond that, the new, post–World War II scientific hypotheses of communication — information theory and cybernetics — both suggest schemes of esthetic understanding. The first, for example, promises a quantitative measure of the experience flowing from a work of art to its receptor — not the content of these transmitted messages, but the size of its channel, the amount of communication precisely measured in "bits," and its quality in terms of essential information versus redundancy. Though several writers — John R. Pierce, Leonard Meyer and Lejaren Hiller among them — have attempted to derive esthetic hypotheses from information theory, no new major philosophy of art has yet emerged. Cybernetics, which emphasizes responsiveness within a closed system, offers ideas less relevant to static art than to that new art form which emerged in the sixties: responsive kinetic environments; but here, too, esthetic theory is more nascent than mature. There is no doubt that a truly persuasive empirical esthetics would represent a great intellectual advance, especially with an artistic generation less eager than its predecessor to rescue art from science; and the result might well supersede previous esthetics much as physics replaced some terrains of metaphysics. While the inadequacies of the forays so far suggest that the procedures used to encapsulate primary physical nature may have little relevance to the artifacts of secondary nature, the philosophy of art probably could profit from emulating the rigor, objectivity, and decisiveness of scientific discourse.

A continuing, but somewhat peripheral, concern of recent American esthetics has been the difference between art and sub-art. The latter is not synonymous with *non-art* or *anti-art*, both of which are by now thought to be historically relative terms (last year's "anti-art" often becoming tomorrow's convention). Rather, the term *sub-art* refers to that kind of commercialized popular or mass art that became prominent in the nineteenth century and, thanks to advertising and mass merchandising, increasingly pervasive in the twentieth. One of the first major analyses of sub-art came from the critic Clement Greenberg (himself an able advocate of modernism in all culture), whose 1939 essay, "Avant-Garde and Kitsch," made decisive distinctions that influenced future esthetic discussion. True arts, in his view, "derive their chief inspiration from the medium they work in" and an awareness of artistic history, while kitsch is subservient both to established artistic formulas and, usually, to the prospect of an imminent sale. Different in intention and intrinsic nature, kitsch and art also vary in effect. Innovative art at first strikes its spectator as puzzling, if not inscrutable, inevitably creating its own audience of admirers, while kitsch exploits stereotyped understanding for a preconditioned public, dealing finally in "the lowest common denominators of experience." In contrast to kitsch, which cultivates the *effects* of art (and often programs an unmistakable response), avant-garde art, as noted already, defines integrity by a capacity for genuine surprise. Greenberg continues, "Avant-garde culture is the imitation of imitating," as "its best artists are artist's artists, its best poets, poet's poets." The difference between kitsch and avant-garde (synonymous in Greenberg's mind with all that remains relevant in contemporary culture) is so great that they have nothing in common beyond cultural ancestry and superficial mediumistic resemblances:

> Kitsch is mechanical and operates by formulas. Kitsch is vicarious experience and faked sensations. Kitsch changes according to style, but remains always the same. Kitsch is the epitome of all that is spurious in the life of our time.

The social origins of kitsch, in Greenberg's view, lie not in capitalism per se, as most "left" critics charged, but in modern industrial society, which on one hand induces mass merchandising of all objects that could be manufactured in unlimited numbers and, on the other, creates the "urban masses" who become the most eager consumers of kitsch. The Soviet Union, he hastens to point out, suffers as much kitsch as the United States.

The issue of mass culture continues to preoccupy many American intellectuals, scarcely a few of whom were also as attuned to genuine art as Greenberg. (Most of them, one suspected, studied tripe because they preferred it to art, or at least found kitsch more susceptible to critical analysis.) Whereas the sociologist customarily studies kitsch's relationship to its audience, esthetic discussion emphasizes its intrinsic nature and purpose; and while critical and moral reasoning could separate one kind of kitsch from another, the esthetic point remained: that kitsch is not art but sub-art. The first real contribution after Greenberg's formulation came from Marshall McLuhan in *The Mechanical Bride*, written during the War but not published until 1951. Here McLuhan examines mass-cultural artifacts with a critical sensibility honed on the close rhetorical analysis of English literature. This approach enabled him to perceive that the representational discontinuity distinguishing modernist painting and literature also characterizes, for example, the newspaper's front page with its discontinuous field of unrelated articles, oversized headlines, and occasional captioned pictures:

> It is on its technical and mechanical side that the front page is linked to the techniques of modern science and art. Discontinuity is in different ways a basic concept of both quantum and relativity physics. . . . Notoriously, it is the visual technique of Picasso, the literary technique of James Joyce.

The Mechanical Bride broached two esthetic themes that McLuhan developed more prominently in his later works: that this discontinuity reflects the impact of electronic information technology (such as, in the example at hand, the wire news service) and that, differences in quality notwithstanding, "the great work of a period has much in common with the poorest work." All this insight into mass culture does not prevent McLuhan from proposing a necessary measure for distinguishing art from kitsch. "How heavy a demand does it make on the intelligence? How inclusive a consciousness does it focus?" (The "pop" paintings of the sixties, it should be noted, do not invalidate this distinction; for though the artist may have appropriated subject matter drawn from kitsch, the best works turn this mundane material to highly sophisticated and uncommon ends.)

Nothing indicates more conclusively the obsolescence of traditional esthetics than the irrelevance of its favorite terms; and as such earlier phrases as "beauty" and "aesthetic distance" lose their currency, the times become ripe for a new esthetic philosophy. Much of this opportunity has been assumed, albeit circuitously, by artists and critics; so that by now, at least in America, a substantial intellectual structure can inform intuitive and/or sensory sympathy for the new art. The result has been a perceptual emphasis that ultimately underscores a highly idealist (and almost solipsistic) philosophy of art, which encompasses such radical propositions as Marshall McLuhan's "Art is anything you [the artist] can get away with," and Cage's hypothesis that art is anywhere and everywhere that the spectator wishes to perceive it. ("Theater takes place all the time, wherever one is. And Art simply facilitates persuading one this is the case.")

The new esthetics has, it is true, won more acceptance from artists than literary people, but the revolutions of modernism have always first occurred in the nonliterary arts. Nonetheless, ignorance of these ideas, like responses proclaiming "hoax" and/or "not art," will usually serve to identify a commentator as fundamentally philistine, no matter how well "educated" he superficially seems. Only this new esthetics, rather than an older one, can assimilate the artistic innovations of the past two decades — not just mixed-means events, artistic machines, and kinetic environments, but also conceptual art, experimental literature, and works revealing the impact of new technologies of mental change. Contemporary art is, in truth, "the only art we have"; and as it continually changes, so there is an unending need for an esthetic philosophy that is, as Croce put it, "always renewed and always renewing."

American Architecture, 1945-65 (1978)

There was no room in such a tradition for diffuseness, there were no resources to spare for the ornate, and it was merely sound sense to design a thing as economically as one could. But in the United States these qualities seem to have become especially characteristic. —John A. Kouwenhoven, *Made in America* (1962)

Architecture is art and science and industry simultaneously; so that an architect's work forges an uneasy path between esthetic ideals and real materials, between spiritual and technical values and such hazards as building codes and unions—among, in short, the demands of commerce, construction, and criticism. A further anomaly is that buildings are often made beautiful for commercial reasons—so units within them will sell or rent at higher rates, or the work as a whole will bestow free publicity upon the client's brand name (Seagram's in New York, for instance): and beauty sometimes comes at the expense of structural quality and creaturely comfort. In a critical history of architecture, the major dividing issue pits beauty against use (since commerce, by definition, is beneath evaluative criticism); and this distinction raises in turn two completely different sets of rationales—one typified in American thought by William James, the other by Thorstein Veblen. As Wayne Andrews draws this useful distinction, in his *Architecture, Ambition and Americans* (1955), the Jamesian believes that a beautiful building will enhance the lives of all who dwell within and around it, as elegant architecture does elegant people make; the Veblenian position argues that since a building's usefulness as a human habitat is primary, technical efficiency and humane considerations create architectural quality and perhaps a certain kind of beauty.

From this distinction also follow two completely different kinds of criticism—the formalist and the functionalist, the former emphasizing esthetic qualities and perceptions, the latter social relevance and habitational experience. Pure formalism would acknowledge, for instance, that designs are added to a structural frame to evoke an esthetic response, while the functionalist accepts only those shapes derived from internal structure. If the latter school of criticism analyzes buildings as primarily "machines built for living in," in Le Corbusier's classic phrase (though he was not himself a hard-line functionalist), the formalist critic is concerned with esthetic properties peculiar to buildings—not only the sculptural qualities evoked by three-dimensional volumes, but also the esthetic character of the space (the "artistic environment," so to speak) surrounding a man inside the edifice. Needless to say, such judgments of architecture's esthetic attributes, particularly its internal environmental qualities, can only be made by direct experience of the building itself; yet the outlines of an empathic description can be gleaned from secondary sources alone. Until better means of three-dimensional reproduction are invented, the most convenient secondhand evidence of a work's particular qualities will remain prose description accompanied by documentary illustration. (Most architectural photographs, however, are taken from straight ahead on a clear and sunny day, thus making the gleaming front, which represents the building at its prettiest, stand for the entire structure—a custom that inspired the historian James Marston Fitch to quip that, "The development of the photograph is the worst thing that ever happened to architecture." Moreover, architecture can scarcely be comprehended from a single frontal view alone.) The formalist position regards individual buildings as the end product of stylistic ideas, as distinct from, say, structural principles or environmental intentions; and another definition of "style" would be visual form that does not derive from structural necessity. Style and structure are not necessarily opposed in architecture, but the evidence suggests that the more formally inventive the architect, the less attention is he likely to pay to the needs of human habitation.

The achievements of today's architecture notwithstanding, one gets general impressions that many contemporary architects often characterize their work or aims with grandiose statements which have little general truth and/or relevance to their work; that most practitioners paying homage to Louis Sullivan's adage of "form follows function" reveal in their buildings more concern with form than function, the functionalist rhetoric masking, so to speak, a design mentality; and that the functional achievements that architects and formalist critics acclaim in beautiful buildings often turn out, after closer examination of the work itself and/or the people customarily using it, to be largely fictitious. Finally, the dominant post–War stylistic persuasions were rather clearly established at the beginning of the period; so that not only did most new formalistic architecture reflect, albeit eclectically, identifiable sources, but even the most adventurous young innovators built within discernible traditions.

The major revolution in architecture between the world wars was called "The International Style," which was spawned mostly in Germany, at the Bauhaus, an art school headed at different times by two masters of the mode, Walter Gropius and Ludwig Mies van der Rohe. The International Style, also known as "The Functionalist Style" or "The Machine Style," stood for six general principles: the marriage of art and the latest technology; the geometric constructivist style whose "streamlining" symbolized the spirit of the machines more than intrinsic technological quality; the building as a volume, rather than a mass (and thus the penchant for glass walls that visually denied the building's massive weight); a rejection of axial symmetry, as in classic cathedrals, in favor of non-centered, asymmetrical regularity, as epitomized by, say, rows of glass walls; the practice of making opposite sides, if not all four sides, resemble each other so that, formally at least, the building has no obvious "front" or "back"; and finally a scrupulous absence of surface ornament. For these reasons, buildings cast in the International Style suggest no-nonsense efficiency and economy, if not a physical environment consonant with both modern technology and bureaucratic ideals, all tempered by geometric grandeur and numerous subtle visual effects produced, for instance, by colors in the glass, or intersecting lines and planes. Technological rhetoric notwithstanding, however, the impact was finally more Jamesian than Veblenian.

Between the Wars, the International Style became the dominant minority viewpoint — much discussed, admired and publicized, even though the attractive ideas were rarely translated into buildings. With the post–World War II construction boom, however, its geometric severity came to signify modernism around the world, as disciples of the Bauhaus constructed a family of related buildings in all the European countries, as well as Latin America and Asia. Particularly among U.S. corporations, forever in competition with one another, glassy geometric skyscrapers became the symbol (or advertisement) of contemporaneity. Gropius and Mies had both immigrated to America in the late thirties, each quickly assuming the chief position in architectural schools at, respectively, Harvard and Chicago's Armour Institute (later to become I.I.T.); and the Bauhaus heritage received the best kind of publicity, ranging from newspaper articles to such highly influential texts as Sigfried Giedion's *Space, Time and Architecture* (1941). By the fifties, the International Style and its descendants had become the dominant new architecture in America, less through the example of the masters than the profligacy of the epigones. While Gropius remained more of an influence than a practitioner (even as a founding elder of the multi-member Architects' Collaborative in Boston), Mies designed at least two post–World War II masterpieces — Crown Hall (1956) on his own campus, and the Seagram Building (1958), generally considered the most elegant of New York City's new skyscrapers. Mies's earliest American publicist, Philip Johnson, coauthor of the first study of *The International Style* (1932), obtained his own architectural credentials after the War and swiftly made his mark with numerous very beauty-conscious but stylistically derivative private homes; in contrast, Eero Saarinen, the son of an accomplished modernist architect and a sometime student of Mies, extended to exhaustion, in such works as the General Motors Technical Center

(1948–56) in Detroit, the post–Bauhaus principles of endlessly repeated glass-fronted grids. (Saarinen's reputation was redeemed somewhat by several posthumously completed edifices, especially the TWA terminal at New York's JFK [né Idlewild] Airport [1962], their sloping roofs echoing Matthew Nowicki's truly innovative [and similarly posthumous] stock pavilion [1953] in Raleigh, N.C.) Johnson and the younger Saarinen were probably the two most influential individual architects during the fifties, when, however, this International Style was most popularized, if not trivialized, by the American firm of Skidmore, Owings, and Merrill, whose numerous slick and sleek glass-and-metal boxes (usually more symmetrical than Mies' masterpieces, as well as more hoggish of their land) functioned inadvertently to inspire by the sixties a fairly general critical interest in modernistic alternatives.

The other primary American tradition grew from Frank Lloyd Wright, who created his first innovative buildings several years before Gropius and Mies even commenced their careers; and though Wright turned 70 in 1939; he lived to 1959, becoming more ambitious, if not visionary, with age. From the beginning, he regarded architecture less theoretically, or with less rationalistic theories, than the other modernists; and possessed of an expressive personality, he made buildings that invariably reflected his prejudices and identifiable personal values. His posthumously completed masterpiece, the windowless Solomon Guggenheim Museum in New York City (1959), at once repudiated the International Style's idea of urban architecture, served as an awkward showcase for most works of painting and sculpture, conquered ventilation problems that typically plagued other museums, constantly impressed its peculiarities upon everyone within it, and attained sculptural qualities by climaxing earlier Wrightian penchants for spirals and inverted ziggurats. The Guggenheim Museum scarcely represents an innovation in Wright's thinking, based, as it is, upon sketches made many years before; but as a masterful architectural work, it had an immense impact, especially as a critical alternative to the International Style.

Actually, the keystone in Wright's architectural philosophy was organicism, or successfully relating a structure to both its intrinsic purposes and the surrounding environment so that "inside" and "outside" blend into each other.

> Thus environment and building are one [he wrote in *A Testament* (1957)]. Planting the grounds around the building on the site as well as adorning the building take on a new importance as they become features harmonious with the space-within-to-be-lived-in. Site, structure, furnishing — decoration too, planting as well — all these become as one in organic architecture.

Especially in his private homes, such as the legendary Falling Water (1936) in Pennsylvania, his works melted into their landscapes and looked as though they *belonged* precisely where they were set. Officially, Wright had no disciples, as, unlike Mies and Gropius, he did not run a degree-granting school; however, several younger architects who passed through his tutelage extended his organicist ideas. Bruce Goff, born in Alton, Kansas, in 1904, has built numerous houses in the middle and far west that closely blend structure into environment. His masterpiece, the Baringer House (1950) in Norman, Oklahoma, has a 96-foot wall that follows a spiral into the living space and ultimately around a pole from which the entire roof, interior stairway and living areas are suspended, while plants inside the structure duplicate those outside; so that the environment literally flows into the home, or vice versa. Paolo Soleri, born (1919) and educated in Italy, but long resident in Arizona, has built several houses embedded in the desert (an advantage in heat protection), as well as designing, since 1948, a hypothetical but conceptually impressive "Mesa City" for two million people on fifty-five thousand acres, to be constructed in similar climate. The truth is that Wright himself and the neo–Wrightians function best not in cities but rural settings; and their stylistic ideas usually succeed best when the surrounding landscape has a particular character.

Most of the other American formalistic innovators did not suffer the Bauhaus, or post–Bauhaus training; or if, like Bertrand Goldberg, they did, it was decades before their innovative masterpieces arrived. Goldberg, for instance, left Harvard in the early thirties to study at the Dessau Bauhaus; but not until the late fifties, in his Marina City (1959) in Chicago, did his work achieve a breakthrough. The innovations here mix structural practicalities with an unusual design resembling a stacked pancake, so that the two similar skyscrapers fit into only three downtown acres. As the lower floors are devoted to stores and then parking lots connected by rams, the private apartments are set on the upper floors, enabling all of them to command a fairly clear view of the city. Second, developing a Wrightian idea, Goldberg has the apartments project and expand outwards from a narrow elevator and utility core in the form of undulating vertical rows that resemble the corn on a cob; so that the major rooms all have outside exposure — a practical advantage indebted to the building's unusual shape.

Louis Kahn descended from rather conventional American-Parisian "Beaux-Arts" sources. Not until he passed his fiftieth year, in the early fifties, did he get commissions encouraging him to do architecture that commanded the attention of his peers. His first major work, the Art Gallery at Yale University, displayed a taste for revealing the heavy structure of the building — the pillars as pillars, the materials as materials, as well as an emphasis on vertical lines that was then very unusual. This vertical dominance, which inevitably incorporates classical allusions, was elaborated in the sprawling Unitarian Church (1962) in Rochester, New York, and the Richards Medical Research Center (1961) in Philadelphia. This last building, generally acknowledged as Kahn's masterpiece (and perhaps the single most imitated work of the decade), has unadorned rectangular columns protruding from heavily windowed walls and towering above the roof of the building. Within the Richards Center, the walls remain unpainted, pipes and ducts are exposed (creating in practice, however, a noise problem), and the windows lack curtains (bringing excessive heat and sunlight to the laboratories facing south). Technical deficiencies notwithstanding, Kahn's imposing and unpretty structures successfully established one alternative within and yet beyond the declining International Style; and it is indicative that Philip Johnson, an opportunist in his eclecticism, chose to emphasize unadorned towers in the Henry L. Moses Research Institute (1965) at New York's Montefiore Hospital.

With the established styles so well defined, the time would seem ripe for the young and wayward; yet so entrenched were the older persuasions that stylistic leaps during the postwar decades were few and usually modest. Several stunning-looking private homes by John M. Johanson, for instance, display a penchant for unusual technical solutions and striking detail, generally informed by a strong, Corbusian sculptural sense, all of which have yet to become a communicable style. Indicatively, when a touted young architect teaching at Yale, Robert Venturi, wrote a dense, allusive polemic on behalf of *Complexity and Contradiction in Architecture* (1966), he meant nothing more radical than transcending Bauhaus simplicities and regularities, as well as perhaps more humbly acknowledging the surrounding styles.

R. Buckminster Fuller is an entirely different kind of architect—a pure Veblenian so different from those already discussed that talk about his achievements requires a different critical language; like other older architects—Wright, Mies and Gropius—Fuller belongs to pre–World War II cultural history as well as postwar. Unlike the others, however, Fuller had to pass his fiftieth birthday (1945) before his pet ideas, mostly formulated many years before, were realized and his sixtieth before his significance became widely recognized. (That he is one of the seminal minds of the era, if not of all American history, is an opinion no longer questioned; so it is hard to believe that not too long ago otherwise "intellectual" people were unfamiliar with his thought.) Fuller's architectural proposals predate his social philosophy; but both incorporate three fundamental ideas first developed and expressed in the late twenties: (1) The dymaxion principle, which is the maximalization of dynamic performance, usually measured per pound of structure, whether in an automobile, an airplane, or a house—an idea related to industrial ephemeralization which is the achievement of increasingly *more* results from increasingly *less* materials. (2) The practical advantages of mass production, so that houses could be assembled more economically on a factory-line, like automobiles or airplanes, rather than, then as now, inefficiently produced on their final resting spot by scores of unrelated craftsmen. (3) The universal applicability of all architectural solutions. Precisely because Fuller came to architecture from some education in engineering and experience in a construction-materials business, his designs lack discernible stylistic antecedents (and the realization of his projects necessitates an architecturally accredited collaborator). Rather than consciously reject "one-of-a-kind" housing or even "The International Style" as "too visual," as some critics have it, Fuller simply established his architectural position from another direction entirely.

His first noted structural innovation was the Dymaxion House (1927) in which a circular multiroom area fifty feet in diameter is suspended by cable from a central unit, forty feet high, that can be set into the ground anywhere on earth. The living space is partitioned into several rooms while the volume between its floor and the ground can be curtained and filled to the owner's taste, its most likely use being an indoor parking space. Above the house is an open-air landing partially shaded from the sun by a suspended roof. Internal innovations include numerous labor-saving devices, several technologies to minimize the use of piped-in water (such as a recirculating shower), and (in certain versions) rotary generators for converting random wind energy into auxiliary power. A larger version of the same general structural scheme was a ten-deck building that, in spite of its weight of forty-five tons, Fuller envisioned as deliverable by dirigible.

> Architects have tended to see the problem of shelter as one, simply, of creating more elegant spatial experiences, whereas Fuller has seen it as one of creating more and better-serviced volumes of habitation [writes the British critic Reyner Banham]. That is why the Dymaxion House project of 1927 . . . was a design that could have delivered what the other [architects] promised but could not produce, a radically new environment for domestic living.

Another early application of the dymaxion principle was a 1933 automobile that saved gasoline, better exploited the spatial area available to a private road vehicle, turned on a near-radius, etc., until one of the three prototypes got into an unfortunate accident that destroyed its public future.

The Dymaxion House also never progressed beyond its model form; but by extending its compositional principles to just parts of a house, Fuller produced in 1937 a model bathroom that, since it has fewer parts than the current version, could be put together in a single manufacturing process and, in 1940, an entire utility core that, if mass-produced, could then be moved into preexistent shelters. Both proposals offered industrial opportunities that were considered but, alas, not pursued. Fuller's first real commercial chance came after the War, with the Wichita House—a circular aluminum shell-plus-utility-core built closer to the ground than its one-family predecessor, designed to be mass produced at six thousand five hundred dollars, if not less. It was commonly anticipated that the airplane industry, demobilizing from the war, would turn its technological capabilities to mass housing; but since this expectation proved unfounded, many orders went unfilled. Indeed, though several companies have since been formed to mass-produce private dymaxion houses and utility cores, it still remains more a proposal for universal housing than an achievement. (Some formalist critics blamed this commercial failure on the domes' supposedly unsightly appearance; but a more likely explanation is the threat they represent to the featherbedding practices of the building industry.)

The commercial failure of the Wichita House drove Fuller into another contemplative period from which he emerged with a new proposal for spanning large spaces. With his standing bias of more for less, Fuller suggested that distances commonly bridged by cables or girders should instead be spanned by a network of three-dimensional triangles (actually, tetrahedrons) often built up into larger tetrahedrons; for Fuller's innovative truth, strangely not recognized by earlier builders, was that the tetrahedron better distributes weight and tension than the rectangular shapes traditionally favored. (Indeed, Fuller's own lectures often include a demonstration that tetrahedrons made of extremely flimsy framing materials, such as bamboo shoots, were capable of supporting surprisingly large amounts of weight.) The best overall form for these tetrahedrons was the "geodesic" dome (stylistically connecting them to Fuller's earlier work), and he claimed that his "tensegrity" structural principles could span spaces of unlimited diameters with unprecedentedly light structures, exemplifying the earlier principle of high performance per pound. (These problems of prefabrication and modular construction also concerned the German-American engineer and sometimes partner of Gropius — Konrad Wachsmann, whose results, especially his "General Panel System," were useful, though less spectacular than Fuller's.)

The first large-scale realization of Fuller's innovation came in 1953, when the Ford Motor Company commissioned a 93-foot rotunda for its Detroit plant; and the following year the U.S. Marine Corps solicited Fuller's advice on mobile shelters. The latter group subsequently adopted a sequence of domes, ranging in size from fifty-five feet in diameter to be delivered by helicopter to a fifteen-foot surrogate tent made of cardboard, all of which could be quickly assembled without expert labor. Called the "Kleenex House," this last envelope for things and people had "one-third the weight of a tent, cost one-fifteenth as much, used less than ten dollars' worth of materials, and packed into a small box." In short, it epitomized the three principles of dymaxion performance, mass production and universal applicability.

As the larger domes began to cover yet greater spaces, Fuller's structures began to assume a peculiar kind of beauty — surely Veblenian at base and yet with Jamesian touches. The Climatron (1960) in St. Louis's Botanical Gardens, a controlled environment housed beneath a Fuller hemisphere 175 feet in diameter, made an elegant universe of lush nature cut off from a larger urban world; and the newly complete sphere over 200 feet in diameter built for Expo '67 in Montreal had an extraordinary grandeur that was surely Jamesian, particularly since the lucite skin changed color in response to the outside climate and the multi-layered interior afforded views from various perspectives. Fuller's domes function to preserve the classic distinction between inside and outside; yet the bigger the dome becomes, the less relevant to felt experience does the old division become. The identical domes built for the Union Tank Car Company at both Baton Rouge, Louisiana (1958) and Wood River, Illinois (1959) span 384 feet, and cover 2½ acres with a steel skin less than ⅛″ thick — an efficiency rate that John McHale estimates as "roughly two ounces of structural weight per cubic foot enclosed." By the early sixties Fuller proposed putting domes miles in diameter over whole cities or neighborhoods — the one proposed for midtown Manhattan would weigh 80,000 tons and cost two hundred million dollars. "It is believed," writes McHale, "that the savings to the city in such items as air-conditioning (dome provides its own natural circulation), street-cleaning, snow removal, and lost man-hours from colds and other respiratory ailments would soon repay initial investment." (Proposals like this extend "architecture" into community planning.)

It was Fuller's singular achivement to extend brilliantly a peculiarly American tradition of magnificent architecture realized primarily through innovative engineering — a tradition dating back to Benjamin Franklin and including William LeBaron Jenney's earliest skyscrapers and the great expansion bridges. To the cultural historian John A. Kouwenhoven, these figures mark "the vernacular tradition in building," which is characterized by "simplicity, lightness, flexibility, and wide availability." Fuller wedded art and technology far more successfully than the Bauhaus, for his domes made grand art out of innovative technology. His works were eminently physical, and thus Veblenian, and yet also spiritual, so Jamesian; and for the future of building they offered not a particular style but a distinctly American example of architectural excellence.

Another scarcely noticed development in modern architecture has stemmed from especially close attention to managing the environment within the building — temperature, humidity, and ventilation; and perhaps because the severe extremes of most American climates demand optimal internal environmental control, Americans have also been the innovators at mediating between interior and exterior. According to the British architectural historian Reyner Banham, in his study of *The Architecture of the Well-Tempered Environment* (1969), Benjamin Franklin invented the principle of heating a room with warm air, and the private homes that Frank Lloyd Wright designed in Chicago early in this century — The Baker House (1908), the Gale House (1908), and The Robie House (1910) "with their easy mastery of environmental control" — made him "the first master of the well-tempered environment."

In Banham's history, no American does as well again without mechanical air-conditioning — not even Wright — until Philip Johnson, in his own country home (1949), a Miesian glass-walled box shrewdly situated on a bluff in New Canaan, Connecticut. (Banham also commends Kahn's Richards Medical Center for environmental considerations which, in my own observations and inquiry, are largely non-existent; and he neglects the environmental ingenuities of such neo–Wrightians as Goff and Soleri.) The other recent example in Banham's citations is the inflatable portable theater designed by the architect Victor Lundy for the Atomic Energy Commission, which first used it in 1959 — "unmistakably architecture [constructed] out of the exploitation of a new technology." Here the elastic skin is blown up into two hemispherical spaces of different sizes, the smaller of which is cut away into an entrance with revolving doors — in sum running 230 feet long, about 100 feet wide and fifty high; and thanks to certain properties of inflated spaces and the construction's internal design ("air balloons kept rigid by internal pressure"), only a small air-conditioner is needed to keep temperatures manageable. (Banham, perhaps the world's most adventurous architectural critic, has also championed impermanent or "clip-on" architecture — an idea that inexplicably had more visible influence in England than America, where the issue of possible impermanence goes generally undiscussed.)

To the rest of the world, American architecture at its best epitomized contemporaneity; yet within the profession were conservative forces constructing the drifts of change. On one hand, Paul Heyer, a British architect-critic traveling through America, could judge unequivocally that, "In the post–World War II years, leadership in the sphere of architecture is generally recognized as having centered in the United States." American examples were, indeed, the most intrinsically successful and influential developments out of the International Style, in part because of such technical achievements as new materials; and the world's cities were, in fact, slowly coming to resemble midtown Manhattan. Nonetheless, the International Style remained an importation to America, a grafting upon native soil and its own structural and environmental traditions; so that this new architecture around the world was curiously imitating the latest American imitations of Europe. Furthermore, in the success of American architecture came a general disinterest in alternatives more radical than, say, Louis Kahn. As James Marston Fitch noted in the 1966 edition of *American Building*:

> In 1964, there were twenty-five firms *each of which* had over $60,000,000 worth of work on its boards. Ironically, this general prosperity has led to the impoverishment of intellectual speculation and artistic invention. The utopian element in architectural thinking has been largely submerged. Theory itself is in disrepute.... The dominant attitude is one of complacent *laissez-faire*, the aesthetic expression of which is a genial eclecticism.

This moribund conservatism is epitomized by the profession's neglect of Fuller himself, his architectural values and the pressing problems of mass housing; for pious proclamations notwithstanding, the dominant attitude within the trade has scarcely progressed beyond the 1928 resolution of the American Institute of Architects "as inherently opposed to any [Fuller] peas-in-a-pod-like reproducible designs." (In recent years Fuller has regularly been placing his bet on students, but at least within the licensed profession his faith has not yet been redeemed.)

A book like John Jacobus' *Twentieth-Century Architecture: The Middle Years, 1940–1965* (1966) demonstrates that a respected academic historian can write an international history of "contemporary" architecture without even mentioning such non-stylists as Fuller and Wachsmann, or their European compatriots, Constantine Doxiades and Kaija and Heikki Siren, or such environmentalists as Goff and Soleri—as though these radical alternatives simply did not exist. Indeed, compared to criticism of other arts, discourse about architecture is not especially good or scrupulous, which is to say that many statements simply do not apply accurately to the works described. One reason for this insufficiency is the frequent disparity, mentioned before, between the architect's stated intention and the building's actual effects; another is the limited number of architectural reviews (and reviewers) and the absence of any architectural periodical as radical as the British *Archigram*; a third is the fact that esthetic reputations are so frequently translated into publicity and monetary values; so that only the critic talking to nobody is allowed the genuine autonomy necessary for his task. Moreover, given these problems intrinsic in architectural writing, one suspects that many speculative designs remain unknown or, if built, unrecognized. All these problems suggest that architecture needs a New Criticism devoted to establishing a substantive index of human inhabitability.

Within the process of professional training are yet other forces discouraging change. The aspiring American architect is subjected to several years of postgraduate education, then a period of internship with an established firm before he or she can take the examination for an official license—a hurdling process nearly as arduous as that required for medicine; and the American Institute of Architects' policies reveal less than eagerness to increase their membership. This explains not only why Fuller's charges get excluded or deflected but also why it is rare for anyone under thirty-five to do his or her own building and impossible for an aspiring architect under thirty. Therefore, the personal or original impulses evident in the youth are likely to be suppressed or lost in the adult. Nothing should discredit this needlessly hazardous system more than the fact that none of the great older masters underwent this sort of initiating ritual. Nor has standard U.S. architectural education yet produced an acknowledgeably great man. Nonetheless, American architecture remains more practical than European; the cultural atmosphere in general is more congenial to individual initiative; in no other country is the structuralist tradition becoming so attractive; so that in spite of all the native conservatism, the best American architecture is genuinely progressive.

Contemporary Painting in America (1978)

The shift in art training in the fifties from the art school and studio to the university art department, which was stimulated by the G. I. Bill, had the effect of imprinting on painting and sculpture classroom modes of inquiry, concerned not with emulating great works but with elaborating problems and solutions. —Harold Rosenberg, "American Drawing" (1976)

The visionaries in art are the people who see ahead, creating alternative new styles that are not only admired by people serious about contemporary art but—and this is the crucial test—also imitated by younger artists. That is, a visionary envisions for art a possibility that has not been realized before, but which will in alternate ways be realized again. In this sense, the history of modern art could be considered the results, the artifacts, of essentially visionary activity.

The first pioneers of post–World War II American painting were Jackson Pollock (1912–1956) and Willem de Kooning (b. 1904), who respectively achieved radical extensions of the two major innovations of early twentieth-century European art—Expressionism and Cubism. In the middle forties, Pollock began to experiment with innovative methods of applying paint to canvas, laying it on the floor, then in a series of rapid movements literally pouring and splattering paint all over the surface. Though he rejected many of the canvases produced by these impulsive and purposeful actions, certain pictures made in this way realized an overwhelming intensity of visual activity. This expressionist density could be found not only in isolated segments but, in a radical innovation, *all over* the nonhierarchical, nonfocused canvas, thereby creating the sense that the imagery could have extended itself well beyond the painting's actual edges, if not forever.

De Kooning, unlike Pollock, was born abroad, in Holland, emigrating to America as a young man. After an earlier career as a WPA muralist, he imaginatively developed and extended a major stylistic contribution of European cubism—breaking up the representational plane to portray an object or field as seen from two or more perspectives simultaneously. The initial

45

paintings in his *Woman* series, done in the early fifties, evoke in impulsive and yet well-drawn strokes (and colors identical to those in the portrayed environment) a single figure regarded from a multitude of perspectives, both vertical and horizontal, in several kinds of light and, therefore, at various moments in time. Not only are the differences between figure and setting, past and present, background and foreground, all thoroughly blurred, but nearly every major detail in this allover and yet focused field suggests a different angle of vision or a different intensity of light.

Pollock's best paintings similarly flash different levels of illusionistic space; but more important for subsequent art was the sense, best seen in retrospect, that his shimmering works surpassed both Cubism and de Kooning precisely by eschewing any reference to things outside of painting. This complete meshing of image and field, content and canvas, even stasis and movement, creates a completely integrated, autonomous and self-referring work which differs radically from the fragmented, allusive, and structured field of post–Cubist painting; and as the picture creates an all-encompassing world of direct, wholly visual communication, a new and fertile vision for painting space was suggested.

Between these two totem figures and recent advanced art stand several visionary painters who, in the middle and late fifties, initiated the directions that others developed — Morris Louis (1912–1962), Ad Reinhardt (1913–1967), Robert Rauschenberg (b. 1925) and Jasper Johns (b. 1930). Louis' innovation, dating back to 1953, consisted of pouring paint directly on unstretched, unprimed and unsized canvas, so that not only is there no shading and no visible trace of the painter's hand, but the color and texture of raw canvas itself remains visible. Given an unusual sensitivity to color values, as well as the ability to mix his own pigments and the willingness to use newly developed acrylic paints, Louis achieved a stunning, perhaps unprecedented optical luminescence, initiating what came to be known as "Color-Field" painting.

Ad Reinhardt was from his professional beginnings a severe abstractionist, who later became a witty polemical advocate of anti–Expressionistic art. His most distinctive early paintings had geometric shapes on a multicolored field, while works of the late forties favored less definite abstract shapes. By 1953, he offered canvases entirely in shades of the same color, at first all red, and then all black and all blue, usually divided into squares whose slight differences in hue became more visible with the spectator's increased attention. That is, his Black Paintings of the early sixties, each 60″ square, contain not a sole black color evenly painted from edge to edge, but nine squares, all 20″ by 20″, each of a slightly different black color from its adjacent squares. Viewing Reinhardt's work from the perspective of subsequent art history, the critic Lucy R. Lippard judges that his "innovations consist largely of the establishment of a valid function for nonrelational, monotonal concepts, progressive elimination of texture, color contrast, value contrast and eventually of color itself, which was replaced by a uniquely nonillusionistic painted light."

If the progress of Reinhardt's career was toward the purification of painting — the elimination of everything that is not of painting itself — Robert Rauschenberg's art developed in the opposite direction, toward the mixing of painting with other things. His distinctive collages of the middle fifties at first incorporated miscellaneous photographs, magazine pages and other found images, creating a diffuse visual field in which, as he put it, there is "nothing everything is subservient to." He then mounted actual objects on fundamentally two-dimensional paintings that implicitly (and skillfully) obliterated the traditional distinctions between materials-for-Art and ordinary junk. In *Bed* (1955), he painted his own bed, transforming another sub-esthetic "found" object into something purchased and displayed by the Museum of Modern Art. In *Monogram* (1959), he put a decidedly three-dimensional figure, a whole stuffed goat, into a painted field. His *Broadcast* (1959) contains a live radio; and to *Third Time Painting* (1961), Rauschenberg affixed a working clock. To characterize painted assemblages that had three dimensions and yet were not quite sculpture, he coined the term *Combine*. "I always thought of them as paintings," he told an interviewer; and so freely did he mix art with "non-art" that critics were forever quoting his most famous aphorism: "Painting relates to both art and life. Neither can be made. (I try to act in that gap between the two.)" By the late sixties, Rauschenberg was working at theatrical pieces and graphics; but historically it was he, more than any other, who established the visionary precedent of combining elements from the outside world (if not the immediate surrounding space as well) with the tradition of painting.

Jasper Johns' contribution to the new sensibility is more subtle; for while he displayed some of Rauschenberg's uninhibited use of materials that were previously forbidden to art, his work has remained largely within the traditional format of painting. A Johns painting is a cool, inscrutable object that induces a multiple inquisitive involvement by the spectator. In looking at his famous *Target with Four Faces* (1955), one cannot help but ask: Is this a replica of a target? A collection of concentric circles? Or something else? What relationship do those four sculpted bottoms of heads (noses and mouths, to be precise) have to the two-dimensional target picture? Why is the target-image represented so realistically, and yet the heads so nonrealistically? Do all meanings exist within the picture, or is there some symbolism here? Is this a "painting"? or a "collage"? or what? "I thought he was doing three things," the composer John Cage once wrote of his painter friend, "but five things he was doing escaped my notice."

By painting a realistic image without a background, Johns followed Pollock in abolishing the discrepancy between image and field that is the core of traditional representational art, again raising the question of whether the target-image was a mechanical copy of the original target, or a nonrepresentational design (and what in this context would be the difference anyway?). In the late forties, Johns was working with subesthetic images such as the American flag, the then forty-eight states of America in outline, and stenciled numbers, as well as such mundane objects as beer cans, a light bulb, a flashlight and a coffee tin filled with artists' brushes. However, it was less Johns' taste in materials than his love of visual ambiguity, puzzle and enigma that became a pioneer possibility for subsequent painting.

The most revolutionary style of the postwar era — the one attracting the most outraged responses — was Pop Art. Its exponents used not only the imagery of popular culture, such as comic-strip figures and hamburgers, but also representational techniques and materials drawn from advertising and other mass media: glossy paint, precise rendering, clean surfaces and sometimes silkscreen reproduction. Quotations are not new in painting, to be sure, but what is unprecedented in Pop Art is the blatantly common character of the quoted materials and the slick manner of representation, which were all so contrary to the painterly expressionism previously equated with "high art."

Pop Art commanded respect and influence, in spite of its representationalism, because it was the first realistic reaction to abstract art that was not primarily conservative (or anti-modernist) in spirit. As the creation of art-history-conscious painters, who had assimilated and revealed the influence of abstraction, Pop Art is primarily about Art rather than about the world, while commercial art, in contrast, is wholly worldly.

One Pop style, exemplified by James Rosenquist (b. 1933), uses both the scale and flat colors, as well as the sentimentally realistic style and visible panel-separating lines, of billboard art (a trade Rosenquist himself once practiced) to create large, glossy paintings which, like his classic ten-by-eighty-six feet *F-111* (1965), are full of incongruous images. As the critic Harold Rosenberg once remarked, "This was advertising art advertising itself as art that hates advertising." Another Pop artist, Roy Lichtenstein (b. 1923), painted enlarged comic-strip images, which were so refined in their realism that they even reproduced the dots characteristic of comic-book illustration; these paintings implicitly ask esthetic questions about image and artifact that clearly reflect the influence of Jasper Johns.

The theme of ironic displacement, which is to say the incongruous relation between the identifiable image and its model, informs not only Lichtenstein's highly comic paintings but also the Pop sculpture of Claes Oldenburg (b. 1929) and the paintings of Andy Warhol (b. 1925). Surely the most outrageous and perhaps the most profoundly American of the Pop artists, Warhol in the early 1960s created works that, in retrospect, seem systematically designed to violate several conventional rules of "high art." Originally a commercial artist with a professional reputation for drawing shoes, Warhol painted popular iconography as early as 1960, and he was probably the first painter to use the silk-screening process to transfer photographs and advertising imagery to fine-art canvas. In his paintings, "found" images, mostly familiar, are transformed — enlarged, recolored, reshaded — to emphasize their pictorial qualities, and often repeated interminably to suggest mental hallucination. Warhol, along with hired helpers, often uses duplicating procedures to make several almost identical canvases or to populate a single canvas with multiple copies of a single photographic image, initially of horrifying public events — *Atomic Bomb* (1963), *Car Crash* (1963), and *Race Riot* (1964), among others. Warhol also uses reductive yet enhancing duplicating processes to make a series of photographically accurate but grotesquely colored portraits such as Jacqueline Kennedy Onassis in *Jackie* (1964) and Elizabeth Taylor in *Liz* (1965), implicitly showing perhaps how these ubiquitous faces have assumed the archetypal qualities of the Blessed Mother.

If Rauschenberg and Johns were, in different ways, the visionary progenitors of Pop, Morris Louis generated an important new direction in Color-Field painting — self-referring works that emphasize not the forms of gestural abstraction but the textures of variously applied paints, the relationships of colors within the field, and, in some cases, the possible subtle shadings of a single hue. Since Louis' premature death, the two younger masters of this method have been Kenneth Noland (b. 1924) and Jules Olitski (b. 1922), both of whom also acknowledge Louis in likewise favoring acrylic paints. However, while Noland generally uses a variety of radiant colors, Olitski deals in fewer, quieter shades in more diaphanous textures (created by spraying his canvases). Thus, not only is the placement of color separated, if not freed, from drawn shapes but his paintings display atmospheric, if not ethereal, qualities that approach subsequent minimal, and even monotonal, canvases. Noland's works are rooted within the painting's frame and a regular design as he divides his canvas into roughly drawn but sharp-edged geometric shapes, such as circles within circles, or a succession of chevrons across a canvas stood on its point, or simple, long horizontal bands (extending as far as twenty feet, or farther than a single glance can apprehend), each of which has its own unmodulated color — in all examples, a precise and sometimes symmetrical structure. Through such scrupulously geometric patterning, Noland avoids reference to earlier ways of structuring a modern painting. Olitski, by contrast, has fields of amorphous shapes, structurally without apparent relation, each with its own color, and then pools of color blending into each other. Later Olitski used just one color articulately shaded into a spectrum of related hues; but on the edge, almost punctuating the field, is usually a solidly painted strip of a different color which either roots the canvas to another world or compromises the painting's preeminently visionary achievement.

The European tradition of geometric abstraction informs not only Noland but also the innovations of Frank Stella (b. 1936). Hailed before he turned twenty-five, his early canvases consist of regularly patterned geometric shapes, such as squares within squares, painted with evenly applied strokes out to the canvas's edge, so that the viewer cannot distinguish any figure from background, or form from content, or image from any larger shape. The spectator's appreciation of these faintly mechanical paintings ideally includes such strictly visual virtues as the relation of one color to another, the solidity of the geometric shapes and the potential complexity of elemental simplicity, as well as Stella's decidedly cerebral deductive solution to certain problems in painting's recent history. In 1960, the twenty-four-year-old artist told an undergraduate audience:

> Finally I had to face two problems: One was spatial and the other methodological. In the first case I had to do something about relational painting, *i.e.*, the balancing of the various parts of the painting with and against each other. The obvious answer was symmetry — make it the same all over. The question still remained, though, of how to do this in depth. A symmetrical image of configuration placed on an open ground is not balanced out in the illusionistic space. The solution I arrived at — and there are probably others, although I know of only one, color density — forces illusionistic space out of the painting at a constant rate by using a regular pattern. The remaining problem was simply to find a method of paint application which followed and completed the design solution. This was done by using the house painter's technique and tools.

In other words, Stella's initial answer to the question of how to organize an abstract canvas now, after all the solutions already posited in modern art, required allover artificial regularity. After establishing a visionary frontier that won admirers and imitators, Stella explored the other solution, espoused earlier by Louis and Noland, of color relations within a regular design. This later work develops another aspect of Stella's earlier painting — the eccentrically shaped canvas, where the shape of the frame usually determines the work's internal forms. "This reduced illusionism to a minimum," wrote Barbara Rose, "and further identified the image with the canvas surface."

The term "minimal" is customarily used to characterize art whose subject matter is insubstantial by traditional standards; and most minimal works tend to combine grandiose physical size with a scant minimum of discernible figuration — perhaps *at most* a large expanse of solid color penetrated by lines or one set of visible marks, so that a painting functions as a visionary field rather than as a composition, and the degree of reduction is a rough measure of its ambition and integrity. For instance, in Barnett Newman's magnificent and yet preeminently subtle *The Stations of the Cross* (1958–66), which is a series of fourteen paintings six and one-half feet by five feet, the traditional Biblical narrative is subjected to minimal imagery (usually two vertical stripes of various widths and shapes, against a background field of raw canvas), where the absence of familiar iconography becomes a commentary on the classic myth as well as an echo of the simple cosmological forms of primitive art.

The inevitable next step has, of course, been the abolition of the stripe of frame for a field entirely in one color—not like Ad Reinhardt's late works, with their rectangles of perceptibly different hues, but truly monochromatic works of art, where painting is the sole reality. The result of such a severe visionary constraint has been not a series of identical paintings but a remarkable variety of ontological explorations that include Rauschenberg's reflecting canvases of white house paint (1952), Barnett Newman's concluding image in *The Stations of the Cross*, which in context inevitably symbolizes the Transfiguration; Robert Irwin's canvases which, if observed fixedly from a distance, reveal tiny specks of different colors forming either their own patterns or an illusory haze floating a few inches in front of the canvas; and particular paintings by Ralph Humphrey (b. 1932) and Robert Ryman (b. 1930), among others—all of which, to quote Lippard again, "emphasize the fact of painting as painting, surface as surface, paint as paint, in an inactive, unequivocal manner."

It was the Abstract Expressionist painter Franz Kline, a contemporary of Pollock and de Kooning, who suggested that, "The final test of painting is: Does the painter's emotion come across?" However, to a subsequent generation of painters, few standards are less relevant than this. The new painting comes from decidedly objective processes—not only is the easel all but universally eschewed and the work usually abstract, but the paint itself is handled in rather anonymous ways (yet still reflecting a human hand rather than a machine). Scarcely will a work reveal much that is personal about its individual creator. Beyond that, in most strains of reductive painting the work demands kinds of perceptions previously regarded as "phenomenal" rather than "artistic" or "esthetic," thereby altering if not repudiating the traditional procedures of painterly comprehension.

In addition to acknowledging the absolute flatness of the canvas, the new painting reflects three major problems of classic modern painting—the use of color (emphasized largely by Matisse), the organization of the canvas' visual field (Picasso) and the potential perceptual experiences peculiar to a painted field (Mondrian). Yet just as the visionary styles of Pollock and de Kooning moved beyond earlier Surrealism and Expressionism, so the visionary painters of the past two decades moved beyond those earlier American masters, in sum suggesting that the tradition of doing art that has not yet been done continues to thrive in America.

Avant-Garde (1966)

Nothing is good save the new. If a thing have novelty it stands intrinsically beside every other work of artistic excellence. If it have not that, no loveliness or heroic proportions or grand manner will save it. — William Carlos Williams, *Kora in Hell: Improvisations* (1920)

Although we are not generally accustomed to think of the United States as hospitable to avant-garde arts, our country now possesses, by common consent, the richest, most varied and most radical agant-garde culture in the world today. The world's artists look not to Paris but to New York to discover original and challenging directions in painting, sculpture, poetry, dance, "intermedia" arts, and music. This achievement is, curiously, quite recent, for America was historically slow in assimilating the avant-garde esthetic that has animated European art for the past century.

"Avant-garde" is a French term originally used to describe the soldiers that move ahead of the mass of an army; by metaphoric extension, the phrase has come to refer to works of art, as well as artists, that are decidedly ahead of the reigning fashions. Admittedly, the concept embodies an historical fatalism; for what is stylistically avant-garde at a certain time will, in the encroaching future, soon become the staple of hordes of hacks — the *derrière-garde*; in art, as in female dress, styles that were outrageously new in 1920 are interred today. New artists climb to eminence on the receding backs of their predecessors.

The possibility of an avant-garde is based upon individualism which is, in turn, indebted to the first painter to sign his canvas and the writer who first affixed his own name to his manuscript. If the anonymous medieval master artist strived to duplicate existing styles, the Renaissance master wanted to deviate from the current conventions and display his individual touch. Contemporary avant-gardists have greater egos; some try even to initiate a stylistic convention. The epithet "avant-garde" also presumes a belief in temporal time — that the future will be different from the past — although it does *not* necessarily presuppose the myth of progress — that the arts of the future will be better than those of the past.

The idea of the avant-garde entered French intellectual discourse about a century ago. The phrase has no single identifiable parent, though among the putative possibilities were the poet and critic Charles Baudelaire, the painter Gustave Courbet, and the poet Paul Verlaine. As its central tenet, the avant-garde ethos presumes that no contemporary artist is significant unless his work offers a style or structure as novel as it is realized and/or an original insight into the changing human situation in our time. This spirit informs not only positive judgments but negative ones, ruling that not only should the artist not repeat his predecessor's works but also that he should not repeat himself. In this sense, all the truly great artists of the twentieth century were, whether intentionally or not, discernably avant-garde at some point of their careers; and the history of modern art and literature, in all genres, can be persuasively interpreted as largely a record of avant-garde activity.

Historically, America has always had vanguard artists, who were usually lone eccentrics creating their unconventional works in spite of a minimum of native response. Walt Whitman's poetry, so important in the modernist revolt against traditional forms, was barely appreciated in his own time. The two initiating American-born figures in the revolt of modern dance, Loïe Fuller and Isadora Duncan, were honored in Europe long before their work was accepted here; Charles Ives heard only one of his major symphonic works performed in his lifetime, although he lived some forty years after finishing them. The tradition of highly individualized eccentricity continues to the present; however, the crucial difference between yesterday and today is that, especially in the past decade, works of art which are truly advanced are more quickly recognized at home. The American public is now more aware of its vanguard culture, though, one must add, it is still hardly aware enough.

In the avant-garde performing arts, the single most prominent figure is John Cage, who is preeminent less for his own musical compositions than for his esthetic ideas and the impact of these ideas upon important young painters, directors, poets, critics, choreographers, and creators of "intermedia" works. In his musical career, Cage has progressively moved away from conventional composition and toward radically different methods for putting sounds together — pieces in which important dimensions are only approximately determined. Some of his works have contributed to that peculiarly contemporary tradition of artistic creations that are distinctly less interesting for their intrinsic merit than for the ideas about art they suggest; and usually these works embody a special quality of being at once superficially comic and ultimately serious.

Surely the most thoroughly radical piece in the Cage canon, if not the most crucially influential, is *4'33"* (pronounced "Four Minutes, Thirty-Three Seconds"), first unveiled in 1952. Here the pianist David Tudor, Cage's most loyal performer, comes to the piano bench and sits — just sits still — for the prescribed duration. The "music" consists of all the sounds that happen to arise in the performance hall during *4'33"*. What makes this rather comic conception so serious and important is less the piece itself — admittedly an unextraordinary experience — than the two implications behind it: first, that any and all sounds, whether intentional or not, are components of the musical experience; and second, that all important aspects — register, rhythm, timbre, volume — are *indeterminate* in performance. (Today, Cage considers even this piece archaic, because its entire length is predetermined. That dimension, too, he would nowadays prefer to leave indeterminate.)

In his more recent work, Cage has continued to explore procedures that encourage similarly unplanned or "chance" mixtures of various and incongruous sounds; indeed, he is conscientiously attempting to renounce completely his own control over the final result. In 1965, he created *Rozart Mix* for thirteen tape machines and six live performers. Here Cage instructs his associates to pick randomly from a pile of tape loops, which are lengths of prerecorded tape with the two ends glued together. They then put the loops randomly on the tape machines, all of which play loudly at once. The aural din continues until the last spectator leaves. Many European musicians have employed aleatoric or chance procedures; but no one else, either here or there, is as thoroughly committed to unintentional results as Cage.

The leading figure in avant-garde American dance, Merce Cunningham, has worked with Cage since they first met nearly thirty years ago at the Cornish School in Seattle, Washington. If Cage suggests that all sounds can be considered music, so Cunningham believes that all movements, in any combination, can be considered viable components of "dance." Cunningham initiated several revolutions in the structuring of dance. First, he extracted dance from its enslavement to the rhythms of the accompanying music; and even when Cunningham does use music, his dancers ignore its sounds — it functions more as an equally discontinuous esthetic parallel to the movements of his dancers. (Cage, incidentally, is the Musical Director of the Cunningham troupe.)

Second, not only do Cunningham's dancers move independently of each other, but he insists that the parts of a dancer's body can also move nonsynchronously. To the untrained eye, these motions might seem uncoordinated; actually, they require the dancer's most concentrated coordination to attain the high grace that particularly characterizes the movements of Cunningham himself and Carolyn Brown, his lead female dancer. Third, he eschews the traditional rule that the sections of a single dance should have a fixed order; sometimes he even adopts aleatoric procedures, such as the tossing of coins, to determine the sequence of its parts. Fourth, as his pieces abandon any reliance upon the climaxes and resolutions of traditional structuring, so they also avoid creating a central focus.

Like Cage, Cunningham rejects the notion of art as self-expression, and they both eschew creating symbolism and other extrinsic references. To them, the purpose of dance is an exploration of the possibilities of movement, just as music is an exploration of sound. Cunningham once said that, when he was young, Fred Astaire was his favorite dancer because he never pretended that "his dances were anything but movement." George Ballanchine has incorporated one of Cunningham's dances, *Summerspace* (1959), into the repertoire of the New York State Ballet; however, the adaptation includes many old-fashioned balletic movements that contradict Cunningham's purposes. People who favor more representational dance often find Cunningham's works incoherent; many artists and writers, in contrast, judge Cunningham the only dancer they can watch with pleasure and interest. Although he has been a recognized force for nearly twenty-years — indeed, he has no equal in Europe — Merce Cunningham still suffers the horrendous indignity of infrequent New York recitals.

The Cagean influence extends to the founders and directors of The Living Theatre, Judith Malina and Julian Beck, who, as director and stage designer respectively, created *The Connection* (1959) and *The Brig* (1963), two of the most truly original and stunning theatrical presentations of our time. In manuscript, *The Connection* seemed a naturalistic portrait of drug addicts; however, Judith Malina's production seems, in retrospect, more about the attempt to force the audience, wholly by theatrical means, to consider whether they would wish to join the players on the stage in taking heroin.

Malina's direction of Kenneth H. Brown's *The Brig,* ostensibly about the brutality of Marine Corps prisons, seems, again in retrospect, a highly effective embodiment of Antonin Artaud's twofold polemical ideal — that theatre should reject its commitment to literature for full exploitation of movement and sound, and that it should move its audience with "the force of a plague." Indeed, the language of *The Brig* held little interest; but its movement was so carefully choreographed and its sound so meticulously orchestrated that it created, in my opinion, the most fully realized and extraordinary American theatrical performance of recent years.

Regrettably, The Internal Revenue Service closed The Living Theatre in October 1963; and Malina and Beck have since chosen exile abroad. Occasional reports that trickle back suggest they continue to field original performances in the Artaud tradition. One of the more imaginative creators of productions in New York today, Lawrence Kornfeld, recently the director of Rosalind Drexler's *Home Movies* (1964) and Gertrude Stein's *What Happened* (1963), indicatively lists as his three major influences: "Cage, Cunningham and Malina."

However, not all that is avant-garde in the performing arts falls within the Cagean ambience. In musical composition there exists a second avant-garde, completely opposed to the Cagean direction but equally vanguard in its development away from traditional procedures. These composers contribute to modernist extensions of Arnold Schoenberg's twelve-tone or serial techniques. Milton Babbitt, among its most articulate and brilliant exponents, has developed what he calls the "total serialization" of musical components.

Whereas Schoenberg applied serial procedures (too complicated to describe here) just to the ordering of pitches, Babbitt applies such organizing principles not only to pitches but also to duration, register, timbre, and envelope (degree of attack and release). The result is a music of unprecedented intensity and complexity, where every note functions in several serial progressions at once. Those who understand this music — their numbers are hardly a legion — claim that a minute of Babbitt's music is to a minute of traditional music as a page of James Joyce's *Finnegans Wake* compares with a page in *Mother Goose*. Within the Babbitt ambience falls the only realized example of avant-garde American opera that I have ever heard, Peter Westergaard's *Mr. and Mrs. Discobbolus* (1966). However, in general, the important contemporary avant-garde operas, from Schoenberg's *Moses und Aron* (1932) to Luigi Nono's *Intoleranza* (1961), are European in origin, perhaps because Americans have never made consequential contributions to this European genre, instead initiating a national style in musical comedy.

The introduction of electronic machines into musical composition has also created music that is distinctly avant-garde; but as the machines lack esthetic consciences, they have been exploited by both the Cagean left and the Babbittian right. That is, composers in the Cagean stream — Nam June Paik, Morton Feldman, James Tenney — use machines to produce unprecedented sounds, while practitioners in the other avant-garde — Babbitt, Mario Davidovsky, Charles Wuorinen — find that the electronic machines give them a greater control over the creation and performance of precisely organized musical structures. (Machines, alas, are more efficient performers of densely complex sounds than human musicians.)

Within the American theatre, too, are numerous playwrights whose works are crucially beyond conventional practice. Edward Albee, in the intensity of his negative vision, is certainly among the vanguard playwrights; the original quality of their humor, in particular, places playwrights such as Lee Baxandall, Robert Head, Robert Hivnor, Denis Jasudowicz, Kenneth Koch, and Arthur L. Kopit far ahead of the Broadway pack. Indicatively, most of their plays are presented way off Broadway. In dance, the avant-garde includes the statuesque static conceptions of Kenneth King, the experiments in graceful discontinuity of Yvonne Rainer, the theatrical mixed-media performances of Ann Halprin's San Francisco group, and the flamboyant, prop-heavy productions of Alwin Nikolais at New York's Henry Street Settlement.

Of all the arts-for-audiences, film has always been artistically the weakest in America; and what is true for our mainstream is also true for our avant-garde. There is neither a single dominant vanguard filmmaker, nor a common radical style; none of the expanding "underground" has created a large body of recognized achievement or initiated a flagrantly revolutionary mode. However, there have been several short films, almost isolated brief flashes of brilliance, that are totally unlike anything else done anywhere to-day. Jack Smith's *Flaming Creatures* (1963), now legally removed from circulation as pornographic, attains unprecedented hallucinatory power. Both Michael Putnam's *The Hard Swing* (1962) and John Cassavetes' *Shadows* (1958) extend unsentimental naturalism without falling into its stylized clichés. In *Dog Star Man* (1964), Stan Brakhage superimposes frames of richly colored texture and cuts his scenes with extreme rapidity. Stan VanderBeek, in miscellaneous shorts, has evolved his own comic style, employing techniques drawn from cartoon animation, on one hand, and the collage tradition of modern art on the other.

Still, so much that is truly original in contemporary performance arts makes traditional categories—dance, drama, music, musical comedy, opera—seem progressively less relevant; and the most exciting recent development in America has been those performances that mix traditional theatrical means. Here, too, the Cagean influence has left its mark, although the movement's impetus is not entirely aleatoric. As many critics have noted, a concert of John Cage's own music has its theatrical values: David Tudor's swift and expansive movements all over and under the piano, juxtaposed against his poker face, sometimes command more interest than the sounds he produces; and Cage himself now calls his concerts a form of theatre, which he defines as broadly as possible: "Something which engages both the eye and ear." Some recent Cunningham dances, such as *Winterbranch* (1964), are theatrical conceptions rather than choreographed performances.

Theatrical performances that intentionally transcend the old boundaries have been called "Happenings," which is hardly appropriate; for not all these works employ chance procedures in composition, nor do they necessarily require audience participation. Instead, I prefer to call the whole movement "theatre of mixed means," which is to say that it straddles traditional categories of theatrical presentation. Under this inclusive rubric, I would list three kinds of mixed-means performances: happenings, kinetic environments, and staged peformances.

In "happenings"—the term coined by Allan Kaprow, one of its leading practitioners—the script is vague enough to allow unplanned events to take place and/or prescribed events to occur in an unplanned succession. The behavior and identity of the official participants is only sketchily outlined; the piece insists upon an unfettered exploration of space and a free attitude toward time. Furthermore, a happenings performance of this kind envelops the attention of the audience by allowing them to feel that they are participants in a process. As Michael Kirby notes, the author is closer to a football coach than a theatre director or choreographer, for he gives his players only general instructions before the event.

In one of his first happenings, Kaprow prescribes the following typical activity. "At another point a young boy goes to a striped pole of black and white hung with red lights and grasping it SHAKES for a while like a victim of palsy [,] returning to his seat when he wishes." The entire script for "Gång-sång," by Dick Higgins is: "One foot forward. Transfer weight to this foot. Bring other foot forward. Transfer weight to this foot. Repeat as often as desired." Some happenings are performed in theatres; others have exploited natural surroundings, such as a woods, or Grand Central Station or an entire city. Some, like Higgins' piece, can be performed anywhere, at any time, before an audience of any amount, arranged in any fashion. Lincoln Center, around 8:30 the night of several performances, would be an ideal setting for, say, one of Ken Dewey's "audience-journey pieces."

Kinetic environments are different from happenings in that they are more closely planned, their space is more defined and constricted, and the behavior of the participants is more precisely programmed; however, they are, like happenings, also open-ended in time, unfocused in structure and capable of encouraging participational attention. USCO, of Garnersville, New York, a group of artists who prefer to remain individually anonymous, create kinetic environments of music, taped noise (such as a television or an oscilloscope), and projected images (both on slides and film). Another kinetic environment is La Monte Young's Theatre of Eternal Music, in which Young, along with three other musicians, creates a constant chord of sound which, as it is electronically amplified to the threshold of pain and projected through several speakers, can entirely envelop one's consciousness. One should add, however, that a recording of Young's performance is not an environment but a piece of music, unless, of course, one re-creates at home the original performance situation of a darkened room, several speakers variously placed, slides of oriental calligraphy, and an odor of incense.

Staged performances are as closely planned in conception and specific in execution as kinetic environments; but here the action is more focused and the audience's role is more observational. Indeed, in all these respects, staged performances resemble traditional theatre; the difference is that the entire new movement deemphasizes, if not totally rejects, the materials of literary expression. In most, there are no words at all; in some, the words are few and barely coherent enough to be expressive. In Ken Dewey's *Sames* (1965), for instance, certain short phrases are repeated over and over; sometimes the same voice is, through duplicating techniques, multiplied into a chorus of itself.

In Robert Whitman's *Prune. Flat.* (1965), "a film-stage event," prefilmed moving images are projected upon both a stationary screen and white-smocked live performers, and the piece develops a thematic motif that a filmed image can often appear more "real" than the live performer. In her *Water Light/Water Needle* (1966), a staged performance, Carolee Schneemann instructs her performers to execute several athletic motions on ropes strung across the area cut off from the audience. She classifies her work as "kinetic theatre" which stems from "kinetic sculpture"; for like many of the creators of theatre of mixed means, she takes her intellectual background, as well as her esthetic terms, from outside professional theatrical circles.

What the various strains of theatre of mixed means have in common, then, is: (1) a distinct distance from literary theatre, which includes a rejection not only of theatre of explicit statement but also the abandonment of plot and the visual clichés of "theatrical" movement and setting; (2) a structure that is comparatively unfocused — the piece lacks a distinct introduction, a climax, and a clear conclusion, as well as a visual focus to rivet the audience's attention; (3) a form of a succession of discontinuous events or images, which are perhaps internally related; (4) performers who do not play roles (others) but merely fulfill prescribed tasks (themselves); (5) elements which move more independently of one another, rather than synchronously; and (6) a variety in the means employed to communicate — film, noise, movement, incense. Unlike the traditional theatre, which is predominantly visual (even the sounds are based upon words visually comprehended), the new theatre of mixed means appeals to the total sensorium; in this respect, it contributes to what Marshall McLuhan has characterized as the contemporary revolt against a predominantly visual existence.

What defines this theatre of mixed means as truly avant-garde is that, at its best, it continually surprises, startling even its most loyal audience. It never ceases to inspire arguments about the nature of esthetic purpose and/or artistic realization. It contributes to the revolution in sensibility that is infiltrating contemporary culture. Most of the pieces described above were unknown a decade ago; and all of them were artistically inconceivable two decades ago. The avant-garde continues to thrive in America; and the only comment about its future one can offer with any surety is that avant-garde artists will continue to surprise us a decade hence.

Technological Art (1969)

The history of avant-garde painting is that of a progressive surrender of the resistance of its medium; which resistance consists chiefly in the flat picture plane's denial of efforts to "hole through" it for realistic perspectival space. In making this surrender, painting not only got rid of imitation — and with it, "literature" — but also of realistic imitation's corollary confusion between painting and sculpture. —Clement Greenberg, "Towards a Newer Laocoon" (1960)

For many years it was the common belief that art and technic were inalterably opposed — that one thrived only at the expense of the other; but more recent thinking and practice have phased this myth into the cemetery of archaic ideas. Instead, technology is now generally regarded as a repertoire of extensions for human capabilities; and just as simple tools extend our limbs beyond normal competence, so more advanced technology can extend artistic ideas and concepts beyond what would otherwise be possible. Furthermore, not only are many of the best contemporary creative figures, in all the arts, appropriating technology to their unique artistic ends, but, more important, much that is consequential in contemporary art is so indebted to technology that, literally, without the machinery there would be no art.

Sometimes technology functions within the creative process, assisting in the making of the art, but disappearing from the final work. An example is electronic tape music, where oscillators and other sound-generators are used to produce sounds that are then recorded on tape, subjected to all kinds of manipulation (including electronic filtering and reverberation), and played back over a tape player attached to an amplification system. Machines of several sorts are used at each step of the process — creation, transcription, and performance; however, the result is articulated sound which, differences particularly in timbre notwithstanding, more or less sounds like "music." Most art indebted to computers, whether musical or visual work, is similarly machine-assisted, for the computer is not present in the work itself.

In artistic machines, as this new form should be called, the technology is embedded in the art, which generally does some kind of "work." The simplest form is electric light, which can be turned to various artistic ends. Dan Flavin specializes in placing long fluorescent lamps horizontally, vertically and diagonally, in bare rooms, so that the surrounding walls and space are considerably subdued, as the exquisitely modulated colors evoke a meditative, almost sacred atmosphere. Other artists dealing in similarly static light have favored neon tubes, sometimes to exploit ironically their commercial resonances, as the pop artist Robert Watts once shaped pink neon into the familiar calligraphy of the classic masters' signatures— Rembrandt, Picasso, et al.

A different use of light occurs in the projection of moving colored images, whether within a framed box—as in the classic Clavilux machines of Thomas Wilfred, or in the "light shows" that are projected on background screens at rock concerts. Perhaps the most accomplished of the latter are the Joshua Light Show at New York's Fillmore East and the Headlights at San Francisco's Fillmore West. In these, as in other artistic machines, the absence of electricity would short-circuit the art.

Another kind of artistic machine is kinetic, which is to say that it moves autonomously in space. The pioneering example, Laszlo Moholy-Nagy's *Light Display Machine* (1922–30), consists of several moving shiny surfaces that reflect whatever light is projected on them all around the surrounding space; and the machine itself is so elegantly crafted that it can survive display as a static sculpture in a museum. (In works of this kind, esthetic standards apply as much to the mechanism itself as the results of its operations.) In the late fifties, the French-Swiss sculptor Jean Tinguely created several much-publicized, highly satirical "drawing machines" with moving, jointed arms attached to crayons that draw jerky, artistically trivial lines on rolls of paper mechanically fed across them; but since these artistically inefficient instruments also emitted atrocious sounds and frequently broke down, they were clearly antimachine machines, implicitly revealing Tinguely's old-fashioned antitechnological bias.

Perhaps the most extraordinary autonomous artistic machine is James Seawright's *Scanner* (1966), an elegant, plastic-ribbed, ball-shaped cage some six feet in diameter, which is suspended from the ceiling. From the ball's lowest point extends a thin metal arm whose fist contains photocells. A strobe light is projected upwards out of the piece's vertical core and then reflected off mirrors at its apex, so that flickering light goes both down the plastic ribs and into the field around the sculpture. The photocells respond to definite changes in the room's lighting by halting the arm and then swinging it in either direction (depending upon whether the alternating current is positive or negative at the precise moment of contact).

The turning of *Scanner*'s arm inevitably redefines the photocells' perspective on the sculpture's field, increasing the likelihood of another decisive change in their perception of light. That switching signal will, in turn, cause the system to halt again and electronically reconsider the direction of its movement. In short, *Scanner*'s movement generates a self-analyzing activity, making it a genuine example of a feedback machine whose output (the movement of the arm) causes the mechanism to intelligently reconsider its input (the field of light) and continually adjust itself accordingly; thus, within its normal operations are the elegant cybernetic processes of response, information processing, selection, and control.

Seawright's machine, unlike Tinguely's, is programmed to respond to stimuli outside itself and vary its activity accordingly; and in this sense it is like a responsive machine, which should be considered yet another genre of technological art. In the pure form of responsive machines, however, the object needs the presence of an outside source, usually a spectator, in order to work. Machines of this kind have a limited vocabulary of possible movements, whose order, occurrence, and/or material depend upon the frequency or pattern of stimulation; but in the most advanced works, the activity is various and variable, if not as mysterious as art has always been. François Dallegret's *La Machine* (1966) has two long, horizontal aluminum bars, one six inches above the other, which invite the spectator to place his hand or anything else between them, thereby activating up to 172 electronic eyes, each turned to generate a particular sound. In Robin Parkinson's charming *Toy-Pet Plexi-Ball* (1968), made in collaboration with the technician Eric Martin, a lucite sphere, slightly larger than a basketball, jerks away from either loud noises or strong light for five seconds and then rests until activated to jump again. As its power source is self-contained and there are, ingeniously, no extrinsic switches, the machine's activity can be stopped only by smothering the bulb in a sound-proof bag.

Robert Rauschenberg, generally acknowledged as one of the dozen major post–World War II painters, has in recent years become increasingly involved with technology. *Soundings* (1968), probably the most successful of his several artistic machines, consists of nine panels, each eight feet high and four feet across, laid side to side in a thirty-six foot row. Each panel has a mirrored surface and two interior layers of plexiglass on which are silkscreened rather usualy and striking images of a single enlarged chair displayed from various perspectives. Suspended above the field in front of the piece are several microphones, and the mirrored surface merely reflects the surrounding scene until sounds near the microphones cause particular lamps to illuminate behind the interior panels, so that flickering process makes simple visual materials become perceptually complex. The pattern of illumination is actually regulated by the pitches of environmental sounds—as in the classic "color organ," where a certain pitch-signal illuminates one lamp rather than another. The experience of *Soundings* is like a conversation with a methodically obedient pet.

The responsive machines discussed so far have rather basic, one-to-one mechanical responses—the ball moves away, lamps illuminate, and so forth; but just as variety is usually a desirable quality in both art and life, so a more various response signifies a major esthetic advance in artistic machines.

Frank Gillette and Ira Schneider's *Wipe Cycle* (1969) contains a bank of nine television monitors in three rows of three. A camera hidden in the monitor bank photographs the area in front of the work (including whatever audience there is) and instantly broadcasts that image to the middle receiver, rebroadcasts it eight seconds later to two screens on either the horizontal or vertical axis, and then at a sixteen-second delay over the other screens on the perpendicular axis. In the four corner screens are two different sets of identical televised images drawn from previously taped materials. To make the system more complicated (and the perceptual experience continually ambiguous and involving), the delayed live images switch axes at periodic intervals, as do the corner images; and the screens are all wiped blank one at a time in a regular cycle. The spectator feels caught in an intelligently watchful system whose persistent and variable observations remain compelling and mysterious even after their operation is explained.

The technology of this work includes a single blank videotape looped through three tape recorders (the first to pick up the image and instantly play it back over the middle receiver, the second to play it back eight seconds later, the third, sixteen seconds later); a second system of prerecorded videotapes and transducers; and finally timing devices to signal all the switching. *Wipe Cycle*'s bank of nine screens superficially resembles Les Levine's *Contact* (1969), which instead trains two cameras, outfitted with close-up, mid- and long-range lenses, on a foreground scene. On the screens appear several simultaneous immediate perspectives of the scene (usually including the viewer), along with prerecorded materials (literally advertising the industrial sponsor's products), and these images shift screens, or disappear-reappear every few seconds. Both *Wipe Cycle* and *Contact*, like certain other artistic machines, were originally built as prototypes for unlimited duplication.

The visual field of Seawright's *Network I* (1969) is an arrangement of small lamps which display various patterns of illumination; so that at any one time some, but not all, bulbs are turned on. Although their imagery is less striking than, say, Rauschenberg's chairs, *Network I* has the esthetic advantage of more various, and thus more compelling, activity. This in turn reflects Seawright's technically more complicated system for transforming sound signals into light. The machine incorporates a small digital computer (which the artist fabricated himself) for translating sounds, measured by frequency oscillations (a combination of pitch and timbre over limited durations), into binary impulses that in turn trigger the light patterns. The ingenious added factor is that only part of the machine's available program functions at any given time; so that the particular composition of the program's active elements (and, therefore, the machine's pattern of activity) changes every predetermined number of signals (which can vary) in a continuous cycle. Therefore, in *Network I*, in particular contrast to *Soundings*, sound signals repeated over and over again do not produce similar visual responses. As a result, the spectator senses that though he can affect the machine's output, his actions can never induce specific changes. For this reason, the man-machine conversation never ceases to be intriguingly unpredictable.

A similar technology informs Seawright's *Electronic Peristyle* (1968), a kinetic enclosed space (called "an environment") that has been touring America in "The Magic Theater"; but here shadows made by spectators within the environment stimulate twelve photocells embedded in the elegantly crafted, plexiglass-covered center globe. These signals are then translated into binary information that in turn generates continually changing electronic sounds; and here too the constantly varying program ensures that the machine's responses remain inscrutable to the spectator, even if he knows how the technology works.

In short, feedback and unpredictable response make both *Network I* and *Electronic Peristyle* more valuable and interesting than traditional casual mechanisms; and Seawright himself believes that these behavioral qualities also make his machines more "human" or "human-like" than less variably responsive machines. "Just as a person you know can surprise you," he once told a reporter, "so can these machines." However, they are less anthropomorphic entities than superior cybernetic systems, realized at a higher level of operational efficiency and perceptual complexity than has so far been common in the art.

These artistic machines, as noted before, all do some kind of "work," yet none has any practical uses. (Not even Flavin's light could be considered "good for reading.") Nonetheless, the best of them perform the useful social function of imaginatively confronting the unprecedented opportunities of modern technology; and these themes, or artistic meanings, inevitably include the possible shapes and uses of industrial materials, as well as, in all kinetic work, the choreographic nature of strictly mechanical movement. Some were made by artists collaborating with technicians; but in the very best the artist performs all his own technical handiwork.

Much new art will grow out of current and future technological developments; for just as many of the technologies used in art are quite new, so nearly all technological artists are under forty. They and others will surely discover yet more artistic possibilities for older machines and appropriate yet newer technologies for artistic uses. The laser, for instance, offers such unprecedented opportunites as holography, or truly three-dimensional photography, and beyond that the possible electronic transmission in three-dimensional form of a live person to another place, so that a distant person's actual movements could be three-dimensionally reproduced in the receiver's presence. Autonomous robots are also in the works, perhaps eventually realizing man's age-old dream of creating a credible replica of himself.

Indeed, there is every reason to believe that the most consequential future art will come not from today's "sensitive" or "esthetic" children but from the tinkerers who love mechanical processes for their peculiar formal excitement (which, since they are not practical, must be classed as esthetic). There is much sense in Seawright's observation that the most enthusiastic audience for his work consists of technical people, who instantly become involved, if not empathetic, with the mysterious operations of his art.

The greatest obstacle now is the fact that by standards familiar to artists, technology is forbiddingly expensive, and the most likely patrons, those corporations manufacturing advanced technology, are only just beginning to extend that beneficence which is ultimately in their own interests. The Los Angeles County Museum, for instance, has persuaded more than forty West Coast industrial corporations to collaborate with artists (not always the best, alas) on impractical projects. This kind of cooperation can bode only well for both man and machine, for the function of machines in art is ultimately not to imitate or supersede human actions, but to provide artistically creative people with the means to extend their creative ideas, as well as their limbs and senses; so that even the most autonomous, if not self-analyzing, artistic machine inevitably reveals the ingenuity of an imaginative human mind.

Technological Art
Reconsidered (1990)

As a sports junkie who read Moholy-Nagy's *Vision in Motion* early in my professional life, I have always admired kinetic art that reflected technological savvy. To my mind, Alexander Calder was and perhaps always will be the greatest, most innovative American sculptor; David Smith's achievement seems stodgy by comparison. Moholy will always be a greater artist for me than the guys who did only static works. Discovering the art world in the middle sixties, I remember James Seawright's 1966 debut at the Stable Gallery, with elegant machines that were sold to significant collectors. I remember that several friends advised me to see Wen-ying Tsai's debut at the Howard Wise Gallery in 1968, and they were right, as good friends usually are, to introduce me to his dancing rods. (It was at Wise's as well, around that time, that I saw my first significant video piece, Frank Gillette and Ira Schneider's *Wipe Cycle*, but that belongs to another story that should include several multiprojections seen at the 1967 Montreal World's Fair. They have made single-screen filmgoing less acceptable ever since.) I remember a Boyd Mefferd plastic layer cake at the Whitney Museum in 1968, its patterns of changing illumination holding my attention. I remember seeing around this time a Robert Irwin suspended disc at the Walker Art Center, the wall behind it reflecting the shadows produced from four strategically placed lamps. I thought this sort of art the wave of the future and said so more than once at the time.

However, by the following decade technological art disappeared from the galleries and thus from the museums supporting them. The last time I saw Mefferd, perhaps a decade ago, he was doing mammoth installations for shopping centers; the last I heard he was repairing yachts. Seawright had only one other one-person New York show, in 1970, though he too has produced kinetic sculptures for shopping centers (and taught at Princeton). Though Tsai continues to live in SoHo, his work is exhibited nearly everywhere else in the world but his adopted country.

There has been a tendency to attribute this unfortunate void to some overpublicized disasters sponsored by Billy Kluver's Experiments in Art and Technology, but that explanation is insufficient. In most exhibition spaces, good technological art was too competitive, stealing attention from paintings and sculptures that only stood still. (The George Segal on the ground floor of New York's Port Authority Bus Terminal has fewer spectators than the George Rhoads in the same building.) Technological art was not only expensive to make; it was expensive to show and to maintain. Once a genuine patron like Howard Wise closed his shop, devoting his resources instead to video, there was no one left to show it, reminding us that we need no more expect "everything good" to get exhibited than "everything good to get published."

And so whenever I come across any recent technological art my first thought is testing whether the best of it is as good as it used to be. One artist to restore my faith has been George Rhoads, who has been depositing his kinetic sculptures — mechanical theaters, actually — in such places as the Port Authority Bus Terminal, La Guardia Airport (temporarily), Terminal C at Logan Airport, the Museum of Science in Boston, and numerous shopping centers across North America. As little balls run along cleverly interconnected paths, these Rhoads machines display color and sound, wit and complexity, humor and pathos, apparently as accessible to children as to adults, all in the great Calderian tradition.

Since Rhoads' art has never sold well, it is not surprising that he has had a patron, and it is not surprising that this patron, David Bermant, is a shopping center developer who realized that he could give his retailers character (and de facto child-minders) wholly without government support. Uncorrupted by any need for a peer-panel system, Bermant has for more than two decades now consistently backed technological artists neglected elsewhere — not only Rhoads and Seawright but Clyde Lynds and Ted Victoria, among others. Should any of his shopping center publics judge a work unsuitable, Bermant is able to move it with a dispatch that our GSA would find enviable. Precisely because no one else supports (or collects) technological art so avidly, the combative Bermant ranks as either "a sucker for bad art," if you dislike this sort of work, or one of the great patrons of our time.

Whenever he decides to sponsor anything, whether in his own name or that of the foundation bearing his name, I await the results. In the spring of 1967 there was a PULSE show, the acronym standing for People Using Light Sound Energy, in the ground floor at 420 West Broadway. There was a Clyde Lynds exploration of fiber optics in the front room, as well as a large Kristin Jones/Andrew Ginzel piece; and in a back room, almost inaccessible unless you knew where to go, was a George Rhoads wall piece, a kinetic sculpture roughly the size of a large painting, that invariably attracted more viewers than its space could comfortably hold. This show's catalogue was, indicatively, not only a book but a videotape (sloppily produced, alas), for photography cannot represent kineticism as well as video. Even though PULSE received few reviews, it was not for nothing that the New York membership of the Association of Art Critics selected it the best local nonmuseum show for the 1986–87 season.

Then in his late sixties, Bermant spoke at the time of moving himself from Westchester to Santa Barbara, where he would announce his arrival with a bigger PULSE show. More than three years later, it has happened, at a far more colossal scale, with works distributed through the transient exhibition space of the Santa Barbara Art Museum, the lobby of the County Administration Building, several galleries at the University of California at Santa Barbara, and local public spaces, including the airport, which now has the *Goodtime Clock* (1984) that was once at La Guardia. (So that is where it went!) And this exhibition likewise came with a book catalogue as well as a videotape.

With eighty-seven works by sixty artists, *PULSE 2* establishes that technological art is scarcely a monolithic entity and thus that understanding begins with discriminations. There is a fundamental difference between those artists who work *with* a technology and those working *through* it. Bruce Nauman's "discovery" is running the letters of "MALICE" backwards in static neon. Lamps embedded in the heads of Jonathan Borofsky's figures project static images. Jenny Holzer uses liquid crystal displays much as any two-bit signmaker would. None of these artists even attempt to explore or alter the peculiar properties of the technologies they choose to use. Epithets such as opportunist or dilletante come to mind, even if you wish they didn't. Tsai, by contrast, discovered how strobe lighting might affect our perception of vibrating rods or falling water, in both cases revealing images not seen before. Ted Victoria explores illusions available to light projectors, such as making water appear to drip upwards. The spinning lamps of Alejandro and Moira Siña display the sculptural presence of light without substance.

Understanding also depends upon accurate classification. The simplest technological art depends upon special kinds of electric light, such as Dan Flavin's neon *Monument to V. Tatlin* (1969), or Robert Irwin's disc that is illuminated from four sides, both of which will always be masterpieces. (However, in the Santa Barbara installation the lights from one work flowed into other spaces, creating unintentional shadows.) A further development in this line is Michael Hardesty's *As If* (1990), in which ultraviolet light is shined upon a globe perhaps two feet in diameter. Put your hand between the light and the globe and then take it away and the shadow of your hand will remain on the globe. (Cute though this procedure is, it should be said that anybody doing it more than twice must be stoned.)

A second category includes work that requires technological assistance, even though the machine need not be visible in the work's presentation. Bill Fontana records the sounds from one place only to broadcast them in another, in this case from the Stroke Bell Tower that is the tallest landmark at the university. All I ever heard were the sounds made by animals from other places in the world, though I expected to hear, as in other recent Fontana pieces, sounds from elsewhere in Santa Barbara. On further thought, all electronic music could be considered machine-assisted, the technology preceding the experience of the work, sound being sound, regardless of its source. Likewise, computer graphics remain graphics.

Autonomously moving sculptures belong to another category. At the Santa Barbara Museum was Dennis Oppenheim's *Four Spinning Dancers* (1989) that functioned only part of the time. Beside this rather simple sculpture was his *Ghost Tantrums/Static Tremors* (1988–89), in which an electric train was supposed to go over a track laid over the large letters spelling out the work's title. Atop the train's engine was a hood that I suppose represented the increment of art. However, it also seemed to upset the vehicle's balance; and rather than allow the train to jump its track regularly, the Santa Barbara Museum marked this display, at least at the opening, "out of order."

Most George Rhoads machines would fall into this category as well, even though their movement is made more complicated by the use of well-balanced distributors that direct the balls down any of two or more possible paths. (Because balls can jump their tracks so easily, Rhoads and his associates won't release a piece until it has been tested for scores of hours.) On further thought, these could have been made in the nineteenth century, because the only machine in most Rhoads pieces is the motor attached to a chain-link hoist that continuously carries the balls to the top of their runs. In the County building he showed the first of his *Lunaticks* (1987) in which many white circles move at various speeds in circular patterns over a black field, creating the impression of autonomous busy bees. Knowing his art, I suspect that subsequent works in this vein will be more complicated. (At O.K. Harris in New York recently was displayed a similar piece with attractively slower movement.)

Machines with variable responses should represent a higher level of technological art. I remember a black Robert Rauschenberg frieze at the Museum of Modern Art some two decades ago. When you made a sound, a light flashed behind the vertical glass, revealing the image of overlapping chairs suspended in space. When you made another sound differing in pitch, a different light came up, revealing another section of the surrogate mural, albeit similar in imagery. Liz Phillips' horizontal *Soundtable I and II (Wet and Dry Landscape)* (1989–90) represents a more complicated, if obscure, extension of the same principle. Roland Brener, a Canadian artist new to me, showed *Life in Quick Basic* (1987), in which two robots move across a single track, perhaps in response to the movement of each other. The moving arm in James Seawright's *Electronic Peristyle* (1966) has a photocell that responds to great changes in illumination, forcing it to stop before proceeding again, making the sculpture a cybernetic system that responds to its own movement. In

Milton Komisar's *The Philosopher's Geometry* (1988), the joints uniting lucite bars change color in a continuous flickering, and continuously changing, sequence.

Bermant's dominance of technological art gives him a monopoly over what should be a free market. Thus, omissions reflecting his blindness recede ever further from public view. There are no holograms in his shows, though holography represents the most energetic use of light, illustrating that holography remains a technology whose esthetic achievements and possibilities are insufficiently understood. Neither PULSE exhibition included a video more recent than Nam June Paik's *Participation TV* (1969). There is no computer-generated kinetic imagery either, even though it too contributes to technological art in our time.

Nonetheless, it was good to see so much technological art on display in *PULSE 2*, even so many old friends, because the whole transcended the best of its parts, reminding me at least that, yes, this genre continues to be valid, filled as it is with a growing variety of interesting works that can, like the best art, be seen again and again, together with art of its kind(s), as here, but also apart, everywhere else art is shown.

The New Arts' Scenes (1970)

The topic of largest interest is real estate: tracking down and/or fixing up a loft, spotting "a place in the country" for the summer. This concern with self-location often dismays visiting friends of art who expect discourses on the "philosophy behind the new art," i.e., transcendental sales talk. — Harold Rosenberg, "Tenth Street: A Geography of Modern Art" (1954)

For every new art, there is a new scene for art; and each art in the sixties has witnessed, in America at least, the formation of new social milieus. In painting, the change has been most conspicuous, as rapidly increasing prices for masterpieces of the fifties have created a boom market for more recent works of any reputation. This means, on one level, that the number of people painting—i.e., painting seriously out of the highest contemporary traditions—has increased enormously; on another level, that there were over fourteen hundred one-man shows in New York City in 1967–68. This affluence means also that a few successful artists under thirty-five can afford to purchase town houses, the time-saving aid of hired assistants and specialized craftsmen, perhaps a summer cottage in the country, and many other luxuries traditionally the domain of older artists, if not the upper classes. As the mores of the profession succumb to affluence, the successful artist is less likely to be ashamed of his extravagant wealth than a comparable figure was only a decade ago. Perhaps because prestige can be swiftly translated into fame, which in turn can usually be translated into money, publicity has become unprecedentedly important to artists and collectors alike, some of whom strive to make fame induce prestige, rather than the reverse. Indicatively, one sculptor of pseudo-note has even hired a press agent, as well as allowed an entrepreneur to found a restaurant in his name; similarly, there is more financial and perhaps professional success to be gained from an enthusiastic mention in the Sunday art news (or gossip) columns of the *New York Times* than a favorable discussion by that paper's art critic. Whether all this money and attention is "good for art" cannot be definitively discerned just yet; nonetheless, much historical truth informs Herbert Read's contention, in *Art and Alienation* (1967), that, "There is no demonstrable connection between the quality of art in any period and the quality of patronage."

It is today possible for a successful artist, even one as critically respected as Jasper Johns and Claes Oldenburg, to become far more of a celebrity than

71

Jackson Pollock or Willem de Kooning, totem figures of the previous generation, ever were (or allowed themselves to be); and the social commentator
Tom Wolfe has written that the highest echelons of New York City society
regard a celebrity painter as the most desirable pulling presence at occasions
intended to induce other kinds of contacts and commerce. The enterprising
collector of new art has also achieved a prominence unknown before, as his
name is sought for the directing boards of museums, he is sometimes profiled
in the slick magazines, his personal collection is frequently photographed,
and he becomes an ersatz critic whose opinion is sought on the current scene
(if not made more influential than the judgments of the acknowledged critics).
"One who landed early on the shores of Abstract Expressionism," quipped
Harold Roseberg, "is invited to lecture on his deed like a Marine colonel in
the first wave at Iwo Jima." While the diversity of American patronage is partially responsible for the stylistic pluralism that allows several styles to thrive
simultaneously, the spectacular appreciation of paintings inevitably persuades some people that their purchase can be not only socially estimable but
more lucrative than speculations in stocks or real estate. More than one old-
timer painter, dealer or art watcher has complained that a "strictly business"
atmosphere has infiltrated the current scene, as well as corrupted the ongoing
critical discussion.

Painters and sculptors, on the whole, are probably less susceptible to
sociological discriminations than other groups of artists. For instance, although New York painters inhabit a cultural world different from non–New
York artists, and homosexuals are different from heterosexuals, these distinctions scarcely separate one esthetic style from another, or pervasively influence either the establishment of reputations or the bestowal of spoils. (Sexual persuasion may influence, however, the immediate propagation of a particular style, which lovers-in-common sometimes female and other times
male, have been known to carry from one artist to another.) There is probably a socioeconomic difference between painters who have a regular gallery
connection, artists who show occasionally, and those who have never
shown — an upper, a middle and a lower class of the profession, so to speak;
but these distinctions scarcely relate to stylistic differences. Birthdates may
divide the first generation of abstract expressionism, born before 1915, from
the second, born largely after 1922, as well as explain why nearly all
technological sculptors were born after 1930; and it is perhaps suggestive that
pop art should come from artists born between 1923 and 1933, most of whom
tend to celebrate popular culture of the late forties. However, such a generational interpretation of recent painting disintegrates before minimal and
psychedelic styles, whose exponents span the years. American artists under
fifty are likely to be more articulate than their predecessors, partly because
inarticulateness is no longer fashionable in the community of visual art, mostly
because nearly all the younger figures passed through college, if not graduate

school, where expository language is the local currency; but the ability to talk incisively is no measure of either stylistic difference or artistic excellence in contemporary art. Of those painters who have earned some recognition and yet insufficient income, most teach in the art schools or universities, usually part-time or on short appointments, moving from place to place, rather than climbing up the academic ladder. Neither an academic connection nor the eminence of the painter's university counts for anything in getting a show or establishing his reputation or even making an artist known, while nothing later than abstract expressionism is regarded, yet, as an academic style. A common artistic aspiration often shapes a friendship, especially if two artists working in the same way have nothing else to unite their interests; and group exhibitions, in both galleries and museums, sometimes serve as occasions for artistically like-minded strangers to establish lasting alliances. Even though people of identical background, age or esthetic persuasion are likely to favor one another's company whenever possible, the world of painting seems genuinely less cliquish than others; and the society of sculptors is more or less similar or tangential to that of painters.

The scene of contemporary music, in contrast, falls rather neatly into sociological patterns, dividing into three distinct communities, each of which has its own compositional outlook, its own totem figures, its own exlusionary membership of composers, its own machinery of spoils, and, inevitably, its own audiences. In the language of descriptive criticism, the three groups are serial composition, which grew out of Arnold Schoenberg's twelve-tone in-novations; mainstream composition, which observes most of the classic pro-prieties of music; and aleatory or chaotic music, which descends from atonality through Henry Cowell and John Cage to the "chaotic music" of non-pitched and non-structured noise; and nearly every composer of note clearly belongs to one or another group. All but a scant few serial composers, for instance, are holders of graduate school degrees, professors at liberal arts universities, sometime recipients of at least one commission from the Fromm Music Foun-dation, subscribers (if not contributors) to *Perspectives of New Music*, heterosex-uals; and their works are generally performed before audiences of a few hun-dred professionals—either fellow composers, musicians, musicologists or music students.

Mainstream composition is the only modern musical language frequently performed in the great concert halls of both Europe and America; its com-posers win the grand commissions, the generous patronage, the sponsorship of a non- or semi-musical high society. Theirs are also the compositional names to become household words. Most mainstream composers are also performers; most composers teaching in the music conservatories (as distinct from the universities) practice and inculcate the mainstream style. It would be neither unfair nor libelous to say that most (but not all) major mainstream composers are homosexual, and that this taste informs their social world.

Aleatory music belongs to a much smaller society, consisting mostly of composers influenced by John Cage; largely impecunious in economic status, they perform to small bohemian audiences, mostly of painters, dancers and other artists, in dowdy, if not makeshift auditoriums.

Most young composers of note — those born after 1930 — subscribe to the compositional predilections of their acknowledged teachers; and this habit explains why the short biographies of rising composers, unlike those for painters, invariably mention the eminences with whom they studied. While published critical opinion influences the reputations of mainstream composers, the informal hierarchies of reputation in both avant-gardes are indebted less to critics than the choices of both the totem figures and the concert impresarios.

The society of film divides, first of all, rather strictly into Hollywood and non-Hollywood; and in this case "Hollywood" includes not only the place itself but those oases of professionals around the country who look toward Hollywood's moguls for both support and approval. The other group coalesces around the phrase "underground cinema," which defines not only an informal network of distribution centers and sympathetic publications but also an increasing number of loosely related people on the campuses, in the bohemias of the cities and elsewhere, whose common marks would be subscriptions to *Film Culture* (even if they regard it skeptically), reverence for the dogged devotion of critic and publicist Jonas Mekas, and insufficient funds for the basic materials of their trade. Although members of the latter group have, largely following Mekas' initiative, taken to calling themselves the "avant-garde" of film, or "The New American Cinema," filmmakers in the Hollywood orbit have produced some of the most original, eccentric and valuable American cinema of recent years — David Lean's *Lawrence of Arabia* (1963), Stanley Kubrick's *Dr. Strangelove* (1964) and *2001* (1968). Here and there are signs of a middle ground, taking esthetic aspirations from the "underground" and yet financing and distribution from Hollywood — examples include John Cassavetes' *Shadows* (1958) and *Faces* (1968) and Shirley Clarke's films; but even after a decade of laying planks, the floor of this position is hardly firm.

The first thing to be said about the society of dance is that it is financially impoverished; according to the critic Clive Barnes, neither Paul Taylor nor Merce Cunningham, two of the major figures in American avant-garde dance, earns as much per year as a bank clerk. Particularly if the choreographer has a company, as most of them do, there are dancers, designers, costumers, technicians and sometimes musicians to support, as well as administrative people; and this kind of expense inevitably demands patronage, both from private foundations and wealthy individuals. Primary patronage for Martha Graham's company has shifted, in recent years, from the Baroness de Rothschild to Lila Acheson Wallace, co-founder of *Reader's*

Digest, while Rebekah Harkness has supported a number of individuals and groups, as well as several series of performances, through the foundation bearing her name; and several successful painters a few years ago donated their own works to help establish a Foundation for Performing Arts, whose primary purpose was supporting not only Merce Cunningham's company but more impecunious dancers. Otherwise, money comes to American dancers from teaching less in colleges (which usually demand a degree in "physical education") than in schools attached to the choreographer's company, in addition to performance tours, mostly of American universities or abroad under the auspices of the Department of State; and even in New York City, the concerts by major groups are rare, while audiences generally number less than the house's capacity. The few regular critics of dance wield unusually great power, affecting not only audiences but the beneficence of the less specialized private foundations. Although there are spectators particularly enthusiastic about dance, the audience for the art still generally overlaps with that for music — mainstream people preferring Martha Graham (who commissions works from mainstream composers), aleatory audiences preferring, say, Merce Cunningham or Yvonne Rainer. (Serial composers, in principle concerned with isolating the materials of their art, rarely attend dance performances.) Most choreographers born after 1935 relate best to the institution in which they were primarily trained — Nikolais dancers giving their recitals at the Henry Street Settlement House and Merce Cunningham alumni invariably performing together. Finally, the mixed-media arts have yet to establish communities of their own, except the collective tribes like USCO or the Merry Pranksters, because most intermedia artists socially still belong to the art worlds in which they were originally trained.

One current argument holds that the traditional avant-garde is dead, primarily because the audience for art picks up so quickly on the latest innovation; but in this criticism the phrase "avant-garde" functions not as an art-historical concept — ahead of the professional pack — but as a sociological term meaning ahead of the cultured society. In the end, this argument is all but tautological, holding that the "avant-garde" cannot be truly vanguard once it is publicly recognized as the "avant-garde" (an error analogous to charging that *Finnegans Wake* loses its complexity once it is explained); but this line of thinking is not only unpersuasive but socially and historically untenable. In fact, while certain new styles in painting and sculpture move with unprecedented quickness into both the established private collections and the art museums, into the slick magazines and even university curricula, all of the figures mentioned in this essay went scorned for a number of years and many still suffer public neglect. On the other hand, the audiences for the new in the various arts have, in general, become more populous, thanks largely to more widespread college education and the general affluence that brings wealthier and increasingly sophisticated audiences — thanks also to the more enlightened tastes of those critics and journalists who disseminate to the larger public. Beyond that, it appears that for every new art there is a new audience, or vice versa; for just as the spectators for an Arthur Miller play presented on Broadway usually average forty-five years of age, so the audience for a mixed-means theatrical event is generally under thirty-five. The same difference in age separates the people flooding an Andrew Wyeth exhibition from those attending a show of the new sculpture; for just as it seems all but inevitable for most people (and even some critics) to admire for the rest of their lives the kind of art they learned to appreciate in college, so it is a young audience that inevitably is more open to the claims of a new art, and more aware of its immediate tradition. And so too, it is the adventurous young artist who is the first to deny, if not eventually disprove, that "everything has been done."

The New Arts in 1968, 1969, 1971, 1972 (1969–73)

If the avant-garde imitates the processes of art, kitsch, we now see, imitates its effects. The neatness of this antithesis is more than contrived; it corresponds to and defines the tremendous interval that separates from each other two such simultaneous cultural phenomena as the avant-garde and kitsch. — Clement Greenberg, "Avant-Garde and Kitsch" (1939)

Both the arts and artists continued to prosper in 1968, as there were yet more grants, larger stipends, higher salaries for teaching positions, huger fees for lectures and other public appearances, even larger audiences, yet higher prices for fresh works of painting and sculpture; in a time of statistical prosperity, the arts in particular have boomed. If someone had invested in a hypothetical Art. Inc. a decade ago, his equity probably would have doubled by now. Economically, established artists are squarely in the middle class; and some of the more spectacularly successful — Saul Bellow, Andy Warhol, Robert Rauschenberg — have the life-styles, as well as the tax problems, of the upper class. Because the critically respected creators of true culture never had it so good in America, one could almost imagine a conventional father telling his artistic son, "If you work hard at your art and do something very good, boy, you'll become famous and rich, too."

Actually, it would be more correct to say the structure of income in the arts resembles that of American society at large — while vast numbers are wealthier than they ever expected to be, a goodly percentage are still indigent, as well as too unrecognized or amateur to latch onto the gravy train. The National Council on the Arts took cognizance of this strata late in 1967, granting minimal fellowships to a few barely published writers; however, support at that level has been, so far, hardly sufficient, while Congress continually threatens to reduce the National Council's budget.

Politics was the primary ecumenical concern of artists and writers in 1968, as they mobilized on behalf of one candidate or another. Most flocked to Eugene McCarthy, largely because of his dovish stand on Vietnam, while Robert F. Kennedy, before his tragic death, could count many eminent culture figures among his supporters. Eldridge Cleaver of the Peace and

Freedom Party won a few and Hubert Humphrey a smaller number; but scarcely an artist or writer of note publicly supported either the Republicans or the newly legitimized Communist candiates. American involvement in Vietnam continued to inspire the protests of writers and artists, though probably to a lesser extent than before; and perhaps the most dramatic gesture was Robert Bly's, upon receiving the National Book Award. He presented his check to a draft protestor who came up from the audience and then excoriated not only American activity in Vietnam but, more courageously, the refusal of his own publisher to protest.

As for books, the best-seller lists for non-fiction included the usual run of manuals for dieting, child raising and other common predicaments; however, among the more substantial volumes were Stephen Birmingham's portraits of the WASP upper class, *The Right People*, a sequel to his Semitic *Our Crowd*; the pseudonymous Adam Smith's wry guide to the hipper sidewalks of Wall Street, *The Money Game*; James D. Watson's memoir of discovering DNA, *The Double Helix*; and Norman Mailer's memoir, *The Steps of the Pentagon*. Samm Sinclair Baker's *The Permissible Lie*, another exposé of advertising, achieved overnight notoriety as the first book to be canceled by a subsidiary publisher, Funk & Wagnalls, because the parent firm, in this case *Reader's Digest*, Inc., editorially objected to its content. In fiction, the big novel for the winter was William Styron's *The Confessions of Nat Turner*; for the spring John Updike's *Couples*; for the summer, Charles Portis' *True Grit*.

Three new films made particularly outstanding impressions in 1968. One of them, *Bonnie and Clyde*, was actually released the summer before, to perfunctory reviews; but thanks to Warren Beatty's one-man publicity campaign and recommendations passed from mouth to ear, it reopened at first-run houses, while several major critics returned to hail it (implicitly raising the question of who leads whom to the movies). *The Graduate* was another charming Mike Nichols film that sporadically scratched some complex feelings and several hard truths; and Stanley Kubrick's long-awaited *2001* was perhaps the first great work of art in cinemascope, the first great "head" film (particularly in its abstract sequence of traveling through infinity), the greatest film made out of science fiction, and much else superlative. In many ways, *2001* was more truly avant-garde than nearly all "underground" cinema, while nothing emerged from the cinematic depths as stunning as Kenneth Anger's *Scorpio Rising* of a few seasons back.

The principal crisis in classical music is the shortage of major orchestral conductors, as Leonard Bernstein resigned from the New York Philharmonic, Jean Martinon from the Chicago Symphony, and Erich Leinsdorf from the Boston Symphony, while Eugene Ormandy intimated his retirement from Philadelphia. Attempts to find successors for these positions led to the discovery that few first-rate musicians relished all the headaches intrinsic in such demanding and diversified jobs. In contemporary composition, the news had less to do with major new pieces, which (except for Milton Babbitt's *Correspondences* and *Relata II*) were remarkably few, than the release of many recordings of recent works that were previously familiar only to a few. Columbia Records, in particular, issued nearly two dozen albums of far-out contemporary works, while RCA put out the premiere recording of Elliott Carter's masterful *Piano Concerto*. If anything is currently happening in the world of jazz, the news has yet to leak out.

The mixed-means rock concert also appeared in 1968 — not the vaudeville-like performance for the screaming teenagers but a genuine concert for a seated, respectful audience which applauds politely after every piece. Here the sound, usually amplified to the threshhold of pain, is accompanied by spectacular and imaginative light shows projected onto a backdrop screen. Perhaps the most tasteful of these theaters was the new Fillmore East in New York, which, unlike the classic Fillmore Auditorium in San Francisco, is not a huge empty space but a sometime movie theater with seats and a recessed balcony. Fillmore East's Joshua Light Show was among the most admired of its kind.

The commanding performers at such extravaganzas were the Doors, whose lead singer, Jim Morrison, became a major sex symbol; Big Brother and the Holding Company, led by Janis Joplin (known as "Big Brother"); Jimi Hendrix, who often climaxes his act by destroying much of his equipment; and certain older black blues performers, such as James Cotton and the legendary B. B. King, both of whom, until a few years ago, performed exclusively to black audiences. In rock music alone, no new songs were quite as universally commanding as the Doors' "Light My Fire" or the Jefferson Airplane's "Somebody to Love" of the year before; and the most impressive new recordings were either rather elemental and hard-driving, like the Ohio Express' "Yummy, Yummy, Yummy" or Big Brother's "Piece of My Heart," or else inordinately complex, like the albums of Cream, three Englishmen with an American blues sound, or a stunningly hyper-electronic group, the United States of America.

No high arts in America today are quite as prosperous as painting and sculpture, perhaps because the rapidly appreciating prices of famous works of the 1950s persuade speculative collectors that there are capital gains to be made. In the wake of abstract expressionism's decline, several discernible styles continue to prosper simultaneously — minimal painting, primary structures, psychedelic surrealism, mixed-media, technological sculpture, assemblage, even Op and Pop art, and much else, along with hybrid varieties between. This is a time when almost anything distinctive sells or earns support (even museums snatch fresh pieces out of the artist's studio); and nearly everything that sells eventually prospers. Among major museum exhibitions, none had as powerful an impact as "Dada and Surrealism," which opened at New York's Museum of Modern Art and then traveled around the country;

and no kind of works drew as much awed and serious interest in the U.S. as those incorporating advanced technologies.

The big event of American dance was Merce Cunningham's first extended season in the city where he has lived and worked for over twenty years, New York, accompanied by numerous major articles celebrating him and his creations. Even though the audiences at the Brooklyn Academy of Music were sometimes less than capacity, they were nothing but enthusiastic, as were most of the major critics. Cunningham's choreography continued to explore that abstract, nonlinear, nonreferential style established over a decade ago, while he continues another, more recent tendency of deemphasizing movement in an expressive setting of props, lights, responsive structures, and sometimes film. The result is ensemble pieces that owe less to the continuous, cohesive dance of classical ballet than the discontinuous, disjunctive mixed-means theater of happenings and environments. Among the other companies, those headed by Martha Graham, Paul Taylor, Alvin Ailey, Robert Joffrey, and Ann Halprin were particularly distinguished; and the New York performances of three younger post–Cunningham dancers — Yvonne Rainer, Kenneth King, and Meredith Monk — commanded respectful discriminating interest.

American theater offered more of the same to its various audiences. On Broadway, there were more slick comedies, a few musicals, several serious imports from England, such as Joe Orton's *Loot* and Peter Nichols' *Joe Egg*, and short runs by respected European groups. In university theaters, the dominant fare was still the classics; and Off Broadway had a number of plays that were neither as pleasing as uptown fare nor as challenging and esoteric as Off Off Broadway. The breakthroughs of the season had less to do with theatrical style than with nudity, mostly but not entirely female, in plays on Broadway, as well as Off and Off Off. Uptown hits were *Rosencrantz and Guildenstern Are Dead*, a clever footnote to Shakespeare by the young Englishman Tom Stoppard; Bruce Jay Friedman's suburban black comedy, *Scuba Duba*; and Arthur Miller's *The Price*. The most successful new musical comedy, *George M.*, starring Joel Gray, promised to join *Hello, Dolly* (now performed by an all-black cast), *Fiddler on the Roof*, and *Man from La Mancha* among the Broadway interminables.

Off Broadway's standbys included Mart Crowley's *The Boys in the Band*, perhaps the first explicitly homosexual drama; *In Circles*, co-adapted from a Gertrude Stein text by Lawrence Kornfeld, who directed it, and Al Carmines, a hip minister who also wrote the music and sang many of the songs; *Hair*, a rather slick musical about hippies that, in the director Tom O'Horgan's much revised and even hairier form, ran on Broadway; and *Your Own Thing*, a rocky musical adaptation of Shakespeare's *Twelfth Night*. The new Negro Ensemble Company, founded with the beneficence of the Ford Foundation, established a fine reputation with several productions, most of them by non–American playwrights. The great shocker of the season—it made nearly everything else in live theater look hopelessly tame—was *Dionysus in '69*, presented way, way off-off-Broadway in an abandoned metal-stamping plant rechristened "The Performance Garage" near New York's Canal Street. Here several young people, known as "The Performing Group," adapted Euripides' *The Bacchae* into a stunning, involving production that filled the available space and at times surrounded, if not implicated, the audience.

On television, the most authentic, appreciated shows are still live presentations of historic events, whether they be professional football games, the activities surrounding the assassinations of Martin Luther King and Robert F. Kennedy, or the political conventions; for all the major television shows of the past season would confirm Marshall McLuhan's thesis that the medium works best not when it offers entertainment but when it extends the viewer's eyes and ears, and possibly his entire perceptual system, to a distant scene.

Perhaps because politics and national tragedies were in the end so distracting, this was less than a glorious year for art and artists; many complained that they were having more trouble than usual in finishing their primary work. Nonetheless, as far as the world's culture was concerned, the U.S. was still definitely, as the hip phrase goes, "where it's at." The most influential modern dance, the most adventurous painting and sculpture, the most persuasive directions in both concert and pop music, and even some path-forging works of literature continue to push America to the world's cultural frontier.

*   *   *

The scene of art in America in 1969 simultaneously experienced the opposite qualities of protest and lull—vociferous outrage over the Chicago atrocities and America's continuing involvement in Vietnam, and a lull in response to the expectation that the Nixon atmosphere would make artistic life more "normal," if not duller and more depressed, than it had been in the hectic and prosperous sixties. What was particularly interesting in the arts in the past year was less at the center of the stage, but along the aisles, where only a few enthusiasts were acclaiming works that would later attract others in increasing numbers.

For instance, scarcely more than fifty thousand people actually saw The Living Theater during their controversial and triumphant tour of their native country; but the publicity and conversation earned by their work, particularly in the "underground" and youth-oriented press, gave their radical political and artistic ideas increasingly widespread impact. This powerful influence extends not only over those who actually saw the plays but people who merely read or heard about them, for in the universities and cities were formed numerous workshops aiming to pursue The Living Theater's kind of performance art. The company's four productions ranged from literary classics to pieces as far-out as theater can get (or has been): *Antigone* adapted a Greek classic; *Frankenstein* displayed spectacular stagecraft; *Mysteries and Smaller Pieces* was a collection of provocative sketches; and *Paradise Now* was an unprecedentedly free enactment of ritualistic liberation that extended itself over the entire theater; so that as the performers continually moved into the audience, so the spectators often flocked onto the stage. The experience was closer to that of a revivalist meeting, where ministers of the church attempt to "freak-out" the unconverted, than anything experienced in American theaters before or since.

Otherwise, the fate of more commercial theater remained rather familiar. There was another import from Britain with a spectacular performance by a great English actor—Alec McCowen in *Hadrian VII*; Howard Sackler's *The Great White Hope*, which portrayed the misadventures of the prizefighter Jack Johnson: innumerable "protest" and "black" plays Off Broadway; and several productions exploiting the previous year's discovery of male and female total nudity: the much-heralded *Oh, Calcutta!*, *Geese*, the Minneapolis Firehouse Theater's imaginative production of *Faust*, and *Che!*, which broke another taboo by portraying various kinds of copulation. Perhaps the most truly distinguished production of the year was also the first true success for Jules Irving's regime at New York's Lincoln Center—Heinar Kipphardt's *In the Matter of J. Robert Oppenheimer*, a theatrical documentary enhanced by Joseph Wiseman's spectacular performance in the title role.

In books, the command still belonged to nonfiction, and the most conspicuous commander was Norman Mailer, now more "the greatest reporter" (and unsuccessful candidate for mayor of New York) than a notable novelist. Not only did his memoir of the October 1967 Pentagon protest, *The Armies of the Night* (1969) cop both the National Book Award and the Pulitzer Prize in 1969, but his hastily written report on the political conventions, *Miami and the Siege of Chicago*, also earned enthusiastic interest, while his essays for *Life* on the moon landing would also become a book. Other important nonfiction included Gay Talese's *The Kingdom and the Power*, a compelling exposé of infighting at the *New York Times*; Robert F. Kennedy's posthumously published memoir of the 1963 Cuban missile crisis, *Thirteen Days*; Eric Goldman's judicious appraisal of *The Tragedy of Lyndon Johnson*; Abbie Hoffman's charmingly incendiary *Revolution for the Hell of It*; and Buckminister Fuller's more substantial speculative program for man's possible future, *Operating Manual for the Spaceship Earth*.

In fiction, the book of the year was the much-publicized *Portnoy's Complaint*, a somewhat pornographic rendering of a 33-year-old Jewish man's neurotic mind; but the more perceptive critics judged that the book's success depended more upon its salacious content, and occasional comedy, than its prosaic literary style. The more valid fiction came from stylistically more imaginative writers—Vladimir Nabokov's inventive but flawed *Ada*, Joyce Carol Oates' highly mythic *them*, and Paule Marshall's *The Chosen Place, the Timeless People*. Fictional best-sellers included *The Andromeda Strain*, a mystery by a young man still in medical school, Michael Crichton; Mario Puzo's *The Godfather*; and Jacqueline Susann's *The Love Machine*. The year's important poetry included three collections of past work by major poets of the older generation—John Berryman, Elizabeth Bishop, and the late Randall Jarrell; Robert Lowell's *Notebook, 1967–68*, collecting hastily written recent work, was a disappointment, perhaps signaling the king's eventual decline from his highest pedestal. There were also significant collections from lesser known but incipiently major poets—James Wright, David Ignatow and David Wagoner.

Sculpture became decidedly more interesting than painting, as the latter floundered over the question of what could still be done to a two-dimensional surface. In recent sculpture, the major concern has been the use of unusual material, displayed in ways that were equally unusual and yet true to both the materials and the situations in which they were displayed. So Richard Serra poured molten lead into the corner of the wall, allowed it to dry slightly, then pulled away jagged strips (leaving some hardened lead stuck to the wall); and Rafael Ferrer, at the opening of the same show at New York's Whitney Museum, put leaves on top of ice cubes that slowly melted away. Pop, the new art of the early sixties, became the stuff of museums, as Claes Oldenburg had an immense retrospective at the Museum of Modern Art and Roy Lichtenstein's paintings graced the Guggenheim.

No film in 1968 was nearly as spectacular and path-forging as Stanley Kubrick's *2001* (1968), which remains a touchstone for the future; and the most acclaimed pictures were rather slick dissections of contemporary characters—the male hustler in John Schlesinger's *Midnight Cowboy,* and the young lovers in *Goodbye, Columbus*. More inventive were the semi-documentaries of adventurous American youth—*Monterey Pop*, which chronicled the performers and audience at the first great rock festival, and *Easy Rider*, which portrayed two young pot-smokers who discover America by motorcycle.

The major events in dance followed the first American tour in years of London's Royal Ballet; and with more modernist endeavor came important younger choreographers, each with a distinct and maturing style—Twyla Tharp, Meredith Monk, Yvonne Rainer, Mimi Garrard, and Kenneth King. Dancers themselves, at least in New York, were particularly enthusiastic about not-young tap dancers reviving an unfashionable but still impressive art in a vaudeville production called *The Hoofers*. The best television shows were still indebted to news events, as though the imaginations of producers could not create programs half as exciting as reality. The televising of the

snail-paced events surrounding the moon landing was such an unprecedentedly popular broadcast, around the entire world, that producers
wondered whether or not those stoned before the tube may not find speed less
of a virtue than lethargy.

The New York Philharmonic, after a prolonged search, finally found a
replacement for Leonard Bernstein in Pierre Boulez, the combative French
composer who in recent years has turned more of his energies to conducting;
and no new compositions commanded as much respect as Luciano Berio's
highly theatrical and dramatic *Symphonia*, and Milton Babbitt's *Relata II*, the
latter being one of the most difficult and precisely complex pieces ever written
for orchestra. In rock, the Rolling Stones established themselves as more relevant than the Beatles; and the third best English group, the Who, finally
earned deserved success in America with their two-record rock cantata,
Tommy. With the decline of the masters of the first great wave of American
rock — Jefferson Airplane, the Doors, and Janis Joplin — came the arrival of
promising new mature stars, such as Credence Clearwater Revival, Johnny
Winter, a freaky-looking spectacular white guitarist with a commanding taste
for Afro-American blues, and Sha-Na-Na, twelve college guys who successfully do studied imitations of middle fifties' rock. The lure of rock stars
brought 400,000 dissident young to a milk farm near Woodstock, New York,
in the socioesthetic event of the year.

Another important new composition, John Cage's *HPSCHD*, filled a
concrete basketball arena with fifty-nine separate tracks of sound, eighty slide
projectors, several motion pictures, and thousands of people. The result was
less a musical composition than a mixed-means theatrical environment; and
much of the most interesting recent art was similarly between or beyond the
old art forms. At New York's best rock emporium, the Fillmore East, rock
bands compete with the most spectacular light display ever projected on a
background screen, the Joshua Light Show; and the totally mechanical
"Magic Theater," which has been touring American museums, forged a New
king of performance art. One intermedium, between literature and design,
mixes words with visual materials, as in "concrete" or pattern poetry (recently
collected in several anthologies) or imaginatively designed books, such as
Claes Oldenburg's *Store Days*, John Cage's *Notations,* and Edward Ruscha's
Thirty-Four Parking Lots, all of which imaginatively combine word with image.
Signs all over suggested that the most adventurous contemporary art was
moving away from not only the old forms but also the old media, into unques-
tionably new territory.

*   *   *

The Arts in America suffered a fairly severe recession in 1971, reflecting
both the economy and the political climate; for not only was there an apparent

scarcity of either first-rate or innovative works, but money available to culture became increasingly tight. As major American publishers issued noticeably fewer books, so writers discovered that contracts for their works were harder to fetch. In the other arts as well, sales were down, all kinds of prior commitments were cancelled, fellowships and similar sweepstakes were increasingly competitive; and as a result young and emerging talents were especially decimated. If there were, for instance, 69 productions staged on Broadway in 1969–70, already at the beginning of the Nixon recession, the number had shrunk to 45 by the following season. Off-Broadway, where the expenses of mounting a production are less, the comparable statistics dropped from 125 to 101; and everyone from producers to stagehands was bemoaning the absence of theatrical investors. The post–Nixon return to normalcy had already undermined the great sixties' energies of the eccentric and the avant-garde, while the forces of more conventional art simply lacked what it takes to fill the vacuum.

There was some good theater, nonetheless, as Broadway never fails to deliver such long-runners as *No, No Nanette*, a nostalgic revival in which remembered stars of the thirties auspiciously reappeared; or Paul Sills' *Story Theater*, which imports a theatrical style and company long established in Chicago. The promising new playwrights appeared Off Broadway, as has become customary by now—John Guare's *The House of Blue Leaves* and Paul Zindel's *The Effect of Gamma Rays on Man-in-the-Moon Marigolds*, both of which, curiously, were written several years before their first successful production. As Off Broadway staging has become more and more expensive, a new set of theaters, housed in cafés, bars, churches, and private lofts, emerged in the late sixties; and in such Off Off Broadway settings have the more experimental recent scripts been produced, such as John Ford Noonan's *Concerning the Effects of Trimethylchloride*, Ronald Tavel's obsessively witty *The Arenas of Lutecia*, and Richard Foreman's uncompromisingly difficult *Total Recall*. In nonliterary American theater, the most acclaimed new "playwright" was Robert Wilson, also known as "Byrd Hoffman," whose *Life and Times of Sigmund Freud* and *Deafman Glance* eschew expository language for performance in which a large number of exotic-looking figures are "choreographed" into a succession of stunning theatrical images. The result has been a theatrical experience that was as successful in Europe, though "untranslated," as in Wilson's native U.S.

Toward the late sixties, emerging young choreographers seemed more interesting than the experienced figures, but that sense of emphasis was reversed in the seventies. The greatest dances of 1971 came from three established choreographers now just over fifty—Merce Cunningham, Alwin Nikolais, and Jerome Robbins. Cunningham's *Signals* suggests yet another step in his multilayered stylistic development, and Nikolais' latest works, *Structures* and *Scenario*, not only belong among the best pieces of his long career, but the latter, by eliminating those props characteristic of Nikolais' works, also suggests a personal stylistic advance. Robbins' new ballet, *The Goldberg Variations*, incorporates modernistic touches into classical conventions; so that the elegantly costumed performers do such peculiar moves as roll on the floor, or just shake their hands, or collectively walk in asymetrical patterns. Not only does this new Robbins piece skillfully deploy a large company of dancers, but it lasts for the unusually long time of well over an hour.

The recession hit music in more ways than one, as the New York Philharmonic floundered through a succession of part-time conductors. The first-rate Cleveland Orchestra suffered the sudden death of George Szell, and Chicago the departure of Jean Martenon, while new pieces of note were few and far between. What slightly revived American opera from its hopelessly European affectations was the New York City Center's imaginative new production of Leos Janacek's *The Markropolis Affair* that also made a prima donna out of the California-born soprano Maralin Niska. In rock, English kings like the Rolling Stones and the Who continued to dominate, as not only were the major American groups disintegrating and/or continually reshuffling their personnel, but three supersingers died prematurely—Jimi Hendrix, Janis Joplin, and Jim Morrison. The scene for live concerts also declined, as Bill Graham closed his Fillmores East and West and violence became endemic at other arenas; and in the aftermath of Altamont, where bystanders got killed, none of the many open-air gatherings ever equalled the "good vibes" of Woodstock in 1969. Symptomatically, the rock newspapers that seemed so exciting and "where it's at" in 1969—*Rolling Stone, Fusion, Crawdaddy* and the like—were floundering by 1971. Interesting new performers emerged, nonetheless, usually from undeserved obscurity—a Berkeley-based group called Joy of Cooking, the balladeer Neil Young, and the pianist-singer Leon Russell.

Movies suffered the doldrums as well, as the new interest in low-budget hip films (following in the wake of Dennis Hopper's *Easy Rider*) petered out in a succession of duds; and nothing in 1971 commanded the popular moviegoing imagination as strongly. Mike Nichols' *Carnal Knowledge* came close, as did in their different ways the year's most popular films, *Love Story* and *Little Big Man*. Among more specialized American achievements were Woody Allen's very, very funny *Bananas*, Peter Bodanovich's highly cinematically self-conscious *The Last Picture Show*, and Melvin Van Peebles' *Sweet Sweetback's Baadasssss Song,* which heralded the arrival of a talented black filmmaker. However, by comparison, such new Italian cinema as Bernardo Bertolucci's *The Conformist* and Elio Petri's *Investigation of a Citizen Above Suspicion*, for instance, seemed more substantial.

The major new craze in modernist visual arts was called "conceptual," as museums across the country, as well as around the world, devoted exhibitions to "Information," or "Systems" and the like. In theory, conceptual art is art (or artistic ideas) that takes the form of print, whether a statement or design, which is photographically enlarged for display so that the kinds of mystery familiar to artistic experience are suggested solely by the words at hand. Therefore, statements like "Perpetuate a Hoax" (by Steve Kaltenbach) gain artistic credence not only from their appearance in an art museum and the fact that their author, as in this case, has been praised as a promising young sculptor-painter, but also from a certain rare kind of resonant suggestiveness. If conceptual art seems to climax a recent tendency toward works that were *less* (in both size and substance) than previous art, the other direction of contemporary art, toward moreness, continued to prosper. The art and technology exhibition at the Los Angeles County Museum displayed objects of immense size and staggering internal complexity, sometimes fabricated with the aid of professional engineers; and this more-like kind of artistic ambition also informed the exhibition "Works for New Spaces," that opened the new Walker Art Center in Minneapolis.

The first symptom of literary decline is the recent absence of a prestigious best-seller comparable to Saul Bellow's *Mr. Sammler's Planet* the year before; perhaps the closest semblance was the late Sylvia Plath's *The Bell Jar*, which was originally published only in England in 1963. In nonfiction, the best best-sellers dealt with incipient social change, not only its likely perils but its unprecedented possibilities — Charles Reich's *The Greening of America* and Alvin Tofler's *Future Shock*; and there were clear enthusiasms for good books about Indians — Vine Deloria's *Custer Died for Your Sins* and Dee Brown's *Bury My Heart at Wounded Knee* — and Women's liberation, such as Kate Millett's *Sexual Politics* and Germaine Greer's far more radical and wittier *The Female Eunuch*. Mike Royko's examination of Chicago's Mayor Richard Daley is a muckraking classic. On lower levels, *The Sensuous Man* came, as expected, in the wake of *The Sensuous Woman's* success. In the fall of 1971 appeared not only good new novels from Irvin Faust and Bernard Malamud but the collected essays of Leslie A. Fiedler, the most brilliant critic of that generation just over fifty. Among the most striking literary debuts rank the first commercial books of poets Clark Coolidge, N. H. Pritchard, and Hugh Seidman, and novelists Frederic Tuten and G. S. Gravenson. Abbie Hoffman's *Steal This Book* became a good seller in spite of seing self-published, after many major houses rejected it and most bookstores refused to stock it. Even in economic and spiritual doldrums, such private pleasures as reading still seemed fairly accessible and reasonably priced.

*   *   *

The arts in 1972 seemed less exciting than they were in the years immediately before, which is to say that fewer absolutely first-rate works appeared and that perceptibly less "was happening." The reasons for the rise and fall of art are largely mysterious, while a single year is simply not a large enough unit to warrant any generalizations. We are, however, now three years into the seventies, and the most obvious conclusion is that the arts in America have not sustained the rapture, inventiveness, and excellence witnessed in the sixties.

What makes this decline surprising is that artists of the seventies were not only inspired but also "educated" by the possibilities of the sixties. In addition, the unprecedented affluence of sixties' artists, along with superior art education, propagated a persuasive faith. It is indicative that far more young people are pursuing serious artistic ambitions today; so that America now has twice as many conscientious poets than a decade before, as well as twice as many painters, probably thrice as many working choreographers, etc. Perhaps because they matured in a thriving, expanding culture, young American artists and writers have become terribly precocious, accomplishing major artistic tasks, such as choreographing their own dances, far earlier in their lives than their comparable predecessors.

The recent recession has caused a severe crunch in art's burgeoning economy, sharply curtailing the amount of money available, while the number of serious artists remained approximately the same. Elementary economics tells us that a lot of artists would thus be financially wanting, especially if they were young and/or unestablished, for recession devastates not the fat cats but the rising underclass. (That development produces, in turn, the increasingly acerbic generational conflict that seems to riddle every art. In-between 35 and 40 lies the sharpest dividing line.) Recession also means that artists feel demoralized, as well as more competitive in ways detrimental to artistic excellence and growth. There were other reasons, no doubt, why the current boom in American art is more quantitative than qualitative. One nagging question remains: To what degree should decline in the arts be considered an index of our cultural condition?

The last few years have also witnessed collective assertions by artists belonging to sociological groups who had previously suffered discriminatory neglect—blacks, Puerto Ricans, Indians, women, etc., all of whom have demanded increased representations in every American cultural endeavor, along with greater public support of their particular traditions. In film, for instance, there were an unprecedented number of films by blacks, apparently for blacks. While the elmination of unjust discrimination was clearly a good thing, one current result of such ambitions has been a lot of inept art, presented less for its intrinsic quality than for its supposed "cultural" value. One secondary fear is that an overflow of bad art from any minority group ultimately undermines their claim to equal status in cultural competition.

What excellences there were in American theater last year emerged largely from the complex enterprise that Joseph Papp founded in the fifties, initially to produce free Shakespeare in New York's public parks. In the mid-sixties, he got a permanent indoor theater with several performing areas, which he progressively turned to the production of new, mostly American plays. His more successful shows, such as *Hair*, have moved out of this downtown showcase onto Broadway, which has, in turn, become ever more reliant upon the Public Theater for its own commercial successes. For instance, Papp's theater has recently supplied Broadway with a musical version of *Two Gentlemen of Verona*, two rather melodramatic plays by young David Rabe, and Jason Miller's *The Championship Season*. One first-rate production that never got uptown was John Ford Noonan's *Older People*, whose thirteen vignettes relentlessly exposed the pains of aging. In New York theater at least, most everything else, except for the productions of Melvin Van Peebles, looked pale by comparison. What Papp's leadership suggests is that not only excellence but theatrical business will become increasingly dependent upon "noncommercial" theater.

Dance has been the rising art of the past few years, winning more critical attention and progressively larger audiences; it capitalizes upon the decline of U.S. drama in becoming the country's premier form of live performance. The high point of the past season was the Stravinsky festival that George Balanchine's New York City Ballet staged to honor the greatest ballet composer (and rhythmicist) of the twentieth century. The series included thirty ballets, twenty-one of which were new — including such masterpieces as Jerome Robbins' *Requiem Canticles* and Balanchine's own *Duo Concertant* — all of which revived a somewhat flagging ensemble. Meanwhile, the young dancer-choreographer Eliot Feld folded his own fledgling company, which lacked enough dates, to return to work auspiciously with the American Ballet Theater.

Modern-dance exists apart from ballet, as modern-dancers have different values and aspirations. It survives as another language, so to speak, of articulated movement, as both pop-rock and folk dancing are yet other languages; for not only does each kind of dance have its own exclusive traditions, but performers rarely excel at, or even perform in, more than one kind of dance. The surprise of last year's modern dance was *Hoopla*, the first truly first-rate piece by the choreographer Murray Louis since his much-repeated *Junk Dances* (1964). Its scene is a circus, its atmosphere that of a carnival, and it is filled with the witty props and parodies that mark Louis' best work. His principal professional associate, the choreographer Alwin Nikolais, has, by contrast, moved away from a dependance upon props for pieces that emphasize light in relation to dancing performers. His latest long piece, *Foreplay*, also introduces a common dance theme that Nikolais had previously made a point of avoiding — heterosexual difference.

Stanley Kubrick's *A Clockwork Orange* was not as innovative in style as *2001* (1968) but among its virtues were crystalline photography, richly detailed settings, and a clearer theme, which examined the meaning of violence in human life. Initially appearing at the end of 1971, it quickly copped the Academy Award for directing, partially in compensation, to be sure, for the Academy's neglect of his earlier masterpiece. The blockbuster of the year was *The Godfather*, and the better foreign films included Vittorio de Sica's *The Garden of the Finzi-Continis*, Jan Troell's *The Emigrants*, and Marcel Ophuls' *The Sorrow and the Pity*. On television, the best programs, both mediumistically and dramatically, remained football games.

The most conspicuous show in music was Leonard Bernstein's *Mass*, which opened the John F. Kennedy Center in Washington and later came to New York's Lincoln Center. A retelling of the Catholic mass, it blended religious values with sociological concern, classical music with rock, drama with Alvin Ailey's choreography, and opera with pop. As classy and yet vulgar as Bernstein's work has always been, it nonetheless succeeded, as Bernstein nearly always has, in winning a large audience. Meanwhile, Boulez assumed command of the New York Philharmonic, and Georg Solti did likewise with the Chicago Symphony, allaying, for the while, the recent crisis in American conducting. Partially in response to the recession's crunch, native record companies were less likely to favor young American composers, or American orchestras, and the big companies were reviving old tapes as "greatest hits." One new craze was piano rags, initiated by Joshua Rifkin's surprisingly successful record, as a whole neglected school of black American music was revived, along with a few of the surviving old-time performers. The highest stars in rock remain the Rolling Stones, who had another awesomely successful tour of the States.

The visual arts were recovering from the dominance in the late sixties of minimalism and conceptualism which seem, in close retrospect, to have been genuine dead ends. There were no taste-setting exhibitions, for instead emerged a variety of moderately interesting styles, none of which has become commanding — a colorful lyricism, a post–Mondrian geometricism, and a new realism. The best practitioners in this last tendency, such as Chuck Close and Janet Fish, realize representational qualities that surpass, in crucial ways, any "realism" done in painting before. Although the recession decreased drastically the amount of money spent on new paintings, the most ambitious visual artists continued to aspire to innovation and change. Whether or not a distinct "new art" will actually emerge seems, increasingly, a question of faith.

The book industry remained economically slumped, as publishers issued fewer books and thus became deleteriously dependent upon a few best-sellers for the profits that might impress absentee conglomerate-owners. Richard Bach's *Jonathan Livingston Seagull* was a best-selling short illustrated fable about a seagull, while Herman Wouk and Irving Wallace rehearsed melodramas already familiar to their millions of readers. The latest publishing craze remained feminism, which has capitalized upon the fact that women dominate the book-buying audience, and the most successful new magazine was *Ms.* For men, the favorite new book was Roger Kahn's memoir of the Brooklyn Dodgers, *The Boys of Summer,* and by autumn it seemed that nearly every professional football star had a new book in print. The young of all sexes made both *The Last Whole Earth Catalog* and Abbie Hoffman's *Steal This Book* into best-sellers. The "big book" that finally never appeared, Clifford Irving's fraudulent "autobiography" of Howard Hughes, inadvertently demonstrated that American publishers will advance huge sums for a book they expect to be a best-seller, no matter how dubious its origins.

On less transient, more serious levels, key novels were Raymond Federman's monumental breakthrough, *Double or Nothing,* Eugene Wildman's *Nuclear Love,* and Ishmael Reed's *Mumbo Jumbo.* In poetry, the major volumes were the retrospectives offered by two older, previously neglected eccentrics— Jackson Mac Low and Bern Porter—along with the posthumous poems of John Berryman. Important nonfiction included Murray Bookchin's *Post-Scarcity Anarchism* and *Things to Come,* an essay on the near future authored by Herman Kahn and B. Bruce-Briggs. However, given the condition of the publishing industry, it seemed likely that many good, uncommercial manuscripts would, for one trivial reason or another, remain unpublished, just as a lot of good art would remain unseen, and good music unheard. A loss of possible communications, along with a decrease of both experience and intelligence, are among the real costs of a cultural recession.

Printout on the New Art (1968)

In the old art the writer writes texts.
In the new art the writer makes books.
— Ulises Carrion, "What a Book Is" (1975)

A new art has been with us for nearly a decade, as it emerged from the void that followed the diminishing achievement of abstract expressionism. One would hope that happenings, pop art, minimal sculpture, and related art are, like the computer and thermonuclear capability, sufficiently established in our common sensibility by now so that we can accept them as subjects worthy of intelligent discussion. Nonetheless, the criticism of an art which is distinctly of the sixties has been just about as baffled and evasive, if not downright ignorant, as say, most writing about computers; for the new art, sometimes masquerading as an anti-art, is so radically different from the dominant styles preceding it that the long-established critics have been less than helpful. In contrast, as the creators of the new art are, by and large, intelligent, educated, and unashamedly articulate people, their own writings often provide the best guides to comprehension and judgment. *Assemblage, Environments & Happenings* (1966) and *Store Days* (1967) are the first full-sized books by two of the new art's most eminent and articulate practitioners; and as their respective authors, Allan Kaprow and Claes Oldenburg, are both adventurous artists, who have created theatrical pieces and prose essays as well as objects to be displayed, so the books they produce are distinctly unlike any tomes we know, and yet as coherent and authentic as everything else they have done. As vanguard artists of diversified talents, both have intelligences integral enough to books that artistically resemble their art, and each possesses in addition a distinct sensibility that colors every page. Whereas Kaprow's book is logical, definite, and accessible, Oldenburg's is cunningly ironic, indefinite, and elusive.

Oldenburg has a literary mind, trained in English at Yale and then honed on journalism in Chicago, that concocts suggestive allusive prose and cultivates perceptual enhancement; Kaprow, trained originally in philosophy, practices clear exposition and champions intellectual reforms. Let me start by saying that his book is, among other things, the most substantial exposition we have of the esthetic aspirations and critical ideas that inform much of the recent scene. If nothing else, it demonstrates why Kaprow became a primary theorist of several tendencies in post-abstract expressionist American art. His 1958 *Art News* essay on "The Legacy of Jackson Pollock" forecast, if not influenced, the styles of art that we now call Pop and happenings, and the manuscript of this new book, which he circulated among friends for six years before its publication, had an enormous influence upon many of the most interesting current talents. American publishing took an unconscionably long time to get his words into print (nearly everyone, rumor has it, enclosed a cutely worded rejection slip, as if to exonerate himself from the industry's Philistinism); and it is even more regrettable that reviewers and review-editors have so far been slow to recognize its seminal significance.

In his essay on Pollock's legacy, Kaprow, then a young painter of some reputation and an instructor in art history at Rutgers, wrote the following prophetic words:

> Not satisfied with the *suggestion* through paint of our other senses, we shall utilize the specific substances of sight, sound, movement, people, odors, touch. Objects of every sort are materials for the new art: paint, chairs, food, electric and neon lights, smoke, water, old socks, a dog, movies, a thousand other things which will be discovered by the present generation of artists. Not only will these bold creators show us, as if for the first time, the world we have always had about us but ignored, but they will disclose entirely unheard-of happenings and events, found in garbage cans, police files, hotel lobbies, seen in store windows and on the streets, and sensed in dreams and horrible accidents.

This belongs among the most important passages in modern esthetics; for not only did his writing influence several students and colleagues at Rutgers who have since established themselves as important artists (George Segal, Lucas Samaras, Robert Watts, Robert Whitman, and Roy Lichtenstein) but it also reached other maturing artists who were then total strangers, among them Claes Oldenburg. In addition, Kaprow successfully coined an epithet—in his case, "happenings"—which so appropriately characterized a certain kind of experience that the term has since entered common parlance. Once a polemical young prophet, he is now, at forty, an elder sage.

As a practicing critic, certified art historian (M.A., Columbia), and recognized creator, Kaprow functions as what the sociologists would call a participant-observer—someone who is very much part of an activity and yet able to achieve the psychological distance necessary for discriminative analysis. *Assemblage, Environment & Happenings* opens innovatively with a long sequence of strategically arranged pictures that have their own story to tell, particularly about how examples of the new art resemble certain older works and how happenings by various practitioners exhibit visual similarities—by implication, how new art, even if concerned with "reality," inevitably comes out of previous art. The text that follows is richly perceptive, invariably sensible, patiently persuasive, and eminently comprehensible; and everything is so thoroughly thought through that Kaprow seems to have considered nearly all problems his new art raises. Although his prose inclines toward excessively long, sometimes "elegant" sentences (perhaps out of stylistic indebtedness to his Columbia teacher, Meyer Schapiro), Kaprow talks about the new art in the common tongue, avoiding the needless complexity and jargon that afflict so much art criticism. No intelligent reader can miss, let alone misunderstand, his major points, or doubt his concluding words:

> If some of the past is still meaningful, as it assuredly is, then what is to be retained in the present work is not archaistic mannerisms, easily recognized and praised for this reason, but those qualities of personal dignity and freedom always championed in the West. In respecting these, the ideas of this book are deeply traditional.

The mixed-means art form that Kaprow calls "happenings" descends from several discernible tendencies in modern painting. The first, probably instigated by Marcel Duchamp, considers any and all materials and subjects as viable for artistic use. Out of this tradition springs not only pop art, junk sculpture, and certain primary structures, all of which employ subject matter previously dismissed as not-for-art, but also the current wholesale rejection of the classical hierarchy which regarded the female nude as the most ideal form and, by implication, disposable junk as the lowest. In his own creative career, Kaprow wanted to see how much "art" he could discover, or create, in seemingly intractable materials; and, after pursuing this interest in his painting, he eventually made a leap to an entirely radical position—that his own art should eschew, as thoroughly as possible, any semblances of the arts we know. This purpose drove him through an "exhibition" of piles of discarded automobile tires, *Yard* (1961), to his present position in which he neither makes nor even compiles art objects. Happenings he now considers a kind of heightened format (a criterion usually signifying "art") in which an indeterminate number of people gather together to participate in certain predetermined activities which may take place in any kind of terrain and over any length of time; as an unprecedentedly open art form, happenings are, for structural precedents, as much indebted to noncompetitive games as to art.

The three words in Kaprow's title outline a second tradition of contemporary painting that likewise culminates in happenings—the imposition of greater dimensionality upon the processes of painting. Whereas assemblage, originated by Picasso back in 1912, is by definition a three-dimensional collage which usually incorporates materials not normally found together or common to the currency of art, an environment escalates the collage-principle to a multiplicity of assemblages that literally encases the spectator—an enclosed space wholly designed as an artistic object. In his own development, creating first cubist paintings in the late '40s, then "action collages" which consist of materials rapidly slapped together into three-dimensional assemblages (which he invariably pronounces as an American word, with the accent on the broadly articulated second syllable), and eventually environments, which took him out of the frame of painting. Kaprow's next step, which historically represents his innovation, came in *Penny Arcade* (1956), where he animated the subjects within that closed space, creating a kinetic environment, and thereby bestowing the fourth dimension of time upon painterly activity.

His next move, as logically derived as all his previous leaps, came in the path-breaking *18 Happenings in 6 Parts* (1959): He introduced into the gallery setting live performers in place of objects and, therefore, created an experience closer to theater than painting. He has since taken his performance work out of the gallery situation entirely, discarding the theatrical convention of an intentional audience along with such other theatrical conveniences as a beginning and an end. "The room," he writes in retrospect, "has always been a frame or format too." (In art-historical retrospect, we can also see that another of Kaprow's leaps consisted of appropriating the *act* of painting, which so preoccupied the earlier generation of "action painters," and making the artist's movement itself into the stuff of art.) As an appendix to his critical text, Kaprow's book reprints the outline-scripts and photographs of several of his own pieces, as well as those of eight other practitioners around the world; and this part too is chosen and presented with taste and care.

My main criticism of Kaprow's book is its presumptuous exclusivity; for although he quite clearly explains his own conception of happenings, he does not sufficiently differentiate them from other theatrical events that occasionally pass under the same name, such as the performance pieces of John Cage, Robert Whitman, Ken Dewey, or Oldenburg, among others. My own suggestion, which is developed in my forthcoming study, *The Theatre of Mixed Means*, is that Kaprow's pure happenings represent only one of the four distinct genres of mixed-means theatrical art—the others being staged happenings, kinetic environments, and staged performances. Each of these achieves a particular mix of the general dimensions of time, space, and materials. Perhaps because Kaprow has the philosopher's preoccupation with correct positions and the necessity of excluding invalid alternatives, he is the only major mixed-means practitioner to devote himself entirely to pure happenings; and the text explains why his own standards persuade him not only to give up painting but to regard the other mixed-means genres as essentially compromised. (This devotion to rationally deduced scruple has led to quarrels with other artists, Oldenburg among them.)

Second, his commitment to the development of his own ideas forces him to create the false impression that happenings historically extend primarily from preoccupations within the traditions of painting (with a dash of John Cage!)—a myth perpetuated in too much early criticism of the art. Actually, there is more evidence that the current mixed-means theatrical art comes from modern eccentric tendencies in all the artistic means it encompasses — painting and sculpture, music and dance, theater and film; and just as every contemporary painter, in Robert Motherwell's phrase, carries the history of modern painting in his head, so the major creators of mixed-means theater are polyliterate and multisensitive enough to be familiar with the relevant esthetic precedents in all these fields. Otherwise, *Assemblage, Environments & Happenings* is an important book, easily the most resonant overview we have of the painting and postpainting of our time; to my mind, it was indisputably more deserving than, say, *all* the 1967 National Book Award nominations under "Arts and Letters."

Oldenburg's *Store Days* is an entirely different sort of publication, designed less as an exposition than as a memento of Oldenburg's first major artistic innovation and first great work of art. *The Store* (1961) was a real lower-East Village store filled with miscellaneous objects, most of which Oldenburg created in the semblance of junk and then actually offered for sale; and this "store" subsequently became the setting for his first major series of mixed-means theatrical events, *The Ray Gun Theater* (1962). In contrast to Kaprow, whose interest is mostly in conceptions, Oldenburg is primarily concerned with image and materials; and his leap in *The Store* consisted of making the stuff within the store itself into an artistic object which bore approximately the same ironic relation to a real store as his miscellaneous sculptural objects did to their respective models. For this reason, just as we can appreciate his mammoth *Giant Hamburger* as a sculptured object that at once resembles a hamburger and yet expresses other archetypal resonances (some of them sexual; as the suggestiveness of familiar objects is a favorite Oldenburg theme), so *The Store* was a store, where things were sold, and yet was much else besides.

His book differs from Kaprow's in another way; though Oldenburg is no less an intellectual than Kaprow, as well as no less skilled with words, he uses his intelligence in an entirely different way. Whereas Kaprow wants to explain, as a teacher might confront his class, Oldenburg weaves an imaginative and thoroughly ironic commentary composed of prose materials as miscellaneous as the stuff of his store—historical data, replicas of important printed matter (such as a business card), sketches, price lists for the objects, photographs (that are not as explanatory as Kaprow's), scripts for his staged performances, various recipes, esthetic statements, ironic declarations and even occasional aphorisms. "Boredom is beautiful, but it is hard to keep awake." The result is an open-ended and semi-satisfying potpourri of bookish materials standing in relation to a real book as *The Store* did to a real store.

"My piece is called a store because like a store it is a collection of objects randomly placed in space." For the words "store," "objects," and "in space," we can viably substitute "book," "phrases," and "between hard covers."

The following passage, perhaps the most famous, should convey Oldenburg's canny style; in addition to parodying Walt Whitman and Allen Ginsberg, his words also echo ironically Kaprow's inventory of viable materials, quoted above, and perhaps the whole tradition of artists' manifestors:

> I am for an art that is political-erotical-mystical, that does something other than sit on its ass in a museum.
> I am for an art that grows up not knowing it is art at all, an art given the chance of having a starting point of zero.
> I am for an art that embroils itself with the everyday crap & still comes out on top.
> I am for an art that imitates the human, that is comic, if necessary, or violent, or whatever is necessary.
> I am for an art that takes from the lines of life itself, that twists and extends and accumulates and spits and drips, and is heavy and coarse, and blunt and sweet and stupid as life itself.

The point, of course, is that the art which he eventually created — the giant hamburger and toothpaste tube, the collapsible "soft" bathtub, and the misshapen bedroom set — has itself an ironic relation to his prescriptions. "What I want to do more than anything else," he solemnly asserts at another point, "is create things just as mysterious as nature."

Squarely in the great tradition of ironists, Oldenburg aims to fuse contraries, usually in the cross-grained fashion of plywood. "My art is a resolution of opposites," he declares in what I take to be a lapse into pure seriousness; and the art critic David Bourdon has pursued this point. "He simultaneously strives for elegant and vulgar forms, animate and inanimate forms, solidity and bodilessness, empathy and indifference. In addition, he is coping simultaneously with metaphor and concreteness, figuration and abstraction, memory and present, mystery and commonplace, individuality and mold, commerce and art." Similarly, I would say that *Store Days* as a book resolves both sense and nonsense. No reader should be fool enough to take everything he says seriously — but in the nonsense lies a clear sense of Oldenburg's incorrigibly ironic and articulate sensibility. In publishing such an unusual book, the Something Else Press does what every truly avant-garde publisher should do — produce tomes that no other house would even consider seriously; for it "explains" Oldenburg's sculptural and theatrical art less by declarative statement than by inferred resemblance.

The Cast of
American Painting (1969)

American art has differed in this respect: that the triumphs of individuals have been
achieved against the prevailing style or apart from it, rather than within it or through
it. — Harold Rosenberg, "Parable of American Painting" (1959)

The desire to define the particularity of American experiences — an impulse that has long informed certain scholarship of our politics and fiction — has recently energized students of other cultural areas; for within the past decade we have witnessed, along with additional reinterpretations of our fiction, the comprehensive work of John Burchard and Albert Bush-Brown on American architecture, Alan Gowans' mammoth and brilliant survey of furniture and habitats in *Images of American Living* (1964), Ishbel Ross' path-breaking, informative but inconclusive *Taste in America* (1967), Wilfrid Mellers' excessively mistaken *Music in a New Found Land* (1965), Roy Harvey Pearce's pioneering but erratic *The Continuity of American Poetry* (1960), and Hyatt H. Waggoner's more definitive *American Poets* (1968). The subject of Wayne Craven's *Sculpture in America* (1968) has not been examined with such chronological completeness for decades, and I know of no similarly thorough studies-in-progress of our cinema, our theater and sports — to name three areas where the Americanness of indigenous work needs a more adequate definition. The development of American painting has also been receiving more attention than before, as several broadly conceived books have appeared recently; and perhaps because their authors cannot rely too assuredly upon past scholarship, the books themselves are unusually various in both critical approach and scholarly detail.

For well over a decade, the accepted histories of native painting have been Edgar P. Richardson's *Painting in America* (1956) and Oliver W. Larkin's *Art and Life in America* (1949), the latter being the more interdisciplinary, the more compendious and the better illustrated of the two. In essence, both are directories of names, dates, sketchy descriptions, and perhaps a rough rating of cultural credit (which is to say reputation), all reported with reasonable objectivity and accuracy. Victimized, however, by an urge to incorporate everything remotely important into their narratives, both Richardson and Larkin resort to patently foisted connectives and hopelessly elastic critical categories. Furthermore, neither of these panoramic books deals with such crucial concerns as changes and elaborations in a particular style; neither conveys much sense of, first, individual creators with personal artistic predilections; or, second, the reasons why their work is American, rather than English or Pomeranian; or, third, the peculiar characteristics of American painting as a cultural entity. If a book on American art is not critically useful, in either whole or part, then how, one may ask, can it be read at all? Mostly, I would think, as a reference guide to the names, dates, and general gist of an individual artist (and, as in Larkin's case, previous scholarship about their work). Another comprehensive telephone book, Daniel Mendelowitz's *A History of American Art* (1960), is more introductory as well as more attentive to both colonial and industrial arts than Larkin, though considerably less sophisticated in its commentary; indeed, Mendelowitz's remarks on American painting (which he concludes with a paean to Andrew Wyeth!) are superficial and/or prosaic. Of the more recent macrohistorical books on American art, only two appropriate this familiar expository format: Henry Geldzahler's stylistically dry, unfailingly humble and analytically nebulous *American Painting in the Twentieth Century* (1965) and Lloyd Goodrich's *Art of the United States, 1670–1966* (1967), which is critically more perspicacious, more intelligently organized and better illustrated (though trivial in its ideas on the Americanness of native painting); and both these surveys were originally written, like much extended prose about art history, to accompany museum exhibitions and, therefore, particular preselected examples of American art. A variation in this chronological scheme is *The Artist in America* (1967), compiled by the editors of *Art in America* magazine and destined for more coffee tables than scholars' libraries; it pastes together the periodical's backlog of sumptuous plates with short, general, and thoroughly obvious essays by several hands (suspiciously identified by name only in the table of contents) on the various periods and movements, and a selection of impossibly brief statements by the artists themselves. This bulk is then prefaced with a 1958 essay by Goodrich (who apparently scavenged from this text for his more recent book), completing a slick package that inevitably lacks any critical direction or historical contribution.

John McCoubrey's *American Tradition in Painting* (1963) has an entirely different emphasis, favoring critical interpretation over the accumulation of facts, its dust-jacket promising an answer to the question of "What is distinctively American about American painting?" However, McCoubrey's interpretative ideas are so conceptually naive that his use of facts is often outrageously cavalier. In contrast to both the revisionist literary scholars (Leslie A. Fielder, Charles Feidelson, Richard Chase, et al) who have found American novelists decidedly disinclined to portray the common reality,

McCoubrey unequivocally asserts that American painting has been realistic. As he tells it, our artists have from the beginning eschewed European stylistic conventions, continental ideas of appropriate subject, and classical systems of patronage to depict unadulterated native reality. "The accuracy with which our artists have observed American scenery," his explanation runs, "has enabled them to ignore or consciously to reject those traditional skills which have been at the heart of the European tradition."

McCoubrey's troubles here stem from using "realism" not as literary critics usually do, as a term characterizing one of many available styles for representing reality (see Erich Auerbach's classic *Mimesis* but as a qualitative measure—to him one picture is more true to a certain experience than another; and precisely because our common reality is so ineffable and our sense of it so personal, *American Tradition* becomes a veritable riot of subjectivity. At times it seems that everywhere McCoubrey looks he finds reality and realism—Robert Motherwell's thoroughly abstract *The Poet* (1947) "does not recall visible nature but, as its title suggests, the unseen processes of thought"; and in classic action painting he discovers "images which sometimes are evoked in Pollock's pictures, the sight of a swallow, or brown leaves and black branches stirred by an autumn wind . . ." whereas most of us find expressive streaks of color that can, at most, be interpreted as representing a particular moment of internal consciousness. In McCoubrey's book so many scenes of social activity, so many symbolic projections of indefinable qualities, so many faintly articulated outlines all and indiscriminately become examples of "realism" that one is reminded of Harold Rosenberg's classic aphorism: "In American painting, the degree of realism in any work is a matter for individual judgement; one man's reality is another man's fantasy and a third man's corn."

At other times McCoubrey finds certain nonrepresentational paintings realistically portray "this essential [American] experience . . . of the individual standing alone in a sea of space and change"; but not only do such interpretations invariably conjure vivid ghosts in the innocent machine but unless McCoubrey can think of an example where alien artsts could handle a culture's most profound themes more effectively than native artists (such as finding, unpersuasively, that Anton Dvorak's *From the New World Symphony* is more indigenously realistic than Charles Ives' Fourth), some of his critical assertions are all but tautological, which is to say meaningless. Even worse, *American Tradition in Painting* is so ineptly written, particularly suffering from an imprecise use of language, on top of conceptual confusion, that the descriptions of individual works are as fuzzy as the exposition of major ideas (all of which raises the question of whether stylistic deficiencies caused intellectual faults, or vice versa). This may explain why, though I read the book several times, I have come across reviews and summaries of *American Tradition* that found the book emphasizing ideas other than those discussed here.

McCoubrey's argument is ultimately so solipsistic that it cannot possibly be wrong on his own terms and will inevitably be unpersuasive, to various degrees, on anybody else's. Nevertheless, if the concept of realism usually defines the accurate representation of the external scene in breadth *and* in detail, one must inescapably conclude that this quality is precisely what the best American artists, as well as the best American novelists, have never been able to achieve. McCoubrey is noticeably reluctant to quote previous scholars — the book's bibliography is short and, even then, mostly peripheral; so let me quote a few, such as Sir Herbert Read, who once generalized, "What I would describe as realism — the humble subordination of the artist before the natural phenomenon — is very rare in America," or Lewis Mumford, who declared of Albert P. Ryder, perhaps the greatest American painter of the nineteenth century, "Ryder, like Melville, was concerned with the depths, the part of experience that eludes statement, that must be hinted at, approached obliquely, rendered in parables." Indeed, at one point McCoubrey himself discovers stylistically nonrealistic symbolism in painting, as he notes that, "[Franz Kline's *Crosstown*] is also pervaded by an American sense of space. His violent strokes of black, as they reach to the very edge of the canvas — and seemingly beyond — imply the continuation of vast distances, the presence of an enormous void, of which the area of the painting is but a fragment." However, the implications of this insight go unremarked.

Indeed, so pervasively obtuse is McCoubrey's argument that a contrary thesis is implicitly suggested, which holds that the best American paintings have focused upon small or hidden phenomena, depicting them with a flatter and yet fuzzier surface, usually to evoke metaphysical essences rather than photographically accurate detail. They often embody what McCoubrey identifies as the major theme (perhaps "myth" would be more apt) of American art — the isolated individual's battle with recalcitrant nature and unbounded space. Even the landscape painters of the nineteenth century, such as Jasper Francis Cropsey and Asher B. Durand, seem more interested in atmospheric and symbolic resonances than natural detail; and how can any student of American painting forget not only that Albert P. Ryder's masterpiece portrays death riding horseback, but that the impetus of nearly all significant twentieth-century art has been counter-realistic. This reality of American artistic practice so strongly cuts against McCoubrey's thesis that he is impelled to dismiss Ryder as "shallower" than Winslow Homer and Thomas Eakins, although Ryder, by most criteria, would seem the more profound artist, as well as the single native progenitor of the consciousness-inspired painting of Pollock, de Kooning, and Jasper Johns. In the end, it is hard not to regard *American Tradition in Painting* as evidence of deep deficiencies in critical taste if not as well of the intellectual immaturity of American academic art history.

Richard McLanathan's more recent comprehensive study, *The American*

Tradition in the Arts (1968), displays less critical ambition than McCoubrey's essay, all but completely evading the thesis implicit in its title; and his commentaries on particular matters are critically thin and often stylistically inept, if not simply platitudinous and/or condescendingly simplistic. The book is a clumsily arranged series of short, introductory essays on various subjects, including architecture and industrial arts, in addition to painting and sculpture. Most of the critical generalizations sound suspiciously familiar to anyone who has read the standard literature: "Essential practicality" and "individualism" characterize early native architecture. "Copley has introduced the theme of man's battle against the forces of nature, which was to be a dominant theme in American art thereafter." "In his grasp of factuality as the basis of his art, Whistler was true to the American tradition." And so on. The text is riddled with extraneous remarks, many of them as ridiculous as the following, in which McLanathan opens the second paragraph on "Early Architecture" by discussing the anonymous portrait of *Anne Pollard* (1721):

> One would have given much to heard Mrs. Pollard's reminiscences of the beginnings of settlement, of the pressing needs of people weakened by disease and the hardship of voyage in tiny crowded vessels that rolled and pitched as they limbered [!] through stormy seas. . .

The verbal refuge of lightweight criticism is platitude. For instance, in closing some scandalously curt and superficial remarks about Alfred P. Ryder, McLanathan says of the many extant forgeries of the master's work: "But more important, the free plastic expression of feeling and idea are absent in the imitations; there is no haunting image, none of the revelation of the truth of vision and of dream that was his unique contribution to American art." (And one trusts that the ladies at the Club applauded enthusiastically.)

Even worse, McLanathan commits the elementary sin of writing descriptions that defy the reader's imagination, such as, to quote a nonartistic example, the one about a painter who "lived largely in a wheel chair and could not move without crutches" (with which to push the wheel chair?). McLanathan's comments on nonrealistic paintings are usually uncomprehending; and he cannot quite bring himself to write what he would clearly like to assert—that varieties of photographic realism establish the primary American tradition. McLanathan may be the first Harvard Ph.D. to hail in print Gutzon Borglum's extravagantly sentimental *Mount Rushmore* as "the most spectacular sculpture ever done by an American," while his remarks about a very recent art reveal a Philistine factuality that takes pride in esthetic imperviousness: "Sculpture has become an open or solid cube, a plastic tent, a clicking box, an undulation of pipe, a compressed automobile body. . . ." But even worse, the pictures illustrating this book are often too small and too fuzzy, though the book's awkward textual design allows excessively wide white-space margins. The following samples of chapter headings — "Thomas Eakins and the Big Tools of Art," "William M. Harnett and the Pursuit of the Real" — devastatingly indicate the general quality of McLanathan's critical language.

Professor McCoubrey contributes the essay on painting to the uneven compilation entitled *The Arts in America: The Colonial Period* (1966) in which his colleagues at the University of Pennsylvania, Robert C. Smith and George B. Tatum, write about architecture and decorative arts respectively, while Louis B. Wright prefaces everything with a superfluous essay in general cultural history. The strategy of dividing the visual art of the period among three critical hands is probably unnecessary and, in this case, less than effective, because neither Smith nor Tatum are as critically competent as McCoubrey. Indeed, the survey of architecture exemplifies the embarrassing circumstance of having fairly large photographs that tell a more distinctive critical story than the text; and Professor Smith's contribution is a detailed but diffuse survey that indicatively closes not with a conclusion but yet another miscellaneous example, in all scarcely supporting his opening contention that "American craftsmen designed and executed some of the finest silver and furniture made anywhere in the 18th century."

McCoubrey's essay is not only more persuasive than his book but also more informed and informative about anonymous artists (even the designers of those marvelous gravestones), lesser talents, and the major figures as well; for his major theme is the development of painterly competence. He shows, for instance, how the representational style of very early painting, reproduced alas only in black and white, reveals the artist's unwillingness or inability to cope with certain representational problems and yet his ambition to do good work within his limited capacities; and his remarks about both the work and personalities of Robert Feke, the key transitional figure, and then the two masters of the age, Benjamin West and John Singleton Copley, are particularly discerning. Another thread of McCoubrey's narrative tells of the assimilation of the recent English style, rather than continental alternatives, followed by a rejection of baroque artifices and other of "art's most elegant blandishments"; "the beginnings of a consistent American modificaton of whatever was borrowed"; and then the development of visionary and spare, rather than realistic and detailed, styles of representation — a trend which McCoubrey, perhaps because of his earlier intellectual commitments, obscurely describes as "the transformation . . . from illusionism to the patent, enumerative techniques of the untrained artist who prefers to paint what he *knows* to be there rather than what the eye records."

The next period of American cultural history, from 1790 to the Civil War, is the subject of Neil Harris' *The Artist in American Society* (1966), which could rival McCoubrey's *American Tradition* as a monumentally defective book. If McCoubrey is the victim of an approach and theme inappropriate to his materials, Harris is simply not the right man for his chosen subject. The problem is less one of formal qualifications than knowledge and experience; trained not as an art historian but in American history (at Harvard, under Oscar Handlin), Harris seems to know little about art — neither his attempts at critical illumination nor his choice of illustrations are effectual — and even less about artists, whether alive or dead, and nothing at all about creativity and the processes of art. The result is a gracelessly written, disembodied narrative, full of names and dates but scarcely any human beings, where the characters discussed could just as feasibly be composers (who are, indicatively, mentioned not at all), academic scholars or dog-breeders, shuttling between both continents and forging a propitious chosen career in a less than congenial environment. If only to avoid any confrontation with their identity as creative people or the processes peculiar to their profession, Harris favors general terms like "the artist" or "artists," rather than dwell too long on individual figures. While the professional fault of the art historian is obscuring jargon, Harris exhibits not only the social historian's irremediable passion for obvious remarks but also a penchant for factual excess, which induces him both to devote eighty-six pages to footnotes and to produce whole fine-print paragraphs itemizing, say, the various illnesses that aspiring American artists suffered in Europe. Perhaps because he never resolves whether his subject demands an analytical essay or a chronological narrative, he appropriates both structures, to the peril of repetition and diffusion. The book is more useful on such previously neglected dimensions as the growth of patronage and the fomation of artists' organizations, as well as the progress of New York City's cultural dominance. No one need subscribe to Oscar Handlin's blurb on the back of the book, "Neil Harris's study of *The Artist in American Society* is the most important contribution we have had to the history of American culture in recent years," for he is probably too committed to the professional success of his former student and younger colleague, as well as perhaps more than a little negligent in his homework. Harris promises a sequel on the American artist from 1860 to the present — a task that his sponsor Handlin might well advise him *not* to undertake.

Barbara Rose's *American Art Since 1900* (1967) ploughs over much of the same painting terrain as her friend Henry Geldzahler, as well as appending one sketchily insufficient chapter apiece on sculpture and architecture; but her commentary is considerably more interpretative, particularly in elaborating the related themes of American artists' changing relation to European examples and the development of an indigenous tradition. Her remarks about the individual artists are both effectively organized and well-informed; for instance, she knows that Stuart Davis was probably the first American to appropriate a French style for distinctly American purposes, or that David Smith, like Picasso, made a sculpture advance by drawing upon stylistic ideas developed in recent painting, or that Alfred Steiglitz and Robert Henri polarized the world of American art to either social realism or avant-garde abstraction, or that not until 1956 did aspiring American painters mostly look to domestic heroes. She also draws generously upon the artists' own statements, which, in accordance with current taste, she always takes literally; and many of these texts, some of them otherwise unobtainable, she has elsewhere compiled into a valuable anthology, *Readings in American Art Since 1900* (1968).

Rose's expository prose is efficient, though stylistically unadorned; and her concise analysis of certain individual paintings, many of which are minutely illustrated, are commendable. (On the other hand, her remarks about things that flow into and out of painting, such as environments and happenings and aleatoric music, are mostly obtuse and/or ill-informed.) At her best she mixes cultural history with technical expertise, as in the following passage about "The Eight," who were fashioning an American painting at the turn of the century:

> Although they admired Whistler's skill, particularly in handling values, they resented his achieving renown as a Europeanized American. Nevertheless, it was Whistler's technique of washing in the background of the canvas with an atmospheric "soup" before working his rapidly sketched figures onto it that Henri imitated in his own paintings.

For a critic as young as Miss Rose, scarcely into her thirties, to attempt such a comprehensive book marks a genuine ambition; and she makes an admirable practice of working outward from her chosen themes and subject, rather than hewing to the major threads and stopping signs.

The book's defects fall mostly between the broad outlines and the particular details. Her major troubles stem from a certain glibness, particularly in addressing those knotty problems of, first, artistic influence and, second, stylistic change that plague those more conscientious art historians who, to their credit, would not avoid them. More than once she is excessively arbitrary in attributing influence: "[Larry] Poons, whose paintings derive in equal measure from Pollock's all-over painting, Newman's chromatic fields, and Mondrian's grids. . . ." And other passages on an artist's sources escalate into a riot of modish pedantry. A related mistake, perhaps so intrinsic in art-historiography, is the strained connective, constantly tying together things that might best remain separate. Second, if an art historian does not deduce in advance general reasons for the rise and fall of artistic styles, his explanations for the demise of a particular way of working are likely to be evasive and platitudinous; and here Miss Rose is especially confused. At first she attributes the evident decline of Abstract Expressionism to a dissipation of internal energies, much as if the style were a biological entity passing into senescence, and then to "internal contradictions [which] could no longer be held together in a viable synthesis." However, on the following page, the demise of this style, as well as others, is blamed upon different, external causes of, first, the challenge of younger artists (which is a bio-psychological analogy) and, second, excessive public acclaim: "As is so often the case in the recent history of art, Abstract Expressionism began to lose impetus as a style at the point when it began to win public acclaim." And the reader is left more befuddled than edified.

Another problem for critical history (particularly of very recent activity) that Rose avoids is revealing her criteria for including (or excluding) an individual artist in her narrative; and she may perhaps take comfort in the sense that the excessively revered Clement Greenberg is no more edifying on this problem. He adopts an earth-tremor metaphor to open his contribution to *The Artist in America*, implicitly rationalizing his subsequent focus: "At the beginning of the nineteen-forties, the strongest new impulses of American painting were making themselves felt in the area of abstract art." Particularly in discussing recent artists, whose reputations are scarcely canonized, Rose is more evasive than courageous. At times the rationale seems tautological — the significant artists are those working in the predominant styles, because the more important styles are created by the more talented artists; but this explanation remains indefinite. Indicatively, in discussing the work of living painters, particularly those she is known to know, Rose rarely commits any negative impressions to print; and precisely because she takes so few risks in championing artists currently unknown or unheralded, this book seems a compendium of currently received opinion. Indeed, one could wager that future scholars will classify *American Painting Since 1900* as a record of reputations established in 1965, which is to say that it is less a definitive history than a summary of how artists and critics important at a certain moment regarded the recent native past.

The primary trouble with these books is that none will greatly enrich our understanding, as distinct from knowledge, of American painting, either in whole or in parts. They are either lacking in unifying threads or erroneous in argument, deficient in taste or embarrassing in emphasis, thin in critical understanding or factually encyclopedic at the expense of close analysis or overarching interpretation. (The difference is that encyclopedias are usually identified as such to make sure that innocents do not attempt to read them as books, from start to finish.) Nearly all these historians avoid the more difficult issues, such as the causes of stylistic transformation, even though a major purpose of scholarly history of art is precisely the representation and explanation of such changes. None, for instance, dares broach such a central puzzle as why American painting in the eighteenth and nineteenth centuries should be less realistic than European, yet not until after the Armory Show did Americans attempt the inevitable result of their earlier predilections, completely nonrepresentational paintings. These historians seem all but completely mystified by the puzzle of transient stylistic dominance — why one way of working rather than another should seem so successful at a certain time; and none consistently attempts to connect the peculiar characteristics of our changing cultural milieu to particular indigenous stylistic developments. (Indeed, only Neil Harris scratches one dimension of this question, the sociology of American artistic reputations.) More than one of these historians seemingly understands little about esthetics and artists; and most of them work in apparent ignorance of the problems and possibilities of their scholarly form, which is a critical history of cultural materials. As a result, we still do not have a book about American painting that belongs beside F. O. Mattheissen's *American Renaissance* (1941) or Leslie A. Fiedler's *Love and Death in the American Novel* (1960; revised, 1966) — persuasive and definitive comprehensive explorations of imaginative artifacts, regarded both individually and collectively, in the context of American cultural history.

One possible reason for this intellectual shoddiness is that the profession of art criticism seems, in some crucial respects, more primitive than literary criticism, which has a longer tradition (and thus higher standards) of both textual analysis and historical rigor; for any considered comparison suggests that the minds of the best literary historians are critically more sophisticated than the major art historians. Another reason is that scholars trained in academic cultural history have usually regarded nonprinted materials as beyond their intellectual competence or professional methods; and even when they decide to talk about artists, as Neil Harris does, they feel more comfortable recording his physical activities than quoting his written statements. (Typically, even Jacques Barzun's *Berlioz and His Century* [1951] contains no musical examples and preciously little critical analysis!) What is also curious is that critical ideas of cultural particularity developed in, say, studies of fiction or film have not been tested against American painting, even though as products of the same collective energy, which is imagination in America, one art is likely to stylistically resemble another. That interdiscipline known as "American Studies" is designed to produce horizontally literate scholars — possessing knowledge stretched across various fields, rather than a vertical mastery of a particular area — who could talk about literature and each of the arts in the same breath (or paragraph); but such polymathic cultural historians have not yet appeared, or at least have not published their findings.

The basic truths are not only that American artists throughout our history have represented subjects different from those favored by Europeans but also that imaginative minds here would seem to function in radically alternative ways. One needs only regard the pictures in a comprehensive book about American paintings to see conclusively how they diverge from European; and among the constant questions for critical scholarship should be the character, the causes and the meaning of this traditional and continuing dissimilarity. And behind these issues ultimately lies a confrontation with the more puzzling and sublime question of the peculiar quality of imaginations in this ineluctably mysterious culture, which is to say finally the imaginative content of our own heads.

Our Continuing Discovery
of Soviet Art (1990)

It's just like deja vu all over again. — Yogi Berra

You would have thought that several years down into glastnost we've seen all there is to see in avant-garde Soviet art both contemporary and modern, but two recent traveling exhibitions initiated in Seattle, on the occasion of the pseudo–Olympian Goodwill Games, would prove that know-it-all sentiment wrong. The more ambitious, *Art into Life: Russian Constructivism, 1914–1932*, cocurated by Richard Andrews and Malina Kalinovska, assisted by Owen Smith, at the University of Washington's Henry Gallery, will tour to Minneapolis and perhaps Moscow. The other, *Between Spring and Summer*, subtitled "Soviet Conceptual Art in the Era of Late Communism," born this past summer at the Tacoma Art Museum, will tour first to the Institute of Contemporary Art in Boston and then to the Des Moines Art Center.

The first virtue of *Art into Life* is that it keeps its eye on the subject, Constructivism in Russia, thereby excluding, among other tangents, such expatriates as Antoine Pevsner and Naum Gabo and suprematists with more fashionable names (e.g., Kasimir Malevich). It keeps as well to the theme implicit in the exhibition's title: in the wake of the Bolshevik revolution these abstract artists participated in social change with applied projects that nonetheless reflected their esthetic heritage. This accounts for the exhibition's scope, including as it does paintings, sculptures, largescale graphics, environments, photomontages, stage designs, and architectural proposals. A second virtue is the inclusion of originals previously unfamiliar (at least to me), such as the El Lissitzky poster that melds male and female heads (which turns out to be considerably larger than I imagined), Alexandr Rodchenko's spectacular environmental *The Workers Club* (1925), and various works of Gustav Klucis, a Latvian slighted in previous exhibitions. Though barely represented not only in the George Costakis collection but in previous surveys of this terrain, Rodchenko emerges as the strongest figure, stronger even than Vladimir Tatlin (represented by the original realization of this *Letatlin* flying machine), if only because Rodchenko's works in various media, beginning with painting, were so extremely innovative. (Now that I think of it, one artist from this period still unknown is Sophia Dymshits-Tolstoya, often photographed in the company of Tatlin but mentioned only in passing in the catalog, even though she reportedly did reliefs at Moscow's Metropole Café before the Revolution. I initially knew about her as my grandmother's sister.)

Art into Life was a crowded exhibition at its original venue, with many individual pieces atop one another; and the Walker will reportedly add several early paintings as well as its own reconstruction of a Constructivist theater set from the early 1920s. This density is reflected as well in the catalog, which is one of those government-sponsored illustrated books good enough to warrant commercial distribution. Handsomely designed, richly annotated, it contains informative, footnoted essays by Anatolii Strigalev, Selim O. Khan-Magomedov, Christina Lodder, Anatole Senkevitch, Jr., and Stephen Bann, among others, in addition to English translations of documents unavailable elsewhere, such as Rodchenko's brilliant "The Line" (1921). In my opinion, *Art into Life* is the sort of show that is best *re*visited after reading its catalog; the reasons for including many lesser works will become more apparent.

Considering that Tacoma is to Seattle as Newark stands to New York City, *Between Spring and Summer* is an admirably ambitious show that, in its original venue, filled a three-story space that was once the City Hall. Curated principally by David A. Ross of Boston's Institute for Contemporary Art, assisted by Margarita Tupitsyn and Elizabeth Sussman here and Joseph Bakshtein in Russia, it features works by twenty artists or artist-collaborators, all of whom are or were Soviet citizens, whose work purportedly resembles American conceptualism: Yuri Avvakumov, Alexander Brodsky and Ilya Utkin, Africa (aka Sergei Bugaev), Collective Actions (Alekseev, Elagina, Kazevalter, Makarevich, Monastrysky, Panitkov, Romashko), Andrei Filippov, Ilya Kabakov, Vitaly Komar & Alexander Melamid, Igor Makarevich, Medical Hermeneutics (Anufriev, Leiderman, Peppershtein), Sergei Mironenko, Andrei Monastrysky (now solo), Timur Novikov, Peppers (aka Ludmila Skripkina, Oleg Petrenko), Dmitri Prigov, Andrei Roiter, Maria Serebriakova, Sergei Volkov, Vadim Zakharov, Konstantin Zvezdochetov, Larisa Zvezdochetova, to slight no one. Once again there is a thick catalog with strong, stylistically various essays unavailable elsewhere by Ross himself, his collaborating curators, and some of the contributors, which is to say a less formal mix than that in *Art into Life*.

American conceptualism at its best held that the idea behind an artistic object could be more consequential than its visual presence. For that reason, conceptual art at its purest favored verbal statements and unadorned geometricism. Even though precursors to American conceptualism could be found in Soviet constructivism (such as the 1921 monochromic Rodchenko triptych, *Pure Blue Color, Pure Yellow Color, Pure Blue Color* that was in the

Constructivist show), the only participants in *Between Spring and Summer* who broach that level of conceptual integrity would be the "paper architects" whose designs were not intended for realization and then the young Leningrad artist known as Africa, whose works both inside the Tacoma museum and outside (including not only its City Hall facade but, among other places, the Book Fair at the annual Seattle festival called Bumbershoot) used advertising techniques (and American English) to mythicize one of his colleagues, Sergei Anufriev.

What was best about *Between Spring and Summer* had less to do with conceptualism than with with theater, particularly of the environmental sort. I asked perhaps a dozen viewers which individual works they thought best, and since unanimity is a rare response to such an anthology, it should be noted that nearly all chose two: the *Site Specific Installation* (1990) of Brodsky and Utkin, whose work here with wire, blackened objects and a reflective pool of water surpasses the similarly intimidating environments shown at New York's Feldman Gallery last spring; the equally dense multimedia installation (1983) of a typically claustrophic Soviet artist's apartment by Ilya Kabakov. I personally liked Andrei Filippov's *The Last Supper* (1990), a 20-plus-foot-long red table with several large plates each surrounded with a hammer and a sickle, and the Africa work mentioned before. These artists transend the academicism, the sense of displaying art school lessons learned too well, that characterizes too much recent Soviet art exhibited here. One striking development, especially to those who have followed Soviet art in America for the past dozen years, is that Komar & Melamid are no longer the obvious stars of such implicitly competitive shows; a less repressive Russia has perhaps undermined their previously awesome irony.

When I saw the mammoth *Paris Moscow* show in Moscow nearly a decade ago, my first thought was how much I had not seen before. I had that sense again when I read Gerald Janecek's masterful *The Look of Russian Literature* (1984) and yet again at the Malevich retrospective at the Stedelijk last year. Now that I've been surprised once more, now that the requirements of a freer market have released previously hidden energies, I wonder how much more major Soviet art still remains to be discovered.

Part II: Individuals

In Esmeralda, city of water, a network of canals and a network of streets span and intersect one another. To go from one place to another you have always the choice between land and boat: and since the shortest distance between two points in Esmeralda is not a straight line but a zigzag that ramifies in tortuous optional routes, the ways that open to each passerby are never two, but many, and they increase further for those who alternate a stretch by boat with one on dry land.

And so Esmeralda's inhabitants are spared the boredom of following the same streets every day. And that is not all: the network of routes is not arranged on one level, but follows instead an up-and-down course of steps, landings, cambered bridges, hanging streets. Combining segments of the various routes, elevated or on ground level, each inhabitant can enjoy every day the pleasure of a new itinerary to reach the same places. The most fixed and calm lives in Esmeralda are spent without any repetition. — Italo Calvino, *Invisible Cities* (1972)

The avant-garde's specialization of itself, the fact that its best artists are artists' artists, its best poets, poets' poets, has estranged a great many of those who were capable formerly of enjoying and appreciating ambitious art and literature, but who are now unwilling or unable to acquire an initiation into their craft secrets. — Clement Greenberg, "Avant-Garde and Kitsch" (1939)

Precursors of
Polyartistry (1969–75)

*Literary Rediscovery has always been a part of avant-garde activity, which insists tradi-
tionally on making revaluation a constant and permanent process. That revivals now
figure so prominently in publishing only shows the extent to which avant-garde practices
have been taken over by the official culture.* —Clement Greenberg, "The State of
American Writing" (1948)

The Bauhaus always had a good press in America—from responses to
a 1931 exhibition in New York through Sigfreid Giedion's supremely influential *Space, Time and Architecture* (1941) to the present; so that when its faculty
fled the Nazi rise, many of the refugees found sponsors willing to re-establish
their eminence in America—officially in Chicago's short-lived "New
Bauhaus" and its successors, respectively the School of Design, and then the
Institute of Design, but unofficially at Black Mountain College, Harvard,
and elsewhere.

The primary reason for our current interest in the Bauhaus is, of course,
the continuing relevance of its ideals. One frequently hears echoes nowadays
of Gropius' favorite slogan: "art and technology—a new unity" and precisely
in the adaptation of technology to artistic uses, there were practical freedoms
(though intellectual confusions) gained by the Bauhaus refusal to distinguish
between fine and applied art. Secondly, not only should the arts be taught
together, but students in every art should be exposed to all the arts; for
literacy in only one form (or only one communications medium) signifies
functional illiteracy before the diversity of contemporary information.

Indicatively, though Gropius, himself already an architect of note,
believed that "all the arts culminate in architecture," and that "the ultimate
aim of all visual arts was the complete building," there was, in the original
Weimar Bauhaus, no course officially in architecture. Nor was there one in
easel painting, though the staff included such distinguished painters as Paul
Klee, Wassily Kandinsky, Josef Albers, and Johannes Itten. These subjects
were added in Dessau, it is true, as the orientation became less experimental
and more practical; but the so-called foundation course remained a general
introduction to materials, from which the individual student could then ideally
concentrate on the material (or art) of his choice.

It follows, of course, that a student, no matter his original ambitions, could and should feel free to work in any and every art he chose. The principle of an integrated polyartistic education was sustained, within budgetary limits, at Moholy-Nagy's Institute of Design; and the same ideal animates, one is gratified to notice, the new California Institute of the Arts in Los Angeles. (The implication is that schools devoted just to dance, or music, or visual arts, are outmoded.) Perhaps the principal achievement of the Bauhaus was a revolution in art education.

If the pioneers of modernism devoted their energies to changing art, their immediate successors, in modernism's second generation, born just before the turn of the century, tried to incorporate art into their mission of changing the world. This fact explains not only why several artists of that generation wrote so much but also why another Bauhaus ideal held that art schools should be concerned not only with art but the society outside. Therefore, just as the uses of technology were incorporated into the curriculum, so an education in painting, say, should be entwined with industrial design or even city planning. One further assumption is that art schools have the opportunity to inculcate a kind of thinking not found in strictly professional institutes of city planning and architecture. At the Bauhaus there was a continuing effort to design prototypes of both pieces of furniture and single-family houses for industrial mass-production, and the Institute of Design made camouflage during World War II, as well as developing programs for the rehabilitation of disabled veterans. The truth here — still very relevant — is that the best politics for artists lies in applying their developed sensibilities and competencies to the improvement of man's physical environment for if artists don't, you know who else will. . . .

How sad, in retrospect, has been the subsequent debasement of Bauhaus aims. Its architecture and design were conceived as anti-stylistic reactions to the beaux-arts ornamentation, with its artificial or imposed prettiness; for the polemical ideal of the Bauhaus philosophy was solid and economical construction, rather than esthetic excellence. The result of Bauhaus influence, however, has been new kinds of uneconomical formalism — in design, artificial streamlining and, in architecture, the slick and pretty glass-walled boxes that have become depressingly abundant on American urban landscapes. Similarly, the anti-academic educational program, emphasizing individual enthusiasm and choice, more than particular results, generated its own academic pieties of stylistic correctness (geometric abstractions in textiles, say, rather than representational patterns) which dominate American schools of design to this day. (In fact, when the Institute of Design itself was incorporated into the Illinois Institute of Technology, one of the first changes was the introduction of uniform testing and grades.) In both architecture and design-education, then, a limited interpretation of the Bauhaus achievement placed an emphasis upon certain end-products, rather than upon an educative process that, particularly today, would probably produce entirely different results. By the 1970s, in short, their intentions, as articulated in the manifestoes collected in Hans Maria Wingler's *The Bauhaus* (1969) and elsewhere, are generally more attractive, and persuasive, than the practical results of their influence.

Gropius and Ludwig Mies van der Rohe had a considerably better press in America than Moholy-Nagy (1895–1946), whose reputation suffered in part because he died so prematurely, but largely because his works did not fit so easily into the established categories of criticism and art-historical scholarship. Believing that artistic commitment was an adventuresome process whose produce could take many forms, Moholy-Nagy made minor contributions to modern painting, sculpture and film, a more substantial contribution to photography, and truly major innovations in arts yet to find their critics and historians — artistic machines (with his *Light-Display Machine* of 1930), environments (especially with his speculative *Mechanical Eccentric* of 1926), and book design. His posthumous book, *Vision in Motion* (1947), established him as also one of the extraordinary critics of modernist art. It is indicative that Moholy-Nagy's governing theme as a critic is the particular intrinsic integrity and extrinsic impact of each art form, and this assumption led him to explore, in turn, the differences between them and the possibilities peculiar to each.

Actively engaged in forging new artistic directions, Moholy-Nagy also had an extraordinary knack for thinking well into the future: On pp. 41–3 of the new English translation of his precocious first book, *Painting, Photography, Film* (1925) is a vision of multiple film projection (or, to be precise, a more mobile cinerama); on p. 60 is a photograph clearly resembling a famous Donald Judd sculpture done in 1965; on p. 25 is envisioned the currently more feasible possibility of facsimile printing of art reproductions on one's home console; and on p. 80 he generously reprints his colleague Hirschfeld-Mack's attempt at prepsychedelic light shows. *Painting, Photography, Film* is also stunningly designed, so that themes introduced in the pithy text are recapitulated in seventy-four pages of shrewdly selected, full-page illustrations; and the book closes with a vividly visualized outline for a film he regrettably never made, *The Dynamic of the Metropolis*. In truth, even in 1925, Moholy-Nagy had ideas that were still "avant-garde" in the seventies.

Lazar Lissitzky, born in Russia in 1890 and commonly known by his nickname of "El," studied engineering and architecture before coming to German cultural circles, just after World War I. His name has been neglected for some of the same reasons that plagued his sometime friend Moholy-Nagy — the diversity of his achievements, and his penchant for innovations in arts that have as yet no standard histories. His historical reputation, in the West at least, was further jeopardized by Lissitzky's unfortunate decision to return to post–Revolutionary Russia. Not only did his work lose its innovative edge, but the Soviets did not make it freely available, while the "Russians" featured in most histories of modern art have been emigrés. Had Lissitzky also belonged to a famous institution, as Moholy-Nagy did, his subsequent reputation might have capitalized on the publicity accompanying its eminence; but on this score too he was unlucky. He died prematurely, like Moholy-Nagy, at fifty-one. It seems that these two major polyartists knew each other best in the early twenties; but since their efforts overlapped and implicitly competed (especially in photography and book design), charges and counter-charges of plagiarism were subsequently made by their heirs.

Though neither as energetic nor as restlessly brilliant as Moholy-Nagy, Lissitzky nonetheless pursued the same kind of artistic adventurousness. In addition to his familiar constructivist paintings (patently indebted to his friend Malevich), Lissitzky realized some of the great modern posters, much good book-design, a children's book entitled *Of Two Squares* (1920) that would be strikingly innovative if published for adults in New York today, several first-rank darkroom-doctored photographs and photomontages, a fertilely speculative esthetic conception in "Proun" (defined as midpoints between painting and architecture), and one of the first great artistic environments, which is to say an artistically defined space. This last precursor was vividly described by Alexander Dorner, then the director of the Hannover Museum, in his neglected but inspiring book on *The Way Beyond 'Art'* (1958):

> The walls of that room were sheathed with narrow tin strips set at right angles to the wall plane. Since these strips were painted black on one side, gray on the other, and white on the edge, the wall changed its character with every move of the spectator. The sequence of tones varied in different parts of the room. This construction thus established a supraspatial milieu for the frameless compositions [i.e., the suspended paintings]. . . . All display cases and picture mounts were made movable to reveal new compositions and diagrams. This room contained many more sensory images than could have been accomodated by a rigid room. Mobility exploded the room, as it were, and the result was a spiritual intensification, proportionate to the evolutionary content of the display cases, which tried to demonstrate the growth of modern design in its urgent transforming power.

Lissitzky also wrote, among other works, an impressively prophetic critical book, recently translated into English as *An Architecture for World Revolution* (1929), whose possible influence was stymied, however, by Josef Stalin's classicist architectural decrees of 1932.

The suspicion remains that Lissitzky could have been a polyartist as pre-eminent as Moholy-Nagy, had his physical constitution been as robust and had he not made political choices detrimental to both his art and its subsequent dissemination. Both men were ahead of their time in several ways, as their writings continue to make clear, and that last fact suggests that it is by print, rather than by "works of art," that certain visionary artists will best be known to later ages. The wisdoms exemplified by their similar professional careers are that creative adventure need honor no imposed limits and that unending commitments to both process and polyartistry, in addition to the excellence of particular work, realizes a Bauhaus-like ideal that sets a persuasive example to this day. No one capable of genuine polyartistry should want to be merely an "artist" anymore.

*   *   *

The Moholy-Nagy exhibition recently at the Museum of Contemporary Art in Chicago is the first large retrospective of his work in America in nearly two decades; and if only because Moholy is perhaps the last great modernist who has not yet been duly honored and whose extraordinariness is less than universally familiar, this presentation intends to repair an unjustified neglect. As such it testifies to the perseverance of Jan van der Marck, director of the new collectionless Museum, once again presenting now what others will handle later; and it is appropriate that the show originates in Chicago, where Moholy spent the final decade of his life (1937–46), founding the New Bauhaus (later renamed the Institute of Design), and producing many of his best works of art.

This large show contains well over one hundred pieces, most of them paintings and related art in the Constructivist tradition, a few Plexiglas sculptures, the justly famed *Light Display Machine* (1922–30), panels of photographs, photograms and typographical designs as well as some slides and several films shown periodically. The emphasis, at least in Chicago, is upon the paintings and the light machine; and it is in this selection, as I shall argue later, that the show disappoints its necessary task.

First of all, this survey of Moholy's career is particularly good at documenting evolutionary themes, some of which were not apparent, to me at least, before. One theme is Moholy's precocious development — within five years — out of Van Gogh-like expressionistic portraiture of 1918 through a form resembling an apple with pins stuck in it (1920), into a brief flirtation in 1922 with collage (indebted to Moholy's friendship with Kurt Schwitters), to, by 1923, a mature Constructivist painting of geometric forms on a sparely organized canvas. And this preference for circles, rectangles and straight lines informed his visual work for the subsequent decade — not just his paintings, but even the best of his abstract films, the manifestly realistic *Port of Marseilles* (1929), and the revolutionary *Light Display Machine*, as well as the abstract film Moholy made about it in 1930.

A second developing theme is Moholy's use of unusual materials on which to paint; and these works are invariably more compelling and innovative than the less distinguished canvases. *Em 1-3* (1922), the famous paintings done by craftsmen to Moholy-Nagy's telephoned instructions (and brought together here for the first time), are made of porcelain enamel on steel; *T1* (1926), as abstract in name as in design, is oil on black bakelite; and in *AL II* (1926), the best of the early paintings, he used oil on faintly reflective aluminum. When Moholy seriously resumed painting again, first in London (1935–37) and then in Chicago, after an hiatus of nearly a decade, he painted more complex and various semigeometric forms, especially the ribbon, on copper and silverit (in a highly reflective work of 1939 that historically precedes Pistoletto), and most spectacularly, on Plexiglas, generally mounted a few inches away from the plywood back, so that shadows become more visible as one moves aside the work and the frame possesses qualities of depth absent from the earlier paintings. In painting on unusual surfaces Moholy displayed remarkable sensitivity to the particularities of his chosen materials as well as forging new esthetic territory with an innovation that has not yet been fully exhausted.

Another theme of the exhibition is the peculiarly expressionistic character of those works done in Chicago in the final years of his life, after the onset of leukemia that killed him toward the end of 1946 — the colors are more aggressive, the forms are more evocative (*Diary of a Fly*, dedicated to Béla Bartók, is almost representational), the titles are untypically macabre (*Leu No. 1, Chi-Finis*, etc.); for while the paintings may strike some as suggesting a rejection of earlier principles, in the context of his life and this exhibiton they also reveal an hysteria that must have been overwhelming.

It is regrettable that this emphasis on the paintings not only produces an insufficiently comprehensive show but also portrays Moholy as considerably less interesting and original than he really was. As this exhibition would have it, Moholy was basically a painter who also dabbled in other materials and forms; and, indicatively, a less-than-hip elderly woman looking at one of those space modulators with me asked, "Was this Moholy-Nagy a painter, a sculptor or what?" Her innocent question raises a real issue which this exhibition avoids. In my own thinking about Moholy's achievement, I would prefer to start with that quality that distinguishes him from everyone else, his variousness. The evidence suggests he was a relentless experimenter who cared less about mastering one or another of the arts than continuing his adventure wherever it took him. "All through his life he was equally praised and blamed for his manysidedness, which was as natural to him as breathing," writes Sibyl Moholy-Nagy, the artist's widow. "He shuffled his different jobs like a deck of cards, getting innumerable new combinations but finding them all part of the same game."

That is to say, Moholy was not just a painter, but also a sculptor, a designer, a photographer, a filmmaker, a writer, a teacher, and a creative figure at a few points among and between — in sum, one of the great *polyartists* of modernism; and these other activities, many of which are more innovative and influential than his painting, get slighted in this exhibition. For instance, though the show includes six of his photograms (or abstract cameraless photography), none of which are particularly distinguished, and six representational photographs only half of which need be shown, there are no photomontages (at which he could excel), nothing about his remarkable curriculum at the Institute of Design, and no visible reference in the exhibition to Moholy's great book, written in English in Chicago and published just after his death — *Vision in Motion* (1947). His activities as a designer are represented by two photographs of the same *Madame Butterfly* stage setting (which was not his best work in this medium), a panel on typography that neglects his innovative and still influential page design for illustrated books, and a carousel of absolutely unmarked sides that mix the "Parker 51 Pen" (based on Moholy's sketches) with work by his students.

The question is which Moholy do we want to see now? While this exhibition presents an indubitably major figure in the history of Constructivism (whose characteristic esthetic syntax strikes the late-sixties sensibility as archaic as that of collage), the other, more versatile and polymathic Moholy strikes me today as one of the dozen great figures of modern art and perhaps the sole member of that generation born before 1900, except of course Duchamp, whose work and personal example remains so relevant to us now.

*   *   *

It is reassuring to see Theo van Doesburg finally receiving some of the recognition that, though indubitably deserved, has previously been denied him. However, Joost Baljeu's new volume, *Theo van Doesburg* (1975), scarcely offers the last word. One reason for past neglect has been the fact that van Doesburg's achievements were easily misunderstood, in part because they are inconsistent, if not somewhat contradictory, but also because he worked in more than one artistic domain. Baljeu does not rectify this last misunderstanding with his blanket assertion that van Doesburg's "main concern" was developing De Stijl philosophy "in all aspects of life through architecture." Thus, Baljeu, himself "a practicing artist and architect," emphasizes the architectural designs and proposals done in the late twenties, just prior to van Doesburg's premature death in 1931.

Rather than see van Doesburg as primarily an architect or painter, I prefer to classify him, like Moholy-Nagy, as a genuine *polyartist*, whose creative sensibility and ambitions were sufficiently diverse for him to excell in several forms. By my count, van Doesburg did important work in painting, architectural design, creative literature, and criticism. His achievements in the first and second domains are familiar, in part because of his backstage role in the histories of Constructivism and even of modern painting. Speaking for myself, I particularly like the rigorously geometric paintings, such as *Composition XI* (1918) and *Counter-Composition XIII* (1924), and his spectacular interior designs for a cinema and dance hall in the Aubette, Strasbourg, France. All of these are adequately illustrated in Baljeu's book.

The real value of this volume, in my judgment, is its partial resurrection of van Doesburg's poetry and criticism, which is generally less well known than his visual art, in part because writings by visual artists are customarily omitted, no matter how excellent, from the histories of literature—even of experimental literature. (Conversely, how many "art historians" acknowledge that van Doesburg's second *De Stijl* manifesto [1920] was devoted to "literature"?) A polyartistic interpretation of van Doesburg would initially identify imaginative proclivities that appear in all the arts he practiced; it would define the core of his sensibility, his real "main concerns," before analyzing the particular achievements.

To obfuscate critical understanding yet further, van Doesburg was, in addition to his polyartistic variousness, *both* a Constructivist and a Dadaist. To deal with this divergence in his creative sensibility, van Doesburg created not one but two pseudonyms for his Dada self, I. K. Bonset and Aldo Camini. The former published poetry, while the latter wrote essays. The best poems in this volume, such as the typographically inventive series entitled "X-Images" (1920), brilliantly exploit the space of the page (apparently as a score for variations untypical in oral declamation), but Baljeu's English translations are inferior to Hannah Hedrick's in *The Structurist 9* (1969). Were Baljeu not so biased toward the visual work, he might have reprinted more of these otherwise uncollected poems. (One favorite of mine is "Voorbijtrekkende Troep" [Marching Infantry, 1916], which I found in Carola Giedion-Welcker's *Anthologie der Abseitigen/Poètes à l'Écart* [Arche, 1965].) Baljeu's introduction speaks of prose fictions, but only one, in drastically brief excerpt, is reprinted here.

Baljeu does not confront the problem of all these pseudonyms, which I conjecture served an important function in van Doesburg's creative life. Given the energetic, peripatetic way he conducted his professional career—he resembled Schwitters more than Mondrian in this respect—I suspect he was temperamentally a Dadaist. In one essay, van Doesburg twice reminds us that Dadaists are born, not made. As he put it, "One cannot become a Dadaist; one can only be one." Thus, the rigors of Constructivism, with its emphasis upon the unified organization of parts, harnessed the inherent volatility of his imagination. Perhaps ashamed of this counter-tendency, however, he concocted several names for his Dada work, often doing and saying things that explicitly contradicted his van Doesburg self. For instance, "Bonset" is opposed to reason and logic in art and literature, whereas "van Doesburg" favors it. By the use of pseudonyms (whose secrecy he labored to preserve), he was able to contain divergent imaginations within a single head.

The most consequential writings in *Theo van Doesburg* are his critical theoretical essays, some of which I have read elsewhere (e.g., Hans L. D. Jaffé's anthology, *De Stijl*, n.d.), but most of them were previously unfamiliar to me. Some are extraordinarily prophetic, even to contemporary concerns: "The Will to Style" (1922), "Toward Elementary Plastic Expression" (1923), "Art Concret. The Basis of Conrete Painting" (1930), "Towards White Painting" (1930). As a superb polemicist, van Doesburg mastered the manifesto-writer's art of stunning, resonant sentences: "We are painters who think and measure." "Only mediocre talents . . . will produce such a thing as proletarian art (that means *politics in painting*)." "In the name of humanism one has tried to justify quite a lot of nonsense in art." "The best handicraft is the one which displays no human touch."

With his comprehensive vision, van Doesburg could distinguish the new art from the old in a sterling list:

Definiteness instead of indefiniteness
openness instead of closedness
clarity instead of vagueness
religious energy instead of belief and religious authority
truth instead of beauty
simplicity instead of complexity
relation instead of form
synthesis instead of analysis
logical construction instead of lyrical representation
mechanical form instead of handiwork
creative expression instead of mimeticism and decorative ornament
collectivity instead of individualism, and
so forth.

Baljeu's bibliography itemizes numerous uncollected and even still-unpublished writings that ought, with this new acknowledgment of van Doesburg's importance, finally to appear in print, ideally in English as well as his native Dutch. The resurrection is yet incomplete.

At his death in 1931, van Doesburg was working on several books of art history and art critcism. Unlike Moholy, who also died prematurely, van Doesburg never got to write his *Vision in Motion*, which is to say his grand summary of his artistic perceptions and interests. One remains smitten by the thought of what he might have achieved, as a polyartist, had he lived longer than 47 years.

The Risk and Necessity of Artistic Adventurism (1969)

Since the painter has become an actor, the spectator has to think in a vocabulary of action: its inception, duration, direction — psychic state, concentration and relaxation of the will, passivity, alert waiting. He must become a connoisseur of the gradations between the automatic, the spontaneous, the evoked. — Harold Rosenberg, "The American Action Painters" (1952)

László Moholy-Nagy continues to live in contemporary art, although the record tells us that he died over two decades ago; for he is the only artist born before 1900 whose work, ideas, and example remain variously relevant in this era of light shows, sculptural machines, abstract film, nonrepresentational photography, radically diverse book layouts, streamlined industrial design, artistic environments, and mixed-means theater. Not only did Moholy-Nagy's writings and ideas espouse most of these distinctly contemporary forms, he actually worked in many of them — three, four, and five decades ago. In contrast to his peers but like some of his prominent juniors, Moholy-Nagy created in several media and joined collaborative enterprises rather than living and dying a specialist in one. He was the best kind of eclectic, which is to say, someone whose various choices are informed by an underlying purpose, a coherent logic, and a highly selective awareness. His history makes him the outstanding exemplar of a particular kind of artistic career — horizontal across the arts, rather than vertical into only one; and as a prophetic precursor of so much that is present, he seems in retrospect one of the most seminal minds of twentieth-century art, in his own way the equal of Picasso, Duchamp, Mondrian, and Klee. "By now," wrote the critic Brian O'Doherty recently, "we have just about processed all the heroes, anti-heroes, and 'figures' of the age of modernism"; but to judge by how generally unfamiliar is Moholy-Nagy's name and work, even among those who would walk in his footprints, he still belongs among the unprocessed, not to say neglected.

Moholy, as he was known to those friends who did not call him "Holy Mahogany," was the great adventurer of modern art, heroically risking not only steps across esthetic boundaries but also lateral movement along several frontiers, and the territories through which he passed include a number of traditional arts, in addition to a few domains partly of his own creation. As he found the taking of next steps to be more consequential than aspiring to intrinsic quality — if one dimension can viably be separated from the other in contemporary art — he also realized early in his career that the freedom granted the avant-garde artist includes the right not only to paint in any style he wishes but also to work creatively in any art or area he chooses.

Since his travels also took him through several countries and cultures in the decades after World War I, the record of his life is as diverse and incomplete as that of his achievements. He was born in Bacsbarsod, in the Hungarian countryside, on July 20, 1895; by his teens, he was publishing poetry in native little magazines. In 1913, he began to study law at the University of Budapest and eventually turned to writing and painting, co-founding the review *Jelenkor* in 1916 and joining the Hungarian art group known as MA (meaning "today"), which later founded a periodical with the same name. Wounded in World War I, he became more serious about painting during his recuperation but still took a law degree; he went to Berlin in the early 1920s, becoming by 1922 a cofounder of Constructivism, coeditor of an anthology on modern art, coauthor of a prophetic manifesto entitled "The Dynamic-Constructive System of Forces," and a contributor to several advanced art magazines. (He began to sign himself "L. Moholy-Nagy" because he regarded "László" or "Ladislaus" as too stuffy — comparable to "Archibald" in English, his widow told me — and he sometimes called himself "Laci," which in English is pronounced like "Lotzi.") Of medium height and stocky build, with peasant features, glasses, and a streak of white through his dark hair, by the early 1920s he was a well-known name and presence in European avant-garde circles. His earliest artistic reputation came from his abstract paintings and nonrepresentational photographs, most of them made without a camera and called "photograms."

In 1923, Walter Gropius invited Moholy to join the Bauhaus in Weimar; thereafter, in addition to his own endeavors in several arts, Moholy taught the basic foundation course (*Vorkurs*) and photography, ran the metal workshop, and coedited, with Gropius, the fourteen Bauhaus books. "He particularly sought," writes the art historian Donald Drew Egbert, "to acquaint students with the revolution in art made possible by modern technology"; and according to Gillian Naylor, in a recent study, *The Bauhaus* (1968), "It was above all Moholy-Nagy's personal interpretation of Constructivist attitudes that contributed to the emergence of a recognizable Bauhaus style [of industrial design]." Five years later, he followed Gropius in resigning from the Bauhaus due to political pressures and returned to Berlin to finish his light machine, to experiment with new materials, to collaborate with Erwin Piscator's theater and the Berlin State Opera, to make films both representational and abstract, and to explore advanced techniques of exhibition display.

The threats of fascism drove him to Holland and, in 1935, to London, where he lived among the Hampstead refugees. During the following two years, he began to paint on Plexiglas and created special effects for Alexander Korda's movie *Things to Come* (1936). He also participated in numerous exhibitions, all the while earning most of his living from book design and commercial displays.

An unexpected telegram invited him in 1937 to create a "new Bauhaus" in Chicago, which closed after one year. (Reportedly, the trustees lost the school's money on stock speculations.) It reopened a year later as the "Institute of Design" and overcame numerous obstacles to become, now, a division of Illinois Institute of Technology. An enthusiastic teacher, who was able to lecture endlessly without a note and sincerely believed that literally everyone could be creative, Moholy earned the loyalty of his students and colleagues, some of whom taught without pay. Despite insufficient funds, cultural unfamiliarity, and inadequte equipment, Moholy persisted with his teaching, also raising money, handling administrative duties, and recruiting a faculty that included such eminences as the sculptor Alexander Archipenko, the philosopher Charles Morris, and the composer John Cage. He regarded teaching as his most natural role, often making great personal sacrifices to pursue this calling. Abundantly energetic and fanatically optimistic, instinctively gregarious and personally generous, Moholy was also adept at making decisions promptly and decisively, at quickly generating ideas and even whole schemes, and at winning, as distinct from buying, competent assistance; yet, uncompromising and abundantly productive, blessed with a quick mind (a faculty more admired in the sciences than the arts), he displayed an inadvertent knack for making enemies and inspiring jealousies. In addition to laboring on his own artistic projects in his spare time, Moholy sufficiently mastered yet another language to write in English the great book that, among other things, spectacularly summarizes all his ideas and interests, *Vision in Motion* (1947), published posthumously the year after his premature death from leukemia on November 24, 1946. His widow Sibyl, in her biography *Moholy-Nagy: An Experiment in Totality* (1950), remembers that he traveled to an educational conference in New York City ten days before he died and that on his deathbed Moholy was energetically drawing pictures of leveraging mechanisms. Although he lived in America less than a decade, becoming a U.S. citizen in 1944, a recent exhibition that the Museum of Modern Art devoted to "The Machine" (1968) lists Moholy as "American, born Hungary."

The bulk and variety of Moholy's artistic activities evade easy summary, partly because he explored so many unprecedented paths that standard classifications are insufficient; beyond that, the historian scarcely knows where to start. First of all, as designer of the Bauhaus publications, he repudiated both conventional "gray, inarticulate machine typesetting" and the highly ornamental "beaux-arts" affectations in typography to originate (perhaps with a debt to El Lissitzky, among others) the now familiar geometric "modern" style of illustrated book design, in which relevant pictures and sometimes epigraphs are mixed in two-page spreads with rectangular blocks of uniform, evenly justified sans-serif type that may vary in size and yet always remains considerably narrower than the width of the page and is sometimes prefaced by sub-heads in boldface type. In his first one-man book, *Painting, Photography, Film* (1925), a sequence of seventy-four shrewdly chosen and arranged pictures abetted by minimal captions successfully retells the argument already elaborated in the preceding text; and the overall design of this book, as well as *Von Material zu Architektur* (1929), had enormous influence upon Continental publishing design. Moholy's favorite maxim insisted on "a clear message in the most impressive manner"; and not only does the design of Moholy's own final book exemplify this clean and efficient style at its very best, but its revolutionary influence continues in such recent illustrated volumes as the two Quentin Fiore-Marshall McLuhan collaborations, *The Medium Is the Massage* (1967) and *War and Peace in the Global Village* (1968). (However, compared to Andy Warhol's *Index* [1967] or Merce Cunningham and Frances Starr's *Changes: Notes on Choreography* [1969], Fiore's neo–Bauhaus style now seems archaic; and Moholy's own curiously conservative preference for "absolute clarity" and impersonality discouraged more inventive, not to say idiosyncratic, typographical expression.)

Yet, books were not the only applied medium to experience Moholy's penchant for revolutionary designs. In Berlin he did several extremely imaginative stage sets, including one with light and sound projections on a continuous strip and another for *The Merchant of Berlin* (1930) with several levels that antedates the Living Theater's similarly vertical staging in *Frankenstein* (1965); and the extraordinary settings Moholy created for Korda's *Things to Come* set an imaginative standard for that art. The asymmetrical but geometric London window displays reproduced in both *The New Vision* and Sibyl Moholy-Nagy's biography would still seem conspicuously abstract and innovative on Fifth Avenue; and incredible as it may seem, while in Chicago he also designed a six-purpose handsaw and other tools for Spiegel's Mail Order House, and a vista dome passenger car for the B. & O. Railroad.

In short, his design esthetics apparently favor the Veblenian persuasion that efficiency and regard for creature comfort in themselves create beauty, in contrast to the position derived from William James that a beautiful object will enhance the lives of those who use it. Moholy characterized his own position as starting with the Louis Sullivan adage of "form follows function," to which he would add the latest "scientific results and technological processes." He once told a reporter from *Time*, "I don't like the word beauty. It's a depressing word. Utility and emotional satisfaction: These are important words. These are the things design should give." More than once his interest in radical design informed an architectural proposal, like the 1922 sketch, also displayed at the Museum of Modern Art "Machine" show (and previously reproduced in *The New Vision*) of a "Kinetic Constructive System," which is a tower with two internal spiral tracks at different angles of incline — "a structure with paths of motion for a sport and recreation." In retrospect, nonetheless, industrial and theatrical design seem the most modest of Moholy's diverse endeavors, and architecture was hardly a sustained ambition for him.

As an artist who assimilated abstractionism from his professional beginnings — he was, after all, just that much younger than, say Kandinsky or Picasso — Moholy applied nonrepresentational syntax to photography by developing the "photogram," or abstract cameraless photography, in 1921, the same year that Man Ray devised a similar process he egotistically christened "Rayographs." In making these pieces, three-dimensional objects were placed directly on light-sensitive paper, which was then exposed for an appropriate duration; and Moholy later learned to complicate the resulting visual field of blacks, whites, and grays by modulating the light and even exploiting such elementary devices of the medium as a negative printing. His purpose was, as he wrote in the catalogue to a 1923 exhibition of his work, "the concretization of light phenomena ... peculiar to the photographic process and to no other technical invention." A few years later he worked with photomontage (or photographic collage), in which some snippets from several prints are placed on a board of fundamentally unrelated images — what he called "a multiple image condensation fixed within a single frame"; and such pictorial collages as *The Structure of the World* (1925) epitomize his masterful exploration of forms and possibilities indigenous to this medium. During the 1940s he envisioned the potentialities of photographic color "understood for its own sake and not as a sign or symbol representing an object," but scarcely realized these aims. Moholy advocated that everyone learn to use a camera or suffer a modern form of illiteracy, and he also emphasized photography in artistic education, because, as his friend Sigfried Giedion wrote, he regarded "the camera as a means of increasing the range and precision of visual perception." In the course of his travels, Moholy also took innumerable documentary photographs, collecting several into books with texts by others on *The Street Market of London* (1936), *Eton Portrait* (1937), and *The Oxford University Chest* (1939), and reportedly appreciating the photos as much for their abstract qualities as their representational accuracy. They bear little resemblance to the precise and harsh realism so fashionable in 1930s American photography. Beaumont Newhall, in *The History of Photography* (1964), reprints a 1928 overhead shot of a Berlin street scene, on the back of which Moholy scribbled, "A bird's eye view of trees which form a unity with the pattern of the street. The lines running in many directions, placed each behind the other, form a rich spatial network." He was clearly less interested in reproducing reality than in discovering an interesting picture when he developed the print. If the historically earliest photography emulated the realistic aspirations of classical painting, thereby eventually making the medium a vehicle of reportage, Moholy imitated the forms and perceptions of more contemporary art, so that his photographs not only define those expressive languages intrinsic to the medium, they also clearly look like they were made in the twentieth century.

Painting was the art Moholy originally pursued, and it was the one he continued, with only one extended interruption, throughout his career. Repudiating a brief juvenile flirtation with Van Gogh–like expressionism, as seen in a self-portrait done in 1916, he rapidly defined an abstract position. Such youthful works as the collages of 1920 reveal a debt to Dada and to Moholy's friendship with Kurt Schwitters, not only in their conglomerate visual syntax but also in their imagery of aimless mechanisms: *ZIII* (1922) announces the pervasive influence of Malevich and Russian Constructivism: several kinds of geometric shapes—rectangles, circles, squares, and, particularly, straight lines—are painted in flat colors and super-imposed on a rather spare field in a style already clarified, though, to my mind, undistinguished. In his supremely suggestive *Transparency* (1921), he took several transparent sheets painted with colored forms and put them on top of one another, so that their colors blended at points of overlapping intersection. A true abstractionist who believed his forms had no representational or symbolic resonances, he boasted that a good painting could be hung upside down and still persuade. He also initiated the custom of giving most of his works either descriptive titles or just numbers and letters.

His paintings in the middle of the 1920s reveal a decided concern with pure color that, though Moholy was not a distinguished colorist, extended into the second phase of his work with paint. After neglecting the two-dimensional medium around 1928, perhaps because the limited syntax and spare field of Constructivist painting were too minimal for his maximal imagination, he took up paint again in London and Chicago, creating a succession of innovative rectangles in which painted Plexiglas stands an inch or two in front of a plywood back, so that images on the front sheet reflect shadows on the back sheet at angles and shapes variably dependent on the extrinsic light sources and the viewer's changing perspective. These paintings realized an ambition announced in his earliest essays on the medium—to move "from pigment to light." Moholy also cut holes in Plexiglas and painted on sheets with wavelike ridges (the brilliant *Papmac* [1943]); later he curved the material into convex and concave sculptural shapes. Moreover, a 1940 work such as *Space Modulator with Fluctuating Black and White Arcs* approaches optical ambiguity, because the spectator's eye cannot definitively deduce whether the black or the white arc is in front of the other. "This kind of picture," he wrote in *Vision in Motion*, "is most probably the passage between easel painting and light display," or between painting and relief; and perhaps because his senses of material and rhythm (in both time and space), as well as his aptitude for invention, were superior to his painterly eye, these "space modulators," as he collectively called them, stand as his most important "paintings."

In 1922, just before Moholy assumed his position at the Bauhaus (and perhaps because of his precocious appointment), in order to warn/challenge his prospective colleagues, he "ordered" five paintings of porcelain enamel on steel, identical in pattern but different in size, from a sign manufacturer by telephoning instructions to the factory supervisor — an innovative experiment that at first strikes us as a Cagean procedure designed to produce an unprecedented, "chance" result. However, since both Moholy and the supervisor were working from the same graph paper and the same color chart, the experimental aim was not at all to create aleatory art but to prove the existence of objective visual values and to emphasize the artistic primacy of conception — two points that, together with the procedure, caused considerable controversy. "In comparison with the inventive *mental* process of the genesis of the work," he rationalized in *Painting, Photography, Film*, "the manner — whether personal or by assignment of labor, whether manual or mechanical — is irrelevant." (The idea of an esthetic work untouched by artist's hand, thereby challenging the convention of "individual touch," has had much recent currency among the avant-garde.) Moholy was also the first major modern artist to regard "multiples," or innumerable copies, as a legitimate form for a serious artist's work.

Though he returned to the flat-surface medium now and then, particularly for a series of almost hysterical expressionistic drawings and paintings executed just before his death — on them, indicatively, he worked not with the usual straight edge but with freehand strokes — painting always remained too limited for both his polymathic bent and his developing interests in unusual materials and light. Back in 1919, as he wrote in his autobiographical essay:

> On my walks I found scrap metal parts, screws, bolts, mechanical devices. I fastened, glued and nailed them on wooden boards, combined with drawings and paintings. It seemed to me in this way I could produce real spatial articulation, frontally and in profile, as well as more intense color effects. . . .
> I planned three-dimensional assemblages, constructions executed in glass and metal. Flooded with light, I thought they would bring to the fore the most powerful color harmonies. In trying to sketch this type of "glass architecture," I hit upon the idea of transparency.

And much of his subsequent work, in painting as well as sculpture, pursued these tendencies toward both greater dimensionality and light modulation.

Moholy's earliest sculptural efforts were more clearly within the Constructivist stream. His *Nickel Construction* (1921) casts materials rather advanced at the time in simple (or "pure") geometric forms. On a metal base is placed a turret with two spokes running through it and an adjacent tower over a foot high; and from the top of the tower to the edge of the base runs a spiraled strip. This form seems indebted to the classic of Russian Constructivism, Vladimir Tatlin's extremely influential *Monument for the Third International* (1920), where the Industrial Age is evoked as a spiral ribbon contrasting with vertical columns — a visual form that Moholy himself subsequently favored. By 1923, he was making constructions of both opaque and transparent glass in combination with nickel and fiber matting (none of which have survived); and continuing to explore materials for their influence upon light, late in his career he turned again to thermoplastic Plexiglas, this time as a lightweight sculptural material that could be shaped to modulate changes in the surrounding light, even though the object itself remained stationary. Such pieces as *Light Modulator* (1943) and *Space Modulator* (1945) realize with particular success Constructivist aspirations of volume implied or enclosed rather than massed, and a spatial presence that does not end at the piece's rim, displaying, in addition, the familiar Moholy manipulations of various hues between darkness and light, his incipient kineticism, and exploiting the translucent object's variable appearance in space; and though Moholy's sculptural syntax is indebted to both Cubism and Constructivism, with a dash here and there of Futurism, his structures by this time had staked a historical position beyond Cubist-Constructivist sculpture. To Herbert Read, in his *Concise History of Modern Sculpture* (1964), a work such as Moholy's *Plexiglas and Chromium-Rod Sculpture* (1946) is thoroughly revolutionary with respect to the tradition of the art, because it lacks "a sensational awareness of the tactile quality of surfaces; a sensational awareness of the volume or (to avoid this ambiguous word) the mass encompassed by an integrated series of plane surfaces; and an acceptable sensation of the ponderability of gravity of the mass, that is, an agreement between the appearance and the weight of the mass." Of course, in being among the first to repudiate all these traditional criteria, Moholy's work became the precursor of much that is radical and interesting — "anti-sculptural" — in recent sculpture. "As a young painter," he wrote in that autobiographical essay, "I often had the feeling, when pasting my collages and painting my 'abstract' pictures, that I was throwing a message, sealed in a bottle, into the sea. It might take decades for someone to find and read it."

"When I think of sculpture, I cannot think of static mass," Moholy once told his wife; and her biography recalls how he sealed their relationship by taking her to see an object he had been sporadically building all through the 1920s. The articulation of light, as noted before, had always been among Moholy's primary concerns; even as a very young man, he wrote a poem that includes such lines as "Learn to know the Light — design of your life." "Light ordering Light, where are you?" "Light, total Light, creates the total man." Although he built *The Light-Display Machine* (1930) as a theatrical prop (to produce by reflection an environmental illumination), rather than as an esthetic object, Moholy's technical collaborator in the project liked the invention more for its intrinsic movement, that is, as a kinetic sculpture. Either way, this light-reflecting machine, four feet high, with vertical spines, a perforated shield, a moving balance ball, and visible gears, belongs among the truly revolutionary exemplars of twentieth-century art. As one of the first machine-driven mobiles, it differs from such nonmechanical kinetic art as the more popular air-stimulated mobiles of Calder and George Rickey (a form Moholy tried himself around 1940) and, also, the illusory kineticism of physically static works by, say, Heinz Mack and Victor Vasarely.

Moholy's *Light-Display Machine,* sometimes known as the *Light-Space Modulator* (depending upon how one translates from the German), is also the first *environmental* light machine, which is to say that it differs from Thomas Wilfred's earlier Lumia machines or his Bauhaus colleague Kurt Schwerdtfeger's *Reflected Color Displays,* in which changing lights (abetted by reflectors and refractors) illuminate by rear projection a fixed screen that is as two-dimensional as a painting—a kinetic technique extended by such contemporaries of ours as Earl Reibeck and the Joshua Light Show. In contrast, Moholy's multireflector can animate any space in which it is situated, blending its imagery with the contours and colors of the environment, while itself remaining visible—a procedure that is more "honest" to the materials of both machinery and projected light; and in this respect, Moholy's machine grew from a 1922 sketch exhibited in the traveling retrospective as "Design for a Light Machine for Total Theatre"; it also stands as a historical precursor of both James Seawright's magisterial *Scanner* (1966) and the environmental light shows of contemporary discotheques. Moholy set up his machine to reflect, as he wrote in *Vision in Motion,* "140 light bulbs connected with a drum contact. This was arranged so that within a two-minute turning period, various colored and colorless spotlights were switched on, creating a light display on the inside walls of a cube." In *The New Vision* he noted that the "great range of shadow interpenetrations and simultaneously intercepting patterns in a sequence of slow flickering rhythm" becomes even more complicated when the light is projected on transparent and perforated screens. Even in its stationary setting, the chrome-finished *Light-Display Machine* looks unusual and distinctly modern; and in contrast again to the Wilfred tradition, in which invisible machines are used to produce more or less familiar art (in this case, abstract painting), Moholy's artwork was the machine itself, whose visibly moving parts produced both visibly intrinsic activity and indigenous extrinsic art. "It seems easy to prophesy," he wrote, "that such types of constructions in many cases will take the place of static works of art." Yet, Moholy himself never finished another artistic machine (although more recent works by his Hungarian compatriot Nicholas Schoöffer are stylistically similar).

Given his preoccupations with both light and motion, it was inevitable that Moholy should become involved with film, whose basic components he judiciously defined as "light, motion, and sound." His major effort in this medium is *Light Display, Black and White and Gray* (1930) — a film literally starring his *Light-Display Machine*; and here the theme is the various degrees of reflected illumination and the overlapping movements of such familiar Constructivist shapes as circles and poles, regarded from various angles and even more various lights. The following summary comes from Istvan Kovacs' essay in *Form* (1968):

> The light machine is introduced in the film [after a stunning presentation of credits, *ed.*] by the focusing of the camera on a perforated sheet through which the rest of the apparatus can be seen, already drawing the viewer into the machine itself. . . . The involvement with the apparatus through spatial manipulation and light moulding increases gradually until the cinema becomes a total kinetic experience. Beginning by simply viewing the machine in its manifold gyrations — but always being so close to it that a separation can never take place between viewer and object — the artist continues by substituting negative frames, juxtaposing negative and positive in the same frame, and proliferating the movement by multiple exposure. While the tempo of the film accelerates through the quantitative increase of the content of the frames, through various photographic illusions and angle shots, Moholy-Nagy probes further the problems he had stated in his photographs. The mirror reappears now as an instrument of interpretation of the total motion. The artist is not afraid to deal with the dazzling, camera-filling light of [reflected] light bulbs. In fact, he observes the gradual rotation of the machine until the camera captures the full, blinding effect of a series of lights.

The result is one of the most compelling exploitations — at once representational (of the machine) and yet abstract — of the kinetic photographic medium that I have ever seen; and even by contemporary standards, some forty years later (!), it would stand as cinematically inventive. Moholy also made several more conventional, yet swiftly articulated silent documentaries about subjects as diverse as *Berlin Still Life* (1926), *Marseille Vieux Port* (1929, the best of this group), *Big City Gypsies* (1934), *Life of the Lobster* (1935), and *The New Architecture at the London Zoo* (1936), all of which ought to be collected into a single program for more popular distribution. In addition, he published several descriptive scenarios for unrealized abstract films. Respecting, as always, the particular nature of each medium in which he worked, Moholy pontificated, "Only a manuscript is film-genuine that cannot be fully understood either in book form or on the stage but exclusively through camera, sound, and color." He even conceived of an aurally nonrepresentational "acoustic alphabet" for application directly on the film's sound track, extending an earlier idea for scratching sounds directly onto a record groove; though the method proved rather impractical, it reveals that, long before he employed

John Cage, Moholy acknowledged the freedom of unpitched, unstructured, and even aleatory musical sounds. He also envisioned all kinds of advances in the medium's technologies, even publishing in 1924 a scheme for three simultaneous projections on a concave screen — roughly equivalent to "cinerama." In *Vision in Motion* is this characteristic prophecy: "The improvement of the film depends on the perfection of color, three-dimensional projection, and sound; upon simultaneous projection; successions of screens arranged in space and smoke, duplicate and multiple screens; new automatic superimpositions and maskings."

Three years after accepting Gropius' invitation to join the Bauhaus, Moholy coauthored a book entitled *Die Bühne im Bauhaus,* recently reissued as *The Theater of the Bauhaus* (1961), that contains other similarly prophetic visions of possible future theaters. Concerned on one hand with the Bauhaus ideal of radically different, but more humanly congenial, environmental structures and, on the other, with expunging each art of impurities derived from foreign media, he conceived of a theatrical performance devoid of "literary encumbrance," that would emphasize "creative forms peculiar only to the stage," and "total stage action," which he interpreted as a "concentrated activation of sound, light (color), space, form and motion." More specifically, Moholy would, first of all, break down the traditional distances between the communicative stimuli, whether human or mechanical, and the audience; for he thought that these theatrical elements, once freed of their imposed contexts, could be used in unprecedented combinations. He also envisioned certain technological innovations still not achieved, such as mobile loudspeakers suspended on overhead wire tracks, and recognized the availability of all materials, including "film, automobile, elevator, airplane, and other machinery, as well as optical instruments, reflecting equipment, and so on."

From these propositions followed visions of two kinds of radical theater. One, which he called "Theater of Totality," is a remarkably direct precursor of the recent Theater of Mixed Means, in which human performers stand, in Moholy's phrase, "on an equal footing with the other formative media." The other vision, called "The Mechanized Eccentric," and characterized as "a concentration of stage action in its purest form," is a humanless environmental field of lights, sounds, films, odors, music, mechanized apparatus (even robots and motorized costumes), and simulated explosions. Both the original German and the recent American edition of the book include a fantastic and suggestive "score" for this multimedia extravaganza. "There will arise an enhanced *control* over all formative media," he declared on behalf of his vision, "unified in a harmonious effect and built into an organism of perfect equilibrium." Unfortunately, Moholy was never able to realize his own theatrical conceptions, though Xanti Schawinsky, a sometime student at the Bauhaus, produced something similar to "Theater of Totality" at Black Mountain College in the late 1930s, and Moholy's own ideas informed nonliterary mixed-means theatrical activities of the past decade.

The German refugees of the 1930s brought to America ideas and examples, often embodied in their own skins; and their presence here crucially shaped the quality and character of post–World War II American culture. Though Moholy had fewer students distinguish themselves in the fine arts than, say, Hans Hofmann or Josef Albers, both of whom lived and taught much longer, his ideas shaped generations of design teachers, who espouse his Chicago curriculum to this day. His example also influenced the creation of both fine and commercial art, as much through the persuasiveness of his writings, teaching, and personal legend as the circumstances of the age. (Of his immediate influence, Lloyd Engelbrecht, who is completing a history of the Institute of Design, judges, "Moholy made a big impact on a small number of people, most of whom went into college teaching.") Historically, Moholy was among the immigrant influences who helped make the key thrust of 1950s American art decidedly abstract rather than as representational as 1930s realism; if nothing else, Moholy wrote some of the most persuasive pages on the social and human relevance of artistic abstraction. Secondly, he exemplified the currently admired idea of the artist as not just a painter or a poet, but someone involved in a creative adventure that may ultimately take him through any medium — where his willingness constantly to explore rather than concentrate on one kind of product becomes the measure of his particular professional integrity. This radical attitude is not without its pitfalls, fostering at times the recently influential but incipiently solipsistic rationale that art is anything (literally anything!) that "artists" do; but the more reasonable benefit is that practitioners today can exploit a lateral freedom practically unknown to their predecessors.

Moholy's own artistic adventurism, along with his characteristically Hungarian capacity for cultural adaptation, may explain his extraordinary ability to keep abreast of the changing historical and artistic situation; for not only did he successfully establish himself in a succession of new cultures and learn at least two new languages, he also stood continually at the frontier of that New World which is twentieth-century art. He died much too soon, missing a contemporary scene characterized by esthetic opportunity and technological access that he would have relished far more than his professional contemporaries. (What other early modern artist would have considered the creative possibilities of television?) He had so thoroughly mastered the processes of an open-ended artistic career and accepted the inevitability of change; unlike most other major figures of his generation, he was not likely to dig his premature grave at some historic position.

Inevitably, the question arises whether Moholy might have been a greater artist had he concentrated on one or another of his enthusiasms; but that is really a useless inquiry, like asking whether steaks should not be pears.

It is hard to believe, as I noted before, that Moholy wanted to create "a great painting" or "classic designs," though his commitment to nothing short of the most significant art and activity shines through all his work; for in the diversity of his experience, as well as the courage of his adventure, is Moholy's greatness most clearly revealed. The point is that his highly defined creative sensibility worked through several artistic media, exploring and yet always respecting the particular nature of each, in some cases contributing significant work and affecting the direction of their modern traditions. In incomparable diversity and persevering eclecticism was, paradoxically, both his coherent totality and singular achievement, as well as an accumulated personal experience that, in the literal sum of his perceptions, marked him as one of the great minds of the age. In the end, Moholy was, in his fashion, as fecund an inventor as anybody in modern art; he was certainly a more various innovator, who made the risk of artistic adventurism a contemporary necessity.

A Mine of Perceptions
and Prophecies (1969)

Ultimately all problems of design merge into one great problem: "design for life." In a healthy society this design for life will encourage every profession and vocation to play its part since the degree of relatedness in all their work gives to any civilization its quality. . . . It further implies that there is no hierarchy of the arts, painting, photography, music, poetry, sculpture, architecture, nor any other fields such as industrial design. They are equally valid departures toward the fusion of function and content in "design." — L. Moholy-Nagy, *Vision in Motion* (1947)

From his artistic beginnings, Moholy was an artist who also wrote, usually in clear and forceful prose; and it is as a writer most of all that he remains with us today. His theatrical ideas would probably have been forgotten long ago, had he not set them in print; and although his efforts in sculpture and photography have been memorialized by the critical historians of those fields, his own ideas and example, expounded in his lifetime by the Bauhaus books and such reviews as *i 10* in Amsterdam, now survive largely in his own prose. His much-reprinted essay on *The New Vision*, originally published in Germany in 1929, translated here in 1932, and subsequently reissued in 1947 in a considerably revised edition, with an autobiographical afterword entitled "Abstract of an Artist" (1944), remains in print and still stands as a fine critical introduction to Cubist-kinetic tendencies in modern art. Less a coherent polemic than a series of related polemical paragraphs, *The New Vision* is a compendium of concise statements (even the illustration captions are pithy), such as an itemized summary of Cubist innovations and wise generalizations about all contemporary art; for Moholy possessed the art historian's competence for discerning the character and drift of the whole. (On the other hand, the more philosophical passages on biological relevance, while ambitious and perhaps necessary to the argument, are less persuasive.) Moholy's writing marks him as perhaps the only major practitioner of modern art possessed of sufficiently broad experience and sympathy to write about more than his few most noted passions; in sheer bulk, he also published more genuine critical prose than any other modern visual artist of note. Moreover, Moholy's writings are rich in such passing prophecies as a reference to film's "unexplored possibilities of projection, with color, plasticity and simultaneous displays, either by means of an increased number of projectors concentrated on a single screen, or in the form of simultaneous image sequences covering all the walls of the room."

The obvious paradox of Moholy's career is that as an adventurer in many arts he was the true master of none, which is to say that in no area except perhaps photography, book design, and kinetic light sculpture was he indisputably a seminal figure and that, though scarcely any of his signed works are outrageously bad, very few of them approach status as masterpieces of their form; the most likely candidates in media other than those noted above are the paintings on metallic and transparent surfaces, the films about Marseilles, and the light machine. The suspicion is that, unlike other artists of his stature, Moholy never really intended to be a "great painter," or a "great photographer," or master of any other specialty, though his intention to be nothing less than a great artist and his uncompromised aspirations to important work inform his activities in every medium. The more unusual paradox is that this artist's indisputably greatest work, to my mind, is his last book, *Vision in Motion*, the consummation of all his ideas and interests, which was written in English (in language sporadically peculiar and yet invariably clear), mostly in Chicago; and since hardbound publication, by definition, brings exploratory processes to a halt, it is perhaps appropriate that the book appeared just after Moholy's death. No other modern artist capped his career with a great book. Though considerably less known than it should be, selling only 40,000 copies in twenty years (mostly to art students) and seldom credited in print, *Vision in Motion* is indubitably among the half-dozen classic studies of modern art, as well as the best example I know, in Moholy's own phrase, of "text and illustration welded toegether." Indeed, I personally regard *Vision in Motion* as one of the most insightful guides available to contemporary art (much as his friend Giedion's *Space, Time and Architecture* [1941] remains the best on its subject), even though it was written twenty-four years ago (and regrettably neglects such issues as reductionism, inferential art, and post-modern dance); for instance, a recent book I did on "happenings," kinetic environments, and related endeavors, *The Theatre of Mixed Means* (1968) was intellectually more indebted to Moholy's masterpiece than to any other single text.

Compendious, discursive, conglomerate, *Vision in Motion* accomplishes several things. It is first of all a summary of Moholy's program at the Institute of Design, enhanced by many generous illustrations of his students' adventurous work (though very few of their names, curiously enough, are familiar to us today); here the theme is the nature and necessity of a truly multisensory education. Literacy, defined entirely by book-learning, is illiteracy in contemporary times, which require genuine polyliteracy. Second, *Vision in Motion* is an implicit record of both Moholy's artistic ambitions and his quest for a perceptual and creative sensibility distinctly appropriate to modern times, and it successfully ties together many strands of his multiple adventure. As a man of artistic and intellectual action, who instinctively translated his ideas into schemes and objects, Moholy frequently illustrated his own endeavors in painting, film, sculpture, photography, light machines, industrial design, and even poetry; this remains the most thorough guide to his own work. The book is finally an illuminating survey of recent achievements and ideas in various separate arts, and even points among and between, not only to define the multiple revolutions of modern art but also to outline a viable tradition behind further work.

While the academic art historian is predisposed to show how recent art draws upon aspects of the acknowledged tradition, Moholy, as a participant-observer, made his thesis the radically different style and opportunites of the modernist moment. He correctly identifies two pervasive tendencies peculiar to contemporary activity — kinesis and inter-media; and these crucial perceptions lead him to predict much that has since become important. The first revolutionary quality he traces back to Cubism and the resulting evolution from "fixed perspective to 'vision in motion,'" which is to say, the process of "seeing a constantly changing moving field of mutual relationship" that he finds exemplified in painting at least as "a new essay at two-dimensional rendering of related objects"; and Moholy concludes an extremely perspicacious analysis of Cubism's conventions by asserting, "From its inception, Cubism became a prime mover in the visual arts. All attempts at visual expression by the following generation have been directly or indirectly influenced by it." His commentary then draws upon the technical morphology of sculpural forms (from stasis to kinesis) elaborated in *The New Vision*; and as cinematic montage is regarded as an extension of Cubism, so film becomes, in Moholy's analysis, the climactic kinetic art. Thus, in all modern arts, Moholy finds "spacetime" or "vision in motion," which he comprehensively defines as "a new dynamic and kinetic existence freed from the static, fixed framework of the past," and Moholy's critical remarks are as true for such contemporary painterly arts as music and post-ballet modern dance, since there are analogies between Cubist artistic space, with its simultaneously multiple perspective, and post–Schönberg serial music. "It is a tribute to Moholy's intellect and visionary powers," noted Jack W. Burnham in *Beyond Modern Sculpture*, "that the outlines of kinetic histories to date have pretty much followed his pattern."

On the second theme of inter-media, Moholy recognizes, for instance, that a light mobile of negligible weight, kinetic form, virtual and changing volume, moving parts, and, thus, "space-time relationships" is not sculpture in the traditional sense but something else; however, Moholy's criticism never quite takes the leap into inventing a new genre, as I would do, of sculptural (or artistic) machines to classify a mechanical entity built primarily for artistic

(or useless) purposes. His imaginative remarks on theatrical possibilities suggest a hybrid between the old theater and spectacular display, and he tends
to place the artistic use of light indefinitely between painting and something
else. While Moholy would encourage the adventurous artist to explore unfamiliar terrains, he also insists that the integrity of each medium be
respected—film cannot behave like sculpture or express essentially literary
ideas, and vice versa.

His section on "Literature," amazingly enough, defines the avant-garde
traditions as we currently know them, twenty-four years later—simultaneists,
Futurists, Expressionists, Dadaists, Surrealists, and James Joyce. Back in the
middle 1940s, Moholy ventured the increasingly persuasive opinion that *Finnegans Wake* was the extraordinary book of the age, and he typically risks a
perceptive analysis of Joyce's language as the key to his multiplicitous theme,
in addition to reproducing an intricate chart (done in collaboration with
Leslie L. Lewis) that I have not seen in print anywhere else. As a critic who
discriminately responded to radical originality, Moholy also knew that one
possibility for language would be in the inter-medium of designed words; and
he identifies precursors of "concrete poetry" or "word-imagery" in Christian
Morgenstern, Apollinaire, and Marinetti. "The ideograms of Apollinaire
were a logical answer to their dull typography, to the leveling effects of the
gray, inarticulate machine typesetting.... Already in Marinetti's Joffre
poems, movement, space, time, visual and audible sensations were
simultaneously expressed by the typography." As Moholy conceived it, the
word-image art at its best would be not a design of letters and other verbal
symbols, in the manner of orthodox "concretism" (most of which, particularly
in anthological presentations, is trivial), or even the visualization of a single
word, such as Robert Indiana's *Love* or the oil painting done of his own name
(*Moholy*, 1921), but a field of words in various type-styles that would "create
a quick, simultaneous communication of several messages"—a conception
close to, say, the Englishman John Furnival's work, if not certain posters full
of words, than anything else. In addition, Moholy anticipates the recent interest in a poetry purely of spoken sounds, even establishing and quoting the
tradition of Hugo Ball's "Verse Without Words," Kurt Schwitters' "Anna
Blume" (but omitting E. E. Cummings' "ygUDuh"). Shrewdly again, he even
looks into the writings of psychotics for alternative ways of structuring linguistic communication.

For his explanation of stylistic change in art, Moholy usually appropriates the theme of technological determinism. The end of Renaissance
representational space, in which a scene is portrayed "from an *unchangeable*,
fixed point following the rules of the vanishing point perspective," is attributed to "speeding on the roads and circling in the skies.... The man at
the wheel sees persons and objects in quick succession, in permanent motion."
He notes at the beginning that, "New tools and technologies cause social

changes," adding elsewhere that "such a 'mechanical' thing as photography" had a similarly revolutionary effect upon the contemporary sensibility.

> One has only to recall the romantic outlook of former generations upon the pictorial presentation of landscape and other objects, and compare it with the way they are perceived now, namely, "photographically." Many people may not realize it but the present standard of visual expression in any field, painting, sculpture, architecture and especially the advertising arts, is nourished by the visual food which the new photography provides.

(This echoes a striking statement in the very first book: "We have through a hundred years of photography and two decades of film been enormously enriched in this respect. We may say that we see the world with entirely different eyes.") And the concern with modulated shading in his own art Moholy also attributes to photography, which "revealed for the first time light and shadow in their interdependence." Needless to say, *Vision in Motion* also has some of the richest pages ever written on the possibilities of the photographic medium.

Technology is also regarded as crucially changing the sum of materials available to an art, so that the innovative design of even something as mundane as home chairs is indebted to "electricity, the gasoline and Diesel engines, the airplane, motion pictures, color photography, radio, metallurgy, new alloys, plastics, laminated materials." At another point, Moholy notes, with an appraisal more applicable right now than thirty years ago, "Today there are more technological sources for light painting than at any other period of human history," and a passing remark acknowledges the artistic potential, only recently realized, of the intermittent, "strobe" light that Harold Edgerton invented forty years ago. At times this bias toward technological determinism lapses off into a contrary Hegelianism; for instance, Moholy writes, "The best representatives of the arts whether in music, poetry, sculpture, or painting, even in their single works, always express the spiritual state of the age." However, this apparent contradiction can be explained by Moholy's establishing, at the beginning of the book, that technology is the primary force informing the spirit and produce of the era.

Vision in Motion is also a profoundly political book, not because Moholy was a politically active artist — publicized agitation was not his style — but because he regarded both the creation and comprehension of modern art as inherently political acts. Indeed, although he sometimes uses Marxian terms to explain certain historical cultural phenomena and favored a more or less socialist economy, Moholy broke with the orthodox Marxists, on one hand, over their resistances to both individual artistic integrity and non-representational modern art and with the artistic "humanists," on the other, over their resistances to technology. As a more organic revolutionary, Moholy favored radical changes in *both* art and life, and both technology *and* psychology,

regarding transformations in each as feeding into the others, so that true
political purpose for the artist lay not in portraying social injustice but in
creating "powerful new relationships. He can do so either by developing
tendencies or by opposing them. The gradual elimination of the still existing
feudal residues, that is, obsolete economic theories, obsolete patterns of individual behavior, obsolete sexual and family relationships is not an
automatic matter." Of a modest Christian Morgenstern ideogram, for instance, he argued, "Still it is an attempt to break the conventions of content
and the customary form of typography, and with it, symbolically, the content
and form of society which applied its great rules of the past only mechanically."

Innovative art is regarded as the anti-archaic force in contemporary
culture, at its best an influence perhaps more powerful than politics. "Tyranny
and dictatorship, manifestoes and decrees will not recast the mentality of the
people. The unconscious but direct influence of art [plus, it would seem, technological change] represents a better means of persuasion for conditioning
people to a new society." As technology ushers changes that make men emo-
tionally behind-the-times, the task of art and education is to reclaim him for
the present. In addition, Moholy regarded technological advance and the
"satisfaction of mass requirements" as more of a blessing than a curse, though
he viewed with dismay both capitalist exploitation and man's reluctance, or
inability, to use all the machines available to him; and a parenthetical
paragraph, set in a broad margin, connects truly functional design with "the
revolutionary spirit of American democracy" and, by converse implication,
pompously excessive ornamentation with "feudal, ornate forms of living."
Moreover, it is by connecting change in art to social evolution that *Vision in
Motion* profoundly comprehends, and advocates, the radical nature of the
twentieth century.

Perhaps the key to Moholy's eclectically radical politics is his list of
favored revolutionaries, grouped in a paragraph sub-headed "the avant-
garde"; for along with Voltaire, "Proudhon, Marx, Bakunin, Kropotkin and
Lenin," are included Pasteur, Einstein, Darwin, Stravinsky, Varèse, "Whitman, Rimbaud, Dostoievsky, Tolstoy, Joyce," Le Corbusier, Gropius and,
of course, Picasso, Malevitch, and Mondrian—all of whom envisioned
radically different ways of practicing their respective arts. Along with his
commitment to innovative revolution, Moholy recognized the importance of
planning, or the implementation of vision; and just as the opening chapter
of *Vision in Motion* calls for "a planned co-operative economy," so the conclusion indicatively proposes the establishment of a college of sophisticated plan-
ners, who would envision and then build a new world.

Moholy also differed from orthodox Marxists by assuming that mind
change (and creations of the human mind, such as technology) precedes social
change, and this induces a particularly revolutionary concern with education.

Since the nature of the new age is defined by kinesis and inter-media, education should be redesigned to respect the new realities. On one hand, he favored training that involved not merely the transmission of information but also "hand and brain, intellect and emotion; the task is to give the student enough opportunity to use his brain together with his emotional potential; to provide for sensory experiences of eye, nose, tongue and fingers, and their transformation into controlled expression." Elsewhere in *Vision in Motion*, he describes the Institute of Design's program, which exposed students to basic materials and concepts of all the arts, as well as including a number of general exercises "mostly built upon sensory experiences through work with various materials. . . . In addition, there is work with sheet metal and wire, glass, mirrors, plastics, drawing and color, mechanical drawing, photography, group poetry, and music — a full range of potentialities." However, the final aim was not dilettante taste but organic integration of diversified competence — what Moholy defined as "seeing everything in relationship — artistic, scientific, technical as well as social." Most of this remains a persuasive and radical vision for future educational reform. As Sibyl Moholy-Nagy observed in a recent article, throughout his life her husband espoused the Constructivist thesis "that perception is the carrier of human emotion and that it is the subtlest awareness of this perception to all phenomena of life that saves men from stagnation and desperation."

As a richly polymathic discourse, *Vision in Motion* teems with miscellaneous aphorisms and genuinely good ideas, some of which are buried in long paragraphs or dropped off in captions; it is one of those rare critical books that yields fresh ideas with repeated reading:

> The simpler [the artist's] medium and the less investment it involves, the easier it is to avoid possible censorship and to preserve the ways of genuinely free expression.
> The finest solutions of functional design usually are found in new inventions.
> Many achievements of the industrial revolution could be praised emphatically if people had not had to pay so dearly for them.
> Art sensitizes man to the best that is immanent in him through an intensified expression involving many layers of experience.
> The higher the window the better it solves its original function, which is to admit light deeply into the room.
> The choice of medium is in the artist's hand; he must have the ability to summon artistic coherence out of the means he uses.
> The illiterate of the future will be the person ignorant of the use of the camera as well as of the pen.
> In 1927 in Zurich I suggested for cinema publicity . . . a gas curtain onto which motion pictures could be projected, through which the public could pass. This gaseous curtain could also, chameleon-like, change colors.
> By analyzing the paintings of these various groups [of modern art], one soon finds a common denominator, the supremacy of color over 'story'; the

directness of perceptional, sensorial values against the illusionistic rendering of nature; the emphasis on visual fundamentals to express a particular concept.

The intrinsic meaning of an abstract painting, as a peculiar form of visual articulation, lies mainly in the integration of the visual elements, in its *freedom from the imitation* of nature and the philosophy connected with it.

Some of Moholy's most memorable comments sketch the interrelationship between technology and design: "The older the craft, the more restraining is its influence upon the imagination of the designer. It is easier to design a new product which is based upon the new sciences and technologies than, for example, to redesign the production-ways and shapes of pottery, one of the oldest handicrafts."

Vision in Motion fires ideas in so many directions that it has inevitably become a mine for plagiarists and popularizers. Gyorgy Kepes, now of M.I.T.'s Center for Advanced Visual Studies, has cribbed freely from it for many of his recent books and anthologies, though he rarely credits Moholy, who not only supervised Kepes in London and Berlin but also brought his fellow Hungarian refugee to America to teach at the Institute of Design. Furthermore, it was Moholy, and not Marshall McLuhan, who noted, in 1947, that the contemporary newspaper, unlike its eighteenth-century predecessor, "tries to organize the many events of the day similarly as the Futurists; the reader should read all the news almost at once." McLuhan and Harley W. Parker note in their extremely interesting *Beyond the Vanishing Point* (1968) that, "Seurat, by divisionism, anticipates quadricolor reproduction and color TV," but this echoes Moholy's perception that "Seurat, for example, with his pointillist art, intuitively anticipates the science of color photography." At times Moholy even sounds like his intellectual successor McLuhan: "With the mass production of autos, the elevated lines became technologically obsolete but were kept on as a cheap means of intercity travel." Although McLuhan is usually generous about acknowledging his more modish sources, he rarely credits Moholy, who clearly stands behind many of the media-sleuth's ideas. (Indeed, it was McLuhan who first told *me* to read *Vision in Motion*.) All in all, though his name is scarcely known, Moholy's ideas still command considerable currency at the present time. He wrote on modern art a critical book that, more than two decades later, still has a contemporary relevance, primarily for its genuine perceptions rather than its style (the customary virtue of enduring criticism); and for how many other books on any modern subject can this be said?

The Truest Polyartist (1986)

Most of the advanced thinkers, writers, and artists of the past century and a half . . .
have preferred to function on the fringe of the avant-garde, rather than as members
of a movement, and even to abandon movements which they themselves initiated.
Harold Rosenberg, *The Avant-Garde* (1969)

If only for his exemplary polyartistic career, Moholy-Nagy was one of
the primary figures of modern art, a unique artistic pioneer who made consequential contributions to the traditions of several nonadjacent arts — painting,
book design, artistic machinery, critical writing, and photography — amidst
lesser achievements in film, theater decor, commercial design, and sculpture.
Given the breadth of his creative experience, complemented by his artistic intelligence, it is thus scarcely surprising that he also wrote in *Vision in Motion*
(1947) the most fertile critical book I know about modernism in the arts — even
after a dozen readings, the book reveals new insights to me. Typically, its
concluding chapter, on "Literature," remains, no less than two generations
later, the best introductory survey to the extreme avant-garde traditions
(literary intermedia) as we currently know them. Since Moholy-Nagy died
nearly forty years ago, you would think him an appropriate subject for a
critical biography updating the memoir, *Experiment in Totality* (1948), done by
his widow Sibyl.

One practical problem is that few scholars have sufficient knowledge, critical intelligence and conceptual language to deal with his polyartistic achievement. A second problem is that Moholy-Nagy was born in Hungary; and
since Hungarian cannot be learned (apparently) — it can only be inherited —
the project had to wait for an Hungarian scholar familiar with artistic modernism, Krisztina Passuth.

Opening at random her new *Moholy-Nagy*, I came across this exercise in
Marxist doubletalk and feared for the rest:

> The Gabo-Pevsner manifesto of 1920 was born in the afterglow of revolution
> [sic lower case]. But Moholy-Nagy had to live with the knowledge of a
> defeated revolution [in Hungary], one in which, moreover, he played no
> role at all [sic]. He adopted the ideas of Constructivism without the
> necessary basis of a social-political background. [So?] Although he was
> regarded as a representative of Constructivism, he himself did not look for

> any contact with the Soviet Union and, unlike other Hungarian emigres [in Western Europe], he never visited there. The new ideas he professed are indeed lacking in roots.

Especially in ascribing deficiency to a putative failure not of commission but omission this reasoning stinks of decrepit Eastern baloney. As we say here, gimmie a break.

However, most of Passuth's *Moholy-Nagy* is, thankfully, better than this, though too often incomplete. Fluently Englished (by several hands), her book has the fullest description of Moholy's childhood that I have yet read, though avoiding the questions of whether his parents with Jewish names were indeed Jewish and of this orphan's actual relation to his two "brothers." She refers to short stories written in Hungarian, but alas does not quote from them. Given the breadth of his activity, it is scarcely surprising that Passuth's appreciation of it is uneven. She speaks well of him as the editor of the Bauhaus books, the first great series on artistic modernism, but then says little about his influential innovations in book design for that series! Passuth reprints several Moholy manifestos (that remind us that few visual artists ever wrote so well, and truly, about their own work); yet as several of these had appeared before in books about Moholy (including mine of 1970), it would have been wiser to reprint (and translate) other writings of his that had not.

The supreme achievement of Passuth's *Moholy-Nagy* is the largest collection of reproductions I have ever seen—of paintings, sculptures, book designs, stage designs, costume designs, and even the Parker 51 pen, which remains perhaps the most collected work by any major modern artist. Nonetheless, the principal fault of the book *per se* is a reluctance to follow Moholy's example in design. "I have always held that" he wrote, "for better visual communication—text and illustration should be welded together. Illustrations should *accompany* the copy and not be searched for." Whereas the illustrations in his *Vision in Motion* appear conveniently adjacent to references to them in the text, Passuth's pictures are gathered together into separate folios, connected only to the text through numbered references. Since flipping the book's large pages can be so inconvenient, most of us are likely to "read" the text and pictures separately.

At times Passuth's commentary rises to meet the originality and adventure of Moholy's best innovations:

> It is clear that as early as 1920 Moholy-Nagy was already captivated by the industrial civilization of Berlin. Paintings and photographs conveyed this only indirectly, but film could express all the tense animation. Since he was unable to make a film in 1921–22 in Berlin, he chose a roundabout route by creating a new genre with his *Dynamic of the Metropolis, Sketch of a Manuscript for a Film*. This genre, which he called "typophoto" and which we might call a scenario, was the unique result of Moholy-Nagy's dual bent for literature

and painting. . . . Real photographs alternated with parts of the text, and the page make-up with its columns showed the influence of El Lissitzky and Hans Arp's *Kunstismen*. The idea of the film—in written form only—most resembles the earlier film experiments of Viking Eggeling and Hans Richter. Their rectangular frames of film arranged vertically show a series of almost unvarying abstract forms. Their works primarily belong to the field of fine arts. On the other hand, by lengthening and condensing individual moments, and by introducing unexpected cuts and changes, Moholy-Nagy created a film on paper—if this is possible at all—in pictures and text.

In combining an appreciation of the visual and the verbal, along with a sense of historical context, this is just perfect. (It prompts me to want to write a book of comparable visual-verbal scripts which, let me tell you, would certainly be a lot more interesting, and less tiresome, than actually realizing films.)

One reason why this *Moholy-Nagy* is not definitive is that Passuth only partially confronts the two toughest questions about his career—collaboration and plagiarism. Since Moholy's education was only in law, he was necessarily dependent upon the contributions of others. Aside from suggesting that his first wife Lucia Moholy did the darkroom work for his best photography, Passuth avoids the knotty problem of identifying consequential collaborators and reapportioning credit. As for plagiarism, the thought appears not to have occurred to Passuth, even though it was a charge frequently made by his contemporaries. I tended to regard the charge skeptically, thinking it alloyed with envy, until I saw in Eberhard Roters' recent *Berlin, 1910-1933* (1982) a 1929 Moholy backdrop stage design that scandalously resembles Paul Citroen's classic photomontage of *The Metropolis* (1922). What compounds this scandal is the fact that Citroen had been Moholy's student at the Bauhaus only a few years before!

Passuth's book surpasses several others on Moholy that have appeared recently, including Eleanor M. Hight's informative catalogue for a film and photography exhibition currently traveling through America; Andreas Haus' *Moholy-Nagy: Photographs & Photograms* (1980); and Irene-Charlotte Lusk's *Montagen ins Blaue* (1980) on the photocollages, if only because Passuth tries to be comprehensive. Partial interpretations, simply by limiting their scope, reduce Moholy to a journeyman, laboring among others similar in kind, rather than an extraordinarily unique creative figure: the truest polyartist of high modernism. Because Moholy's achievement transcends the pigeonholes of American scholarship (and, worse yet, of our scandalously narrow-minded channeling of scholarship-support), perhaps it is not so surprising that this, the best book so far, should come from behind the Iron Curtain. In truth, reading *Moholy-Nagy* gave me chills, reminding me of my first discovery of his heroic example and reconfirming my earlier estimate of his continuing importance.

Protoholographer (1987)

Photography is a new medium of expression. Since its working rules have not yet been frozen into unalterable dogma, it has experimental potentialities. Moreover, by analogy, one may [by working in photography] find clues, may approach other media with fresh insight. —p. 177, L. Moholy-Nagy, *Vision in Motion* (1947; also the source of all other indented passages)

Just before World War I, Guillaume Apollinaire wrote "conversation poems" culled from snatches of talk overheard in Parisian cafés. Looking back on such efforts now, we can think, poor Kostro, as he was then known — too bad he didn't have access to audiotape with which he could have not only recorded the café conversations but edited them into audiopoems that would add an acoustic dimension to his first rate poetic idea. Recently rereading the epigraph above in Moholy-Nagy's greatest book, my first thought was, poor Moholy, too bad he didn't live long enough to use holography. Four decades after *Vision in Motion* was written, holography epitomizes his notion of the new medium of expression, offering experimental possibilities, at a time when the procedures of photography seem ever more codified.

The progressive painter who is struggling with his traditional element, pigment, feels that very soon a transition will come, a transition from pigment to light. The knowledge for this understanding can hardly be acquired accidentally. It must be based partly upon scientific research and a new technology. [163]

For those unfamiliar with holography, let me offer some basic guidance. There are two kinds of hologram — reflection and transmission. The first is more common, referring to display material that will reveal an image, with modest degree of depth, when illuminated by surrounding light. The hologram commonly seen on a credit card falls into this category; so do those that appear from time to time on shiny surfaces in magazines. By contrast, in a transmission hologram, the image, customarily embedded in a pane of glass or other clear material, is illuminated from behind, usually to a greater degree of illusory depth. Most holograms seen on public display are of this type.

Within this latter category are two kinds of holograms, one involving

146

motion picture film, the other involving the process of laser beam splitting
seen in all holography instruction manuals. The first, called a holographic
stereogram or multiplex, is comprised of numerous vertical slivers that are
actually anamorphically compressed film frames. The multiplex is appropriate for representing subjects that will move as the viewer crosses its path. As
a two-eyed viewer looks at two different sets of slivers, he or she sees material
suspended from two slightly different perspectives, thus creating the appearance of depth. Perhaps the most famous multiplex is Lloyd Cross and
Pam Brazier's *Kiss II* in which, as the viewer moves from left to right, the
woman in the semicircular cylinder appears to blow him or her a kiss. My
On Holography (1978) shows five syntactically circular statements about
holography suspended in the middle of a cylindrical drum that is placed atop
a revolving stand, the letters marching from right to left as the cylinder turns.
Because multiplex involves motion picture film, it is sometimes dismissed as
"not-holography" by those who make traditional holograms. While there is a
point to their discrimination, it is difficult to think of another category where
such three-dimensional imaging belongs.

> There is no more surprising, yet, in its naturalness and organic sequence,
> simpler form than the photographic series. This is the logical culmination
> of photography — vision in motion. [208]

It was lamentable that Moholy did not live to use holography, which extends from photography, on one hand, and from film, on the other. Within
a stationary object holography is able to represent motion; but unless the
hologram moves, as in the revolving cylinder mentioned above, the requirement is that the viewer move. In my *Antitheses* (1985), for instance, four
distinct planes of words emerge forward from each side of a suspended glass.
As words are visibly situated behind other words, the viewer must move from
side to side, as well as up and down, to read them all, one theme of mine being
that holographic reading differs from conventional reading. (The trade term
for such body movements is "laser limbo.")

In *Vision in Motion* (207) Moholy brilliantly enumerates "eight varieties
of photographic vision," which I reprint in summary because all his rubrics
are applicable to holography now: (1) *Abstract seeing* by means of direct records
produced by light; (2) *Exact seeing* by means of camera records; (3) *Rapid seeing*
by means of the fixation of movements in the instantaneous snapshot; (4) *Slow
seeing* by means of fixation of movements spread over a period of time; (5) *In-
tensified seeing*; (6) *Penetrative seeing;* (7) *Simultaneous seeing*; (8) *Distorted seeing.*
While holography was an incredible development, beyond the capacities of
Moholy's imagination a half-century ago, it is another sign of his prophetic
critical intelligence that his terms of understanding should be relevant to
something he did not know. One additional quality special to holography,

that would have interested Moholy, is that light turns on the image. A photograph or a film has an image visible to the eye, while a hologram looks blank until it is appropriately illuminated.

Most of the early holograms were essentially photographic in subject matter, such as portraits rendered with the illusion of depth reminiscent of that available from stereo cameras; and most viewers approached them as they would photographs, glancing at an image that could be quickly grasped, with an option of more extended examination. Within holography are now working several artists, including myself, who consciously eschew producing work that allows this kind of hasty perception. For example, in my work mentioned above, five sentences must be read one at a time, or words must be seen behind other words; it was important for me to discover how to make holographic experience different from photographic.

> The photogram exploits the unique characteristic of the photographic process — the ability to record with delicate fidelity a great range of tonal values. The almost endless range of gradations, subtlest differences in the gray values, belongs to the fundamental properties of photographic expression. The organized use of that gradation creates photographic quality. [188]

With the photogram, we remember, Moholy avoided the camera entirely, simply placing objects on photographic paper and then exposing the array to light. His intent was to discover a pictorial language unique to photography. Something similar is already happening in holography, where Fred Unterseher, the pioneering principal author of *Holography Handbook* (1982), has been making objectless holography whose imagery of colored tones unique to holography is generated from within the technology itself. In principle, the "organized use of [such] gradations" should rank among the most fertile current options for holography.

> In the successive stages of sculptural development the main characteristic is the reduction and lightening of the heavy mass so that even the normal characteristics of the material disappear. In mobiles, material is utilized not in its mass but as a carrier of movement. To the three dimensions of volume, the fourth, the time element, movement, is added. [237]

The Moholyan works closest to holography are the light modulators of the 1940s. Here, we remember, Moholy placed a plastic sheet above a canvas so that holes within the sheet, as well as shapes painted on it, made shadows on the background canvas. To appreciate their variable structure, the viewer had to move from side to side, as well as up and down, broaching the choreographic vocabulary of laser limbo. Had Moholy lived to use holography — remember he would have been only seventy when the technology first became available — my own suspicion is that he would have filled it with the same kinds of geometric imagery that appear not only in these light modulators but also in his photographs, his paintings, his films, his book designs, and much else. Among contemporary holographers, the one coming closest to doing such Moholyan work also ranks among the best — Sam Moree. A characteristic of his work, as you view it holographically, is the radically changing relationships between foreground shapes and background; it must be seen in person to be believed.

> The development of the visual arts from fixed perspective to "vision in motion" is *vision in relationships*. The fixed viewpoint, the isolated handling of problems as a norm is rejected and replaced by a flexible approach, by seeing matters in a constantly changing moving field of mutual relationships. [114]

A cultural puzzle that mystifies me is the disparity in the public careers of video and holography, which were two new arts, both based on technological developments that became publicly available approximately a quarter-century ago. While video added picture to radio, holography added depth and motion to photography. While the former has entered the mainstream of art culture, with its practitioners given museum exhibitions, critical articles and academic jobs, holography has remained a comparatively marginal enterprise. (Oddly, video has allied itself with film, though it eschews film, while all forms of holography depend upon film.) What holography now needs is a figure comparable to Moholy, in his relation to photography — a practitioner and critical advocate, encouraging innovation and suggesting standards, long before the art becomes academicized.

> Most of the visual work of the future lies with the "light painter." . . . It is difficult to go into details yet, but in the coming experiments, research into the physiology of the eye and in the physical properties of light will play an important part. [168]

One measure of the richness of Moholy's commentary in *Vision in Motion* is that, even after two decades of reading it, I continually find new ideas in its pages. Rereading the book recently, I came across this gem, ostensibly regarding film: "The root of all evil is the exclusion of the experimental creator, of the free independent producer" (273). It made me think of one problem in the practice of art holography today, which is that the field is dominated by people who work only in holography, who are "holographers," as they like to call themselves. They stand in contrast to independent producers like Moholy who came to a new art after involvements in other arts and who, like me, following Moholy's example, do holography alongside work in other arts. After all, the people who made films an art were not professionals steeped in the technique, but adventurers trained in other fields.

Finally, as a great fan of Moholy's writing, I wish he had lived long enough to have written about holography, because I am sure he would have made discoveries that have so far escaped me. Need I conclude that as a writer and artist, or a writer/artist, Moholy's example remains an abiding inspiration.

To End in a Book (1991)

Tout, au monde, existe pour aboutir à un livre [Everything in the world exists to end in a book]. —Stéphane Mallarmé.

I've long ranked L. Moholy-Nagy among the greatest contemporary artists, not only for the value of individual works but for the incomparable quality of his esthetic adventure, with exploratory consistency, through several media. Because he excelled at several nonadjacent arts, among them painting, kinetic sculpture, photography, film, book design and writing, Moholy should be considered a modern exemplar of the *polyartist*. Asked to identify a single work that epitomizes his achievement, that represents the sum of his imagination and intelligence, I would choose, without intending to deprecate anything else, not a work of primarily visual art but the big book written in Chicago that, appearing posthumously, concluded his short life as only a book can do — *Vision in Motion* (1947).

It is first of all one of the major critical essays about artistic modernism, documenting as it does the new developments not only in painting and sculpture, but in photography and even literature. The general intelligence as well as the quality of Moholy's insights is so great that you frequently pause and take notes or mark profusely. Take this passage on modernist painting:

> But in analyzing the paintings of these various groups one soon finds a common denominator, the supremacy of color over "story"; the directness of perceptional, sensorial values against the illusionistic rendering of nature; the emphasis on visual fundamentals to express a particular concept.

Or this on modernist sculpture:

> In the successive stages of sculptural development the main characteristic is the reduction and lightening of the heavy mass so that even the normal characteristics of the material disappear. This is most effectively realized on the "mobile" or moving sculpture. Here the problem of virtual volume relationships is posed.

Or this on classic photography:

151

The photogram exploits the unique characteristic of the photographic process—the ability to record with delicate fidelity a great range of tonal values. The almost endless range of gradations, subtlest differences in the gray values, belongs to the fundamental properties of photographic expression. The organized use of that gradation creates photographic quality.

Or this forecasting of the principles of computer sound composition:

To develop creative possibilities of the sound film, the acoustic alphabet of sound writing will have to be mastered; in other words, we must learn to write acoustic sequences on the sound track without having to record real sound. The sound film composer must be able to compose music from a counterpoint of unheard or even nonexistent sound values, merely by means of opto-acoustic notation.

Or this on the politics of art and the function of art education:

Art may press for the sociobiological solution of problems just as energetically as the social revolutionaries do through political action. The so-called "unpolitical" approach of art is a fallacy. Politics, freed from graft, party connotations, or more transitory tactics, is mankind's method of realizing ideas for the welfare of the community.

To my mind, the concluding section on "Literature" is one of the strongest in the book, identifying as it does the most extreme modernist developments as we know them to this day. (It is not for nothing that I reprinted it in a 1982 anthology on *The Avant-Garde Tradition in Literature*.) The highest point of this chapter is Moholy's pioneering analysis of *Finnegans Wake*, which was published only a few years before. Not only did he understand Joyce's extraordinary work better than anyone else writing at that time, but Moholy also provided a chart that, as it uses his favorite visual forms of the rectangular grid and circles, remains to this day the most succinct (and inspired) presentation of the Joycean technique of multiple references. (Need it be said that no other modern artist wrote as well about literature?) What Moholy established in *Vision in Motion* was a model of writing about all the arts as a single entity, to be called art, whose branches (literature, painting, etc.) were merely false conveniences conducive to specialization and isolation.

Though he had come to America only a few years before, Moholy wrote *Vision in Motion* in English, in contrast to his earlier books that were originally in his second language, German (and thus translated by other hands for their appearance here). Though his spoken English was reportedly imperfect, Moholy's prose in *Vision in Motion* is (or was made) remarkably vigorous and clear, as the above examples demonstrate. Indeed, you can feel Moholy's thrill in communicating his favorite post–Bauhaus ideas in yet another language new to him for a new audience in his adopted country; you can feel his evident pleasure in writing an American book as a newly American artist. As a Hungarian critic perceived, "Each line, each analogy, each phrase in the book is, in spite of the influence of the Bauhaus tradition, one hundred per cent American."

What he understood back in the 1940s was that kinesis would become a predominant quality in contemporary visual art and thus that much innovation would occur in areas between the old arts. As a result, Moholy became a remarkably prophetic guide to the future. In writing my 1968 book on happenings, kinetic theater and other mixed-means events, I found myself citing him often. Two decades later, in writing an essay on the esthetics of holography, I turned to *Vision in Motion* again, for conceptual insight into a medium that didn't arrive under twenty years after his death! Though I have read the book perhaps two dozen times, every time I return to it I find myself, amazing though it seems, recording an insight that escaped my attention before.

It is scarcely surprising, remembering Moholy's pioneering realization of Bauhaus book design, that *Vision in Motion* should represent the epitome of his book-making style in all respects but one (the use of serif typography, rather than the sans-serif he traditionally favored). Its blocks of type, both roman and bold, with different widths, are distributed among shrewdly selected rectangular illustrations, usually in close proximity to commentary about them, under the assumption that text and image should be seen together. The pictures included modern masterpieces along with examples of his own works and, generously, those of his students. For all of its intelligence about modern art in general, *Vision in Motion* is also an "artist's book," or bookart of the highest order, about Moholy's rich esthetic experience, and needless to say perhaps it is a book that only he had enough experience to write and design as well. If we accept the revelations of Conceptual Art that a prose description of artistic experience could constitute, in and of itself, an esthetic object, then *Vision in Motion* has other resonances that not even Moholy could have foreseen.

USCO (1967)

Environmental art is without doubt the most avant-garde art mode of the nineteen
sixties — if we take avant-garde to mean the type of art that, regardless of art values,
makes all other kinds of art seem a thing of the past. — Harold Rosenberg, "Lights!
Lights!" (1969)

USCO, USCO — those mysterious initials that magisterially appear in
various places and contexts signify US Company (or company of us), a collective of artists who operate out of a forsaken church in Garnerville, New York,
about an hour north of New York City. USCO functions as a frame, as well
as a signature, for individual artists who move in and out, contributing to the
collective effort and yet preserving their personal identities. The quickest
measure of USCO's impact is the relation between its age and achievement;
for in less than four years, it has completed a multiplicity of projects and
established an international reputation.

The core members of USCO are its founders — a painter in his late twenties named Steve Durkee; a younger man with a considerable aptitude for
electronics, Michael Callahan; and a thirty-eight-year-old poet who had occasionally plied conventional trades, Gerd Stern. Their paths crossed in the
early sixties, as they helped one another with their respective works. "Gerd
was living near here," Durkee remembers, "and he was just turning his poetry
into on-the-wall objects. As I had been making objects on the wall for a long
time, I helped him. Since I understood that very thoroughly, he was able to
say X, Y and A, and I was able to say A, B and Z. That was how the relationship started." A short while later, Stern, then in San Francisco, needed some
technical help in making an audio tape collage, and Michael Callahan, as a
technician at the local tape music center, became his collaborator. Not until
1964, however, did they all gather in Durkee's studio-home, the Garnerville
church, to combine their collaborative instincts into USCO.

As each moved out of his respective art into collective work, the results
of their collaboration became intermedia — works that straddled the walls
which traditionally divided one art from another. USCO has produced objects of all sorts — posters as well as machines — but their primary medium has
been the theatrical event. Some have been conventional performances where
an audience arrived at a certain time, paid an admission price and then took

their seats, but USCO prefers to work in what Stern calls "the environmental circumstance," where "you take a space and an open-ended piece of time, and you see what you can make it do to people." In producing an environment USCO metaphorically creates a world of activity—just as, Durkee adds, "God created the universe."

The best USCO theatrical pieces contain a plethora of communicative stimuli—slides, films (sometimes looped), colored and/or pulsing lights, sounds, objects and even odors—all of which usually function to evoke archetypal themes; a particularly successful piece they characterize as "a beautiful mix." The four-room environment USCO constructed at the Riverside Museum in May, 1966, was probably their most elaborate and brilliant exhibition.

USCO designed this "system" to be a "meditation room," full of basic symbols and materials—male and female, heartbeats, and above, seven spheres representing seven planets. "We also had five elements," Durkee remembers. "We had sand in the box in the middle; fire in the candles; we had air; we had water in the fountain around the periphery of the column, which was also the lingam inside the yoni—a psychosexual situation. There was an 'om' tape playing on a stereo tape recorder. Have you heard of 'om'? Dome, home, womb, tomb, bomb; the 'om' is in a lot of important things. 'Om' was the original sound of the universe. What we had in that room, in short, was everything that is." Most of USCO's oldest admirers consider the Riverside Museum display its greatest single work, and the exhibition has been memorialized in Jud Yalkut's color film, *Down by the Riverside* (1966).

The effect of an USCO environment is somewhat similar to the psychedelic experience, for in both an awareness of sensory overload disrupts all attempts at concentrated focus and also initiates a gamut of emotional and psychological changes. An intrinsic purpose of such an environment is challenging linear habits of organization. "We're dealing with the question of how you can get into the mind with information and images and whether literary, sequential ordering is really the only decent, rational and reasonable input," Stern remarks. Therefore, the connection with psychedelics, while valid, does not explain everything. Although Durkee once extensively lectured on the new drugs (which he has since given up), USCO's pieces are designed to turn people on not to themselves but one another. Their principal theme, Durkee says, "is that we are all one. Once we have the understanding that you're not threatening to me and I'm not threatening to you—in other words, that you are myself outside of myself—then we can begin to work together." USCO's environments present a field of elemental images precisely to make everyone undergo a common reception and then experience a shared awareness. Indeed their conception of art's possible purposefulness evokes echoes of the American thirties, but the content of USCO's message is more ecumenical than parochial.

The close connection between electronic media and shared awareness has McLuhanish overtones, and sure enough McLuhan's ideas are conspicuously among USCO's influences. Back in 1960 Gerd Stern read an early draft of *Understanding Media* (1964) in the form of a report McLuhan submitted to the National Association of Educational Broadcasters in 1959, and that experience persuaded Stern to consider the artistic potential of the new media. Soon after, his own poetic impulses took off from the problems of black words on white paper and were channeled into tape collage. McLuhan himself has joined USCO for two performances, speaking after and sometimes before a mixed-media presentation. USCO concurs with his prophecy that today's cities will soon disintegrate into small communities, electronically interconnected; and from him, they also recognized how sensory overload in their home environment could recircuit their own sensibilities. "When you live in a twenty-four channel system, day in and day out — as we did when we were doing our things at home, running them for twenty-four hours a day, almost," Durkee judges, "you can become pretty much omniattentive."

From McLuhan, along with the Indian esthetician Ananda K. Coomaraswamy, they took the theme that the contemporary artist should be as anonymous as the medieval artist; but interpretations of "anonymity" create a constant argument within the USCO house. Their work is clearly anonymous in the sense that it contains neither an individual signature nor earmarks of personalized expression. However, to Stern, their impersonal result does not deny individual artistic contributions.

USCO has done so many things in its short life that future historians will have difficulty collecting all the data; what I list below is merely a rough summary of their produce:

1) Psychedelic posters and other graphics.

2) Various kinds of machines and electronic devices, such as strobe lights and programming units.

3) Electronic audio-visual aids, such as a counting unit for the New York production of Norman Mailer's *The Deer Park*.

4) Mixed-means presentations for corporation sales conferences.

5) The setting up and operation of a mixed-media discotheque.

6) Kinetic artistic-informational displays, such as a much-appreciated media-mix about the Lower East Side for New York's Jewish Museum and, this autumn, the Smithsonian Institution in Washington.

7) Miscellaneous sound and light effects for all kinds of hippy and pacifist benefits.

8) Theatrical performances in dozens of museums and universities.

9) An elegant kinetic meditational tabernacle in their own house.

10) The construction of a communal village in the New Mexican desert.

11) Consultation in environment creation, including hyped-up rooms intended for psychiatric purposes.

The more USCO does, the further from convention it goes; the more imitators they have, the stronger is their desire to move beyond even media mixes. They will probably move out of quasi-art objects and even theatrical displays into larger and more comprehensive creations. "If we are concerned environmentally," Stern says, "we might as well plan our own environment." The New Mexico project will be their first attempt at building a human community from scratch.

Home base for USCO is still the one-time church in Garnerville. A rather large building, it has one huge room which was formerly a workshop but now houses *The Tabernacle* (1966), a kinetic environment that USCO opens to the public every Sunday afternoon. A hexagon, about twelve feet in diameter, *The Tabernacle* has such a rich gallery of sensory effects that the experience of sitting in it confirms Stern's promise that, "*The Tabernacle* stimulates people, shows them things they haven't seen before, makes them contemplative."

All receipts from USCO activities go into maintaining the establishment, purchasing new supplies for pieces, and transportation. The telephone rings a lot, and a collective passion for long-distance conversations earns Mother Bell several hundred dollars each month. USCO's annual income runs about thirty thousand dollars per year, mostly from Maverick Systems, Inc., a subsidiary in electronic manufacturing. As expenses invariably run more than income, donations fill the deficit. "We have all the same administrative problems of a small business," Stern judges, "and none of the conventional incentives—no fringe benefits and time off." The building itself has a legal identity in New York State as "The Church of the Tabernacle, Inc.," whose "ministers" are USCO. To earn a tax-exempt "free church" status, USCO must keep the Church's pews, which is to say *The Tabernacle*, open free to the public one day every week. Within the shell of an old church thrives a new kind of religion, as a new Church.

The core members of USCO are hardly anonymous and amenable types who could facilely blend into an organization, let alone a crowd; yet their diversified talents and personalities make everyone, Stern insists, "mutually supportive." About a dozen years ago, Stern had a reputation as an undistinguished poet on the fringe of the Beat Movement. He went to Black Mountain College for a spell, and he met both Allen Ginsberg and Carl Solomon in a psychiatric hospital in the late forties. Born in 1928 in the Saarbasin, and a few years later a refugee from Hitler's Germany, Stern came with his family to New York City in 1936 and later attended the Bronx High School of Science. He has worked as a carpenter, a mucker in a gold mine, a public relations executive and a travel writer for *Playboy*; to the USCO division of labor, he brings competencies developed in all these experiences. He is the poet and the carpenter, as well as the coordinator and the publicist. It is Stern who usually deals with the outside world; and perhaps because he is considerably older than his partners, he usually assumes the mediator's role in intra–USCO squabbles. Medium in height and build, he has an imposingly long, untrimmed and unfurling reddish-brown beard, thick unkempt black hair and thick eyeglasses, which have a small reflecting disc at the zenith of their bridge. His appearance conveys a faintly Hasidic image which Stern sometimes cultivates; usually in demeanor he is disciplined and responsive, generous and practical.

Steve Durkee is so different from Stern that their relationship strikes some outsiders as an inexplicable puzzle. Born in 1938 in Warwick, New York, about fifteen miles from Garnerville, he grew up in New York City, quit high school at fifteen and soon embarked on a career as a painter. Some of his early work incorporated English words into an abstract field; and perhaps because he also lived near Robert Indiana, Robert Rauschenberg and Jim Rosenquist, the critic G. R. Swenson included Durkee in his pioneering survey of Pop Art, *Art News* (Sept.–Oct., 1963). Objecting to this premature classification, Durkee abandoned that way of painting to concentrate on large, cleanly executed pattern paintings — in general, objective creations designed to induce subjective responses. In 1962, soon after their marriage, the Durkees purchased the abandoned church from a patriotic organization. He considers himself a follower of the mute Indian prophet Meher Baba, whom he calls "The Avatar of the Age;" and it was a personal directive from Baba himself that persuaded Durkee to terminate his use of psychedelic drugs. In USCO's work, he is not only the painter but the ideologue and visionary; statements of principle and ideals are his specialty. His appetite for mystical literature is almost scholarly. When presenting his ideas, he speaks with the surly intensity and commanding presence of an incipient prophet.

Michael Callahan is considerably younger than his partners, as well as possessed of distinctly different habits and competencies. Born in San Francisco in 1944, he joined Durkee and Stern at Garnerville just before his twentieth birthday. Prior to that, he had attended San Francisco City College for nearly two years, intending to major in psychology. He also helped design and construct the Bay City's first tape music center, eventually becoming its vice-president. The son of an electrician, he learned precociously the languages of switches and circuits; as he puts it, "Although I don't have a degree, I've always known people who have needed something electronic done." As chief maker of the strobe lights and other breadfetching equipment, Callahan is officially president of Maverick Systems; and electronic manufacturers and distributors occasionally give or lend him instruments that USCO cannot yet afford. The machines and devices he realizes for mixed-media displays are often more intricate than his limited budget would allow a lesser talent.

The producer-consultant John Brockman does so much work with USCO that he is an associate in all but name, and along with Gerd Stern and Michael

Callahan, Brockman is coauthoring an introductory textbook on intermedia. At one time anyone was welcome to join USCO, and strangers who can contribute to the current activity win cordial hospitality. Nonetheless, by now USCO seems more of an example of what can be done — a recognized avant-garde revolutionary elite; and just as their innovations in the arts of media-mix have influenced scores of other artists and groups of artists, so USCO itself has become a model for other new American tribes in sync with the electronic age.

Joshua Light Show (1968)

The new plastics allow a new type of visual expression to develop. Glass-like sheets, pliable, can be curved convex and concave. They can be perforated so that light and pigment will be fused into a new unity. Artificial light sources (spotlights, moving lamps) can continuously change the composition. This kind of picture is most probably the passage between easel painting and light display, a new type of moving picture.
—L. Moholy-Nagy, *The New Vision* (1938)

At every Fillmore East concert, which I rank among the liveliest theatrical experiences in New York, the music is accompanied by the Joshua Light Show, offering frenetic pulsations for "acid rock" and appropriately more subtle "light paintings" for less aggressive music. Their lights are projected from backstage onto a rectangular translucent screen, twenty feet by thirty feet, that stands behind the performing musicians. Generally, the entire screen is filled with bright and moving imagery—in the middle, usually within a circular frame, are nonrepresentational, brilliantly colored shapes pulsating in beat to the music and changing their forms unpredictably; around their frame is a less blatant, fairly constant pattern whose composition and colors mysteriously change through variations repeated in a constant rhythm. Across the entire screen flash rather diaphanous white shapes that irregularly fall in and out of patterns. From time to time also appear some representational images—sometimes words, other times people; sometimes stationary, other times moving. For instance, while the musicians are tuning their instruments on stage, on the screen is likely to arise a "gag" image of, say, Arturo Toscanini hushing his orchestra.

Esthetically, the Joshua Light Show is two-dimensional, abstract, and kinetic, as well as live; and this distinguishes it, on at least two counts, from the conventional discotheque light display which is both environmental and mechanical (or not-live). Critically, the group provides what is, to my mind, the best example of that two-dimensional illuminated (or "lumia") kinetic art that includes the classic work of Thomas Wilfred and the more recent "light boxes" of John Healey and Earl Reibeck, among others; and the Joshua Light Show has become noticeably more inventive and fluent in nearly two years at the Fillmore. Only a few particularly compelling musicians can entice the spectator's eye down from the screen; and at times the performers themselves furtively look at the screen behind them during their sets. Members of the stage crew make a point of telling the light artists what routines did or did not succeed that evening, and the show itself is so intimidating that no one awake can miss being mesmerized by it.

Joshua White and his five associates create their art from a narrow thirty-foot platform high up the back wall of the Fillmore stage; and as in jazz, each member of the group improvises intuitively within a frame of artistic convention and collaborative experience. The kinetic background patterns come from eight carousel slide projectors, each customized to take a 1200-watt lamp, all of them containing identical slides in identical order (so that all are usually projecting the same image on the screen), while spinning multicolored celluloid wheels create that illusion of rhythmical movement mentioned before; and in switching the slides from one pattern to another, White changes the projectors one or two at a time, gracefully blending the metamorphosis.

The pulsating and abstract shapes come from up to three "overhead projectors": On top of a base lamp is put a portable plate of liquids of various colors and materials—glycerine, alcohol, oil and water (which do not mix with one another, explaining why the colors stay separate). By placing another plate on top of the mix, someone in the group can manipulate the mix's imagery by hand, usually in sync with the music—a technique at which Bill Schwartzbach is especially skilled. The image made by the "wet show," as this is called, is then projected up into a box of lenses and then out onto the screen. Not only can two or three wet shows be projected onto separate areas of the screen, but their kinetic images can also overlap. The visual frame around these pulsating colors comes from a "matte"—a sheet with a circular pattern cut away—that goes between the base lamp and the plates.

The flashing white shapes are the work of Tom Shoesmith, stationed alone on a higher platform with a collection of mirrors, with which he reflects various light sources onto the screen. "Tom is autonomous," White told me. "No one down here can turn him on or off." The group once used a closed-circuit television, rented last February for the Janis Joplin concert (to project the grand dame's enlarged image on the screen); and although this technology was at the time more detrimental to their art than not, they would like to try a similar system again.

They pick the slides of words and pictures (like Toscanini) off an illuminated board running along the back wall, and put them into a central slide projector. Suspended in front of this board are a collection of film loops (where one end is tied to the other) which can go into either of the two projectors. Along the ledge of the ramp is hung a strip of multicolored lights, three white strobes and those rich blue lamps that customarily illuminate the stilled screen between acts. Collected together in one low board are all the dimmer switches, with handles running between the numbers one to ten, to control all the light sources except Shoesmith's — no illumination switches suddenly on and off. At this control post is usually stationed White himself, who thus retains ultimate control over what appears on the screen. At the left end of the ramp, near the door exiting to backstage, is an imposing metal cabinet containing power supplies for the dimmers; and next to it is a closed-circuit television screen with a view of the front stage, as well as a loudspeaker "we can turn down mercifully; the music isn't getting softer." The lamps make the area so hot that all of the men but White tie up their long hair and some work without shirts, while the liquids emit a faint stink. Out of all this machinery they make their art; and without the technology there would be no light art.

The examples of both earlier mechanical lumias and Hirschfeld-Mack's Bauhaus endeavors notwithstanding, the live improvised light show is a brand new art, no more than five years old; and most of the people involved in it are still shy of thirty. Joshua White himself is 27, a New Yorker by birth, son of the theatrical and television producer Lawrence White, and a graduate of Elizabeth Irwin High School; and he attended Carnegie Tech for two years and the University of Southern California's film school for two more, taking no degrees. Back in New York in 1963, he found himself unable to relate to "underground cinema" and so became associate producer on more conventional projects, as well as making some short films "which were terrible." In the summer of 1966, he worked with Robert Goldstein at L'Orsin, a Southampton discotheque that reportedly pioneered the environmental light display, and by the end of the following year he organized the group bearing his name. Of medium height, slender, bespectacled, well-dressed, well-spoken and faintly patrician, White functions largely as the group's manager and craft-conscious overseer. "My responsibility is primarily to keep ourselves working. We started as a business; now we begin to take our art more seriously."

It was at a commercial venture that he met Shoesmith and Schwartzbach, both also 27, both of whom had been working in theatrical lighting; and in the fall of 1967 they were asked to assemble a one-shot two-screen light display for Bill Graham, the founder of Fillmore West, who was then producing a program in Toronto. "It was there that we saw a real light show for the first time," Schwartzbach remembers, bemused by his earlier innocence, "and we knew then we wanted to devote ourselves to this." So, when Bill Graham decided to open a Fillmore East in New York, in the spring of 1968, he hired the Joshua Light Show, gave them headline billing along with the transient acts, and sealed with a handshake a permanent contract for a thousand dollars a week. Remembering earlier bad experiences with older entrepreneurs who failed to pay the promised amounts — the exploitation of young people so endemic nowadays — Schwartzbach judges, "There is no question that Graham delivers what he promises; this makes a difference when people are working creatively. He is our patron." (Most rock groups also tip the light show, British groups customarily favoring a bottle of wine, the great B. B. King once offering thirty dollars, which they refused.)

The Joshua Light Show also creates enterprise where none existed before; and White himself devotes considerable thought to what else the group might do. They have already designed the light displays at discotheques, accompanied "Switched-On Bach" on the Today Show, created an environmental light show for a classical concert at Carnegie Hall, turned on parties of various kinds, toured Europe with the Chambers Brothers, created visuals for the Lincoln Center production of *King Lear*, and illuminated both the hip part scene in John Schlesinger's *Midnight Cowboy* and something similar in the forthcoming *The Magic Garden of Stanley Sweetheart*. For the moment, "We'll do anything for money, exposure and the opportunity to do something fine, as long as the people who hire us know how we can contribute to what they want. We'd particularly like to do television."

Thinking further into the future, Schwartzbach, who is probably the group's creative fount, told me between sets, "We'd like to work in more than lights, to do something as thorough, involving and transforming as Disneyland — an environment that would play on all the senses. We'd like to start in bright sunlight, with the environment that God gave us, and put the fantasy all around, in all elements — where every novel, interesting and arresting experience a man can have is presented to him. Of course, you can't put dope and sex there, but you should allow everyone to be free." And his quick mind leaped to another vision involving holography, or laser-assisted light that produces the illusion of three dimensions. "I know the technology is available; and with enough money or technical support, we could do it."

As art as well as enterprise, the Joshua Light Show is an adventurous creation; and they are still exploring artistic possibilities. In the beginning, most of the visual ideas were determined by the technologies of slides, wet shows, and film loops — what each technique is most inclined to do; so that only Shoesmith's abstract reflections made a truly innovative contribution to the established repertoire of artistic articulations. Nonetheless, they are the best light show I have seen, less because they are more imaginative than, say, Glenn McKay's Headlights in San Francisco or the Pablo collaborative in New York than because they are visually the richest, most tasteful and continually inventive within the course of both a long evening and nearly two years at the Fillmore. "This theater needs a visual experience which is as involving as the musical experience," White told me. "Ideally, the audience should not remember a single thing but experience the music and the theatrical situation more thoroughly."

One esthetic problem stems from the fact that several dimensions of light pulsate in sync with the music, while the eye also tends to impose synchronous order, even if illusory, on a chaotic field; however, the critical bias of all modern art distinctly devalues such obviously unison activity. To this change, White rationalizes, "I'm not an artist, working within the traditions of modern art, but a theatrical performer; I must be more concerned with the audience." More conservative critics, particularly those whose taste was honed on music without light, tend to judge the Joshua Light Show as either unnecessary or distracting; but I for one find it hard to imagine such a rich theatrical experience as the Fillmore without the illuminated screen.

The more serious problem is that the screen imposes a two-dimensional limitation on light's possible expressiveness because the Fillmore's theatrical layout requires people to sit in seats and look straight ahead; but perhaps the Joshua Light Show's likely adventures into other situations will include occasions for illuminating other kinds of space in yet other ways.

Ben Shahn: Master "Journalist" of American Art (1969)

The artist Ben Shahn lives not where one might expect, in the big city where he grew up (New York), but some sixty miles to the south, in Roosevelt, New Jersey, a one-time garment workers' cooperative of built-alike houses near Princeton. His home there is, appropriately enough, very much like his artistic career, which is to say a magnificent edifice built upon 1930s foundations. Shahn was first hailed in 1932 for his now-familiar portraits of Nicola Sacco and Bartolomeo Vanzetti. As an employee of, first, the Works Progress Administration and, then, the Farm Security Administration, he painted some of the most memorable murals ever to grace American buildings.

In the course of working on one of his best murals, for a neighborhood community center, he moved to Roosevelt, then known as "Jersey Homeland" (only to be renamed, by popular ballot, after FDR's death), partly because the monthly rent there cost only sixteen dollars, but mostly because his and his wife Bernarda felt their growing family of four children needed fresh air. They planned to stay only a year; but though he remains the sole noted artist in their neighborhood, the environment proved so congenial that the Shahns have never left Roosevelt for long. "Until I was thirty-five," he confessed, "I had no use for people who did not paint, play music, or write books; but I've changed completely since then." Out of his house and its backyard studio, he has produced a remarkable number of artifacts, including paintings, sculpture, graphics, stained glass, book designs, prose essays, even photographs and stage settings.

Dressed in a button-up flannel shirt and sport slacks, Shahn greeted his guests in a spacious, beautiful room built nearly a decade ago literally on top of the flat-roofed thirties house that originally looked like all the others on its block. "Hope you had no trouble finding us," he said coming up the stairs, probably knowing that most of his neighbors had also embellished their housing stock and we had indeed to ask a passer-by. He then sat down in the least plush of several unmatched chairs, while Mrs. Shahn excused herself to an adjacent room to type her husband's letters. Large clean windows on two sides looked out upon snowy woods. An Alexander Calder mobile was suspended from the ceiling directly above Shahn's head; the walls were filled with paintings, each with its own story, one of which, an expressionistic portrait by his youngest daughter Abby, looked like "a Shahn" except for its consistently thicker brush lines.

A compactly built, blue-eyed, gray-haired, gray-bearded man of medium height, with ruddy lines on his cheeks and an easy smile that revealed a gold-capped tooth, Shahn seemed younger than his seventy-plus years. Looking more like a farmer than an artist, he also resembled certain photographs of the elder, bearded Ernest Hemingway. Although suffering from slight discomforts that kept him from reading in bed that morning, he talked vivaciously for several hours, unashamedly prefacing most of his remarks with that ubiquitous first-person pronoun. "I like to tell stories," he said of his paintings, which usually capture moments in events that existed before and after his image (while abstract art, in contrast, deals in representations of timelessness). Also a charming raconteur in a voice free of either mannerism or accent, he likes to articulate his pet stories and attitudes far more than exploring issues and ideas. He halted his quick and easy flow only when he sensed resistances, or a question asked him to define more precisely a fuzzy assertion.

Contained and confident, he spends most of his days in his studio, returning to the main house only for lunch with his wife, who solicitously guards his regimen and cares for his needs; and he resists most invitations to leave Roosevelt, even skipping the recent opening of a one-man show at his New York gallery. "I knew exactly what I'd see," he declared through puffs on his pipe. "I've been a pro since I was fifteen. And I don't often take vacations, as my threshold for doing nothing is two and one-half days." Like all people who spend most of their waking hours at their chosen work, Shahn enjoys describing his procedures. "In the studio, I keep notebooks of visual and verbal ideas, sometimes a word and sometmes a pattern; and I'll often jot down a note on the back of an envelope. I don't believe in random inspiration, for my inspiration comes when I begin to work. I start work with an idea, which combines technical details, like the quality and texture of the paint, with that which I can verbalize."

When I asked if he were "a quick worker," Shahn nodded affirmatively. "Yes, yes, sure, sure," but then paused to stir his tobacco. "I can usually tell after the second line whether it will go or not. I abandon a lot. You know that famous drawing I did of Ghandi. I started somewhere in the garment and then knew everything would turn out well. It often goes that way. I've done one hundred drawings for a book in a week or ten days, and that *Partridge in a Pear Tree*, which the Modern Museum publishes for every Christmas, I did in thirty-six hours straight, including all night awake." One reason for his facility is that his distinctive style is based upon an economy of means—"to do," as he put it, "in one line what others need twenty lines for."

Shahn is not a painter of rare masterpieces but a steadily working artist whose best recent work has been in graphics, which is to say visual designs to be reproduced into many copies. Not only is his reputation based less upon a few works than the sheer bulk and variousness of his personal achievement, but it is as a representational graphic artist — a prolific commentator in the tradition of Hogarth and Daumier — that he still commands the attention of fellow professionals and has no real peer in America. Few other graphic artists, anywhere, possess such an instantly identifiable personal style.

Of course, artists scrupulously devoted to producing only rectangular canvases tend to put Shahn down as "essentially a journalist" (an epithet used by Mark Rothko, among others). It is true that Shahn's work, like journalism, unashamedly betrays its hasty creation and relates to particular moments, rather than transcending its time. His work courts sentiment sooner than challenging it; aims for clarity and simplicity, rather than complexity and ambiguity (except perhaps in his drawings of human hands); and directs itself to a larger audience rather than a few.

However, Shahn contends that paintings is not *per se* superior to graphics and that a "first-rate design is better than a second-rate painting, a fine piece of journalism better than a second-rate essay and so on. It's self-evident that they are different, but I don't have a hierarchy. I don't like to make distinctions between graphics and painting." Pausing to make sure that his words were recorded accurately, he continued, "I want to destroy the traditional sense of difference, I look upon all media as images. I'm as moved by the studies Picasso made for *Guernica* as by the entire work. He used every medium of graphics in all his painting."

These distinctions notwithstanding, Shahn is clearly a master of that rare art, encompassing both graphics and painting, that would combine word with image — "illuminated manuscripts" to the medievalists, "concretism" to some contemporaries, "word-images" to others. He has invented several alphabets of original lettering styles, at least one of which is instantly identifiable as his; and he has freely incorporated hand-drawn words into his paintings and designs. "I use words," he explains, "because I want to use everything I can." He picked up from the table the most spectacular of his several books, *Love and Joy about Letters* (1963), and started to read from his commentary:

> I began to use letters now, not as local color, and not as subordinate parts of paintings, but for their own sake, for their beauty and their own meaning. Words and letters may amplify and enrich the meaning of the painting. They are at the same time independent and integral to the painting, a contrapuntal element.

He flipped familiarly to another page.

> I realize that such a practice tends to roil the people who believe that painting should remain strictly within the confines of its own parish. But I believe that

sensitivity is not departmentalized. [He paused to repeat that last marvelous line.] Art itself is not to be confined within hard boundaries. The inclination to see, to feel, to hear, to apprehend, and understand form, to make new shapes and meanings out of the materials at hand, is simply human capacity, and it appears in all sorts of unpredictable ways.

What distinguishes Shahn from nearly every other noted American painter is his sense of audience, as he creates not for the pace-setting few — experienced collectors, museum directors, periodical critics — but a larger populace; and the sheer number of available reproductions of his handicraft may make him the most familiar serious artist in America today. "Art should be available to the public; they should be able to see it." He repeatedly remarks that every beginning artist must ask himself not only "Who are you?" but "With whom do you wish to communicate?" His own answer to the second is quite clever: "People with whom I can talk about other things. I can't separate art from life."

Indicatively, Shahn's work is never about art alone, but other things; and his pieces strike one as moments in a particular kind of conversation between himself and the viewer. "Without being boastful or egotistical, let me say that I'm the most American artist there is. I think I can speak more about America, to more Americans, than anyone else. That is not a qualitative judgment, but an accident that perhaps has something to do with being a convert to America, rather than a native."

Like so many other successful elder artists, Shahn views the current scene with dismay, first of all criticizing the increasing influx of speculative money into a world that should not be about money at all and, secondly, deploring the emphasis upon abstraction in recent art. He particularly condemns shifty opportunism, which he contrasts with stylistic integrity (though Shahn's critics charge opportunism in his endlessly repeating his most successful manner). His verbal criticisms are, like his paintings, simple, concise, and pointed. One leading graphic artist young enough to be his son is dismissed as "a plagiarist, who stole from everybody." He sneered at another recently dominant style, "I was reproducing 'psychedelic art' when I started as a lithographer, except we called it 'Art Nouveau' then." Roy Lichtenstein's famous Pop works are perversely dismissed: "I can't take the enlargements of cartoons as works of art, although the original comic book was." And minimal art, to Shahn, offers not esthetic puzzles but "communicates that the person has nothing to say." Rather than insisting that representational styles should dominate again, Shahn holds for stylistic pluralism — the coexistence, with both artists and publics, of abstract and representational art.

"Art exists under patronage, whether the Medicis or the Church; or as things are now, the art collectors; but it is my opinion that the federal government was the most tolerant patron there ever was. In the thirties, side by side on a WPA exhibition, there would be an Anatole Gorky and a Raphael

Soyer, without anybody questioning it. I honestly believe in diversity. It still exists in Paris, but not on Madison Avenue, except for a few exceptions. The danger of isolating one style, as happened in the late fifties, is that it becomes a cult to which a youngster must accommodate or become a washout. He'll show one slide to a gallery director, and they'll know everything. This kind of cultism is more dangerous. The government is more tolerant than the 750–1,000 galleries in New York." Rather than the current program of the National Endowment for the Arts, which disburses grants to several score selected artists (most of them incipiently fashionable), Shahn proposes that all federal, state, and city agencies hire "those who profess to be artists" to work for the government, as happened in the 1930s.

Shahn is commonly identified as a "socialist painter," but as an individualist, rather than an economic revolutionary, he now regards himself as more of an anarchist, more of a perpetual radical than a visionary utopian. "The tradition," he told me twice, "is best kept alive by those who have rebelled against tradition." He did anti–Goldwater posters in 1964 and a popular pro–Eugene McCarthy poster in 1968, as well as affixing his name to anti-Vietnam petitions. "Nobody hires me to do political things," he declared, and then chuckled. "They are done out of the goodness of my heart. No, that's such a cliché; leave that out. I believe in taking part. I don't remove myself. Yet, I'm not a pacifist. As the Arab countries threatened Israel with destruction, then the Israeli attack of 1967 was probably justified. A war of destruction was forestalled. I think the same thing should have been done just after the Spanish Civil War began in 1936 and after Hitler took over the Ruhr." Though Shahn speaks proudly of all the lucrative invitations he avoided and of all the prose and art he gave away gratis to those who could not pay, he now earns more money than he needs, living well beneath his means and putting the excess into trust funds for his children (three of whom, he should be flattered, are now professional artists).

Illnesses of the past two years have curbed his legendary energy, though his right leg no longer needs a brace. Then, Shahn has recently been plagued by a professional problem that never haunted him before. "Every door I open shows me some place I've seen before." How sad, but Ernest Hemingway's advice to A. E. Hotchner is relevant to Shahn. "Retire? How the hell can a writer retire." The habits of forty-five years drive him to work as much as possible, on his self-initiated work as well as commissions; as his wife put it, when her husband was away, "The length of a man's career reflects the depths of his roots." He returned, declaring, "I'm designing a mosaic for Syracuse University, and it will be on the way to the stadium, where everybody will see it." He recently did a portfolio of lithographs for a very plush edition of Ranier Maria Rilke's *The Notebooks of Malte Laurids Brigge*, and a few years ago he incorporated a Wendell Berry poem into a good-selling graphic memorial volume for JFK. "I do books all the time, often just as a gift for my wife; and

and sometimes they get published." He stirred his pipe again. "You know, if I could do it again, I would have gone into movies. It has everything — image and after-image, music and speech. Everything. Everything. Its communication is pretty total. I never read anything that has the power of Rossellini's *Open City*."

"I think I've had it," he declared just before dinner. "I've not pontificated so much recently." He paused to recompose himself, gratified to see the tape-recording machine go off. "I will, of course, deny every word of mine you quote in print, because what I say here is true only now."

He died a few weeks after his interview, and that accounts for why the profile did not appear when it was written.

Robert Rauschenberg
Conversation (1968)

One who landed early on the shores of Abstract Expressionism is invited to lecture on his deed like a Marine colonel in the first wave at Iwo Jima. — Harold Rosenberg, "Past and Possibility" (1964)

Although painting is Robert Rauschenberg's dominant interest, throughout his career he has kept an informal connection with theater. Back in the summer of 1952, at Black Mountain College, he participated in John Cage's "prehistoric" happening, an untitled event that established an American precedent for subsequent theater of mixed means. From 1955 to 1965 he designed sets and costumes, as well as controlling the lighting, for the Merce Cunningham Dance Company; and in the early sixties he participated in theater pieces by Yvonne Rainer and Kenneth Koch. *Pelican* (1963) was his own initial piece; and when he all but abandoned painting in 1965, he initiated a series of mixed-means theatrical works — among them *Spring Training* (1965), *Map Room I* (1965), *Map Room II* (1965), *Linoleum* (1966), and *Open Score* (1966) for the New York Theater and Engineering Festival. He was born in 1925, in Port Arthur, Texas.

Interviewer: *In high school you had a reputation as a person who could draw or at least do certain kinds of drawings.*

Rauschenberg: I never thought of it as much of an ability. I thought everybody could do it a little bit. Some people could draw a little better than other people, but I never took drawing or painting any more seriously than that.

Later, [Josef] Albers told me I couldn't draw — that my whole childhood was wasted. I had an awful time pleasing him. I was too messy for collage, and I was too heavy-handed in my drawings.

He would like open spaces and thin lines.

The Matisse kind of thing.

He would teach a course in form, which he gives year after year, refining it more and more, and a course in the performances of color — a really clinical method. We worked in drawing from the same model week after week. Once a week or once every two weeks, someone in the class at Black Mountain would pose for us. Then, he would talk about the valleys and the mountans and things like that about the figure. Other than that, it was an aluminum pitcher—a shiny volume without a straight line and you couldn't do any shading. It is really the outside and inside that you got to say. You do it with one line, and you can't do any erasing. You feel that there is air on this side of the line and on the other side of the line is the form. In watercolor, we had it again—one model we used month after month; and it was a terra-cotta flowerpot.

I figured out, at least in the watercoloring classes, that what he really had in mind was something like Cézanne. I found Albers so intimidating that after six months of this, during the first year, my whole focus was simply to try to do something that would please him. I didn't care what I got out of class. All I wanted to do was one day walk in there and show him something and hear him say, "That's pretty good."

I have noticed that you wish to avoid historical interpretations of yourself. In general would you prefer not to say that someone influenced you?

No, I've been influenced by painting, very much; but if I have avoided saying that, it was because of the general inclination, until very recently, to believe that art exists in art. At every opportunity, I've tried to correct that idea, suggesting that art is only a part—one of the elements that we live with. I think that a person like Leonardo da Vinci had not a technique or a style in common with other aritsts but a kind of curiosity about life that enabled him to change his medium so easily and so successfully. I really think he was concerned with the human body when he did his anatomical work. His personal curiosity, apart from any art idea, led him to investigate how a horse's leg works so that he could do a sculpture of it.

Being a painter, I probably take painting more seriously than someone who drives a truck or something. Being a painter, I probably also take his truck more seriously.

In what sense?

In the senses of looking at it and listening to it and comparing it to other trucks and having a sense of its relationship to the road and the sidewalk and the things around it and the driver himself. Observation and measure are my business.

I think historians have tended to draw too heavily upon the idea that in art there is development. I think you can see similarities in anything and anything by generalities and warp.

They are concerned with identifying influence and, thereby, continuities.

There's another thing. Now we have so much information. A painter a hundred or two hundred years ago knew very little about what was going on in painting in any other place except with his immediate friends or some outstanding event. It wasn't natural for him also to take into consideration cave painting and fold it into his own sense of the present.

I think, if you want to make a generalization, there are probably two kinds of artists. One kind works independently, following his own drives and instincts; the work becomes a product, or the witness, or the evidence of his own personal involvement and curiosity. It's almost as if art, in painting and music and stuff, is the leftover of some activity. The activity is the thing that I'm most interested in. Nearly everything that I've done was to see what would happen if I did this instead of that.

You would believe then that art is not a temple to which you apprentice yourself for future success.

It's like outside focus and inside focus. A lot of painters use a studio to isolate themselves; I prefer to free and expose myself. If I painted in this room — the stove is here and all those dishes are there — my sensitivity would always take into consideration that the woodwork is brown, that the dishes are this size, that the stove is here. I've tended always to have a studio that was either too big to be influenced by detail or neutral enough so that there wasn't an overwhelming specific influence, because I work very hard to be acted on by as many things as I can. That's what I call being awake.

People are enormously impressed by the variety of your work. How do you look upon your past work as a painter — as an evolution, or merely a succession of islands upon which you've put your foot?

Looking back, I can see certain things growing, as well as a slackening of interest in another area because I am familiar enough with it. So far, I've been lucky enough always to discover that there's always been a new curiosity that is also feeding and building while I'm doing something else. I can figure out some logical reasons when I look back far enough, but I never do when I'm making the work.

Let me take a particular example that interests me — say, the White Paintings *(1952). Here you have created what, if you believe in linear notions of art history, is a dead end. Did you look upon it as a gesture toward a dead end?*

No. It just seemed like something interesting to do. I was aware of the fact that it was an extreme position; but I really wanted to see for myself whether there would be anything to look at. I did not do it as an extreme logical gesture.

But wasn't there an idea there — not a notion derived from art history but of a simple experiment, which was to see if a painting could incorporate transient images from outside itself? Therefore, once you discovered the result of that idea, then you could go on to another.

You could speculate whether it would be interesting or not; but you could waste years arguing. All I had to do was make one and ask, "Do I like that?" "Is there anything to say there?" "Does that thing have any presence?" "Does it really matter that it looks bluer now, because it is late afternoon? Earlier this morning it looked quite white." "Is that an interesting experience to have?" To me, the answer was yes. No one has ever bought one; but those paintings are still very full to me. I think of them as anything but a way-out gesture. A gesture implies the denial of the existence of the actual object. If it had been that, I wouldn't have had to have done them. Otherwise it would only be an idea.

Claes Oldenburg said that he has a dream that someday he would call all his things back, that they had not really gone away.

I have another funny feeling that in working with a canvas, say, and with something you picked up off the street and you work on it for three or four days or maybe a couple of weeks and then, all of a sudden, it is in another situation. Much later, you go to see somebody in California, and there it is. You know that you know everything about that painting, so much more than anybody else in that room. You know where you ran out of nails.

You can look at it then as a kind of personal history.

It's not like publishing, for each one is an extremely unique piece, even if it is in a series. I like to look at an old work and discover that is where I first did a certain thing, which may be something I may just happen to be doing now. At the time I did that earlier piece, I didn't know it was the lower right-hand corner that had the new element — that that part would grow and that other parts would relate more to the past.

Have you ever started something that you couldn't finish?

Yes, but I really try hard not to. I work very hard to finish everything. One of the most problematic pictures I ever made was something I was doing for a painters' picture series in a magazine. I had started the radio sculpture thing, which became *Oracle* (1965). My mind was more in sculpture or objects free of the wall. I found I was uncomfortable from the new difficulties metal afforded, because I really didn't know what to do with it. So I figured that if I was to be scrutinized, I'd do a painting instead. I said I'd do it, and I try to do what I say I will do. That painting went through so many awkward changes, unnecessarily. It was large, it was free-standing. Then I put it against the wall, then I finally sawed it in half and made two paintings out of it. I wrecked one of them.

I didn't know what to do when Rudy Burckhardt came up and said, "How far did you get today? Can I take the picture tomorrow? Why did you do that? What do you have on your mind?" It just didn't work out. I knew I was compromising at the tme; and when the article went in, I insisted that they photograph what I was not doing too. If those things are going to mean anything, they somehow ought to be the truth. In those days, it seemed like that would be your only chance for the next twenty years to get your picture reproduced in color. Now I have this lousy painting.

In looking at your career, critics customarily tote up all the stuff you have used: blueprint paper, white painting, black painting, collage, assemblage. . .

I call those things "combines," because it was before the museum show of assemblages. Earlier I had this problem with the paintings that would be free-standing—not against the wall. I didn't think of them as sculpture. I actually made them as a realistic objection; it was unnatural for these to be hung on a wall. So when the sculptural or collage elements got so three-dimensional, then the most natural thing in the world was to put wheels on it and put it out into the middle of the room. That gave two more sets of surfaces to work on. It was an economical thing. I think I've been very practical. Sometimes the underneath surface is also a painting surface, because that would be viewed. In that one there is a mirror on the side so that you can see what is underneath there without bending down, or you're invited to.

I thought of them as paintings, but what to call them—painting or sculpture—got for some people to be a very interesting point, which I did not find interesting at all. Almost as a joke I thought I'd call them something, as Calder was supposed to have done with "mobiles," and it worked beautifully. Once I called them "combines," people were confronted with the work itself, not what it wasn't. Sometimes you can choke on these things; people have called my drawings "combine drawings." The word does really have a use—it's a free-standing picture.

Just in passing, let me say there is one work of yours I can't deduce. That is the set Factum I *and* II *(1957).*

There I was interested in the role that accident played in my work; so I did two paintings as much alike as they could be alike, using identical materials—as much as they could be alike without getting scientific about it. Although I was imitating on one painting what I had on the other, neither one of these paintings was an imitation of the other, because I would work as long as I could on one painting and then, not knowing what to do next, move over to the other. I wanted to see how different, and in what way, would be two paintings that looked that much alike.

How, then, did some critics consider this a comment on action painting?

I think Tom Hess said that. Again, you see, if you do anything where an idea shows up, particularly in those years when an act of painting was considered pure self-expression, then it was assumed that the painting was a personal expressionistic extension of the man. The climate isn't like that now. We've had a history of painting here now, and I think it's unfortunately getting to be a lot like Europe. We have enough reserve work so that it is very easy for a tradition to exist here which also includes any new ideas, which are immediately tacked onto where we were yesterday.

A painting is pushed into historical perspective before it has become history, as well as critically classified before it is perceived.

I would like to see a lot more stuff that I didn't know what to do with.

In several earlier statements, you said that your paintings were not the result of ideas. What you've said now, however, suggests that they stem from a certain kind of idea.

I think the ideas are based upon very obvious physical facts—notions that are also simpleminded, such as, in the *White Paintings,* wanting to know if that was a thing to do or not, or in *Factum*, wondering about what the role of accident is. Those aren't really very involved ideas.

That is different from the idea, say, of doing a painting about war, or the idea of realizing a premeditated form.

They are more physical than esthetic.

Rather than posing a thesis, you are asking a question and then doing some artistic experiment to answer it or to contribute to an answer.

But I do it selfishly. I want to know.

What kind of idea, if you can remember, was present in, say, Monogram (1959), which contains a stuffed Angora goat?

I have always worked with stuffed animals, and before that, stuffed baseballs — and other objects. But a goat was special in the way that a stuffed goat is special, and I wanted to see if I could integrate an animal or an object as exotic as that. I've always been more attracted to familiar or ordinary things, because I find them a lot more mysterious. The exotic has a tendency to be immediately strange. With common or familiar objects, you are a lot freer; they take my thoughts a lot further. Not only for content was the goat a difficult object to work with, but also because Angora goats are beautiful animals anyway. I did three versions of that painting. For the first one, it was still on the wall; I got him up there safely attached to the flat surface. To make him appear light — and this is the way my mind tends to work — I put light-bulbs under him, which erased the shadow of the normous shelf that supported him. When I finished it, I was happy with it for about four days; but it kept bothering me that the goat's other side was not exposed; that it was wasted. I was abusing the material. So, I did a piece where he was free-standing on a narrow seven-foot canvas that was attached to the base that he was on. I couldn't have him facing the canvas, because it looked like some kind of still life, like oranges in the bowl. So I had him turned around, which gave me another image which didn't occur to me until, this time, only two days after I had finished it — a kind of beast and vehicle. It looked as though he had some reponsibility for supporting the upright canvas or that pulling a canvas or cart was his job. So, the last solution stuck, which was simply to put him right in the middle — to make an environment with him simply being present in it.

How dominant is he?

He is dominant but I wouldn't worry about that as much as how dependent is everything else on him. I think that the painted surface and the other objects were equally interesting, once you see what the goat is doing there.

But doesn't this presume that you forget about the goat to a certain extent?

You forget about how arbitrary a goat is in the picture; that was never the point. It was one of many challenges, but it wasn't a function of the work to exhibit an exotic animal interestingly. Also, the tire around the goat brings him back into the canvas and keeps him from being an object in himself. You don't say, "What is that goat doing in that painting?" but "Why the tire around the goat?" And you're already involved.

This, like so much of your other work, reflects a decided interest in working with unusual and challenging materials. What was your painting Pantomime *(1961) about?*

I thought of it as making a surface which would invite one to move in closer; and when you move in closer, you discover it has two electric fans which then join you. I thought of it as kind of an air relief. Any physical situation is an influence on not only how you see and if you look but also what you think when you see it. I just knew that if you were standing in a strong breeze, which was part of the painting, that something different would happen. If I did make a point, it is that even the air around you is an influence.

It's a way of saying to the spectator that the Metropolitan Museum right now, with all the pollen in the air, is a lot different from midwinter.

Also, looking at pictures from one place to another, and also from one season to another, makes them different. That's why, then, the business about masterpieces and standards is all archaic.

The notion of masterpieces presumes that if someone puts the Mona Lisa *in a stuffy New York museum and you have to push your way through a large obnoxious crowd to see it, you should still be greatly impressed.*

Put it in the Greenwich Village outdoor show and see what happens. Put it in the Louvre and send it in with an armed guard, and people will see it. I like the idea of that kind of dramatic carrying-on, for that's part of our time, too.

Now that you have become so involved with theater, have you given up painting?

No. That was a mistaken rumor. Giving up painting is all part of that historical thing.

Will you be able to work on a painting while you are doing theater work?

Absolutely, I always did that. You see, it sounds interesting for the painter to give up painting.

It's the myth of Duchamp. Actually, I was thinking more of Claes Oldenburg's statement that when he did a theater piece he temporarily gave up painting.

The last year before I went away with Merce [Cunningham] when I was doing a lot of theater [1963–64], I did more painting than I ever had before. If you're working on something, it seems to me that the more you work the more you see, the more you think; it just builds up.

You would prefer, then, a more varied regime than a single setup.

Absolutely. I find that when I'm working on paintings, I can do drawings I like very much, although I am forced to adjust to a flat surface and a different scale.

How did you become involved with theater?

I've always been interested, even back in high school. I like the liveness of it — that awful feeling of being on the spot. I must assume the responsibility for that moment, for those actions that happen at that particular time.

I don't find theater that different from painting, and it's not that I think of painting as theater or vice versa. I tend to think of working as a kind of involvement with materials, as well as a rather focused interest which changes.

How did you become the author of your own theater pieces?

That skating piece, *Pelican* (1963), was my first piece. The more I was around Merce's group and that kind of activity, I realized that painting didn't put me on the spot as much, or not in the same way, so at a certain point I had to do it.

In some places, like London where [in 1964] the group was held over for six to eight weeks, and we did the piece of Merce's called *Story* three or four times a week, well then it was very difficult to do a completely different thing every night. A couple of times we were in such sterile situations that Alex Hay, my assistant, and I would actually have to be part of the set. The first time it happened was in Dartington, that school in Devon. The place was inhabited by a very familiar look — that Black Mountain beatnik kind of look about everybody; but they occupied the most fantastic and beautiful old English building, all of whose shrubs were trimmed. There was nothing rural or rustic or unfinished about it. For the first time, there was absolutely nothing to use; you can't make it every time. There was a track at the very back of the stage that had lights in it; so the dancers couldn't use that space. About an hour before the performance, I asked Alex whether he had any shirts that needed ironing, which is a nice question to ask Alex because he always did and he always ironed his own shirts. So, we got two ironing boards, and we put them up over these blue lights that were back there. When the curtain opened, there were the dancers and these two people ironing shirts. It must have looked quite beautiful, but we can't be sure absolutely. But from what I could feel about the way it looked and the lights coming up through the shirts, it was like a live passive set, like live decor.

Would you do it again?

I won't do that. You see, there is little difference between the action of paint and the action of people, except that paint is a nuisance because it keeps drying and setting.

The most frequently heard criticism of Map Room Two *(1965) is that it was too slow.*

I don't mind that. I don't mind something being boring, because there are certain activities that can be interesting if they are done only so much. Take that business with the tires in *Map Room*, which I found interesting if it is done for about five minutes. But something else happens if it goes on for ten more minutes. It's a little like La Monte Young's thing [*The Tortoise, His Dreams and Journeys*]. At some point, you admit that it isn't interesting any more, but you're still confronted by it. So what are you going to make out of it?

However, there is a difference between intentional boredom and inadvertent boredom.

I'd like it if even at the risk of boring someone, there is an area of uninteresting activity where the spectator may behave uniquely. You see, I'm against the prepared consistent entertainment. Theater does not have to be entertaining, just like pictures don't have to be beautiful.

Must theater be interesting?

Involving. Now boredom is restlessness; your audience is not a familiar thing. It is made up of individual people who all lead different lives.

I've been with people who have speech problems. At first it made me quite nervous, later I found myself listening to it and being quite interested in just the physical contact; it can be a very dramatic thing. I've never deliberately thought about boring anyone; but I'm also interested in that kind of theater activity that provides a minimum of guarantees. I have often been more interested in works I have found very boring than in other works that seem to be brilliantly done.

What was it that made them more memorable to you?

It may be that that kind of pacing is more unique to theater-going. The role of the audience, traditionally, I don't find very interesting. I don't like the idea that they shouldn't assume as much responsibility as the entertainer does for making the evening interesting. I'm really quite unfriendly and unrealistic about the artist having to assume the total responsibility for the function of the evening. I would like people to come home from work, wash up, and go to the theater as an evening of taking their chances. I think it is more interesting for them.

I'm bothered about this juxtaposition of interesting and boring. What you're doing, I think, is setting up an opposition to entertainment.

I think that's it. I used the word bored to refer to someone who might look at a Barnett Newman and say there ought to be more image there than a single vertical or two single verticals. If someone said that that was a boring picture, he was using the word in relation to a preconceived idea of what interesting might be. What I am saying is I suspect that right now in theater there is a lot of work described as boring, which is simply the awkward reorientation of the function of theater and even the purpose of the audience. Just in the last few years we have made some extremely drastic changes. Continuity in the works that I am talking about has been completely eliminated. It is usually different from performance to performance. There is no dramatic continuity; the interaction tends to be a coincidence or an innovation.

What else do you think is characteristic of mixed-means theater?

An absence of hierarchy. The fact is that in a single piece of Yvonne Rainer you can hear both Rachmaninoff and sticks being pitched from the balcony without those two things making a comment on each other. In my pieces, for instance, there is nothing that everything is subservient to. I am trusting each element to sustain itself in time.

What do these changes imply?

All those ideas tend to point up the thought that it would be better for theater that, if you went a second night, you found a different work there, even though it might be in the same place and have the same performers and deal with the same material. I think all this is creating an extraordinary situation that is very new in theater; so both the audience and the artist are still quite selfconscious about the state of things.

You would agree with John Cage, then, that one of the purposes of the new movement is to make us more omniattentive.

I think we do it when we are relaxed; all these things happen naturally. But there's a prejudice that has been built up around the ideas of seriousness and specializing. That's why I'm no more interested in giving up painting than continuing paintings or vice versa. I don't find these things in competition with each other. If we are to get the most out of any given time, it is because we have applied ourselves as broadly as possible, I think, not because we have applied ourselves as singlemindedly as possible.

Do you have then a moral objection to those dimensions of life that force us to be more specialized than we should be?

Probably. If we can observe the way things happen in nature, we see that nearly nothing in my life turned out the way that, if it were up to me to plan it, it should. There is always the business, for instance, if you're going on a picnic, it is just as apt to rain as not. Or the weather might turn cold when you want to go swimming.

So then you find a direct formal equation between your theater and your life?

I hope so, between working and living, because those are our media.

You would believe, then, that if we became accustomed to this chancier kind of theater, we would become accustomed, then, to the chancier nature of our own life.

I think we are most accustomed to it in life. Why should art be the exception to this? You asked if I had a moral objection. I do, because I think we do have this capacity I'm talking about. You find that an extremely squeamish person can perform fantastic deeds because it is an emergency. If the laws have a positive function, if they could have, it might be just that—to force someone to behave in a way he has not behaved before, using the facilities he was actually born with. Growing up in a world where multiple distractions are the only constant, he would be able to cope with new situations. But, what I found happening to people in the Navy was that once they were out of service and out of these extraordinary situations, they reverted to the same kind of thinking as before. I think it is an exceptional person who utilizes that experience. That's because in most cases the service is not a chosen environment; it is somebody else's life that they're functioning in, instead of recognizing the fact that it is still just them and the things they are surrounded by.

So you would object to anyone who finds the Navy an unnatural life.

It is a continuation of extraordinary situations. We begin by not having any say over who our parents are; our parents have no control over the particular peculiar mixture of the genes.

Looking back over your involvement with theater, do you see any kind of development, aside from the obvious development that you have now become the author of your own theater pieces, rather than a contributor to somebody else's? Also, do you see any development in your company of more or less regular performers?

Well, that last is mostly a social thing of people with a common interest, and we have tended to make ourselves available as material to one another. It is in no way an organized company, and it changes from time to time — people move in and out. However, where a play could be cast with different actors and you would still get the same play, if I was not in constant touch with these people, I could not do those pieces. The whole concept would have to be changed, if I had new performers — if I let Doris Day take Mary Martin's part in a musical or used the Cincinnati Philharmonic rather than the New York Philharmonic.

You write for these performers, and they have learned to respond to the particular language of your instructions.

It goes beyond interpretation or following directions. From the outset, their responsibility, in a sense of collaboration, is part of the actual form and content and appearance of the piece. It makes them stockholders in the event itself, rather than simply performers.

In *Map Room Two*, a couple of the people involved said that they had now gotten some kind of feeling about what I was after. Because this is my fourth or fifth piece and these people, if they weren't in them, had seen them all, then I think there is a body of work. If someone is working with an unfamiliar kind of image and if you see only one, it looks like a lot of things that it isn't and a lot of things that it is; but you don't really understand the direction. In five of those new things you're more apt to see what they are doing. It's like signposts; you need a few to know that you are really on the right road.

Do you feel stronger and more confident now in approaching a theater piece?

Confidence is something that I don't feel very often, because I tend to eliminate the things I was sure about. I cannot help but wonder what would happen if you didn't do that and if you did this. You recognize the weaknesses in *Map Room Two*, for instance, that weakness of the neon thing coming last. *Linoleum* is probably one of the most tedious works I've ever done, the most unclimactic. If you're in the audience, you simply move into it with your attention and live through this thing. At a certain point it's over.

How did you conceive Oracle *(1965), your multipart sculpture?*

I finished it after I got back from Europe, after touring with Merce Cunningham. Technically, it had to be completely rebuilt, because ideas which had been impossible when I started in 1962 later became possible.

In the technological sense?

Yes. It is a single work with five pieces of sculpture. Each piece has its own voice. The controls are a console unit which is embedded in one of the pieces; and all five have a sound source. Each piece can be played independently, because the console has five volume controls, one for each piece. A scanning mechanism goes across the radio dials and provides a constant movement, so that what you control is the speed of scanning. All this gives you the maximum possibilities of varied sound, from music to purely abstract noise and any degree in between. Each piece can be adjusted accordingly. One of the ideas was to make it so simple that you would not have to be educated to do it — so that the thing would just respond to touch.

When this sculpture is displayed, is someone working the dials or are they merely present?

Anyone around it can change it; and it can also be set up so that the sound is constantly changing, independently of anyone's control.

One of the pieces, a cement-mixing tub, is also a fountain, because I wanted another source of sound too in running water. I didn't want to imply that these sounds all had to be electronic.

Do you consider this an "environment" or a "combine"?

Sound is part of the piece; it is not a decoration. It is a part of the climate that piece insists on. You really do get a sense of moving from one place to another, as you shift from the proximity of one piece to another piece.

Because the field of sound is constantly changing. Several questions come to mind: Why the field of sound? How does the sound relate to the visual elements?

The sound relates to the pieces physically by the material interaction — the peculiar kind of distortion the sound of a voice has as it is shaped by its context. "Why sound?" — because hearing is a sense that we use while looking anyway.

One of the myths of modern culture — I associate it particularly with Lewis Mumford's Art and Technics *(1952) — is that art and technology are eternally opposed to each other and that one succeeds only at the decline of the other.*

I think that's a dated concept. We now are living in a culture that won't operate and grow that way. Science and art — these things do clearly exist at the same time, and both are very valuable. We are just realizing that we have lost a lot of energy in always insisting on the conflict — in posing one of these things against the other.

In contrast to nearly all contemporary artists, you did not need to find your own style by first painting through several established styles — by taking them as your transient models. From the start, you were, as we say, an original.

I always had enormous respect for other people's work, but I deliberately avoided using other people's styles, even though I know that no one owns any particular technique or attitude. It seemed to me that it was more valuable to think that the world was big enough so that everyone doesn't have to be on each other's feet. When you go to make something, nothing should be clearer than the fact that not only do you not have to make it but that it could look like anything, and then it starts getting interesting and then you get involved with your own limitations.

As an artist, do you feel in any sense alienated from America today or do you feel that you are part of a whole world in which you are living?

I feel a conscious attempt to be more and more related to society. That's what's important to me as a person. I'm not going to let other people make all the changes; and if you do that, you can't cut yourself off.

This very quickly gets to sound patriotic and pompous and pious; but I really mean it very personally. I'm only against the most obvious things, like wars and stuff like that. I don't have any particular concept about a utopian way things should be. If I have a prejudice or a bias, it is that there shouldn't be any particular way. Being a complex human organ, we are capable of a variety; we can do so much. The big fear is that we don't do enough with our senses, with our activities, with our areas of consideration; and these have got to get bigger year after year.

Could that be what the new theater is about? Is there a kind of educational purpose now — to make us more responsive to our environment?

I can only speak for myself. Today there may be eleven artists; yesterday there were ten; two days ago there were nine. Everybody has his own reason for being involved in it, but I must say that this is one of the things that interests me the most. I think that one of my chief struggles now is to make something that can be as changeable and varied and alive as the audience. I don't want to do works where one has to impose liveliness or plastic flexibility or change but a work where change would be dealt with literally. It's very possible that my interest in theater, which now is so consuming, may be the most primitive way of accomplishing this, and I may just be working already with what I would like to make.

How will our lives — our ideas and our responses — be different after continued exposure to the new theater?

What's exciting is that we don't know. There is no anticipated result; but we will be changed.

Merce Cunningham (1973)

You have to love dancing to stick to it. It gives you nothing back, no manuscripts to store away, no paintings to show on the walls and maybe hang in museums, no poems to be printed and sold, nothing but that single fleeting moment when you feel alive. It is not for unsteady souls. — Merce Cunningham, *Changes* (1969)

Merce Cunningham has been modern dance's principal choreographer for the past decade, if not longer; and what makes his eminence so remarkable is that it is rarely challenged and thus remains as undisputed as any superlative position in art can be. For more than twenty-five years, he has been the major dance-maker on America's avant-garde fringe, but only in recent years has the mainstream acknowledged his excellence and acclaim for his work become international. Even in conservative London, a critic for the *Dancing Times* recently dubbed him "the greatest of modern-dance choreographers."

From his professional beginnings, over thirty years ago, Cunningham showed extraordinary promise. Accepting Martha Graham's 1939 invitation to join her company, he quickly assumed leading roles in her pieces, playing March in *Letter to the World* (1940), the Christ figure in *El Penitente* (1940), and the revivalist in *Appalachian Spring* (1944). Audiences were awed by his spectacular leaps and general physical lightness (which contrasted with the floor-rooted quality typical of Graham's choreography), as well as by his "all-American good looks," and some still remember him as "America's finest lyric dancer." The dean of American dance critics, Edwin Denby, noted at the time, "As a dancer, his instep and his knees are extraordinarily elastic and quick; his steps, runs, knee bends and leaps are brilliant in lightness and speed. His torso can turn on its vertical axis with great sensitivity, his shoulders are held lightly free, and his head poises intelligently. His arms are light and long, they float and do not have an active look. These are all merits particularly suited to lyric expression." Photographs made prior to 1955 customarily show him suspended in mid-air with spectacular grace.

Though Cunningham performed with Graham until 1945, he was pursuing his own choreographic interests. As early as 1943 he stopped taking the dancer's "daily class" with others, in order to develop his own regimen and his own dance technique—literally to teach himself the basics of movement.

In April, 1944, he presented, in collaboration with the musician John Cage, his first New York recital of self-composed solos that, in Denby's minority judgment, "combined such impeccable taste, intellectually and decoratively, such originality of dance materials, and so sure a manner of presentation." Once on his own, Cunningham gave an annual self-financed New York recital. In addition to renting the performance hall, he usually printed the tickets and peddled them as well. Unlike Denby, however, most dancers and dance fans attending these early concerts did not come back; and not unlike other post–avant-garde heroes, Cunningham revealed superhuman persistence in overcoming the scandalous neglect that had plagued his early career.

Since New York offered few opportunities, Cunningham and Cage wrote letters to colleges, soliciting performances; and the dancer spent a summer in Paris, in the late forties, working with a pick-up group that included Tanaquil Le Clerq and other incipiently prominent ballet dancers. Cunningham began to teach, every summer at Black Mountain College and in New York during the year; and out of these classes emerged the beginnings of a loyal performing group. It then included Carolyn Brown, Viola Farber, Paul Taylor (who soon quit to form his own company), and Remy Charlip (who has since authored well-known juvenile books and choreographed his own pieces). Though the local dance public ignored him, Cunningham's concerts began to win a loyal audience consisting largely of painters and poets, many of whom would soon become famous. By the mid-fifties, he remembers, half the New York spectators had familiar faces.

The Cunningham Company's first New York season, at the end of 1953, precipitated a crisis that had an unfortunate effect upon his subsequent career. Although the theater was filled every night, with sophisticated people, not one local critic reviewed these performances. This disappointment partially explains why Cunningham was, until recently, reluctant to stage another season in New York. Other reasons were an absence of both subsidized performance situations and suitably equipped platforms. Several pieces, mostly solos, were never performed in the city; and as recently as 1963–64, his habitual New York fans had to journey as far as Hartford for their annual dose.

The source of Cunningham's professional predicament was, in short, the originality of his art; and not unlike his colleague Cage in music, Cunningham became the once-favored son whom the American dance establishment felt obliged to exile. Not only did his work go unreviewed, but it was frequently excluded from "series" where it might deservedly belong. Or, included in a series one year, he was excluded the next, "with a note I thought impolite." It is hard to believe, but true, that not until a few years ago did major dance schools invite him to teach or perform; the U.S. State Department has to this day never sent him abroad. More than once he suffered doubts about pursuing his career, "but I decided I couldn't do anything else."

Since he survived with integrity and glory his years in the wilderness, no eminent artistic career could be more classically avant-garde.

The dispute was artistic, rather than personal, as Cunningham himself
has always been more cordial and polite than antagonistic, for at issue was
not just a difference in "style," but his radical departure in compositional approach. Since his works "broke the rules" and thus were different in more ways
than the dance world could understand, they were dismissed as "unserious"
or "absurd," and it was commoningly said: "He dances so well; it's too bad
he does those funny things." (In truth, innovative art nearly always seems
ludicrous at first.) Since the well-known critics were unsympathetic (and
Denby wrote less and less), much of the New York dance audience simply remained unaware of his annual performances. The turning point came in
1964, when enthusiastic responses to the company's first extended world tour
boosted interest (and business) at home. Not until then, to cite one key index,
was the *New York Times'* dance critic at all predisposed to Cunningham's
choreography. Therefore, people who liked his pieces came to *advocate* them
(and care about *him*); and such advocacies made acceptance of his art *the*
crucial issue that, during the sixties, distinguished the square from the hip,
the fogies from the future.

In brief, Cunningham's departures broached a third generation in
the evolution of modern dance. The first generation, led by Isadora Duncan,
rejected the tone and devices of classical ballet, with its fixed vocabulary of
positions and movements, to put the dancer's feet flat on the floor and to use
freely formed gestures that were more expressive of human emotions than
the strict conventions of ballet; and the work of this pioneer generation initiated a choreographic tradition that has developed largely apart from ballet, and apart as well from folk dance, ethnic dance, social dance, jazz
dance, chorus lines, vaudeville dance, television dance, and "water ballet."

The second generation of modern dance, to summarize again, introduced
more definite vocabularies of movement (Graham, for instance, favoring
contractions and releases), and their work customarily had particular subjects, such as *Appalachian Spring* or *The Moor's Pavane* (José Limon), that evoked
a plot and/or depended upon a familiar literary allusion. Like Duncan before
them these choreographers danced on standard theatrical stages to conven-
tionally tonal music, the rhythm of their movements relating to the predict-
able musical beat; and their typical gestures served to mime identifiable emotions or meanings.

The reason why Cunningham's pieces looked so different, both on stage
or in photographs, was that he had drastically reworked every dimension of
dance-making — not only the articulation of time, but the use of space; not only
the movements of dancers' bodies, but their relationship to each other on the
stage. First of all, if most ballet and even most modern dance has a front and

a back, Cunningham's works are designed to be seen from all sides; and though theatrical custom has forced him to do most of his performances on a proscenium stage (which has a front and a back), his pieces have also been successfully performed in gymnasiums and museums. They could be feasibly staged in a hockey rink or a ballpark.

Time in Cunningham's work is nonclimactic, which means that a piece begins not with a fanfare but a movement, and it ends not with a flourish but when the performers stop. Since he avoids the traditional structure of theme and variation, the dominant events within a work seem to proceed at an irregular, unpredictable pace; their temporal form is, metaphorically, lumpy. "It's human time," he explains, "which can't be too slow or too fast, but includes various time possibilities. I like to change tempos." In this respect, his pieces resemble basketball games or soccer matches.

It is also true that they generally lack a specific subject or story, although interpretation-hungry spectators (and critics) sometimes identify particular subjects and/or the semblance of narrative. It follows that his performers eschew dramatic characterizations for nonparticularized roles, which is to say that a Cunningham dancer always plays himself and no one else. The titles of these works tend to be abstract (*Aeon, Winterbranch*), or situational (*Rain-Forest, Summerspace, Place*), or formally descriptive (*Story, Scramble, Walkaround Time*). Since heterosexual themes are as *verboten* as other specific subjects, the most visible difference between the men and the women, aside from physical appearance, is that the latter rarely lift the former off the floor.

As his dancer's gestures have been ends in themselves, rather than vehicles of emotional representation, Cunningham freed himself to explore the unlimited possibilities of human movement; and in this respect in particular, he has been incomparably inventive. His dancers reveal an unprecedentedly large vocabulary of movements, including all sorts of everyday activities. He also defied tradition by allowing parts of the dancer's body to function disjunctively and nonsynchronously. Once, for *Untitled Solo* (1953), he listed the movable parts of the body and enumerated their possible actions. He then tossed dice to determine theoretically possible combinations that he might be reluctant to try on his own initiative. Since exploration, rather than refinement, is his ideal, Cunningham then took months to learn all his aleatory results, until he found, after repeatedly trying, that a few hypothetical combinations simply could not be done. "I was always interested," he noted recently, "in discovering ways in which the body could move." Precisely because such experiments resist emotion-equating interpretation, his choreography has been called "unnatural" or "anti-human," but Cunningham insists that any activity done by a human body reveals its "natural expressivity."

Since Cunningham's movements are not symbolic, they are meant to be appreciated as ends in themselves. His dance thus demands not empathy of the spectator but, as his closest colleague, the composer John Cage, once explained, "your faculty of kinesthetic sympathy. It is this faculty we employ when, seeing the flight of birds, we ourselves, by identification, fly up, glide and soar." His dances generate, to extend Cage's point, the kind of experience we get from watching sports events or frolicking children. In the end, what seems at first inscrutable about Cunningham's work is quite comprehensible, providing one does not strive too hard to find "meanings" that are not there. What you see is all there is.

There is no fixed center in Cunningham's stage craft, as crucial events occur all over the performing area—even in the corners; so that the spectator's concentration is often confused, or diffused. The distribution of performers, as well as the lines of their movements, resembles a soccer game again—or the closing moments of a football play, rather than the beginning. The result is organized disorganization, so to speak, that seems "chaotic" only if strict forms of order are expected. Cunningham's works have been compared to Jackson Pollock's "all-over" paintings, but Cunningham finds them "more like Bob Rauschenberg's, in that he takes a canvas and puts various things in different places." Sometimes his dances are quite funny.

Like Rauschenberg, Cunningham also challenged the traditional hierarchies of art; and although some of his dancers were more skilled than others, his works avoided the format of leader-and-chorus that is typical of ballet and much modern dance. Unison activity, when used, is rarely sustained in his art, and individual dancers move at different speeds, often simultaneously. "They are both independent and dependent," he explains. His company is an ensemble of equals, whose various members dominate at different times; and rather than looking and dressing alike, as is customary in most companies, his collaborators accentuate their individuality in both appearance and activity. "I try to emphasize what's interesting in each of them." (The other major choreographers of his generation—Alwin Nikolais, Ann Halprin, and Jerome Robbins—have also shown comparably counter-expressionistic, counter-hierarchical tendencies; but none has been as comprehensively innovative.) One might say that Cunningham took the fluff out of modern dance by returning the art to its indigenous, mediumistic essentials. "My definition of dance," he announced, with cunning simplicity, "is movement in time and space."

All these artistic departures might have been more acceptable, had not Cunningham committed an even greater outrage in his use of music. Whereas most choreographers drew their inspiration from particular scores (which were often specially commissioned), Cunningham composed all but a few of his pieces without music, which was usually added after the dance had been finished, and seemed shockingly atonal and rhythmically irrelevant to the movement. To make fortunes still more hazardous, Cunningham remained loyal to his friend Cage, whose own egregiously dissonant scores distracted attention from the dance, as well as offending "music lovers" even more than Cunningham's art disturbed the dance regulars. He also celebrated the arrival of electronic sound for "avoiding the usual phraseology," and long before such technology became fashionable, he was the first choreographer to dance to electronic music. Typical Cagean scores of the sixties consisted of silences punctuated by earsplitting amplified cacophonies (or vice versa) or disconnected electronic sounds generated by the dancers' random proximity to metallic poles visible on stage (*Variations V*, in 1965); or Cage himself and/or the actor David Vaughan reading funny stories at a varying pace.

Rauschenberg handled lighting and costuming until 1964; but once he left the company, Cunningham and his current "artistic advisor," the painter Jasper Johns, invited eminent painters and sculptors to *add* decor to new works. Settings have since included a row of industrial fans lined up across the front of the stage (Bruce Nauman's idea for *Tread* in 1970) and helium-filled silver pillows attached by string to the floor (Andy Warhol's, for *Rain-Forest* in 1968). Though each of Cunningham's works has a distinct collection of movements, most of the audience remembers them not in terms of choreography but setting and score. That truth may indicate a defect in dance-education or an inadvertent compromise in communication.

The key difference between Cunningham and his predecessors is that their dances were mostly derived from a central idea or score that informed all the parts, which reinforced in turn the initial concept (*Appalachian Spring* again), while Cunningham's works are assembled from disparate, independently created materials that remained perceptibly separate, and yet artistically complementary, in the final performance. "The relationship between the dance and the music," Cunningham said, his hands carving shapes in the air, "is one of co-existence. That is, they are related simply because they exist at the same time." It is the spectator's job to comprehend the quality of time and space, the kinds of movement and organization, used in each piece.

One of the most famous, *Winterbranch* (1964), originated with the spatial idea of "entering the stage and doing a configuration," and the physical idea of falling, or "going to the floor," which then suggested that the performers would either need to get up under their own power or, perhaps, be dragged off the stage. This last requirement ruled against dancing in tights, which twist uncomfortably and do not adequately protect the body. Rauschenberg suggested that the dancers wear sweatsuits and tennis shoes with white socks (to protect their feet from the sneakers) and without laces (so that, while kneeling, they could easily bend their feet back along the floor). Rauschenberg also proposed that the dancers fall on dark canvas sheets that could be pulled off the stage without worrying about splinters. Here, as elsewhere, many choreographic decisions were determined by physical necessity, rather than any initial artistic design.

Cunningham suggested that the piece might take place at night, "but not in moonlight, because it implies something romantic and all that. Our nights are artificially lit, with lights that can be turned on and off at will." So Rauschenberg proposed that the stage be darkened, except for occasional beams of light that would be trained autonomously across the stage. (Surprisingly, the darkness that seems so essential to the final piece was not a core idea, as it seems, but a later addition.) Rauschenberg also suggested that the dancers put black smudge under their eyes, much as baseball and football players do on sunny days; and Cunningham donned a black bathing cap, so that his hair would not get caught as he dragged himself across the floor. He originally intended to vary the order of falling sequences, but discovered it was hard for the dancers to remember the different falls and their temporary sequence too. Thus, the order of action was fixed.

He then asked Cage to suggest a piece of music, and he chose La Monte Young's *Two Sounds* (*April, 1960*), in which two abrasive sounds, perceptibly different, are repeated interminably. The dark and raucous qualities of *Winterbranch* seem almost representational, and critics have regarded the work as portraying race riots, or concentration camps, or bombed cities, or blackouts. To Cunningham, all these interpretations "are not invalid, but idiosyncratic. I didn't have any of those ideas in mind, but that shouldn't prevent people from finding them there." There is no doubt, however, that one theme is perception in sporadically illuminated darkness. A British art critic noticed a formal resemblance to American football, which Cunningham had not intended but reluctantly acknowledged. (He especially recommends watching the game against a background of classical music — so that the result is "the best ballet you can find in America.")

The result of all his choreographic departures was an artistic mix that was well beyond the bounds of "acceptable" modern music and/or dance and/or theater. At the first Cunningham concert I ever saw, at Philharmonic Hall in the summer of 1963, the spectators devoted to José Limon and Donald McKayle (whose companies shared the same subscription) would, with every Cagean cacophony, rise and angrily file out, efficiently reducing the audience to the true Cunningham afficionados. The *Times* critic suggested that Cunningham would fare better without Cage; but Jill Johnston, then the principal dance critic for *The Village Voice*, replied that such bowdlerization would be comparable to "the Bible without God." By 1968, however, Cunningham's work had become so acceptable that another critic, Arlene Croce, could note, "Today it seems just as preposterous to make a mental effort over Merce as it does to make one over Fred Astaire."

The man who changed modern dance is scarcely the ogre his art (or antagonists) suggest. A cordial steady soul with a ready laugh and a twinkly manner, Cunningham is a tall, lean, solidly built man (6'1", 168 lbs.) with a long torso, strong hands and rather muscular forearms. His legs are sturdy, his feet pigeon-toed, and his ankles unusually thick. Strong in his eyes, he is very observant. What makes his erect head so striking is that his long, vertically-lined face has comically broad expressive features: a wide mouth, flared nostrils, large eyebrows, high cheeks, broad forehead, and jawbones that run wide back to his ears. Grey-brown curls run over his thinning pate, and down both his cheeks and the back of his neck. He seems ready-made to play Shakespeare's Puck, and the theatrical makeup he favors on stage accentuates his singular appearance.

He was born Mercier Cunningham around 1920 — the exact date remains a secret — in Centralia, Washington, the son of a lawyer; and his two brothers, one younger and the other older, have respectively become a lawyer and judge. Originally wanting to become an actor, he took tap-dancing lessons as a child and became good enough to tour with his dancing teacher's daughter. He developed a love of reading and of nature, both of which have remained with him; and his favorite sport was long-distance swimming in Washington's lakes. Not unlike other young Americans of his generation, he went often to the movies. "When sound came in, I liked musicals." Upon graduating from high school in 1937, he went to the Cornish School, a progressive art college in Seattle, initially to study theater, and there learned about modern-dance for the first time. Encouraged by Bonnie Bird, a sometime Graham dancer who then headed the Cornish dance department, he journeyed in the summer of 1939 to Mills College in Oakland, where the Bennington School of Dance was temporarily in residence. Martha Graham, then a member of the Bennington faculty, recognized his talent, and invited him to join her in New York. His subsequent rise to professional eminence was meteoric. Certain idiosyncracies of his choreography can be attributed to an initial interest in theater and tap-dancing, rather than the more typical background of ballet and modern dance.

The *eminence grise* in Cunningham's art has been the composer John Cage, whom the dancer initially met at the Cornish School, where Cage was a faculty member hired especially to play the piano in dance classes. When Cunningham began to make his own dances in New York, he asked Cage, then teaching in Chicago, to compose a percussive piece. When Cage moved to New York in 1943, Cunningham was among the first and closest friends he made. The dancer identifies the composer as the greatest single influence on his work "because of his ideas about the possibilities of sound and time and the separate identities of music and dance." As early as 1939, Cage had advocated "the simultaneous composition of both dance and music." (Another early influence was Fred Astaire, because he made steps for their own sake, rather than trying, like Graham, et al., to express particular emotions.) After years of living apart, though usually touring together, Cage and Cunningham now share a large, sparsely furnished, plant-filled loft in the West Village, and their circles of friendship overlap.

The disconnected qualities of Cage's music complement Cunningham's choreography, not as a synchronous accompaniment, of course, but through esthetic similarity—the ordered disorder of one formally resembling the other. As Jill Johnston, who was once Cunningham's most profound critic, noted of Cage's music: "Each sound is heard for itself and does not depend for its value on its place within a system of sounds. Similarly, a typical Cunningham movement is a series of isolated actions, and the connection is simply that of sequence or juxtaposition, or whatever the observer wishes to make out of it." From Cunningham-Cage collaborations have come the currently popular customs of keeping apart those elements that might normally be expected to coincide, or of simultaneously offering materials that otherwise have nothing to do with one another; for their great, much-imitated idea was presentational noncongruence.

What was never disputed, however, was Cunningham's own competence as a dancer; even in his fifties, he remains the most accomplished exponent of his particular kinds of individual movement—original in gesture, often awkward in both form and balance, and yet graceful and fluent in execution. In the judgment of Carolyn Brown, his partner for two decades, "no one else can approximate the thrusts of energy, the quick changes, the subtle rhythmic variations, the counterpoint of torso and arms and legs and head that occur in his own dancing." A consummate performer, he is also a masterful soloist, who can infallibly fill and capture all the theatrical time and space he allots for himself. Though his theoretical critique of hierarchy supposedly discounts egotism, Cunningham becomes *primus inter pares,* first among equals, by virtue of his intellectual leadership and physical competence.

One weekday afternoon, early in 1973, he was working with the nine other members of the performing company. There were three new colleagues who had to learn earlier pieces in the active repertory, and they were helping one another, as well as soliciting advice from the veterans. One couple who had learned a new duet the day before were teaching it to a second couple, just in front of the tall mirror that runs along one wall. They were counting the rhythm aloud, though this mnemonic device would be dropped before the final performance. By that time, they would know from experience precisely when to move and how quickly. A seemingly exhausted dancer was lying alone in the middle of the floor, occasionally doing a stretching exercise and moaning with fatigue; but no one else seemed to notice him. Cunningham himself was working with two other dancers, or talking to me, while alertly watching the entire perspiring, heavy-breathing, motley-dressed group—all with the proximity, attention, and authority of a basketball coach overseeing a practice.

He said remarkably little, as his demonstrations communicated desired movements far better than words; and occasionally he would clap his hands or count aloud to a rhythmic beat. "One two. One two three. One two three four. One two three four five. One two. One. . . ." He sat on a battered piano bench, looking down at a stopwatch, until circumstances required him, as player-coach, to give another demonstration. If his colleagues looked clumsy or uncertain, he suggested another way of doing it. "I'm making this up as we go along," he told me, and from time to time he would peek into a notebook that contains sketches for the new piece. As no music was used, one could hear feet rhythmically bouncing off the floor. He was working that afternoon on a new piece whose tentative title was *Changing Steps*. Like his other works, it originated not with a plot or an emotional idea but certain conceptions of space and time, physical movement and interpersonal organization. He wanted the dance to exist within a smaller performing area than his other works, in part because certain spaces they found on tour were too tight for the pieces currently in the repertoire. Secondly, Cunningham wanted to concentrate on some quick leg inflections he had just developed.

Thirdly, it would consist of solos, duets, trios, quartets and quintets; and since the company now had ten performers, there would be ten solos, five duets, three trios, two quintets, and two quartets. A further hypothesis was that each of these five forms would have the same duration — all solos would run one length of time, while each quartet would be as long as the others. Having made these essential compositional decisions, Cunningham was now working on the sequences that would be assembled into a final dance. Passages that did not finally suit *Changing Steps* might be saved for a future piece. "That sounds like a long work, with all those combinations," I remarked. "Yes," he replied, "but they might do several of them at once. It would change in time, or change its density, or it could have a different continuity. Those are ways of being flexible."

The general characteristics of Cunningham's choreography have remained the same for over two decades. The pieces are many-sided, nonlinear, nonexpressionistic, spatially noncentered, temporally nonclimactic, and compositionally assembled. The decor and sound are supplementary, rather than complementary; and the dancers are highly individualized. Though his art is avant-garde, his sensibility is classical, which is to say precise, constructivist, and severe. He reveals the enormity of his choreographic intelligence through his profound knowledge of dance and dancers, coupled with his limitless capacity for invention. Though one can feasibly generalize about Cunningham's work, his pieces are so various, and his imagination so free, that they defy absolutely encompassing formulations, for one or another piece sticks out as a contrary example. *Walkaround Time*, for instance, is filled with allusions to Marcel Duchamp's life and work, and the women performers in *Story* (1963) have been known to lift the men off the floor.

Most pieces were composed with the help of "chance" procedures, which serve to accentuate all these general characteristics. Cunningham likes, for instance, to create structures whose parts can be varied in performance *without* the whole losing its particular identity; chance operations, such as throws of dice, can provide a means of determining changes for a particular presentation. However, the initial scheme — the decor, the prearranged steps, the choice of performers, etc. — will ensure that, though certain details and combinations may vary, the result will resemble work X rather than work Y. "Chance" is not a real issue in comprehending Cunningham, though many critics emphasize it; for "chance" cannot be perceived. Instead, aleatory operations are a device for realizing certain perceptible forms of choreographic structure. The validity of those structures, however, is a genuine critical issue. In Arlene Croce's critical opinion, "Merce gives you that complete freedom to enjoy the nonrelatedness of things as they are in life."

His choreography changed in the late fifties, as he introduced props — not as bodily extensions, as Nikolais does, but as physical foils (such as strapping a chair to his back) — until his works were closer to mixed-means theater. *Winterbranch,* for instance, differs from traditional dance in that the aggressive sound and light do not accompany the performers but realize a theatrical status equal to movement, each element accompanying, so to speak, all the others. *Walkaround Time* freely mixes movement and stillness, sound and light, costume and props. The epitome of this mixed-means tendency was *Variations V* (1965), which includes Theremin-like metallic poles, films, video projections, slides, and a bicycle (that, in a brilliant stroke, Cunningham rides off the stage to conclude the piece). Subsequent works reveal, however, that Cunningham returned to Dance. "I got interested in making up steps again, as distinct from theatrical structures." Another difference is that his late sixties pieces used more people than ever before, for one practical effect of prosperity was an interest in choreographing for larger ensembles.

In a more recent development, Cunningham has come to favor the scheduling of "Events" rather than a group of particular pieces. An event consists of passages excerpted from previous pieces — a self-anthology, so to speak; and different passages are selected for each performance. Cunningham developed this open-form concept in the middle sixties, as a response to the demands of touring in unfamiliar places. The disadvantage of scheduling certain pieces, he told me, is that the company might discover that crucial performers were ill, or that the auditorium was inappropriate for one or another of the promised works. The stage might be too small, or the lighting inadequate, or the floor too hard. ("When will someone invent a more resilient cement?") Thus, if the company promised just "an Event," Cunningham could decide on the spot what would be best for this particular situation. One esthetic reason that Cunningham prefers Events is that "no two are alike. They could have the same material, but the continuity would be different. This can be seen, if you come again, as you should."

Another advantage is that Events, which customarily run about ninety minutes, "eliminate the intermission, which doesn't seem to function anymore.

My friend Lois Long says they're of no use unless you smoke. I like Events because they have an openness and flexibility that interests me, and they can be done in both proscenium theaters and gymnasiums." He paused to broach a confidence, "I don't like printed programs, which are useless, because so much can happen between the time you plan a program and the time you get around to performing it. Theaters ought to have a scoreboard, which would tell you what the piece is called and who was dancing. They could be instantly changed in response to changes in the situation. A scoreboard would encourage flexibility."

In part because his choreography has been so comprehensively innovative, even "dance critics" have failed to understand his work (which may also explain why they neglected it), and more nonsense has been written about Cunningham than any other choreographer. He tries to repair such ignorance with "lecture-demonstrations," and he even authored a book entitled *Changes: Notes on Choreography* (1969). However, this volume is less the "introduction" that his work needs than a highly original and enlightening supplement assembled from photographs, programs, diagrams, notes (both handwritten and typed), reproductions of chance charts, etc., in addition to a spectacular 1958 letter addressed to Rauschenberg. Though the book lacks a table of contents, it becomes clear that various sections are devoted to particular dances. On the inside front cover is a photo of Cunningham looking at three female dancers. Lines of brown type run up the page, over the photograph, while two sets of green type run diagonally. Such superimpositions echo, of course, the compositional character of Cunningham's art, which the book illuminates not through step-by-step exposition (like *this* profile) but through esthetic semblance. "I wanted to make a book," he disclosed, "that was not an explanation but a process, like a dance, so the complexity of the material about a certain dance depends upon the complexity of the original work. I found that it is possible, with a fair amount of concentration, to understand everything."

Cunningham has composed so many dances—about two every year for the past decade—that one would think choreography his principal occupation; actually, it is economically avocational. His principal source of income for all these years has been teaching. He has given private classes in New York lofts borrowed from friends or rented by the hour; he has taught in George Balanchine's School of American Ballet. At Black Mountain, his classes included such cultural eminences as Charles Olson (who was physically immense), the painters Elaine de Kooning and Robert Rauschenberg, the potter-poet M. C. Richards, the novelist James Leo Herlihy. When the company performed at a university, he generally taught its "master class," no matter how good (or bad) the students were; and he would sometimes spend a weekend teaching alone at nearby schools so that his company could continue its tour during the week. He has been the principal professor in his own school, which was founded in 1959; and if the company is residing in New York, he usually teaches at least one class a day. The fifty pupils in each class include incipient professionals, exercise-nuts, and local dance teachers, who, incidentally, propagate his gospel.

He recognizes that instruction is essential to his art, which can rarely be successfully self-taught from scratch (unlike writing or painting) and that his performing company must be trained by himself. "If you really want to be a dancer, you must study with a professional. Nothing else will do. Classes in the colleges are not taught in any professional sense. If a choreographer didn't train dancers, he'd have to accept dancers trained by another, or accept untrained people. I chose to train them." He paused to watch one of his dancers at work. "What you study is less important than the teacher—how good he is. A good teacher will stay out of the way, opening your mind or imagination, rather than pinning it down." Out of his classes (and his company) have come most of the notable young avant-garde choreographers, including Twyla Tharp, Yvonne Rainer, Barbara Lloyd, Steve Paxton, Tina Croll, Rudy Perez, and Gus Solomons, Jr., all of whom reflect his limitless, constructivist ideas about movement and organization. Perhaps the initial artistic problem for them—and all that intends to be avant-garde—is finding choreographic terrain that their master has not already appropriated.

Needless to say, Cunningham's existence has been impecunious. In the forties and fifties, he lived in the East 17th Street loft where his company also practiced; the rent was $40 per month. The company traveled in Cage's microbus, with six dancers, two musicians and a technical person filling all the seats. Suitcases were put on the back ledge, while the sets and equipment went on the roof. Cunningham paid all the lodging and dining expenses out of his own pocket, to ensure that his otherwise unpaid penny-pinching colleagues would not scrimp on their essentials; and since receipts rarely equalled the company's costs, he also assumed all indebtedness. When he received his first Gugenheim fellowship in 1954, a friend asked Cunningham what he would do with the money. "I'm going to eat" was his reply.

This bus survived until 1964, when it was sold "to help defray expenses for our first European tour." In the early sixties, he lived in Little Italy in a 2½ room apartment whose rent rose from $35 per month to $57 when the landlord installed heat and hot water. In the middle sixties, his residence was above the rickety, since-demolished studio on Third Avenue, near Thirty-Fourth Street. In 1965, when we first met and fortunes were not yet so fine, he noted how truly awesome it was, given persistent financial hardships, that American choreographers such as Ruth St. Denis, Martha Graham, and Ted Shawn worked steadily into their seventies and eighties. "The kind of energy that Merce has sustained," Barbara Lloyd once noted, "has been extraordinary, both humanly and artistically."

His recent eminence has changed circumstances a bit. There is now a larger studio, which can take more pupils (who pay $20 each for eight ninety-minute classes), and a Cunningham Dance Foundation, which has a full-time administrator. It frequently receives grants from the National Endowment for the Arts and the New York State Council on the Arts, as well as private tax-deducting donors; but expenses have progressed apace. His company members now earn about $200 per week, apiece, for half the year, and the rent at Westbeth is several times that on Third Avenue. The Foundation gives Cunningham a weekly salary which equals that of a junior university professor or a beginning lawyer.

New eminence has also brought the mixed blessing of more requests to perform. One problem is that his company colleagues are not as predisposed to travel as before, and some of them would like to work as well in other situations, or by themselves. Just as the audience for modern dance has grown immensely, so have the number of performing companies, the populations of talented young dancers, and the quantity of showcases, especially in New York. Having helped make dance a much more popular art, and increased the flow of talent and sophistication through his own classes, Cunningham now suffers a peril of prosperity — losses of exclusive allegiance. Though the quality of the whole company remains as strong as ever, members are continually quitting — the most recent alumna being Carolyn Brown, who has long been Cunningham's only true peer and partner. Since pieces are generally composed with the current company in mind the departure of a certain dancer may necessitate the premature retirement of a particular work.

In response to such transience, Cunningham is developing a new schedule that would disband the company for the summer months, leaving both Cunningham and his colleagues totally free to pursue other activities. Their chief has thought about teaching his pieces to other dance companies, or going to the beach more often, or working on his own. "I have a feeling that people like to do more than one thing, and I'd like to establish a situation that encourages variousness and personal flexibility." Those last two nouns — flexibility and variousness — remain the key ideals in Cunningham's esthetic and his life.

Robert Whitman (1978)

Robert Whitman is a master of performance art that coheres in terms of imagery, rather than language or narrative. He was fifteen years ago regarded as a sometime visual artist who had exhibited his paintings and sculptures, but had, unlike, say, Claes Oldenburg and Robert Rauschenberg, abandoned those crafts to concentrate exclusively on theater; his willful concentration was, at the time, seen as a measure of serious theatrical purpose.

His masterpiece a dozen years ago was *Prune Flat* (1965), which was then curiously spelled "Prune. Flat." It opens with the screen image of a movie projector (implicitly declaring that one theme would be cinematic images). Then comes a grapefruit (that nearly fills the screen) being cut by a knife. After other images, a tomato appears, which is also cut, black egg-like objects pouring out; and when the tomato-cutting sequence is repeated, two young women dressed in white smocks and white kerchiefs walk in front of the screen, the filmed blade apparently cutting through them. As the film shows the two women walking down the street, one slightly behind the other, so the same two women walk across the stage, but in the same formation. Later in the piece, the image of a woman undressing and showering is projected directly on the full-length body of one of the women performers; but once the film shuts off, the woman who appears to be undressed is suddenly revealed to be definitely besmocked. One theme of *Prune Flat* is the perceptual discrepancies between filmed image and theatrical presence, and it differs from other mixed-means theater pieces not only in its precise control but in its visual beauty.

Whitman staged other nonliterary theatricals at the time, including the spectacularly scaled *Two Holes of the Water* (1966) on a Long Island lake; but these tended to be diffuse and temporally flaccid. I had heard of earlier performance pieces of his, but did not see them until the Dia Foundation presented a retrospective in the spring of 1976. The best innovation in *American Moon* (1960) was the positioning of the audience, which is divided into groups of ten, each assigned to a cubicle within a circular structure that looks into the performance area. In other words, this is "theater-in-the-round" with the audience subdivided by partitions. Translucent cloth screens separated each audience group from the stage before them, and film is at times projected from

198

behind on these individual screens, so that each section sees a different part of the movie. Once the curtains are raised, the climax of the piece is a cellophane structure that is blown up from an unseen (and unheard) source, the plastic filling the center space. Two performers walk through it. As a man is suspended in a swing above the space, the piece closes. *American Moon* struck me as the best of the other works in the retrospective that included *Flower* (1963), *Nighttime Sky* (1965), *Salad P. N.* (1974), and, of course, *Prune Flat*, in addition to a new work, *Light Touch* (1976). Though each of the others includes stunning particulars, it is still *Prune Flat* that in my experience remains the most extraordinary of Whitman's theatrical creations.

His work has always been uneven, and always exploratory. His forte has been evocative, memorable imagery; his recurring failings include a leaden sense of theatrical time and sado-masochistic undertones. Though I have already seen *Prune Flat* perhaps a dozen times, I would gladly see it again.

Tsaibernetics (1990)

Intellectually, art in our time is oriented toward science and technology — as is almost every activity in modern society — and to values of functionalism, rationality, and economy of means. On a less visible level, however, art has never ceased to expand its searches into those areas of experience formerly considered to be the province of religion and metaphysics. — Harold Rosenberg, "Metaphysical Feelings in Modern Art" (1975)

Wen-ying Tsai, commonly known only by his family name, came to America early in 1950 to attend William Penn College in Oskaloosa, Iowa. His father, a businessman in pre–Communist China, advised the sixth of his eight children to study science and technology; an uncle already in America advised doing so in "the heartland of America." Uncomfortable in such a small rural school, Tsai, by birth a city boy, followed another Chinese student's advice and transferred to the University of Michigan, where he earned his B.S. in mechanical engineering in 1953. For the following decade he worked in New York City as a consulting engineer and project manager on various architectural projects, most of them industrial; by 1962 he had taken American citizenship.

Interested in visual art from childhood, he painted in his spare time until 1963, the year he received a John Hay Whitney Opportunity Fellowship. Quitting engineering work, he wandered through Europe for three months and, upon his return to New York, began to work not in two dimensions but three. Within a few years, his reliefs were included in "The Responsive Eye" ("Op Art") exhibition at the Museum of Modern Art; his sculptures gained international renown.

In the heady 1960s, he deduced that he could combine his engineering training with his artistic interests, producing sterling examples of avant-garde technological art. "I wasn't satisfied with something static," he told me recently. In an USCO exhibition in the mid-1960s, he rediscovered the flickering strobe light that was to become an essential element in displaying his work. "In engineering school, it was used in laboratory tests of material — modular elasticities, waveform amplitudes. I never thought the strobe could be part of artistic expression."

More than two decades later, I can still remember walking into the Howard Wise Gallery in 1968 and being knocked over by examples of his most famous sort of work — shiny flexible rods with tops the size of bottle caps. Thanks to a motorized base, these rods could shake at variable speeds before a physically separate strobe light that, rapidly flickering at a slightly different frequency, caught these vibrating rods in a succession of striking postures that created the anthropomorphic illusion of dancing. The illusion was that firm material, steel, was made to look as though it had lost its rigidity. (One autobiographical source of their choreographic quality was Tsai's studying modern dance with Erick Hawkins for several years.)

A further innovation was that the flickering speed changed in response to either sounds in the surrounding space or the spectator's proximity to a sensing device in the sculptures themselves, making them a pioneering example of responsive or cybernetic art (that I take to be more advanced than artistic machines that move autonomously). At the time I responded to such work as an excellent example of *kinetic* or moving sculpture in the tradition of Naum Gabo and Moholy-Nagy, on whom I was then doing a book. It was scarcely surprising that Tsai's work won second prize in a 1967 international competition sponsored by E.A.T. — Experiments in Art and Technology — and was later included in "The Machine," a monumental 1968 exhibition at the Museum of Modern Art.

After such auspicious beginnings, Tsai's public career stalled. Howard Wise closed his gallery in 1970 and no one else followed his initiative. Tsai and his wife Pei-de Chang left New York, first for M.I.T., where he spent two years as a fellow of the Center for Advanced Visual Studies, and then moved to Paris to prepare for a museum exhibition that never happened. "I never felt at home there," he told me recently. "It was difficult to find materials for my art. You had to be a registered engineer or belong to a guild or company before you could be qualified to purchase components of a professional quality. You had to pay a value-added tax plus import duties, so everything cost 50 percent more. Here you can call a big company and get everything delivered the next day." In 1976 Tsai returned to his downtown Manhattan studio, settling his family on Roosevelt Island and then in SoHo just as it was becoming recognized as a coherent art community. He has lived there and on a Catskills farm ever since.

Tsai himself is a slender, unusually tall oriental, over six feet in height, with clear tanned skin and a very full head of graying hair. He seems self-contained and almost aristocratic, even when he laughs softly, as he often does, at his own jokes. His handsome wife Pei-de, whom he met on a blind date in the late sixties, worked as a biochemist before their marriage; she has since run cultural exchanges between the United States and China. (Since the disappointments of 1989, she is avoiding contact with the mainland.) Her English is more accessible, as well as wittier, than her husband's; he tends to odd grammar and incomplete sentences. They have twin sons, Lun-Yi and Ming-Yi, both yet taller than their father; each is half-way through a Boston college, drawn to science on one side and the humanities on the other—just like their parents.

It is unfortunate that technological art disappeared from the commercial galleries in the 1970s and hasn't returned since. Some artists working in this way have, instead, done industrial projects for such patrons as the shopping center developer David Bermant, who long supported George Rhoads, today the most visible machine artist, his noisy and witty glass-enclosed arcades inhabiting bus terminals, airports and shopping centers across the country. "I don't go to galleries anymore, other than friends' openings," Tsai told me recently. "I want to see a work I can interact with, like a being of any kind." He once gave me a Chinese protective talisman that, he admitted, had been given him. "I can't hang that. I have only high-tech art."

As a result, works like Tsai's aren't exhibited here as often as they should be. His last one-person show in the United States was in Houston over a decade ago. One-man shows of his work have since appeared, instead, in Paris, Dusseldorf, Brussels, Montreal, Hong Kong, Tokyo, Caracas, Taipei—everywhere, it would seem, except anywhere in his adopted country. The last major American group show in which he was included was "Computers and Art" (1988), which was organized by the Everson Museum at Syracuse University and toured to the IBM Gallery of Science and Art in New York. Though several dozen dealers have galleries within a stone's throw of his studio, none represents him now, as much by his choice as theirs, he insists. Though examples of his art are included in many collections around the world, he has retained much of his best art, selling one or another from time to time. "My fax is open," he jokes.

Thus, the best place to see his sculptures, to begin to understand his extraordinary artistic achievement, is in his own five-thousand square-foot SoHo loft, which happens to be around the corner from mine (which is considerably smaller); the place must be experienced personally, with all one's senses, to be believed. With high windows, whose bottoms are above eye-level, it feels like another world, inhabited by spirits unknown outside.

Behind the dining area is an example of his most successful early painting, *Random Field* (1963), in which a plane of unmodulated flourescent red is mounted one-half inch in front of a field colored only with fluorescent green. Circular holes cut into the front board reveal the green background. When seen under ultraviolet light, the green appears to shimmer above the red.

In the next space are two elements from his *Multi-Kinetic Wall* (1965) in which motors make circles suspended within other circles spin in various directions. When all thirty-two elements are assembled together, the work measures eight feet high by sixteen feet across and twenty inches deep. Beside these samples, hanging on a wall, is Tsai's *Multi-chromics* (1971), a sort of painting three feet square, in which he embedded reflective circles, called defraction gratings, that appear to change color as you move from side to side. (Tsai speaks of them as technically having "color without pigment.")

On the other side of the *Multi-Kinetic Wall* is *Computer Column* (1980), which has a vertical row of flippers, much like those in a train station. The plates in this piece have various colors, and the speeds of the various flippings, from one color to another, can be controlled from an early Radio Shack computer. To my senses, such sculptures are more theatrical than painterly — they function in time as well as space; that explains why most of us can spend a generous amount of time looking at them. He reveals his engineering training not only in neat workmanship but in his sense of how elements might interact together.

In the Tsai living room are several examples of his most famous innovation — the vibrating rods mentioned before. Some are over ten feet tall; others the height of shrubs. Some have squares on top of their rods; others, circles. In some, two rods emerge from a single base, resembling tuning forks. One later development was substituting fiberglass for metal in the upright rods. Though no two are identical, they resemble one another much like siblings. With several sculptures operating in the same space, Tsai is able to get different responses from each. To show how the speed of the strobe light can be changed, he generally claps his hands before admiring "the dancing rods," as he calls them.

For such responsive works Tsai claims a *fifth* dimension for sculpture — not only width, depth, height and movement but artificial intelligence. "My research in cybernetic art," he explained, "inevitably led me into an ever deeper involvement in electronic technology — memory chips, computer interface, random generator, feedback sensor, audio control and computers. All these components create an essential interacting intelligence hitherto unknown to sculpture-making."

In a corner of his living room, behind a couch, is a work that resembles an umbrella with a single vertical rod supporting a collection of loose-limbed rods dangling from its top. When turned on, this shakes like leaves on a tree. It was very hard to make, he insists, because of balance problems. (In his workshop were several examples that didn't work out.) In an anteroom on the way to his workshop is a circular piece whose name he has forgotten. (His catalogue says *Quasar* [1973/81], which, like other names for his work is descriptive, rather than symbolic or tangential.) When he turns *Quasar* on, the ends vibrate, flickering faster than the eye can register, creating the illusion of several arms in the place of every one.

Between his front door and his kitchen is a sunken tub that receives water from vibrating showerheads attached to the ceiling. As the falling water is illuminated by a strobe, the droplets dance up and down; at certain strobe speeds, the droplets appear to be moving upwards, violating all rules of gravity. *Upwards-Falling Fountain*, as he calls it, creates an illusion that must be seen to be believed. This sculpture, like others of Tsai's, move so gracefully that, as the British art critic Jonathan Bentall wrote, "His creations look effortless and spontaneous."

Though he once obtained a patent for the technology behind his illusion, his works are fundamentally inimitable. "Technological art can be easily copied," he surmises, "unless the technique is so profound it is difficult. You can make it so complicated or so subtle that nobody else would have the combination of artistic sensitivity and patience to do it. In my case, people who try to copy can't do it, so I retain my uniqueness." Copy? hell. Their mystery comes from the sense that most of us can hardly deduce how they might work.

In his workshop is a yet larger water sculpture, *Living Fountain* (1980–88), with a showerhead three feet in diameter plus three concentric circles of water jets all installed above a basin twelve feet by sixteen. Here the strobe is designed to respond to combinations of changes in audible music, random sensors, audio feedback controls, and a computer program. For the traveling "Computers and Art" exhibition mentioned before, Tsai chose G. F. Handel's *Water Music.* (He'd like to use music more contemporary next time.) In my opinion, this is the second indisputable masterpiece in the Tsaibernetic oeuvre.

Across from it in his workshop is a new wall piece that likewise caused him considerable technical difficulty — an orb with extending vibrating tentacles that Tsai called *Sun Dial* (1988), whose first word is what it literally resembles. From the ceiling Tsai hung a sculpture that has lightbulbs that flicker on and off in various arrays, all in response to the changing music — *Light Computer Array* (1985). Also in this workshop are the tools of the kinetic sculptor's trade — piles of shower heads, pipes, electrical wire, cartons of new strobe lamps, and a wall full of boxes with screws and other small implements of various sizes. Kinetic sculptures so finely tuned often break down, especially when moved and reinstalled; and no one can fix them as well as the artist.

Sitting in his office space, surrounded by books about art and materials, Tsai speculated, "Science and technology can create alternatives in life. And in art. I'm not trying to recreate birds and plants. Someone more talented than I could use this material, the technology, to create new physical, artistic creations that you can touch, can feel, can hear, can see — wonders that would make us feel this universe is more complex than we know, an unknown never seen before." Pausing to look around the only public room in his house devoid of his machines, he continued, "Metaphysical feelings come from science and technology at the highest levels. When a person is confronted with something unknown, that involves decisions beyond ourselves and our understanding, the feelings within ourselves, you can say, are metaphysical."

What his best sculptures are fundamentally about, in my opinion, is the esthetics of electricity, which is to say possible artistic properties that depend upon electricity. Beyond that Tsai is also interested in ideal kinds of person-machine experiences. As he wrote in 1971, responsive sculptures have "been created to effectuate an instantaneous interaction of Man with his art, his environment, using scientific instruments as a tool. By virtue of this interaction, the cybernetic sculpture evokes a spontaneous vigor and response in the participant, thereby awakening in him the inner curiosity and sensitivity toward the poetic unfathomable wonder of the universe."

Though his works are on permanent display at the Kaiser Museum in Krefield, Germany, the Ontario Science Center in Toronto, and the Orlando Science Center in Florida, among other places, it is here in his own house, more than anywhere else in the world, that we can see the sum of Tsai's powerful vision: to make cybernetic sculptures that exploit twentieth century electrical-electronic technologies (in contrast to the mechanical and thus nineteenth-century Rhoads), more variously and successfully than anyone else has done. In the most fundamental sense, Tsai is avant-garde, forging ahead a path that others will take, continuing to suggest what else might still be done in modern sculpture's four-plus dimensions.

James Turrell (1991)

Is there a wall of silence around me, I will make the silence audible! — Karl Kraus.

The most remarkable thing about James Turrell's career, when you look back on a quarter century of it, was that he knew from the beginning that his medium would be light. He didn't discover light after a career of exhibiting objects or a period of theorizing. His first exhibition, in 1967, just two years after his graduation from college, consisted entirely of projections within a museum space. The best sense that we can get of his earliest works now is to read between the lines of the chapter about them in Turrell's single book, *Occluded Front* (1986), which began as the catalogue of a retrospective exhibition in Los Angeles. He then created in his own Southern California studio a series of light-based installations by cutting slits into the walls and ceiling to let sunlight sweep through his space in various experimental ways; he used lenses to refract it strategically. What he never did was make objects.

The first Turrell I saw was *Laar* at a 1980 exhibition at the Whitney Museum of American Art. On the other side of a darkened room, opposite the elevator and stairway, appeared to be a large gray monochromic painting. As you moved closer, it retained that identity, its surface shimmering, much as good monochromic painting sometimes does. Only when you were literally on top of the work, close enough to bump your head into it, did you discover that, surprise, the monochromic rectangle is really a hole in the wall — or, to be more precise, a window onto a three-dimensional space painted gray. If only to accentuate the illusion of entering a palpably different world, you could feel that the air behind the aperture had a perceptually different weight — heavier to my senses. According to Adam Gopnik in *The New Yorker*, "What Turrell had done was to define 'the approach space' with direct light from four seventy-watt tungsten bulbs mounted and pointed at the side walls, while lighting the rectangular aperture entirely by indirect, 'ambient' light." In a later variation, *Daygo* (1990), shown at the Stein-Gladstone Gallery in New York in 1990, I stuck my head through the rectangle and noticed purplish light fixtures. In either case, the effect was not only magical, it was unlike anything else anyone had ever seen.

206

For over a decade now, Turrell has been working in remote Arizona on remaking a volcanic crater into a celestial observatory. The "Roden Crater Project," as he calls it, should be a masterpiece; but until it is complete, as well as more popularly accessible, my Turrell nomination for the contemporary canon would be *Meeting*, as installed in 1986 at PS 1 in Long Island City. You are asked to come no earlier than an hour before sunset and to stay no later than an hour after sunset. You're ushered into a former classroom, (22' 6" × 19' 8" × 18' 3" high), most of whose ceiling has been cut away into a smaller rectangle, 49" less on each side, leaving the sky exposed. (It looked like very clean glass to me until I felt the temperature change.) Benches are carved out of the walls, but it is perhaps more comfortable to lie on the rug floor, looking skyward. Along the top of the benches runs a track behind which is a low level of orange light, emerging from tungsten filaments of thin, clear, meter-long, 150-watt "Osram" bulbs. (Having no visible function at first, these lamps later contribute crucially to an illusion.)

What Turrell has done is framed the sunsetting sky, making its silence audible, its slow metamorphosis visible, in an unprecedented kind of theater that proceeds apart from human intervention. You see clouds move across the aperture; at times, an airplane, a helicopter, or some birds. It all looks familiar until the sky begins to turn dark. Lying in the middle of the floor, I saw the sky pass through a blue reminiscent of Yves Klien. Above me developed, literally out of nowhere, the shape of a pyramid, extending into the sky; and as the sky got darker, the apex of the navy blue pyramid descended down into the space.

Eventually it disappeared, as the square became a flat dark gray expanse, looking like nothing else as much as a James Turrell wall "painting," before turning a deep uninflected black that looked less like the open sky than a solid ceiling. Now, I know as well as the next New Yorker that the sky here is never black; there is too much ambient light. What made it seem black was the low level of internal illumination mentioned before. (You can see the same illusion at the open-air baseball stadium where, because of all the lights shining down onto the field, the sky likewise looks black.) I returned on another day, cloudier than before, to see textures different from those I recalled. On both occasions I remembered the epithet of a European art official who, getting up from two hours on the floor, exclaimed, ironically, "This Turrell is a great painter."

On the simplest level, what Turrell had done was manipulate the natural changing colors of the sky, first through the frame that required you to look only upwards and then with the internal illumination that redefined its hues. How he discovered this I do not know, as he is reticent about his working processes; I can imagine him setting up experiments with light and *then patiently sitting with them long enough to see what happens*. Otherwise, remembering my own skepticism about reading about Turrell before seeing, I would be remiss if I did not say that no less than experiencing *Meeting* in time is believing; descriptions always sound insufficient.

What is also remarkable is how much intellectual resonance the work carries to a wealth of contemporary esthetic issues, such as illusion/anti-illusion, painting/theater, unprecedentedly subtle perception, the use of "found objects" (in this case, natural light), and conceptualism (bestowing meaning on apparent nothing), all while transcending all of them. I personally thought of John Cage's *4'33"*, his notorious silent piece, in which he purportedly put a frame around all the miscellaneous accidental sounds happening to be in concert hall for that duration, much as Turrell frames unintentional development in the sky. *Meeting* is theatrical in that it must be experienced over a requisite amount of time; no passing glance, as well as no single photograph, would be appropriate. Indeed, though *Meeting* could have been realized technically prior to the 1950s, there was no esthetic foundation for it before then. It is indicative that though most artists agree Turrell is "doing something special," he has no well-known imitators; what he does must be hard to do.

Don Celender (1980)

If history can make into art what is now not art, it can also unmake what is now art.
— Harold Rosenberg, "The New as Value" (1964)

Don Celender's annual O. K. Harris shows arrive as comic relief in an otherwise earnest art season, and no one in the galleries today is funnier. His recent exhibitions have been horizontal eye-level mountings of the results of cunning questionnaires that he sends to circumscribed groups of people. These responses are sometimes also bound into 8½" by 11" books published by his gallery. It is Celender's ingenious method to submit straightforward and superficially innocuous questions on academic stationery that inform the recipients that he is indeed a chaired professor of art at Macalaster College in St. Paul and a Ph.D. Since his queries look like serious scholarship, most of his respondents answer them seriously, the process sometimes prompting them to reveal their characteristic selves in a concise way.

In the better of his two recent displays, artscene celebrities were asked, "If reincarnation were available to you, what form would be your preference?" Many of the responses betray assertive bravado, sometimes tinged with irony. Richard Serra: "I'd like to return as a Richard Serra clone." Arakawa: "You ask too late. I've already done." Ivan Karp: "I have no plans to depart this life." Others are perhaps self-revealing. John Kacere: "I would like to return as Florenz Ziegfeld." Mel Ramos: "First-string catcher on the New York Yankees." Some responses are drowned in picayune digressions that are no less characteristic, or amusing (e.g., Jules Olitski and Clement Greenberg). Celender's "investigation" must be a work of art, not only because it is exhibited in a gallery, but also since its pleasure must be defined as *esthetic* because it certainly is not *scholarly*.

Oddly, it is the other, weaker exhibition piece that Celender chose to bind into his 1979 book. To produce his *National Architects Preference Survey*, he asked a thousand American architects: "If you were to advise students of architecture to see one significant structure in the world that would be the most inspiring and instructive for their future careers, which structure would you recommend?" For both the exhibition and the book, Celender has retyped their answers, added a photograph of the recipient and the work he or she selected. Not unexpectedly, the Parthenon is recommended more than anything

209

else; the only other structure that is not an idiosyncratic favorite is the National Museum of Anthropology in Mexico City. This Celender survey turns out to be less comic than instructive, especially about the enthusiasms of architects in small-city America. The surprises come from those recipients who refuse to play Celender's game:

> Dear Dr. Calendar [sic]:
>
> I am shocked by the question. It is inconceivable that students should be directed to any one structure as being able to give them a clue to their future. The process of developing a design philosophy cannot be reduced to simplistic answers.
>
> Ulrich Franzen

Whereas this architecture survey asks artists to talk about art, most of Celender's other pieces mix art with something else (e.g., reincarnation). His earliest works of note were two packs of cards, both entitled *Artball* (1971, 1972). The first was twenty baseball cards with artists' faces pasted over baseball players' bodies; on the back were poorly reproduced examples of their works. The second *Artball*, a slicker production, is a complete pack of 54 playing cards with the faces of art-world celebrities superimposed over football players in action postures and then their names and putative positions also pasted over the originals. Thus, uniform #41 getting ready to pass is "Stella — Running Back," #74 with a football cupped in her raised hands is "Parsons — Quarterback." Some of the juxtapositions are funnier than others, it is true; but in both *Artballs* the wholes represent a bigger joke than the sum of their parts. A third undated box, *Holy Cards*, puts artists' faces into paintings of religious figures; on each backside is a religiously suggestive prose passage by or about the featured artist. His *Olympics of Art* resembles a jokebook in that superlative captions appear under people's pictures, one to a page. Thus, "The Leading Copycat Artist of an Artist Father" appears under Jamie Wyeth. "Most Over-Celebrated Living Artist" appears under Victor Vasarely. And so forth. Part of the charm of this collection of one-liners is that gossip and art-historical scholarship are posing as each other.

Museum Piece (1975), the second of Celender's works in the current questionnaire-response form, is still the best, and fortunately it exists as a book as well. Museums around the world received this query: "I am developing a research project dealing with museum architecture. May I request a photograph of your loading dock, or receiving area?" This request was open and yet unprecedented enough to prompt officials of each museum to respond in a revealing manner. One wrote that it has no "loading dock" because its collection is permanent; another asks its staff photographer to comply with the request, while a third begs Celender for funds to hire someone to photograph their dock. A fourth apologizes for the garbage stacked on the photographed platform which he piously assures Celender "looks much better after the garbage men have been here." The reply from the National Museum of Korea might seem tasteless, did not Celender reprint the accompanying letterhead and signature as well:

> We removed new building in 1972. But this museum has not any receiving area. The loading dock is imperfection. Anyway inveloped photos are loading dock from outside to inside. Dock is basement.

As a native New Yorker I still collapse with laughter every time I read the double-spaced response from the Brooklyn Museum: "We are very sorry that due to the Musem's security policy, we are not permitted to forward a photograph of our loading dock as requested." Perhaps because I would rather read language on my butt than on my feet, I prefer my Celender compilations between covers, which is to say that I think the most appropriate medium for exhibiting his work is the spine-bound book. (On the other hand, every book artist envies his having an annual wall show at a West Broadway gallery.)

Other recent Celender pieces likewise mix art with non-art. In 1976, he wrote trucking companies that he wanted to ship from North Dakota to New York City, in time for the bicentennial, a giant statue of Myron the Discus Thrower, thirty-five feet high, made entirely of cake. (This one has not yet become a book.) In 1978, he asked travel agents to identify their favorite work of art, and then reprinted their professional mug shots alongside larger reproductions of their selections. (This has not become a book either.) His first book, *Political Art Movement* (1971), is leaden and needlessly contrived; a later suvey, *Opinions of Working People Concerning the Arts* (1975), suffers from repetitious responses that are limited in range. *Observations, Protestations and Lamentations of Museum Guards Throughout the World* (1978) is also a middling work, again limited and repetitious, redeemed only by occasional flashes of surprise and revelation, usually from a respondent who objects to the questionnaire. *Observation and Scholarship Examination for Art Historians, Museum Directors, Artists, Dealers, and Collectors* (1977) comes as a multiple-choice exercise book that asks the reader to identify a whole painting from only a rectangular fragment. Four possible choices are given, and the whole paintings (the answers!) are reproduced in the back of the book. What I expected to be funny turned out to be a serious exercise for visual idiot savants. Scrutinizing these books suggests that Celender cannot securely tell in advance the esthetic value of each questionnaire, but some of his results are clearly more successful than others.

Destiny in a Name (1978), also an exhibition that became a book, is a Celender anomaly, for neither the subject nor the respondents are necessarily connected to art. People whose surnames reflect their occupations were asked to comment on the connection. Thus, Mr. Rockwell, the music critic of the *New York Times*, for instance, received a questionnaire asking, "Did you feel destined by your family name to assume your present occupation?" So did Mr. Reveal the psychologist, Dr. Cure the physician, Mr. Houseworth the architect, Mr. Fangman the dentist, Messers Law and Case the attorneys, Mr. Pieper the plumber, Dr. Butts the colon and rectal surgeon, and Messers Blood, Deer, Eagle and Stear, all veterinarians. However, since everyone is so irately anxious to deny any name-determinism, their responses are rarely funnier than the initial connection of their names and professions.

What Celender has done in these recent projects is construct shrewd response-devices that encourage people (and institutions) to display themselves merely by providing answers that they think are "normal" to them; but by assembling their responses into a single context, Celender not only makes a "found art" that is uniquely identifiable with his name, but he allows his respondents to contrast and augment one another in a burgeoning irony that is obviously marvelous and yet quite unlike anything else I know in either art or literature.

Paul Zelevansky's Trilogy (1991)

There is a familiar tradition of the book as a repository for words, customarily set in uniform typography that is cast into rectangular blocks, sometimes accompanied by illustrations; there is a secondary tradition of books with pictures, customarily captioned. Whereas the first could be described as words sometimes accompanied by pictures, the second exemplifies the principle of images sometimes accompanied by words. There is another, less familiar tradition in which words and pictures have equal status, accompanying each other, so to speak; so that the words remaining in your head long after you have read the work — the *after*image — are as strong as the visuals, or vice versa. The classics in this third tradition include *The Book of Kells*, Hebrew illuminated manuscripts, and the visual books of William Blake; and though most of us are familiar with such contemporary popular examples as the comics, the higher examples are less known. In this last respect, I'm thinking of Tom Phillips' *The Humument* (1980) and Bern Porter's *Found Poems* (1972) as the contemporary masterpieces, to which should be added Paul Zelevansky's trilogy, *The Case for the Burial of Ancestors* (1981, 1986, 1991). All have epic structures; all took years to become complete; all mix classical materials with contemporary moxie; all regard the book as a medium capable of containing a multiplicity of interests.

*   *   *

It seems odd in retrospect that Wyndham Lewis, who was a great painter as well as a major writer, never broached this third tradition; but given the compartmentalization of contemporary criticism, it is scarcely surprising that none of his critics, to my recollection, address this omission.

Other contemporary American books that realize this visual/verbal balance (and likewise tend to mix fact with fiction) are Arakawa and Madeline H. Gins' *The Mechanism of Meaning* (1979), Alain Arias-Misson's *Confessions* (1974), Emmett Williams' *Sweethearts* (1967), Merce Cunningham's *Changes* (1969), Dave Morice's *Poetry Comics* (1982), J. Marks' *Rock and Other Four-Letter Words* (1968), Jean-François Bory's *Post-Scriptum* (1970), Claes Oldenburg's *Store Days* (1967), Warren Lehrer's *French Fries* (1984); but the obvious difference between them and the Zelevansky trilogy is scale. The last is not only bigger but touches on more dimensions of experience.

The principal sources behind the Zelevansky trilogy are the Old Testament, the major myths, *Moby-Dick, The Magic Mountain,* hieroglyphics, Georges Seurat, Fra Angelico. He once told me that his favorite composer is John Coltrane; his favorite movies, François Truffaut's *Shoot the Piano Player* (1962), Martin Scorsese's *Raging Bull* (1980), Orson Welles' *Citizen Kane* (1941). You need not look too far in Zelevansky's trilogy to see reflections of all this eclectic collection of sources—reflections not only in specific textural details but in the variety of representational styles.

Zelevansky has done painting as well as performance, just as Phillips has composed music and painted canvases and Porter has done various arts (not to mention physics); but it is in books that we find the sum of their intelligence and imagination.

Pic Adrian (1984)

Abstraction in art should be born of reality and lead back to reality evoking new visions, fresh insights, new levels of perception and consciousness of both nature and art. — Eli Bornstein (1977)

What makes Pic Adrian interesting, as well as different from 99 percent of the visual artists in the world is his commitment to principles, as well as rational processes, to make visual art that appeals first of all not to the eye but to the mind. Even though several of us are working in this way, to the art world we will always be heretics.

Precisely because his discoveries in visual formats have no practical use or academic value, it is fair to call them not Philosophy but Art, and fair as well to classify our response to them as principally esthetic.

Although the moves of Adrian's art are rational from point to point, the end results go beyond; that is one crucial difference between the deduction of a logical conclusion and what he does.

Adrian is the only artist I know to be attracted and inspired by Albert Einstein's testimony that, in Adrian's summary, "He formulated his ideas in psychical entities, signs and images, which were more or less mythical, and which could be reproduced and combined 'at will.'" It is in that prelinguistic intellectual domain that Adrian has ambitiously situated his own art.

Even now, at the end of a century that has witnessed more artistic innovations than any other, we have every reason to honor and respect those who, by doing what has not been done before, expand our sense of esthetic possibility.

One immediate sign of Adrian's esthetic integrity is, paradoxically, severely limited pictorial content.

In considering the world's religions Adrian typically sees not convergent ideas but similarities in visual symbols, which, typically again, he documents not with words but images abetted by few words. Like the founder of Esperanto, Adrian wants not just to see the world as one; *he wants the world to see itself as one.* This spectacular idealism of his work makes the "politics" of other artists seem parochial, if not childish.

The coherence of his art is established not by a consistent look — an art-world strategy that is coming to seem increasingly cheap — but by a consistent intelligence.

215

We identify "an Adrian" not by how it looks but by the character and quality of the polemic informing it.

To my mind, this kind of esthetic coherence *per se* signifies higher purposes. One subsidiary benefit of our acceptance of Conceptual Art is better preparation to appreciate this kind of art-making.

At a time when we are inundated with visual artifice, much of it spectacular, we have a great reason for appreciating visual work that stands to traditional Art as metaphysics stands to Physics.

One challenging question raised by Adrian is whether Principle Art, as he calls it, represents not only a realm beyond Art but an advance over Conceptual Art. If only to acknowledge his ambitions, I am, on both these issues, more inclined to agree than disagree.

Given his esthetic principles, it is not surprising that Pic Adrian should want to support his work not only with essays and manifestoes but with elaborate illustrative charts. (Some of them document his purposes; others locate himself in contemporary art.) In this respect, he belongs to a distinguished modern tradition of artists whose self-explanations are every bit as stylish and important as their work—Moholy-Nagy, Mondrian, Ad Reinhardt.

The American art audience tends to find such principled esthetics either suspect or incomprensible, which is unfortunate; for at its foundation is an unfashionable counter-craziness that, in spirit at least, reminds me of no artists more than Walt Whitman and Charles Ives, who were likewise artists so principled in their devotion to an unfashionable vision of their art that their work could not find its optimum audience until after their deaths.

Adrian's art is ethical in ways that other art is not; it is also Jewish in ways that Chagall, among others, could never be. (Remember the commandment proscribing graven images; remember the quest for truly universal relevance.)

Adrian wants to make an art devoid of excrescence; and now that so much of the most prominent new art seems full of shit, this quest for purity becomes more and more attractive.

Andy Warhol (1988)

Minimalist paintings and sculptures reiterated the functional style of the Constructivists, but without the social aims of that movement, as Pop Art repeated Dada, but without its social criticism. — Harold Rosenberg, "Lyric Steel" (1975)

Though we know for sure that Andy Warhol was a celebrity for more than fifteen minutes and that he died a multimillionaire, much about him remains mysterious. What were his deepest ambitions? How bright was the man who entered college at fifteen and yet, as an adult, seemed to prefer appearing dim? How did his intelligence function in the making of his art? What was his relationship to the Church whose loyal communicant he was? What should be made of his inability to depict depth? What in his *oeuvre* will survive as contributions to the history of art? The last question should particularly interest an art historian like Rainer Crone, a German now teaching at Columbia University; but his *Andy Warhol: A Picture Show by the Artist* ignores these issues for other stuff.

Appearing here less than a year after Warhol's death, *A Picture Show by the Artist* is not a new book but, rather, the American edition of the catalog to an exhibition at the Württembergischer Kunstverein in Stuttgart in 1976. As that exhibition was confined only to Warhol's earliest work, the reproductions all but end with his 1962 portraits of Hedy Lamarr in which there are hints of the saintly presences that distinguished the great paintings that came a few years afterwards. Those origins account for why the book's decade-old text, cleanly translated by Martin Scott, is less about issues of quality in Warhol's art than, in Crone's phrase, "a summary of the literary and general cultural situation" in the 1950s and then the beginnings of his art career. The former is best skipped over, filled as it is with familiar interpretations and semidigested quotations attached to footnotes (segregated to p. 107, where misspellings abound—"Kernau" for Alvin B. Kernan and "Ria" for Elmer Rice); the latter depends upon Crone's conversations not with Warhol, it seems, but with those around him. Crone also makes a brief case for the early Warhol as a caricaturist, missing, however, not only any explanation of the relationship between this early interest and the mature Warhol painting but, say, Harold Rosenberg's critical understanding of the possibilities of caricature in his *Saul Steinberg* (1978).

It is reasonable to distinguish high art, with its lasting values, from commercial art, with its essentially journalistic motives, and then to classify Warhol as a commercial artist who for a remarkably brief period in his career, entirely in the middle 1960s (just *after* this survey ends), made works that belong to the history of painting (and perhaps book-art and experimental film). His repetitious portraits of myth and terror will always be with us. However, once his niche in art history was established, Warhol reverted to the working regime (and mentality) of a commerical artist, producing mostly to order, working with a staff of assistants, etc., but charging more money than before, thanks ironically to his reputation as a high artist. (Inexplicably, the survey of reproductions ends not with the Lamarr drawings mentioned before but with a leap forward to 1973 sketches of Mao Tse-Tung that are distinctly inferior.) In 1975, Warhol wrote, with uncharacteristic frankness, "I started as a commercial artist, and I want to finish as a business artist. After I did the thing called 'art,' I went into business art."

No other American major painter in history learned to capitalize so well upon what was once called selling out, and none ever made so much money. For those dubious achievements alone he will always be remembered. Though the subversive point of Warhol's esthetic strategy was obliterating the distinction between high art and graphics, I think that the former survived and, more to the point here, that many patrons-come-lately who thought they were commissioning high art have been stuck with decoration. Why he gave up serious painting remains a mystery to me; perhaps he thought he could not sustain his excellence and feared becoming, say, another Willem de Kooning, who would spend half of his adult life haunted by an inability to produce work equal to his acclaimed masterpieces. (Remember that high art is far more competitive and success is scarcer — for every hundred who make a living at commercial art, only one survives solely from making high art.)

Given the sumptuous production of Crone's book along with a comparatively cheap price (that must have depended upon outside beneficence or a large print-run), it is reasonable to ask whether it is about an artist who was also a celebrity or a celebrity who was also an artist. If the former, it would try to isolate excellence; if the latter, it would present materials simply as embossing the celebrity. Except for the portraits of Lamarr and "A Gold Book by Andy Warhol," an eight-page sequence of drawings handsomely printed on gold paper and bound into this book as a separate signature, there is little of distinction here. Most of the drawings, if presented without attribution to a panel of professors, would barely get passing marks. What the book illustrates, alas, is that even publishers devoted to art books are prepared to pay more for Celebrity than Art.

Another element of the Warhol mystery is that he had nearly continuous celebrity for a quarter-century, which is not easy to do in this fickle country. He survived the dire predictions of those who accorded him no more than an hour or two of fame, if only because his entourage had an air, at once self-destructive and homosexual, that would never sell in the provinces. The final tragedy of his life was that much of his time was spent amassing an art collection that will never be shown intact, because his executors have decided that it should sooner be auctioned away! (It could have been the single most distinguished collection ever belonging to an American painter whose name was in the history books.) One of the perils of becoming a bachelor celebrity is that you accumulate odd friends and odder executors.

Curiously, the most compelling images in the book are the photographs and portraits of Warhol as a young man, enigmatic photographs that raise those questions about intelligence and motives mentioned before. (And when you find photographs of an artist to be more interesting than his or her art, your subconscious is trying to tell you something, in this case that the latter will be sooner forgotten.) The life he lived, the mechanics of his success, the separation of excellence from junk in his work are all more interesting than these reproductions of his juvenilia. By such discrepancies this "Picture Show by the Artist" suggests the need for substantial critical, biographical, and cultural analysis that, alas, isn't here.

Two Ways of
Polyartistry (1990)

All through his life he was equally praised and blamed for his many-sidedness, which was as natural to him as breathing. He shuffled his different jobs like a deck of cards, getting innumerable combinations but finding them all part of the same game. — Sibyl Moholy-Nagy, *Experiment in Totality* (1950)

Laszlo Moholy-Nagy was, throughout his life, tortured by the problem of professional definition, which was less an issue to him than it was to those around him. Some thought of him as a painter who also dabbled in other things, yet others saw him as a writer who was a painter manqué. Moholy, as he was commonly called, also did book design, made both films and sculpture, and developed a revolutionary program of artistic education. In my 1970 documentary monograph on him, I regarded Moholy as the great adventurer of modern art, my introduction to the book speaking of the "risk and necessity of artistic adventurism." The book itself is structured not to emphasize one or another of Moholy's activities as primary but, instead, to give each of them roughly even weight. Thus, the chapters of my book have titles such as painting, photography, design, sculpture-architecture, film, light machines, educational ideas and social philosophy. Whereas most of us compartmentalize to various degrees, Moholy worked across both the constraints of preparatory education and the conventions of professional careerism. He made arts he was not trained to do; he realized acceptable professional work in domains where he had neither specialized schooling nor apprenticeship. He worked on several projects, often simultaneously.

What that old book of mine lacks is the magical critical term *polyartist*, which is magical, because, like all good critical terms, it not only clarifies a concern that is otherwise inchoate, but it dispenses with false issues and irrelevant caveats. To call Moholy a *polyartist* is to say that he excelled at more than one nonadjacent art or, more precisely, that he was a master of several unrelated arts. The principal qualifier in my definition is *nonadjacent*. By contrast, sculpture and painting are adjacent visual arts, so someone excelling at both painting and sculpture is not a polyartist; similarly, poetry and fiction are adjacent arts. So are photography and film. However, painting and poetry are not adjacent, music and fiction are not.

220

Once we have this term in mind, we can distinguish the polyartist not only from masters of two related arts, of which there are many. We can distinguish the polyartist from the master of one art who dabbles in another, such as Picasso who, we remember, wrote modest poetry and plays; we can distinguish the polyartist from the dilettante who, as I understand the term excels at nothing. We can also see that Moholy was scarcely the only polyartist in high modernism. The term characterizes as well the activities of his friend Kurt Schwitters, who did inventive poetry as well as visual art; of Theo van Doesburg, who likewise wrote poetry in addition to making visual art; and of Wyndham Lewis, who is remembered not only for his novels but his Vorticist paintings. Jean Arp was a polyartist. So, in different ways, were Marcel Duchamp, Jean Cocteau and William Blake. These figures are adventurous and different, because of their variousness; all of them were judged deviant and unacceptable in their times, in part because of this variousness.

Now that we accept this magical word polyartist, we can recognize that the great movements of classic modernism — Dada, Surrealism, Futurism and the Bauhaus — were all essentially polyartistic enterprises. It follows that the best way for a critic to deal with the polyartistic purposes of collective endeavors would be to identify the core esthetic ideas of each movement and then the particular forms these basic ideas take in various media. To me, the key ideas of Dada were the disruption of conventional forms, producing a literature of parody and semantic nonsense, an art that incorporates images not normally found together, a theater of absurd chaos. Surrealism was concerned with the representation of dreams and related interior states, Futurism with the clashing of elements, and the Bauhaus with rigorously relational structures and the absence of inefficient frills. (Each of these last characterizations could become the thesis for a long essay, if not an entire book.)

The key ideas of Moholy's sensibility had their origins in the Bauhaus-constructivist synthesis. Nearly everything he did favored rectangular forms — his book designs, his stage designs, his paintings, his photographs, his films, even his few sculptures — for one senses that he regarded nonrectilinear structuring as decadent. As the designer of the first great series of modern art books, the Bauhaus editions, Moholy repudiated both "gray inarticulate machine typesetting" on one hand, and the highly ornamental "beaux-arts" affectations in typography on the other. His alternative was the now-familiar, geometric, hyper-rectangular "modern" style of illustrated book design in which relevant pictures and sometimes epigraphs are mixed in two-page spreads with rectangular blocks of uniform, evenly justified sans-serif type that may vary in size and yet always remain considerably narrower than the width of the book's page. These paragraphs are sometimes prefaced by subheads in boldface type. Visually, the design of a typical Moholy page could be characterized as rectangles within rectangles; there are no disruptive ornaments. The epitome of this style is Moholy's needlessly forgotten master-piece, a book he designed as well as wrote in American English, that is not only worth looking at but also merits reading from cover to cover — *Vision in Motion* (1947).

The rectangle was scarcely the only geometric form to which Moholy was devoted. In both his photography and his paintings, we see a prolifera-tion of straight lines and regularly curved lines that are either circles, parabolas, or spirals. Take, for instance, one of Moholy's very best visual works, *The Great Aluminum Painting* (1926), which was, like several other works discussed here, illustrated in my 1970 monograph on him. With this painting, he incidentally discovered the esthetic usefulness of industrial material quite different from the stretched canvas of traditional painting. Here we see three circles, a panoply of straight lines that are both parallel and diagonal to the frame of the painting, and then overlapping parallelograms that create other, smaller parallelograms wherever they intersect. In its characteristic forms this work echoes an earlier oil, painted on cardboard, *Landscape with Houses* (1919), which is composed all but entirely of straight lines and regularly curved lines. Even in this early, essentially representational work, painted when he was twenty-four, Moholy reveals an absence of jagged, undulating or other-wise irregular lines (except, of course, for his signature in the lower right-hand corner).

A similar idea of rectangles within rectangles all within the larger rec-tangle of the painting's frame also informs *C XII* (1924), which is 36″ by 28″ in size. Here the rectangles created through overlapping are defined by different colors. The tendency toward an unbalanced picture is tempered by the rigorous geometricism. In a later oil painting, *A 19* from 1927, bands of color large enough to seem rectangular intersect with one another, creating other geometric shapes, both triangular and intersect with one another, creating other geometric shapes, both triangular and rectangular, by their overlapping. Superimposed above this, almost as if it came from a spotlight, is a white circle which imposes circular edges wherever it shines. One quality of this work is the anomaly between the predominant imagery of stripes, in contrast to a single circle; but the work as a whole does not seem visually anomalous.

From here consider a later oil, Moholy's *Copper Painting* (1937), which also has lines that form rectangles and a small yellow circle almost in the mid-dle, and then a yet later painting, *Chi Feb II* (1943), which is, as its title says, the second painting Moholy completed in Chicago in February, 1943. Here we find an ellipse, encircled by a hoop, over an object resembling a basket-ball, itself over an object resembling an egg — in short, almost an anthology of Moholy's characteristic imagery.

One of Moholy's many artistic inventions was the space modulator, which he made by putting a sheet of Plexiglas a few inches above a background canvas, so that any shape either painted on the Plexiglas or cut out of it would leave shadows on the surface underneath. Even in these works, such as *The Ovals* of 1943–45, Moholy favored his idiosyncratic iconography.

As we turn to the other media in which Moholy worked, we can now see how obsessed he was with his geometric vocabulary. In one of his earliest experiments in cameraless photography, a 1922 photogram, we find again the circle surrounded by strips of roughly even width. In the brilliant photomontage, *The Shooting Gallery* (1925) — really a masterpiece of its genre — we see again the rectangles, the lines and the strips, with spare representational imagery. In *Structure of the World*, another photomontage, again we find the strips creating rectangular frames within a larger frame for imagery of human parts. Even in his representational photography, which is clearly distinct from his photograms and photomontage, Moholy often perceived the world in terms of geometrical shapes. The subject of *The Dolls* (1926), which takes a full page in *Vision in Motion,* is dismembered toys, to be sure; but the principal visual motif is the rectangular grid of lines. In *Boats in the Old Harbor* (1929), which I rank among Moholy's greatest representational photographs (and thus reprinted in my book), we find again the ellipses, this time aligned in rows punctuated by diagonal strips. These Moholy forms, as we should by now call them, also appear in his stage designs, like that for the *Tales of Hoffman,* done in 1929, for the Berlin State Opera, and in the special effects done in 1936 for the Alexander Korda movie *Things to Come,* as well as in his poster designs for, among other things, automobile tires, all of which are reproduced in my book.

It is by now scarcely surprising to us that even in his sculptures are the Moholy forms. In *Nickel Construction* (1921), the strips are both straight and spiraled. His *Light-Space Modulator,* which he made between 1921 and 1930, is a complicated machine with rectangularly arrayed ribs, spirals, and circular holes within a larger circular plane. Though this *Light-Space Modulator* is certainly elegant on its own, Moholy designed it not to stand or even work by itself but to reflect light projected on it — thus, its title is no less explicit than other Moholy titles. In fact, it became the subject of a Moholy film in which, though fields of white are projected in various ways, the geometric forms continue to dominate the screen.

Moholy's vocabulary had, it seems, a way of showing up in much that he did — not only in his catalogue outline of the curriculum for the New Bauhaus in Chicago but even in his literary criticism. Here I am thinking of his brilliant charting of James Joyce's *Finnegans Wake*, which appeared initially in *Vision in Motion*. Here Moholy discovered in his favorite forms a way of representing the multiplicity of James Joyce's most extraordinary book. Along the left-hand column are listed the various dimensions of experience that are incorporated into the *Wake*. Along the top are the five major characters —

Earwicker, his wife, Anna Livia Plurabelle, their daughter and their two sons, Jerry and Kevin, who are on another level known as Shem and Shaun. The rectangular grid thus identifies the various forms that each of these characters (or prototypes) assumes in the different experiential levels of Joyce's novel. On the cabalistic level, for instance, HCE is Adam, Anna Livia is Eve, their daughter Lilith, and the sons Mercy and Justice. Over this rectilinear grid Moholy imposes circles that signify four sets of related subjects and issues. The diagonal strips refer to certain themes that run through much of the book.

What seems most extraordinary about Moholy is the strong unity amid all the variety—how similar artistic ideas infiltrated his creative work in various media. Everything he did relates to other things, and ultimately to his encompassing vision of rectangular, circular, and comparable geometric regularities, in which he saw not just a compositional truth worth repeating polyartistically, as he did, but perhaps an ideal order of existence.

II

The [painters influenced by Piet Mondrian] all underplay the center, they underplay the constraints of boundary and format, and they replace hierarchy with coordination. They approach the structural level of homogeneity and thereby point to an undifferentiated state of being. In the world at large, the curtain walls of the so-called International Style provide the architectural equivalent. They, too, dispense with organization around a center and could expand and contract their limits without modifying their character. — Rudolf Arnheim, *The Power of the Center* (1982)

John Cage, born in 1912 and thus a generation younger than Moholy, born in 1895, was likewise the subject of a documentary monograph of mine that appeared in the same year as did the one on *Moholy-Nagy*. (It too lacks the magical term, alas.) In Cage's work in music and visual art, in theater and in writing, we find a similar pattern of unity amid all the activities; but with him the generative idea involves nonfocused, nonhierarchical agglomerations that lack definite beginnings and ends. That is, Cage's works are constellations of elements, none of them more important, more climactic, or more cohesive than any other. Though his pieces in various media necessarily begin and end, neither the opening element nor the closing element makes a firm impression; indeed, often any one of many possible elements can function as the beginning or as the end.

The radicalness of this kind of structuring should not be underestimated; for whereas classical notions of artistic form deal with centering and focus and thus favor arclike forms that organize emphases and have firm beginnings and ends, Cage has been doing something else. There are glimmers of this alternative structure in his early music, such as *Construction in Metal* (1937) in which the emphases come so thick and fast that the entire work is finally nonclimactic in overall form. To get a sense of what I am talking about here, listen to the performance of *Construction in Metal* on the three-record album entitled *The 25-Year Retrospective Concert of the Music of John Cage* (1958). To get a further sense of the difference between classical structure and Cagean structure, contrast J. S. Bach's *Well-Tempered Clavier* with a comparable exhaustive Cagean piece for a comparable instrument, the *Sonatas and Interludes* for solo piano of 1947, which is available on several recorded performances. Bach's short pieces are traditionally structured, with clear beginnings and ends as well as cumulative linear interweavings; Cage's, by contrast, represent a radical departure from such classical forming. (Incidentally, there is some important critical work to be done on those modern exhaustive keyboard pieces that reflect Bach's late masterpiece — not only Cage's *Sonatas and Interludes* but Philip Glass' greatest work, *Music in Twelve Parts* (1974), which is essentially a keyboard work, and William Duckworth's more recent *Time Curve Preludes* (1977–78), and behind them Dmitri Shostakovitch's *24 Preludes and Fugues* (1950–51) and Paul Hindemith's *Ludus Tonalis* (1943).

However, not until the early 1950s did Cage fully realize his characteristic structure — not only in *4'33"* (1952), the notorious silent piece in which the inferred aural experience must likewise be unfocused and nonhierarchical, but in *Williams Mix* (1952), a tape collage that I personally take to be the principal neglected masterpiece of Cage's musical oeuvre. Here we find, in the scrupulously uninflected succession of unconnected moments, a most thorough repudiation of classical ideas of structuring. (It too can be heard on the twenty-fifth anniversary record mentioned before.)

Oddly, it was in his visual work that Cage more rapidly realized his characteristic structure. Consider the drawing entitled *Chess Piece* that Cage contributed to a 1944 exhibition of works related to Marcel Duchamp's interest in chess (and reproduced in my 1970 Cage monograph). It has a checkerboard pattern, at once reminiscent of both the chess field and the artistic constructivists with whom Cage initially had an affinity — remember that by 1944 he had already spent a year teaching at Moholy-Nagy's Institute of Design in Chicago. However, look closer and you will notice that no part of this work is more important than any other — the white does not predominate over the black, the center squares have no more emphasis than those on the outside. Moreover, not even the professional musician would know in which direction to read this collection of staves, because no square is intriniscally superior to any other; the array of squares has neither a definite beginning nor a definite end. A later visual work, descending from unintentional purposes and yet eminently Cagean in its artistic style, is the untitled drawing made by Cage while cleaning his pen during the composition of *34'46.776"* in 1954. (A reproduction of it appears in my monograph.) The scattered ink lines create noncentered, nonhierarchical space, incidentally resembling, more than anything else, not painterly constructivism but expressionist paintings by Jackson Pollock who, we remember, was likewise concerned with the possibilities of noncentered, nonhierarchical visual space.

Before returning to Cage's music, I want to look at certain scores from the 1950s, which are in a different way visually nonhierarchical and nonfocused. That is, where a conventional music score consists of horizontal staves that function to direct attention from left to right and from top to bottom, the Cagean score from this period is a field of aggregates that can be played in any order; and further to eschew structural climax, the pages of *Winter Music* (1957), for instance, are unnumbered, which means that they can be played in any order. By such initially visual devices, Cage has ensured that the aural experience of the entire piece will likewise be noncentered and nonclimactic. (Listen to the recorded performance in which *Winter Music* is played simultaneously with *Atlas Eclipticalis*; the piano is predominantly heard as clusters.)

Like Moholy before him, Cage has moved freely from art to art, nonetheless bringing his personal signature of esthetic structuring to new media and the new problems they pose. Of all the performance pieces he has done for the past three decades, none was more spectacular, none was more exemplary of his radical esthetics, than *HPSCHD* as it was done at the University of Illinois at Urbana in May of 1969. I went to Urbana to experience it, and in the *New York Times* the following weekend filed this report:

> In the middle of the circular sports arena were suspended several parallel sheets of visquine, each 100 feet by 40 feet, and from both sides were projected numerous films and slides whose collaged imagery passed through several sheets. Running around a circular ceiling rim was a continuous 340-foot screen, and from a hidden point inside were projected slides with imagery as various as outerspace scenes, pages of Mozart music, computer instructions, and nonrepresentational blotches. Beams of light were shrewdly aimed across the interior roof, visually rearticulating the modulated concrete supports. In several upper locations were spinning mirrored balls reflecting dots of light in all directions — a device reminiscent of a discotheque or a planetarium; and the lights shining directly down upon the asphalt floor also changed color from time to time. There was such an incredible abundance of things to see that the eye could scarcely focus upon anything in particular; and no reporter could possibly write everything down.
>
> The scene was bathed in a sea of sounds that had no distinct relation to each other — an atonal and astructural chaos so continually in flux that one could hear nothing more specific than a few seconds of repetition. Fading in and out through the mix were snatches of harpsichord music that sounded more like Mozart than anything else; this music apparently came from the seven instrumentalists visible on platforms raised above the floor in the center of the Assembly Hall.

With these images in mind, listen to the musical component of *HPSCHD*, which has been available on record, for you will hear the most sustained example of densely chaotic, absolutely uninflected music any of us has ever heard. (I remember Aaron Copland, who once had a modern music program on New York radio, characterizing *HPSCHD* as beyond the bounds of music. Needless to say, history has since moved beyond Copland.) While *HPSCHD* represents a great change from *Winter Music*—a change from spareness to abundance, from minimalism to maximalism—there are still the same Cagean structural devices conducive to the creation of noncentered, nonhierarchic, nonfocused time and space, full of activities that have neither a definite beginning nor a definite end. Indeed, the only feasible way to begin *HPSCHD* is to turn it on, as one might a switch, and the only way to conclude it, in this age of electricity, is simply to pull the plug.

Cage's later visual art is similarly unfocused and nonhierarchic; and here, as in his musical-theatrical works, Cage veers between visual fields that are very full, as in the two drawings we saw before, where the imagery fills the entire space, and visual fields that are very sparse. An example of the maximal is Cage's principal visual work of the late 1960s, *Not Wanting to Say Anything About Marcel*, which is a series of Plexiglas structures done in memory of Cage's long-time friend. For this Cage wrote remarks about Duchamp, and then took them apart, distributing these verbal fragments on sheets of Plexiglas that were then stacked one behind the other. There are few images other than letters and parts of letters. One leverage of this work is that as you move from side to side, or come closer to it, the relationship between elements on each successive Plexiglas sheet changes, sometimes radically. Cage also derived a single lithograph from this work, and it too has the dense, all-over field reminiscent of Pollock. Cage's prints of the 1980s, made mostly for the Crown Point Press, suggest the counterstrategy of spareness. Cage's veering between these two strategies of moreness and lessness reminds me of a generalization I have made often in the past two decades—that avant-garde art nowadays tends to have either much less stuff or much more stuff than art used to have.

John Cage has always been writing; and in spite of his vehement objections to literariness, especially in the 1940s, he has been making consequential contributions to the experimental tradition of American writing. His first successful poetry, in my opinion, appeared in the *Diary* pieces of the late 1960s. The initial three *Diaries* were reprinted in *A Year from Monday* (1967). It can be observed that they are a series of disconnected remarks, none more important than another, about a variety of subjects—art, reading, recent experiences, Cage's friends. Each remark is set in a different typeface, and the lines of poetry appear to break in an eccentric fashion.

In my documentary monograph is reprinted a worksheet from this project, along with this explanation from Cage:

The roman numerals identify the stanzas, the arabic numbers the amount
of words permitted to each typeface, the symbols refer to results derived
from chance operations, as translated into terms suitable for consulting the
I Ching.

Now that I have acknowledged Cage's use of the *I Ching*, let me confront
Cage's notorious interest in "chance." It has been my assumption, in over two
decades of writing about Cage, that his use of chance is a minor issue and
thus that critics of Cage who emphasize it, whether to praise or to blame, are
missing the point. Chance is a method of composition—not a characteristic
structure; chance is not perceptible—certainly not as perceptible as uninflected structure is, or the serial row is. Indeed, it is more useful to identify
Cage's typical compositional strategy as fixing some parameters of a piece,
while allowing others to be left unspecific, which is to say left to chance. For
instance, in *HPSCHD*, he requires that the fifty-one prerecorded tapes should
consist of tones randomly produced within scales divided by every integer
from five tones to an octave to fifty-six tones to an octave (except for the standard twelve tones to an octave). In brief, a computer is instructed to generate
random tones within each of these fifty-one scales. However, once that requirement of fifty-one different divisions of the octave is established, it simply
does not matter what sounds are laid on the individual tapes or in what order,
or how loudly each tape is played at any point in the piece; the only possible
result of playing all (or even half or some) of those tapes together could be
microtonal din, which is precisely consonant with Cagean esthetics. As the
result of purposeful purposelessness, not purposeless purposelessness, this is
ordered disorder, which is quite different, in both construction and perception, from disordered disorder. Similarly, once Cage ruled that a performance of *HPSCHD* would contain a large amount of slides drawn from
many sources, in addition to an abundance of films and a wealth of screens,
he determined many essential characteristics that would always be evident,
regardless of particular details. Of course, chance methods are conducive to
ensuring that the space and time within Cage works will be nonhierarchic,
nonfocused, etc.; but it is also possible that he (or anyone else) could realize
such structural signatures without the use of chance methods. Indeed, as we
have seen and heard, Cage's characteristic form precedes his involvement
with that strain of oriental philosophy that encourages the acceptance of
everything, without connection and without discrimination.

In those books of his that he designed, as well as authored, Cage likewise
favors his signature form. I am thinking here not of *Silence*, where someone
else had selected the work to be included, or even the later collections of his
own fugitive writings, but of *Notations* (1968), which has always struck me as
the quintessentially Cagean book. Here he published in alphabetical order
sample pages of the works of several dozen contemporary composers. He

invited the composers to choose their single-page contributions, rather than select them himself, because he felt he could trust them to represent themselves at their best. No contribution is billed as more important than any other; none is given more space than any other. This nonhierarchical structure represents a radical departure from the traditional notions of anthologies or magazines, which require that the editor "responsible for the book" put the best stuff toward the front and the weaker stuff toward the back. And the responsible editor further indicates importance by featuring certain contributions on the magazine's cover or in the table of contents. Cage's *Notations,* by contrast, refuse the editorial options of focus and hierarchy. As he told an interviewer, his book "has this character of no value judgment," so that, he continues, "in one and the same collection there are good things and what people would say are poor things. And there are all kinds of things, and they're not organized into any categories. So that it's like those aquariums where all of the fish are in one big tank."

In his more recent poetry, Cage has drawn largely upon the language of others, first Henry David Thoreau and then James Joyce. For *Mureau,* the first of his Thoreau pieces, he extracted Henry David Thoreau's remarks about music and then reworked them by chance processes into continuous language that in certain qualities resembles prose more than poetry. (This can be heard as well — not on a record but on an audio cassette that is likewise publicly available.) Cage's later work with Thoreau, *Empty Words,* is more poetic, as Cage is now using four classes of elements: phrases from Thoreau, words, syllables, and finally letters; and in the four sections of the piece, the material becomes progressively more sparse. Nonetheless, *Empty Words* is, like its predecessor, finally nonhierarchical, nonfocused, uninflected, etc.

Cage's more recent poetry is derived from *Finnegans Wake,* from which Cage has extracted Joycean words in a succession of inventive ways. It seems indicative to me that Cage should be drawn to a major work of modern literature that is likewise scrupulously nonfocused and nonhierarchial, a work that characteristically ends with the direct suggestion to return to its beginning. It ends, we remember, "A way a lone a list a loved a long the" and begins "riverrun, past Eve and Adam's, from swerve of short to bend of bay, brings up by a commodius vicus."

To my taste, the richest of these Cagean workings with *Finnegans Wake* is *Roaratorio* (1979). Here the plan was to gather local sounds from all the geographic locations mentioned in the *Wake*; and since roughly half of the places are in Ireland, most of these location sounds are audibly Irish. More than two thousand separate acoustic elements were mixed on three sixteen-track machines and then four sixteen-tracks into an hour-long piece. Underneath this dense chaos you can hear, as a sort of ground bass comparable to the Mozart harpsichord music in *HPSCHD,* Cage himself reading from one of his reworkings of *Finnegans Wake*. (A cassette of *Roaratorio* is available in a boxed book published in Germany.)

My interpretation of Cage has been reductionist, I admit; for while acknowledging his diversity, I have sought to identify his imaginative signature in a variety of artistic forms. The reductive suggestion is that Cage, like Moholy before him, confronted each new medium with a definite set of artistic strategies. But this curt summary is not quite true. It is more accurate to say that whereas a monoartist attempts to invent variations on his personal style, the polyartist finds new media for his signature. The polyartist imposes a profoundly different interpretation upon the critical issue of consistency amid variousness — his unities are horizontal, across the arts, rather than vertically down into a single one. In Sibyl Moholy-Nagy's phrase, the polyartist makes "innumerable combinations" that are "part of the same game."

III

The anarchist believes in a state of society wherein there is no frozen power structure, where all persons may make significant initiatory choices in regard to matters affecting their own lives. — Jackson Mac Low, "Statement" (1965)

With that image of anarchism in mind, we can see that there are political implications to Cagean structuring, just as there were political implications to Moholy's characteristic forms; for whereas Moholy and his Bauhaus colleagues would appear to want to wrap up the world in geometric structures (and for that reason were often charged with being fascistic), Cage is interested in creating models of diffusion and freedom. That is what makes him a libertarian, in short an anarchist libertarian. What makes Cage's art special, and to my senses politically original, is that his radical politics are expressed in decisions not of content but of form. For instance, one quality of *HPSCHD*, as well as many other works of his for large ensembles, is that they do not need a conductor. By extension, Cage is implying that outside of music, as well as in, it is possible to create social mechanisms that likewise can function without conductors, without chiefs. In other words, in the form of his art, in the form of performance, is a representation of an ideal polity.

It is precisely in relinquishing traditional opportunities for authority that Cage is making political decisions. As we know, his scores are designed to encourage variety of interpretation. There is no "right way" to do them, though there are wrong ways, especially if a performer violates instructions that are not left to chance. (To my mind, the major problem for Cage criticism in the future will be comparative evaluating of performances. I know this well because I recently avoided this problem in doing the liner notes to yet another recording of his *Sonatas and Interludes*.) A second reflection of his politics is writing music for an ensemble of equals, even when he is one of the performers, thereby resisting such conventional hierarchical forms as a soloist with a backup group. (The fact that this last feature was always true, except for a single work from 1957–58, indicates to me that Cage subscribed to his egalitarian politics long before he was conscious of them.) Thirdly, the principle of all notes being equal extends to objects, as all instruments are equal, regardless of their tradition. In *Credo in Us* (1942), for instance, the piano has no more presence than the home radio or phonograph; all should be equidistant from the audience. Fourth, he has performed his music in gymnasiums as well as opera houses, the assumption being that all venues are equally legitimate. Fifth, his ideal universe is less a state than the preconditions for society. As Paul Goodman put it, "The libertarian is rather a millenarian than a utopian." In another context, Robert Nozick, wrote, "Utopia is metautopia: the environment in which utopian experiments may be tried out; the environment which must, to a certain extent, be realized first if more particular utopian visions are to be realized stably."

One assumption of a compilation like *Notations,* with its equal portions of contributor-selected works in alphabetical order, is that the editor has no more authority than the reader in assigning value. The absence of hierarchy in this book likewise reflect his politics; yet a traditional editor would huffily characterize a book like *Notations* as "an abdication of professional responsibility." Anyone who has ever worked in theater with Cage knows that he believes every performance venue should have convenient exits so that spectators can leave whenever they wish. Capturing anyone's attention, as we say, is to him no more justifiable in art than in life. (Thus a space in which anyone's leaving would be noticed is politically disagreeable.) One truth of Cage's own functioning is that no one loses anything by relinquishing power, but the essence of his method is not to tell but to show.

With that last point in mind, it is instructive to contrast the anarchism of Cage's art with another masterpiece of anarchist art in our time, the Living Theater's production of *Paradise Now,* which was staged two decades ago. Those of us who saw it will remember that *Paradise Now* was structured as a series of sketches designed to elicit audience participation. Thus, it opened with the performers reciting testimony of their own imprisonment: "I can't travel without a passport," they repeatedly proclaimed, confronting and challenging the audience to respond with argument or shocked acceptance. "I am not allowed to take off my clothes." "I don't know how to stop the war," they kept on repeating. From this purgatory the performers progress to sketches of liberation, which is paradise, culminating with members of the audience being invited onstage to leap into the locked arms of male company

members. Structurally, this play is dialectical, moving from antithesis to synthesis; and in this respect, it differs from Cage who hasn't presented any antitheses, as far as I can tell, in at least forty years.

   Another difference is that *Paradise Now* is preachy, Julian Beck even telling us that we've been offered glimpses of the postrevolutonary age. Cage, by
contrast, shows instead of tells, for his assumption is that, in his art at least,
the Promised Land has come. When asked about his response to such programmatic political music as Frederic Rzewski's, Cage said, "I have difficulty
with it, because it's so pushy. It has precisely in it what government has in
it: the desire to control; and it leaves no freedom for me. It pushes me toward
its conclusion, and I'd rather be a sheep, which I'm not, than be pushed along
by a piece of music. I'm just as angry, or refusing to go along with the
'Hallelujah Chorus' as I am with the Attica one [by Rzewski]. The moment
I hear that kind of music I go in the opposite direction. And they use the
technique of repetition, and of sequence, incessantly [as did the Living
Theater, I should add]. And I can do without that."

   One thing that fascinates me about Cage is the purity of his anarchism.
His perceptions are true to his politics; in neither his speech nor his behavior
do I find the kinds of contradictions and compromise that some political people think are opportune for ultimate ends. He is utterly free of pretenses to
superior humanity or false snobbism (and in these respects so utterly different
from his sometime protégé Morton Feldman). I've always regarded Cage as
epitomizing the noncompetitive life, where no one is regarded as a threat who
must be eliminated, where you can afford to be generous with your own work
as well as your possessions, with work so extreme and idiosyncratic that
plagiarism need not be feared. As he has always made a point of publishing
his writings in small magazines as well as large, it is not surprising that his
recent piece on the Satie society bypasses book-publishing entirely to become
available, via a modem, only on your home computer. Even his philosophy
is true to his politics, at a time when, to paraphrase Barnett Newman,
Philosophy is for the artist, especially for some painters nowadays, much as
the Bible is to the minister, which is to say a respectable source that can be
used to justify anything. I recently read scores of interviews with Cage and
have never found him saying anything about his art that was demonstrably
false.

   It is scarcely surprising that in his own professional life he has resisted
not only titles and accompanying power but servility, being neither a boss nor
an employee but instead, both, or more precisely a small businessman with
a peripheral relation to another small business that didn't give him much
power (or until recently make much money) — I'm thinking of the Merce Cunningham Dance Company. In other words, even in his own life there has been
an absence of antitheses. For the academic year 1988–89 Harvard University
offered him a professorship, which gave him one of those titles purportedly

raising its bearer above the nonprofessors. "This is false to our politics," I told him at the time. "Especially if you are to be talking about anarchy, as I've heard, you must insist upon being called the Charles Eliot Norton *Person* of Poetry." Several months later, I asked him, "What is it like to be a Professor at Harvard?" He replied appropriately, "Not much different from not being a professor at Harvard." Right on, comrade.

Another thing I admire about Cage is that, especially in contrast to many post-socialists of his generation, he has never doubled back. He has never said that an earlier position of his was now unacceptably radical. As a result, he's never been an ex-anything in either his esthetics or his politics. His art, as I noted before, has always displayed the anarchist characteristics I'm defining here. I would judge that one reason for his confidence now, in politics as well as esthetics, is that he knew from the beginning that he was never wrong, which I hasten to add is not the same thing as being always right, especially in politics.

I should also add that simply becoming a polyartist is itself a libertarian gesture, an assertion not only that the old pigeonholes should be exploded, but that no one art has a necessarily higher status than any other. (I don't participate in many university conferences, in part because I remember an earlier one where a poet tried to argue that literature represented higher knowledge than that available in the other arts—no, it's just different knowledge in a universe where we all do the Lord's work in different ways.) Need I say that given the professionalism of the arts in America now, it is also a libertarian act to publish poetry without benefit of an M.F.A. —the literary license, so to speak—or to produce scholarhip without benefit of a Ph.D.

In my second, more recent book on Cage, *Conversing with Cage*, which is a mosaic of passages from interviews he has given over the years—an ur-interview, so to speak—the concluding chapter is called "Social Philosophy." Here Cage is asked about having power: "I think we should go over our language and remove all words having to do with power. There are a number of composers who are interested in music becoming more political. They say that our social situation boils down to who has power and who doesn't. If that were so, I'd want to be one of those who were powerless." He continues, "I don't like the words 'greatest' or 'strength.' People are simply different from one another."

When he is asked, "Do you vote?" he answers, "I wouldn't dream of it. I'm looking forward to the time when no one votes. Because then we wouldn't have to have a president. We don't need a president. We can get along perfectly well without the government," which is the modern wisdom that the apolitical can be wiser, or less dangerous, than those who claim to be politically engaged.

Elsewhere Cage objects to the idea of total employment as a social goal: "What we need is a society based on the final possibility; finally we are able

to have unemployment. Most people will tell you that this idea of lov-
ing unemployment is foolishness, because they are afraid that all those people who have nothing to do will go out and murder one another. This is
simply like the bankruptcy of the city, the bankruptcy of the whole society;
we don't have confidence in one another. Think of yourself and imagine
whether you would murder other people if you had nothing else to do. You
know perfectly well that you wouldn't. Why should we think so badly of other
people?"

The last example is more subtle, but profound in showing how his
political bias leads him to question a shibboleth of conventional philosophy.
Bear in mind that here Cage is participating in a symposium moderated by
C. H. Waddington. Someone else says, "I have a feeling that at present the
world has lost a sense of unity at almost all scales, from the individual through
these intermediate neighborhood groupings right up to the world scale." Cage
replies, "I don't find the notion of unity . . . ," but he is cut off by his questioner:
"I should not have said 'unity'; I should have said 'wholeness.'" Cage continues: "Well, how was it that you should have said 'wholeness' and you did
say 'unity'?" I have been thinking about this question of unity and multiplicity,
and for myself I prefer multiplicity. It seems to me to conform more with our
circumstances than unity does."

So the other guy replies: "Unity was a mistake; come on to wholeness."
Cage continues: "But the mistake is very revealing. Wholeness — the only objection I see to wholeness is that it suggests that there are boundaries to the
whole, and then wholeness is like unity. I would rather have 'open-ness,' not
unity or wholeness but open-ness — and open-ness particularly to things with
which I am unfamiliar."

One Cagean tactic that always puzzled me in reading interviews with
him is how he will often rationalize an esthetic move in terms not of ideology
but simply of social benefit. Let me quote an example from my new Cage
book (p. 93), where he says of his *Freeman Etudes* for violin: "They are intentionally as difficult as I can make them, because I think we're now surrounded by very serious problems in the society, and we tend to think that
the situation is hopeless and that it's just impossible to do something that
will make everything turn out properly. So I think that this music, which is
almost impossible [to play], gives an instance of the practicality of the impossible."

Once I recognized this tendency toward social rationalization in Cage's
commentary, I was skeptical about it, thinking it might have represented a
certain opportunism; but the more often I see it, I have come to recognize
Cage as someone who came of age in the 1930s, when ideas about social bet-
terment through art were more plentiful. Indeed, that ethos is the center of
his polyartistry. To me, Cage is essentially a 30s lefty, more interesting than
others who came out of that period because he made some original percep-

tions not only about art but especially about the place of politics in art, and then the possible role of art for politics, all the while remaining true to the sentiment of that time. In my sense of Cage, Zen and chance and everything else came afterwards; they are merely icing on this anarchist cake.

Art Autobiography (1985)

Toward the end of his career, Moholy-Nagy described the purpose of a retrospective exhibition as that of making the spectator "travel" as far as he [the artist] had traveled himself and added, "What a long way to go!"—Frank Popper, *Art-Action and Participation* (1975)

The thought of doing my own visual poetry initially came to me while bored with Antonioni's *Blow-Up* early in July 1967. The next day, I wrote—rather drew—my first poem, "Tributes to Henry Ford," using rulers, French curves and stencils that I purchased at a neighborhood store; and the fact that this five-image poem remains among my most reprinted, most familiar works both pleases and depresses me. I had already seen some visual poetry, initially at London's Institute for Contemporary Art two years before and again in the then-current "concrete" issue of the *Chicago Review*. Even though most of the work collected under that "concrete" label did not appeal to me, the idea of casting language in an alternative visual form struck me as very suggestive.

Much of the glorious summer of 1967, just after my twenty-seventh birthday, was spent working with my new art, producing many pieces that have since become more familiar—"Disintegration," "Echo," "Nymphomania," and the "Football Forms," among others. Some of these early works are explicitly mimetic, my drawing enhancing the legible words in representational ways; for my aim then was the creation of a visual form so appropriate to a certain word that the whole would make an indelible impact—an *afterimage* that would be implanted in the viewer's mind, primarily because the shape endowed the word with certain resonances that would otherwise be unavailable. Though limited by a lack of artistic training, I nonetheless felt obliged to do all the drawing myself; for since my works were poetry, rather than commercial design, they should visibly reveal the idiosyncracies of my amateur hand.

Toward the end of that summer, I discovered the technology of photostating and then began to submit clean, camera-ready copies of my work to periodical editors I knew, mostly because they had published critical essays of mine; but nearly all of them were unresponsive, some even suggesting that I was wasting my time with this poetry. The first editor to accept them was

Paul Carroll, who was then putting together his pioneering anthology, *The Young American Poets* (1968); and my appearance there served the crucial professional function of certifying, in my own mind at least, my status as "a poet" as well as "a critic." To celebrate the publication of his anthology, Carroll sponsored a series of "readings" in New York; and in response to his invitation to participate, I developed the presentational form I still use — "an illuminated demonstration," in which a carousel slide projector throws my visual poems up on a screen, while I, their author, standing behind the audience, declaim a nonsynchronous, voice-over narration that is filled not with specific explanations but general concepts that the audience may or may not choose to relate to what they see. Seventeen years ago, I had only enough slides to fill a single carousel tray; now I can fill several and often project two different sets of images simultaneously.

Since a book's worth of poems existed almost from the beginning, I decided, early in 1968, to dedicate the volume to my most inventive teacher at college, S. Foster Damon, and even announced the dedication that February at Foster's 75th birthday party. Copies of my pioneering collection were submitted to several publishers, some of whom had previously issued books of mine; none of them took it. By 1970 I reluctantly recognized that commercial publishers in America were not yet hospitable to visual poetry. (Many years later, none of them have yet matured that far, even though this sort of poetry has by now been published and exhibited widely.) It was thus inevitable that *Visual Language* should be published under the imprint of Assembling Press, which I had confounded that summer; and in printing the book, I had two ulterior motives in mind: I wanted to see this work reviewed (it wasn't) and I needed sufficient copies to distribute to anthologists and friends. Photostats were becoming an unnecessary nuisance and expense.

The publication of *Visual Language* also forced me to consider alternative ways of making nonsyntactic visual poetry. I tried to make a complete visual alphabet, parts of which are reprinted in my second collection, *I Articulations* (1974); I also compiled collections of synonyms that were then visually enhanced, such as the "Live-Kill" pair (1972) that I personally consider among my very best pieces. Another new development, begun in 1970, is the handwritten visual poem, such as "The East Village" (1970–71). Here I wanted to get away from the centered space and single perceptual perspective of my earlier work. Since I am scarcely able to invent a situation from scratch — or, to be more precise, since my mind is more inventive with materials than imaginative with situations — I chose a familiar subject: the neighborhood in which I then lived. As my theme was the variousness of the individual side streets, each of which has its own characteristic spatial qualities, its own details, and its own sounds, I did a one-page portrait in language and space for each block. I thought of hiring a professional calligrapher to redo my peculiar handwriting, but the single sample I saw reminded me too much of the rigors of linotype. And *that* was precisely what I was trying to avoid. So, once again, the best solution was letting the work reveal my own hand. I originally wanted Assembling Press to publish "The East Village" as a single book, on large 11″ by 17″ pages. However, since twelve images seemed insufficient for a book, even in such a large format, I eventually incorporated the work into the 7″ by 10″ pages of *I Articulations*. A later, longer handwritten poem, "Portraits from Memory," appeared as an entire 35-page book (1975), in which each page contains a verbal-visual portrait of a woman I might have known. Here, as elsewhere in my work, the titles of individual pieces tend to be rather explicit.

I had always thought that my best visual poems should appear in enlarged forms, not only to make them available for gallery exhibitions but also to enhance their afterimage capabilities. Back in 1970, I made a large photostat of "Concentric" for a two-person exhibition. In the summer of 1974, I took a silkscreening course which resulted in a few enlarged prints; but since my technical competence remained limited, in the following year I commissioned a printmaker to produce *Word Prints*, a set of seven, 26″ by 40″. By 1976, I got into photolinens, with images even larger than the prints, and had them stretched, much like paintings, over wooden bars. As I have never painted, just as I've eschewed sculpture, I feel of two minds about the fact that these photolinens look very much like black-white paintings.

By the time my third collection of short poems, *Illuminations* (1977), appeared, I felt that my previous ways of making poetry were no longer so fertile, which is to say that the new variations were no better than my earlier work and did not advance it in any discernible way. As my esthetics incorporate an ethics of transcendence, not only of my previous work but of myself, it became necessary for me to go on to something else. Two new solutions for poetry came to mind in the summer of 1979, when I was an artist-in-residence at Mishkenot Sha'ananim in Jerusalem. The first I call Strings, which are extended lines of letters composed of overlapping words. To be precise, each new word incorporates at least three (or, in one earlier case, two) letters of the preceding word. Typed out, these strings are roughly 100 inches long, and they have been published in literary journals with their extended lines broken by hyphens. However, remembering my interest in transcending the typewritten or printed page, I began to think about how else these Strings might be published. Since the long word is really one unit that should not be broken apart, I hand-lettered them on continuous adding machine tape and exhibited them in that format.

Early in 1980 I received from the National Endowment for the Arts a Visual Arts Planning Grant for Art in Public Spaces, and that got me thinking. I figured that the best place to "publish" these Strings—to make them available to the public—would be in an extended public space, such as the wall or a long hallway, like that at an airport or, better yet, the floor along the edge of a train platform. As I envision the latter, the letters should be brass and they should be embedded in the platform floors with their bottoms away from the train, perhaps three feet in from the edge of the platform; and I calculate that if these letters were 4" high, in a lower case condensed typeface, the piece would be 200 feet long, which is roughly the length of a New York City subway station. Because these Strings are, to be frank, linguistically difficult and thus cannot be fully comprehended in a few minutes — in this last respect they are not like most public sculptures or wall murals — they need an audience with time to spare, which is to say people waiting for a train. I imagine that travelers will observe the section in front of them, fully aware that they can be disturbed by friends or by the oncoming train, because the work with all its variations on the three-letter constraint will be available to them again the next time they return to the station. I also wrote a String in French and then others in German and Swedish, partly because I wanted to see how the same techniques would work in another language, but also because I hoped that sponsors in Paris, Berlin, Montreal, or Stockholm might be interested. To several American cities that have recently held competitions for public art, I have made proposals; but none have scored yet. My assumption is that just as it took me years to publish my poems in books, so it will take years for them to appear in public spaces. Precedent suggests that happen they eventually will.

Whereas the Strings are not visual poetry, as I understand that term, but verbal poems whose optimal form of publication is visually unusual, especially for poetry, the other new development in my poetry is, in certain respects, closer to my earlier work. I began by putting individual words in each of the four corners of the rectangular page, attempting to discover how four spatially distant words can make more than the sum of their parts. As before, once I determined my constraint, I did numerous variations. Sometimes, it seems to me, the four words reinforce one another through complementary relationships; other times, one word stands out from the others precisely because it is not a complement — perhaps an antonym or perhaps a word that comments critically upon the other three. Sometimes as well, the words cohere in terms of sound, other times in terms of visual qualities, such as length or common neology. These poems are dedicated to Anton von Webern, because they descend from my love and experience of his style of an aural pointillism informed by linguistic rigor. Ideally, in pages so dominated not by black but white, the *poetry* arises between the words.

Later I made two more sets of poems in this vein — one set with eight words to a rectangle and then another with sixteeen words to a frame; and in these as well, the words within each poem relate to each other in various ways. While I feel, on one hand, that four words to a page may be too sparse for poetry, I am not so sure that the more populous poems are necessarily more poetic. The first selection of just four-word poems, a diminutive chapbook entitled *Turfs/Arenas/Fields/Pitches*, appeared in 1980; the first full collection of all three strains, *Arenas/Fields/Pitches/Turfs*, appeared in 1982. I should like to see two more collections that would complete this phase, "Fields/Pitches/ Turfs/Arenas" and "Pitches/Turfs/Arenas/Fields." More recently, I have been working with just two words and three words laid across the page, and then groups of words in circular forms; the collection of these is tentatively titled "Duets, Trios & Choruses." I still enjoy visual poetry more than the movies.

II

Each novelist, each novel must invent its own form. No recipe can replace this continual reflection. The book makes its own rules for itself, and for itself alone. — Alain Robbe-Grillet, "The Use of Theory" (1955)

Probably from the time I began to read I had am ambition to write fiction, but everything I drafted between my freshman year of college and early 1968 eventually struck me as an obvious echo of some text I already admired. At least seven times I began a novel that, upon close inspection, was clearly an imitation of Nathanael West's great work, *The Day of the Locust*; and so this ambition subsided, along with my dreams of becoming a professional football player or a rock musician. I felt no need to recapitulate what had already been written, and did not yet know how to write what had not.

In doing poetry, I had discovered early the idea of a constraint so severe that it would prevent me from using language in familar forms; and that primary initial restriction was the use of only one word that would then be visually enhanced. An imposed constraint, I discovered, serves to force the creative imagination to resist convention, if not cliché; and like meter in traditional poetry, the constraint I chose also encourages puzzle-solving and other forms of playfulness. This approach struck me as rather useful at generating original work; and perhaps the easiest measure of the difference or newness of my work is whether or not the reader feels challenged to discern sense and significance in what at first seems inscrutable.

Early in 1968, I began to think about a similar kind of severe constraint for writing fiction; and after a few abortive experiments, I hit upon the hypothesis of writing a story with no more than two words to a paragraph. For a subject, I chose the conveniently familiar one of boy meets girl. This plot appears frequently in my fiction, not because I have anything particularly profound to say about heterosexual encounters, but because a familiar, transparent subject makes both myself and my readers more aware of the technical issues that really interest me. Once the two-word paragraphs of "One Night Stood" were drafted, I typed them out, indenting alternate lines;

and the following winter I realized that each two-word phrase could take up the entire page of a book, thereby expanding the story into a minimal novel (that was not published until 1977). Subsequent verbal fictions are similarly skeletal — "Excelsior," with only one word to a paragraph; "Milestones in a Life," in which chronological numbers are followed by just a single word or sometimes two; and "Dialogue," which is composed of only two words, "Yes" and "No," repeated in different ways.

In the summer of 1969, I discovered how to make visual fiction, realizing an implication of my much-reprinted "Football Forms" — that images in sequence could tell a story, whose temporal rhythm is based upon the time a typical reader takes to turn the page; and that perception informed not only my alphabet novella, *In the Beginning* (1971), but also my first abstract fictions — those consisting only of lines, lacking words, save for their titles. That summer I also drafted the theoretical statement, "Twenty-Five Fictional Hypotheses," that even a decade and a half later is still reprinted for its radical possibilities. It suggests, among other things, that anything can be used to tell a story, not only nonsyntactic language but visual materials as well; and of course I practiced what I preached. I also noticed a crucial difference between poetry and fiction, even on the avant-garde fringes: Whereas the former tends to concentrate both image and effect, fiction creates a world of related activity.

A further development in my storytelling is the work composed of sequential four-sided symmetrical line-drawings that metamorphose in systemic sequence. Begun in 1974, these "constructivist fictions," as I call them, presently include two published collections of short stories, *Constructs* (1974) and *Constructs Two* (1978); two novellas that are discussed later, *Modulations* (1975) and *Extrapolate* (1975); and two more unpublished collections, in addition to two full-length novels that will both soon be published — *Symmetries* and *Intermix*. Remembering my NEA Planning Grant, I have also proposed putting some of these in public spaces, such as the floor of a long hallway or even on a private roadway; so that people in transit could inadvertently experience visual fiction as they moved from one point to another. (Imagine experiencing stories overhead or underfoot!) However, no luck yet, although I expect that they too will sometime be.

Another variation of this Constructivist theme is *And So Forth*, a visual fiction in which the geometric images are, by contrast, *not* perfect symmetries and their order is *not* fixed. These were published not in a perfectbound book, like the other Constructivist fictions, but loose in an envelope in 1979. They have also been exhibited over the walls of a fairly large space.

In the summer of 1970, I drafted another verbal fiction, entitled *Openings & Closings*, which remains, in one crucial respect, the most conventional imaginative piece I have ever written — it contains full sentences! Nonetheless, it resembles my other verbal fictions in observing a truncating constraint; for whereas the earlier stories had one or two words to a paragraph, here I decided to suggest, within single sentences, either a story that might follow or one that could have gone before. The isolated sentences are literally either the openings (of hypothetically subsequent stories) or the closings (of hypothetically previous stories). These could be considered incomplete stories, it is true; yet it was my aim to make a single sentence be artistically sufficient (and let readers imagine the rest). As there is no internal connection between any particular opening or any closing, I thought from the beginning that the stories should best be set in two different styles of type—italics for the openings, roman for the closings— with plenty of white space between them; but not until 1975 was the book published. Invited, in 1976, to exhibit *Openings & Closings* in a gallery, I typed the sentences out on individual cards—one card to a sentence—again using italic for the openings and roman for the closings. These cards were then scattered, in no particular order, initially over a display board and later around a gallery's walls. I like this work for its leaps in space and the changes of its voices and tones, from item to adjacent item.

In an earlier version of this essay (prepared for the catalogue of my first retrospective), I declared that I would never again use expository sentences in fiction; but fortunately, the practice of art comes before my principles or even my theorizing. Early in 1979, I began writing single-sentence stories that would be not the beginning of a story or its end but its epiphany, which is to say the supremely resonant moment that, in James Joyce's theory, locks the rest of the story into place. Once again I had to tell the whole story, or at least suggest the remainder of the story, within a single sentence. I have written over two thousand of these and have likewise put them on individual cards that could fill an exhibition space with an abundance of stories; for this work, *Epiphanies*, like *Openings & Closings* before it, is in part about the exhaustive experience of the experience of fiction. Selections from this text also became the base for my first theater piece, likewise entitled *Epiphanies*, which will be discussed later.

III

Beyond the style of an individual, a period, or a race, there are higher forms, a language common to all human intelligence. Without some trace of this universal language, art is not possible. . . . This universal language depends on the science of numbers (especially of simple ones); of Mathematics, whose application to the plastic arts, necessarily spatial, constitutes geometry. —Paul Serusier, "ABC of Painting" (1921)

In my first numerical work, "Accounting," drafted early in 1969, I wanted to see if numbers could be used in lieu of words or letters; and that numerical piece was also the first of its kind to appear in print, initially in my anthology *Future's Fiction* (1971) and then as a separate booklet (1973). The profession of accounting, like this numerical piece, documents processes of accumulation; but not until 1972, when preparing a revised version for chapbook publication, did I realize that this incremental sequence should end, like an accountant's tabulation, with a row of zeroes. That new numerical conclusion gave the narrative an ironic twist that, in my judgment, enhanced the work considerably. *Accounting* visually resembles my novella *In the Beginning*, composed around the same time; but whereas the former comes to a definite end, the final page of the latter suggests that the narrative could continue forever. That diametric difference in their sequential form indicates, of course, comparable differences in meaning.

Late in 1972, I set everything else aside to see how far I could take my growing interest in numbers—to see whether I could create a literature composed of numbers alone. I thought at the time that I was making a book of "poems & stories," remembering my earlier distinction. However, by the following year, I realized that these works were actually becoming something else—a "numerature," perhaps; a *numerical art*, to be sure. My aim in working with numbers was no longer the writing of poems and stories but the creation of a numerical field that is both visually and numerically coherent, with varying degrees of visual-numerical complexity. These works do not merely incorporate numerals within visual concerns, like, say, certain Jasper Johns paintings; my pieces are literally about the language of numbers. A principal difficulty in communicating this work, I belatedly discovered, is that audiences must be *numerate* to comprehend them, much as they must be *literate* to read modernist poetry and fiction.

My opening arrangements were numerically simple. "1024," for instance, incorporates both the parts and the factors of that variously divisible number, while "Indivisibles" is a field of visually unrelated numbers whose common property is that no number can be divided into any of them (except, of course, themselves and one). As before, titles in my works tend to be explicit. Realizing that I wanted arithmetical patterns that could, like art (and unlike puzzles), be numerically appreciated again and again, I then tried to create numerical fields whose relationships were more multiple and less obvious. In works like the diamond-shaped "Parallel Intervals," I began, I think, to approach the levels of complexity that I admire in serial music and *Finnegans Wake*, for numbers were more conducive than words to my penchants for rigorous systems, structural complexity, and geometric order. (Simply because one number can go next to any other number, numerical syntax, unlike that of words, is also infinitely permissible.) In addition, these number pieces realize an empirical ideal that, though esthetically heretical, has long haunted me—that all the artistic activity that one identified in the work could be *verified* by another observer and yet be rich enough to be appreciated again and again. My first numerical prints were done in 1974 and the first numerical photolinens in 1975. *Numbers: Poems & Stories* (1976) reprints several works in a large newsprint format, while *Numbers Two* (1977) collects several more in an envelope. *Exhaustive Parallel Intervals* (1979) is an elaborate book-length sequence — a novel of sorts — composed entirely of the magical diamond mentioned before. I sometimes think that with these numerical pieces I have made the most rational art that anyone has ever made.

IV

A correct interpretation of Webern requires absolute rigor and an utter contempt for expressive lights and shades. Webern was the forerunner of an "abstract music" which was later to be developed by Boulez, Stockhausen and a few others. He was the first to reject every kind of sentimental appurtenance, distilling beauty from form alone. — André Hodier, *Since Debussy* (1961)

In the spring of 1974, I completed *Recyclings*, the third and most successful of my initial experiments with nonsyntactic prose. *Recyclings* was made by subjecting earlier essays of mine to selective processes that destroyed their original syntax, while retaining their characteristic language. (Another example from this period is the shorter text "Declaration of Independence," in which I freed myself from syntax, declared myself independent of it, by writing the historic American document backwards, word by word.) These pages of *Recyclings* literally recycle my language, but destroy the original linearity of these words. Thus, these new pages can be read not only horizontally, like normal prose, but also vertically, as the eyes, moving down and around the page, can perceive not only consistencies in diction but repeated words that usually indicate an identifiable ulterior source or subject. I subtitled this work "A Literary Autobiography," as it recapitulates everything I have written. An inaugural volume of 64 pages was published as a chapbook in 1974; the complete text, all 320 pages, appeared a decade later. A collection of my other experiments with prose should appear sometime soon, under the characteristically descriptive title of *Prose Pieces*.

Considering how to declaim *Recyclings* aloud, I hit upon a performance structure that would aurally incorporate both the horizontal and the vertical: recruiting a chorus of readers, each of whom would speak the text horizontally, one word after another; but rather than read in unison, each new reader would begin to speak approximately one line behind his or her predecessor. Since I was aiming not for any specific vertical juxtapositions, but just for constant vertical relationships, each speaker could go at his own pace, and in his own manner. I assumed that an audience listening carefully would hear vertical relationships — words spoken simultaneously, much like chords in music — amid the horizontal polyphonic declamation.

When invited to be a guest artist at the new radio studios of WXXI-FM, Rochester, NY, March, 1975, I realized a seven-track *Recyclings* in which all the declamatory voices are my own, each one amplified differently from the others. Although it was my opening intention to realize aurally certain qualities that were visually present in *Recyclings*, I found that the experience of listening to this audiotape was really something else. This is not poetic declamation, as we customarily know it, but something closer to the performance of a musical score, probably because it mixes a language text with compositional structures more typical of music. Though "sound poetry" to some and "text-sound" to others, I prefer to classify this particular audiopiece as "sound prose," because the basic material is not poetry but prose.

V

In neue Hörspiel, *the author mostly does not write a text for someone else to produce but produces it himself. You can compare it with the history of filmmaking. That medium began with authors and texts. Now we have filmmakers. The authors of* neue Hörspiel *must familiarize themselves with the techniques of the mass media. They can change the mass media with their imaginations.* — Klaus Schöning, in an interview (1981)

My other early audiotapes were largely straight declamations of my truncated stories, amplified and enhanced in various, comparatively modest ways. For *Openings & Closings*, I put the opening sentences on one side of a stereo system, and the closing sentences on the other; and in *Foreshortenings*, a later verbal fiction, a voice clearly identifiable as mine swaps single-sentence lines with a chorus of my voice, both sides speaking the same repertoire of eighty-four simple sentences in increasingly different ways. (The principal reason why my own voice takes both sides of this and other early audio conversations is that most of my early tapes were done late at night, with only an engineer and myself present in the studio. And someone else had to watch the voice levels on the recording machines!)

In a later group of works I favored familiar religious and political texts, such as the "Declaration of Independence" (1976) or the Lord's Prayer, that are electronically modified in ways that would make them aurally incomprehensible to most ears, were not the texts already familiar. Indeed, religious materials strike me as especially suitable for electronic enhancement, which generally increases the implications of sacredness. Sometime after completing the first version of "Praying to the Lord" (1977, 1981), where a single voice speaking a familiar text is electronically multiplied into a vibrantly cacophonous chorus, I came across R. Murray Schafer's observation, in *The Tuning of the World* (1977), that "it was not until the Renaissance that God became portraiture. Previously he had been conceived as sound or vibration."

In the back of my mind, when I began this piece, was the experience, that previous summer, of seeing the valley to the west of Mount Sinai, and then imagining the presence of thousands of noisy Israelites waiting for Moses to return. Vibration, I now thought, could also be interpreted as the sound of the multitudes venerating God. Schafer's remark also reminds me of Marshall McLuhan's observation that electronic media of communication recreate the sensory experience of preprint peoples.

In 1981, I began to do longer, more complicated audio pieces. While a guest of the DAAD Kunstlerprogramm in Berlin, I taped over sixty Berlin ministers speaking prayers in over two dozen languages. These tapes were then sent to the Electronic Music Studio of Stockholm, where I mixed them on a twenty-four track machine into overlapping solos, duets, quintets, and choruses that were then assembled into a piece one hour long. After years of doing only short works, I wanted to make a piece as long as an oratorio is long and actually had in mind the structural example of J. S. Bach's *St. Matthew Passion.* Another theme in my head at the time I associate with James Joyce's *Finnegans Wake* — the theme of telling the same story in many languages that are interwoven. In this case the subject was that sound that makes all prayers sound ultimately alike, which is to say the metalanguage of prayer. One quality I like about *Invocations,* as this piece is called, is putting into the same acoustic space prayers that would not otherwise be heard together, and for that strategy alone the work is meant to be ecumenical. When it was first played on New York radio, the composer Tui St. George Tucker telephoned to suggest, appropriately, "This must be what God hears."

Back in 1977, inspired by the audiofugues of Glenn Gould's radio documentary, *The Idea of North* (1967), I thought of experimenting with the experience of hearing simultaneously four different voices speaking the first four books of the New Testament. The Gospels struck me as an appropriate text for such a speech quartet, not only because they tell the same story in four different ways, but because that story and its phrases are so familiar that the audience need not follow the plot or understand every word to recognize it. I also wanted to create a sound piece that would be so long, while its purposes would always be so present, that the listener could neglect it for a while — even walk away — and still fluently resume the experience when he or she returned. This constant presentness is a radical structure I associate with John Cage's musical theater pieces of the past two decades, as well as Merce Cunningham's dance events. The reason why the spectator can miss any passage in passing is that each work is continuously about the same thing, which is the style of itself. In my piece, the "thing" is, simply, the fugal experience of the four Gospels or, to put it differently, the experience of Matthew-John-Luke-Mark, which is perhaps the Ur-Gospel from which the others are descended. My proposal was commissioned by Westdeutscher

Rundfunk in 1981. Since my knowledge of German is scanty, Klaus Schön-ing, my producer at WDR, was kind enough to commission an English ver-sion that became a sort of warm-up for the German version. The German is 60 minutes long; the other, 120 minutes long.

Another 1981 audiotape draws upon a story entitled "Seductions" that was published in *More Short Fictions* (1980). There the story appears as con-tinuous prose in sixteen different styles of typeface. Each typeface contains a continuous narrative that is here, one sentence at a time, intermittently in-terwoven with the others. All sixteen stories deal with the narrator's memories of his seductions of women, for the fiction as a whole is about unity (of a single repeated plot) amid diversity. For audiotape I duplicated the printed struc-ture, so that each story is told in the acoustic analogue of a distinctly different typeface—in an audibly different version of my voice. The individual recorded stories were then cut apart into sentences that were, as in the printed version, reassembled into a continuous stream, now a tape, that jumps from one voice to another, until all the stories become a single story with sixteen interwoven voices. The tone of *Seductions* is ostensibly erotic, much as the tone of *Invoca-tions* is continuously religious; for Audio Art, even at its most experimental, can deal with the most important human subjects.

In a more recent work about the sound of my hometown, *New York City* (1984), I took hours of field recordings of both speech and other sounds into the Stockholm studio where I worked before. In these field recordings, I tried to focus upon sounds that I thought unique to New York—that announced New York merely by their acoustic presence. However, in putting them together, I was less interested in documenting scenes than in combining sounds, often from disparate sources, to evoke sonic qualities that I likewise regarded as indigenous. Because the producer commissioning it, Klaus Schöning, wanted a piece much shorter than what I had in mind, *New York City* presently exists in two versions—one 140 minutes long, which I call the American version; and an International version 60 minutes long, with con-siderably less speech, that was broadcast over Westdeutscher Rundfunk in April 1984. Because this work has an associational, incremental structure, I have also been able to excerpt sections from it, for concerts and for an exhibi-tion. However, what I ultimately have in mind for it is a full-evening's piece, a kind of oratorio, where the longer tape will be accompanied by perhaps 3,000 or 5,000 slides of images that were likewise unique to New York. Another possibility in the back of my mind is making my American *New York City* the soundtrack of a film that would likewise be composed of distinctly hometown images.

The main distinguishing characteristics of my audiotapes so far have been, first, the use of inventive, uncommon language structures, whether truncated lines or nonsyntactic or scrambled sentences; the exploitation of the technologies available in a sophisticated multitrack studio; and then the realization of aural experiences that would be unfeasible, if not impossible, in live performance. It makes no sense for me or anyone else to do in one medium something that could be done better in another.

VI

Each electronic medium has come into its own only when we recognized its newness and stopped trying to use it as a container of the old. — Tony Schwartz, *Media: The Second God* (1981)

Late in 1975, I was invited to be a guest artist at the Synapse video studio of Syracuse University. Here I worked not with a single engineer-producer, as I had at WXXI-FM, but with an institutional staff of young instructors, graduate assistants, and undergraduates. With their help, I realized video versions of four earlier texts. To do "Excelsior," a truncated story in which two people make love in one-word paragraphs, I created a circular visual image for each character. As voices change from one gender to another, the screen flashes rapidly from one moving image to the other. In "Plateaux," with its single-word paragraphs, each relating a different stage (or plateau) in the development of a love affair, we used video feedback to create a kaleidoscopic moiré pattern that changes slowly in no particular direction, complementing visually the pointless, ultimately circular development of the fiction's plot. For *Openings & Closings*, I instructed the large crew, first, to alternate between color cameras for the openings and black-white cameras for the closings, and then to make each new image (mostly of me reading) as different as possible from the one before, thus realizing visually the leaps of time and space that characterize the radically discontinuous prose text. Finally, whereas the audio *Recyclings* has nonsyntactic prose read by nonsynchronous voices (all mine), for the color video I hit upon the image of pairs of speaking lips (all mine again) — one pair of lips for the first "Recycling," two pairs for the second text, etc. We went up to eight pairs of lips in the studio; however, one-inch videotape that has been passed, or superimposed, eight times has an electronically unstable signal, so not only were the last two generations lost completely, but the next two (counting backwards) had to be reshot in black and white to survive on tape. Were *Recyclings* to be redone in a professional quad (two-inch tape) studio, all the images would have a much surer chance of surviving in their optimal form.

In 1977, long frustrated in my desire to work with the sophisticated video equipment necessary for my technologically complex ideas, I began to think about working with the more limited possibilities of ½" or ¾" videotape. Most of the short pieces I made in this format exploit a contrast between words that are heard and facial images that are seen, as the camera's close-up eye assimilates only part of the speaking figure.

In 1979, I discovered a video technology whose artistic possibilities have scarcely been utilized—the character-generator, which is the machine that creates letters that appear on the screen, most familiarly in the credits at the end of a program. Remembering my "Declaration of Independence," I sat before a camera only inches away from my lips and then read the nonsyntactic text four times in approximate unison, with each successive declamation allowing the camera to show a little bit more of my bearded mouth. Since this text is, to be sure, inscrutable on first hearing, especially if read by a chorus of identical voices, I used the character-generator to run a silent commentary about the piece across the bottom of the screen—the letters "crawl," as they say, from right to left.

Later that year I took some of the epiphanies mentioned before and with a character-generator set them in various typographical arrays, white letters against a dark background, mostly one story to an image, duplicating an idea I had developed earlier in a film composed entirely of words, which thus must be *read*, quite rapidly, to be "seen." The common joke is that these imageless films and videotapes are "all titles, no action." What makes such entirely verbal tapes and films interesting to me are two complementary phenomena: the inordinate concentration required of the viewers, who realize that they must pay constant, strict attention if they are to see everything, and then the experience of reading in unison, with a crowd of strangers, in contrast to the conventional literary experience of reading a text of one's own choosing, at one's own speed, by oneself. The second set of early films, made in collaboration with Peter Longauer, shot the Constructivist Fictions in negative, so that four-sided symmetries of white lines appear on the black screen in sequences that are systematically composed (complementing the systematic composition of the individual images). I returned to film in 1981 with *Epiphanies*, which will be discussed later. Of all the media in which I have worked, film requires the most laboring time and seems, in terms of what I should ultimately like to do with it, the least maturative.

VII

Abstraction is not only a product of artistic creation, it is already present and primary in our intuition of reality. We just do not see reality as it simply presents itself. . . . What is seen is something quite different from a photographic image, because in intuition we grasp something abstractly, that is, by doing away with the inessential, the incidental, and manifold, and by laying bare the essential simple form of the figure. . . . Finally, wholly abstract forms are attained, such as circles, triangles, squares or crosses, the geometrical elements of all forms, which thus result as more developed abstractions of real figures. —Robert Havemann, "Learning to See and Learning to Think" (1964)

In the summer of 1977, I finally completed photographs worth preserving. I had been thinking about the art of photography ever since doing my documentary monograph on *Moholy-Nagy* (1970), for the example of Moholy taught me not only that I could work in several arts at once but that, if I chose to do photography, I should create images that could exist only as photographs — that would not be "moments" from films, say, or extensions of documentary reportage. After several abortive experiments, I hit upon the idea of taking a single 8″ by 10″ photograph of myself, cutting it apart into eighty equally sized squares, and then recomposing these squares into eighty new pictures which I called *Reincarnations*. Given that my feelings about exact systems were vacillating at that time, the geometric rearrangements of these photographs are only roughly, or incompletely, systemic, while the order of the images is not fixed. (The structural analogue in my Constructivist Fiction is *And So Forth*, which was done around the same time.) For a second sequential piece, *Recall*, completed in 1979, each of the photographs is recomposed within slightly varying, scrupulously systemic principles; and the order of the pictures is fixed. At the time that examples of *Reincarnations* first appeared in print, I did not own a camera and never had; but one theme of this Moholyan memoir is that the lack of such prerequisites, let alone "education," should never prevent me, or anyone else, from working in any art.

VIII

Nor is it altogether an illusion to suppose that each artist, no matter how self-willed, is in some degree used by his genre for the purpose of elaborating its own possibilities. —
Harold Rosenberg, "The Vanishing Spectator" (1967)

The next step would take me into holography, a new technology for three-dimensional photography that surpasses the stereoscope of photographic history. I had followed the development of this new art for over a decade without generating any ideas for working with it until I saw a circular (360°), cylindrical, rotating hologram. Then, it occurred to me that I could use one of my favorite artistic materials, the English language, to write syntactically circular, grammatically seamless statements. I had used this circular form before, in the "Manifestoes" that opens *Visual Language* and was subsequently reprinted as a broadside poster (1975); so I recognized that it would be appropriate in a 360° hologram. Since the words of my earlier circular work dealt with my theories of visual poetry, it followed that my initial hologram should contain syntactically circular statements about holography and that it should likewise have an explicit title, *On Holography*.

In their original, typed-out form, the statements looked like this:

holos = complete; gram = message;
representation in depth = hologram =

The hologram creates a world of incorporeal activity that exists only within
the illusion not only of depth but of equal focus to all distances are
characteristics particular to holography which creates
by capturing on photo-sensitive material the amplitude, the wave-length
and, most important, the phases of light reflected off an object a
hologram reconstructs a three-dimensional image

In the hologram, the ends of these lines are attached to each other, making
the statements visually circular and linguistically continuous. As these
statements have different word-lengths, they inevitably vary in circumference. As the largest one is at the bottom and the shortest one on top, the
five statements visually make a pyramidal form.

Rather than having the statements turn in unison, as a stationary
pyramid, I wanted each line to revolve at a different speed. Given the nature
of the circular hologram, they had to move in ratios of 1:2:3:4, with the
longest statement at the base. Thus, at the same time the longest statement
runs once around and the entire circumference of the cylinder, the second
statement is repeated twice around the cylinder and the third statement three
times around and the shortest statements, placed atop each other, move in
unison four times around the cylinder. Therefore, during the time it takes the
cylinder to complete one revolution, the bottom statement can be read once
in its entirety, the second statement twice, the third statement three times and
the top pair of statements four times.

However, since the circles made by these statements have different cir-
cumferences, a contrary effect occurs: Their words *appear* to move before
one's eyes at roughly the *same* speed. That is, at the same time that the bottom
line traverses its entire thirty words, the second line moves 20×2 words, and
the third line 12×3 words and the top two lines each 4×4 words. At first I
thought this unanticipated result of visually equal progress might sabotage my
original desire for the appearance of different linear speeds. However, I later
realized that, had the lengths of the upper levels not been respectively doubled,
tripled and quadrupled, the movement of the top line's words would have
been very slow, if not boring, while that of the bottom line would have been
intolerably fast. In any case, *On Holography* was indubitably holographic in
that its effects could exist only within a hologram.

For its initial exhibition, at New York's Museum of Holography, I added
an audiotape of five voices reading the same words on individually continuous, aurally seamless audiotape loops. These voices were then mixed
down into a single cassette that went through stereo speakers beside the
hologram, so that spectators could hear in five-voice unison the same words
that they might see in five-line unison. In more extravagant circumstances,
these voices might emerge from four different speakers that would surround
the spectators.

IX

In the old art the writer judges himself as being not responsible for the real book. He writes the text. The rest is done by the servants, the workers, the others.

  In the new art writing a text is only the first link in the chain going from the writer to the reader. In the new art the writer assumes the responsibility for the whole process.

  In the old art the writer writes texts.

  In the new art the writer makes books. — Ulises Carrión, "The New Art of Making Books" (1980)

Books edited by me began appearing in 1964, books authored by me in 1968; but only with the publication in 1970 of *Visual Language* did I begin to design certain books of mine as well. Concomitantly, my critical interest in alternative forms of book-making goes back to critical essays I published in 1968 and 1969 (and subsequently reprinted in the last section of this book). Not until 1975, however, did I realize that Book Art as such was a conscious creative concern of mine, and by "book art" I mean books that are not just rectangular vehicles for their contents but works of art in themselves, usually because of their unusual and yet appropriate forms. Once I understood what I had been doing, I immediately produced a set of volumes that explore alternative book forms: the accordion books, *Modulations* and *Extrapolate* (both 1975); the handwritten book, *Portraits from Memory* (1975); a chapbook with horizontal images spread over two open pages, *Come Here* (1975); a book composed of cards that can be read in any order, *Rain Rains Rain* (1976); the book with two fronts, *Prunings/Accruings* (1977); and two tabloid-sized newsprint books, *Numbers: Poems & Stories* (1976) and *One Night Stood* (1977). That last title also appeared as a small paperback book, 4" by 5"; for the existence of both editions offers the illustrative contrast of reading the same fictional text of two-word paragraphs in two radically different book forms and thus, perhaps, how perceptibly different the two formats can be.

More recently I have done two blank books, one a collection of stories entitled *Inexistences* (1978) and the other a novel, *Tabula Rasa* (1978), each of which has a single-page preface that connects it to my earlier work — these are Constructivist Fictions of an escatalogical sort. I also did a book, mentioned before, of sheets gathered in an envelope, *And So Forth* (1969); and a novel composed entirely of numbers, *Exhaustive Parallel Intervals* (1979); and I am presently completing *Symmetries*, a Constructivist novel of 384 images whose 96 pages will be a 4½" high and 17" wide and thus open to be 34" wide across one's lap, as the sequence of slightly evolving images will be eight abreast. My newest full-sized book-art book is *Autobiographies* (1981), which is not a sustained continuous narrative but a multiperspective collection of bits, written both recently and long ago, not only by me but by others; for it was my experiment to discover if this kind of piecemeal, cubistic autobiography could be more true, not just to myself but also to my history, than a more conventional self-narrative. In certain respects, it is the most traditional of my book-art books, being 288 rectangular pages that are bound along one side; in other ways, it is the most audacious in using the book medium for a radical reinterpretation of the epistemology of biography and, by extension, of all historiography.

X

In the Renaissance an artist who was, for example, exclusively a painter could not possibly be recognized as a truly significant personality. Many artists of the period excelled in a variety of skills. — Alexis Rannit, in *New Directions 38* (1979)

Of the current projects, *Epiphanies* is the most ambitious and most suggestive. It began as a text of single-sentence stories that were offered to literary-magazine editors, who were invited to select whichever ones they preferred and then to publish their selections in whatever order they wished. (Some editors, needless to say, spurned this cordial invitation to exercise their editorial intelligence, two even returning the manuscript to me as, they insisted, "unedited.") These *Epiphanies* were then also typed on over two thousand cards for an exhibition that could fill a fairly large space, and the stories appeared as well on the small screen in the character-generated videotape mentioned before.

In addition, the text became the basis for a theatrical experiment. I had known since the middle 1970s that I wanted to write performance texts that would be structurally radical: They would not have dialogues, they would have no instructions for setting or costumes; they would avoid plots, characters and all those other crutches that conventional playwrights use to push the evening along. My scripts would simply be lines — resonant lines that were hopefully so vivid and compelling they could command theatrical attention merely by being evocatively spoken. I wrote several texts in this vein, a few of them reflecting the influence of Gertrude Stein, and then put the entire project away for later work (that I still expect to do). By 1980 I realized that *Epiphanies*, already a year in progress, was incidentally a text that fulfilled my playwrighting goals. It was offered to theater directors with these general instructions: Since the stories are designed to be the most important sentences within larger fictions, the performers should be asked to speak them with a sense that they know what the entire story is. Secondly, since these sentences are discrete items with no ostensible relation to one another, the director should either allow plenty of space and time between them, or separate them in other ways. Thirdly, the performers should be widely distributed over the performance space. I even proposed putting the audience in the middle, while the performers were scattered around them (thereby inverting the convention of "theater in the round"). The first performance, at the University of North Dakota, was done in this way; the second, at Vassar College, was done with the performers distributed throughout a seatless exhibition space where the audience was free to move about. In the first production, the sentences were read formally, with pauses between them, for forty-five minutes; in the second, less formal production, perhaps thrice as many stories were read, sometimes in duets, trios, or choruses, also within forty-five minutes! From time to time I also work on an operatic *Epiphanies* that will have an appropriately epiphanic musical score by Bruce Kushnick. Here some *Epiphanies* will be of words alone, others of music alone and yet others of both words and music, used in the widest variety of complementary ways. The samples we have done so far persuade me to think that Kushnick, of all the composers I know, has the greatest musical imagination for this sort of curtly episodic structure.

During my DAAD residency in Berlin, the Literarisches Colloquium asked to publish a selection of my *Epiphanies* as a book. A translation had to be commissioned, and this turned out to be more of a problem than anyone expected. Most translators are skilled at realizing consistency, at transforming a style in one language into an approximately similar style in their own language. However, the premise of *Epiphanies* is just the opposite — that the sentences should be different from one another. After approaching individual translators who were appalled by this last requirement, I realized that the best way to translate the text would be to gather a large number of translators, offer them the English Epiphanies on cards (or slips of paper), ask them to select the stories they wanted to translate and then return with their German renditions. One charm of this unusual translation procedure would be that similar elements, such as the same phrase, in two different stories could thus be translated in two different ways, while a variety of individual German styles would further accentuate differences in the stories. A second charm is the efficiency of mass-production — with a large enough group of translators, all two thousand *Epiphanies* could be done in a day. (Indeed, if the voices of the translation turn out to be more various than the voices in the original, perhaps it would be appropriate to translate these new *Epiphanies* back into English, again not with one translator but another populous team.)

The English text of *Epiphanies* also became the script of a radio play that was recorded in 1982 but has been only partially edited. Here I recruited thirty-six readers, with voices as different from one another as possible, and asked them to come in either one of two shifts to a radio studio with six microphones. On the anteroom floor for each shift was roughly a thousand cards, numbered in sequence, with one story to a card. The eighteen performers for each shift were asked to select cards they wanted to read and to make sure that they would not pick two successive numbers. Once in the studio, I instructed my readers to speak the stories in numerical sequence and, like the theatrical performers, to say them as though they knew what the whole story was. The result was several hours of audiotape that I have been editing into two different versions. One audio *Epiphanies* will be several hours long and will, like other recent audio works of mine, have this quality I want of something that can be left and returned to. The other version will be a series of very short tapes, ranging in length between, say, twenty seconds and five minutes, for public radio stations to broadcast whenever they wish (such as places where, on a more conventional radio station, commercials might be). In this last format, the experience of *Epiphanies* will not be continuous but, perhaps more interestingly, split apart into bits and pieces heard throughout the year.

The principle of *Epiphanies* also informs a film that I have been making for the past few years. For visual material I am using found footage, gathered from as many sources as possible, both amateur and professional. From masses of 16mm film, I select sequences that visually strike me as being epiphanies of larger stories. (What function these bits might have served originally is, of course, another matter.) Precisely because these cinematic epiphanies must be as various as possible, it is more appropriate for me to collect footage than to shoot it; other people's film would inevitably be more various in subject, style and even picture quality than the footage I could shoot myself (if I knew how to shoot film — I don't). At last count, this film *Epiphanies* is ninety minutes long, including footage gathered in both Berlin and New York. I want it to be at least 240 minutes long and to have footage gathered from around the world, for the visual materials should be as universal and encompassing as I want my verbal stories to be. Thus, for the sound track, I drew upon the long tape made for the radio performance (and for a twenty-minute version presented on German television in 1982 had sixteen speakers read selected translations); for since there is no connection between any film story and any verbal story, this sound track need not be synchronized with the film. (Likewise, sound tracks in yet other languages could be produced without altering the images.) This film *Epiphanies* could be projected in the normal way, as a continuous image on a single screen, or it could go into an environmental installation where one-hour segments from the film are projected continuously in one-hour cycles on screens at four corners of the compass, while the sound track is played continuously in four-hour cycles. Or the full film could be divided into many short films, each with its own sound track, that might, among other possibilities, become a sort of serial preface to other films in a particular moviehouse, or at a festival; for just as the images need not be watched in any particular sequence, so they need not be seen at one time (or one at a time). No matter the medium, one quality intrinsic in *Epiphanies* is the exhaustive experience of the experience of fiction.

No doubt other possibilities for "publishing" *Epiphanies* will be discovered before this project is laid to rest.

XI

But nothing is more irritating to an artist who expresses himself in various media (as did the artists of the Middle Ages and the Renaissance) than the modern habit of arbitrarily confining the artist's reputation to one medium. [Hans] Richter is a total artist, a universal artist, and whether he expresses himself in painting, in printing, in abstract films or documentary films, it is always the same artist, freely expressing a unique vision. It is only possible to appreciate the significant place he occupied in the modern movement if we bear in mind the extraordinary range of his creative activities, and at the same time realize that they are all expressions of the same poetic vision. — Herbert Read, Introduction to *Hans Richter* (1965)

In my creative work so far, there has been a continuing concern with alternative materials for traditional genres, such as poetry and fiction, and then with language in alternative media, such as audio and video, which sometimes enhance the preexisting materials and other times function as a cunning constraint. Predisposed to invention, I had intended from the beginning to make imaginative works that looked and "read" like nothing else anyone knew; and since my reasons for making art were quite different from those behind my critical essays, separate fundamental concerns insured that my professional functions were not confused. In doing things differently, I have accepted the likelihood of losses with the gains; and should people protest, as they sometimes do, that certain qualities they like in my criticism are absent from this creative work, my reply is that the latter stems from different purposes in myself and hopefully exhibits certain qualities absent from my criticism. "In contemporary art," Moholy-Nagy once wrote, "often the most valuable part is not that which presents something new, but that which is missing. In other words, the spectator's delight may be derived partly from the artist's effort to eliminate the obsolete solutions of their predecessors."

One fact I should like to note about my creative career is the absence of any early conventional work; there is no juvenilia — no poetry in either traditional or modish forms, no linear fiction, no representational drawings, which is to say none of the trappings that indicate that I learned some academic lessons. I began my creative career at an extreme position and have, simply, moved only further out. The idea of imitating what is taught in school — or either proving myself or establishing my credibility through the mastery of classroom exercises — has never interested me. One reason for this absence is that I came to creative work not from an apprenticeship in poetry and/or fiction and/or visual art, as nearly all creative writers and artists do nowadays, but from the neutral territories of intellectual history and expository prose which, of course, I continue to do as work distinct from my art.

Though superficially diverse, not only in media but styles, my creative works still exhibit certain unifying marks, such as riskiness, rigor, clarity, structural explicitness, variousness, empiricism, and conceptual audacity — qualities that might also characterize my critical writing, perhaps because they define my personal temper (and are thus as close as the work can be to being me); and my creative concern with innovative structure is also a principal theme of my criticism and my anthologies. Two goals in mind for both my art and my criticism are that they be more complex and yet more accessible, if only to prove that these aims need not be contradictory.

All my creative work can also be seen as the dialectical result of pitting my traditional education and professional experience (with expository writing) against a series of antithetical efforts to transcend conventional forms — to write a poetry of intentionally limited language, to make a fiction exclusively of lines, to compose literature with numbers, to multitrack declaimed language, etc. Since much of the work involves the mixing of different artistic materials, the process of perceiving it customarily combines at least two perceptual modes — the visual with the verbal, the verbal with the aural, the fragmentary with the linear, the numerical with the visual, the static with the kinetic, etc.; for the work is usually meant to be perceived not just in one traditional way but, more likely, in a few ways. It could also be said that I have endeavored, first, to synthesize my education in literature and history with a growing interest in music and the visual arts and, second, to test my inventive proclivities against the resistances of several unfamiliar media. This background may explain such idiosyncracies as why even my Constructivist Fictions, which are totally devoid of language, usually embody a strong narrative line, why all my music so far is based upon the spoken word, or why my works seem at once so intellectual and so anti-intellectual; or why I am more interested in results than in processes, or why I find myself so often talking and writing about the work, and finally why this memoir is as it is.

One might also characterize my art as premeditated, impersonal, experimental, and intelligent, although eschewing traditional symptoms of how intelligence functions in art, such as allusions to past literature and history. My works are particularly indebted, in different ways, to such precursors as Moholy-Nagy and Theo van Doesburg, in addition to my friends John Cage and Milton Babbitt; and I will gladly acknowledge the influence of such earlier cultural movements as Constructivism, Dada, and Transcendentalism, in addition to the intermedia developments of the past two decades. Except for my video art, I have so far favored black and white as the sole colors indigenous to art, believing with some irony that all other hues belong primarily to "illustration."

Though I once said that my creative work made me "a poet," I now speak of myself as an "artist and writer," nonetheless wishing that there were in English a single term that combined the two. "Maker" might be more appropriate, its modesty notwithstanding. The variousness of all the work confuses not only the art public but also those critics who still expect someone to be just "a poet" or just "a composer" or just "a visual artist," rather than *all* of these things, and *much else besides*. On further thought, the principal problem with person-centered epithets such as "painter" and "writer" is that they become not descriptions but jails, either restricting one's creative activity or defining one's creative adventure in terms of one's initial professional category (e.g., "artist's books"). As Ad Reinhardt put it, "Art disease is caused by a hardening of the categories." In truth, it should be possible for any of us to make *poems* or *photographs* or *music*, as we wish, and, better yet, to have these works regarded, plainly, as "poems" or "photographs" or "music." Perhaps the sum of my artworks is ultimately about the *discovery of possibilities* initially in the exploitation of available media, and then in art and, by extension, in oneself as a creative initiator.

Another reason for *my* discarding narrow terms is to suggest, if not ensure, that the work as a whole be finally judged not just as Literature or just as Art but as something among and between; for it is only with my own kind, rare though they be, that I wish my total creative self ultimately to be compared. Perhaps the most accurate term for my imaginative endeavors should be "Language Art"; the title of a recent traveling exhibition of this work was *Wordsand*.

Part III: Positions

When he enters the territory of which Eutropia is the capital, the traveler sees not one city but many, of equal size and not unlike one another, scattered over a vast, rolling plateau. Eutropia is not one, but all these cities together; only one is inhabited at a time, the others are empty; and this process is carried out in rotation. Now I shall tell you how. On the day when Eutropia's inhabitants feel the grip of weariness and no one can bear any longer his job, his relatives, his house and his life, debts, the people he must greet or who greet him, then the whole citizenry decides to move to the new city, which is there waiting for them, empty and good as new; there each will take up a new job, a different wife, will see another landscape on opening his window, and will spend his time with different pastimes, friends, gossip. So their life is renewed from move to move, among cities whose exposure or declivity or streams or winds made each site somehow different from the others. Since their society is ordered without great distinctions of wealth or authority, the passage from one function to another takes place without jolts; variety is guaranteed by the multiple assignments, so that in the span of a lifetime a man rarely returns to a job that has already been his. — Italo Calvino, *Invisible Cities* (1972)

Picasso, Braque, Mondrian, Miró, Kandinsky, Brancusi, even Klee, Matisse, and Cézanne derive their chief inspiration from the medium they work in. The excitement of their art seems to lie most of all in its pure preoccupation with the invention and arrangement of spaces, surfaces, shapes, colors, etc., to the exclusion of whatever is not necessarily implicated in these factors. — Clement Greenberg, "Avant-Garde and Kitsch" (1939)

The End of Art (1969)

A vehemently hostile reaction is almost always a sign that habits of taste are being threatened. — Clement Greenberg, "Art Chronicle" (1952)

With each passing year, with each outrageous new step, with each apparently terminal piece, with every new invention and every repudiation of esthetic piety, there is an increasingly persuasive sense that everything in the arts has been done—that no more frontiers can be forged, that the end has been reached. However, in this year, like last and next, there arrived works of painting and sculpture, dance and music, film and mixed media, as well as forms among and between, that did succeed in pushing the frontier ever further ahead.

While the arts themselves change drastically within our own artistically conscious lifetimes—my own still runs less than a decade—the reasons for their transformation remain more or less constant. One cause of change is the inevitable depletion of an established style, which has a life cycle of its own. Fathered by one or a few people, it earns admirers and eventually imitators until its intrinsic, or apparent, opportunities are thoroughly exhausted and its children expire through excessive display. Since people in general and artists in particular are always doing things in inventive ways, the social demise of a recently dominant style inevitably grants an opportunity to other kinds of work: so that a number of alternatives compete in the free market of critical admiration and artistic imitation, and rising creators climb to eminence on the receding backs of their once-famed predecessors. To put it differently: Either out of cussed rejection of established procedures or out of the impetus toward innovation that is perhaps intrinsic in man and the times, there are distinct leaps in art; and the new way of rendering that persuades most effectively, usually by its intrinsic relevance or its art-historical relevance, establishes a transiently dominant style.

To move to the frontier of an art is to risk poverty, as well as failure and scorn; yet not all first-rate frontiersmen are necessarily scorned and poor. Personal income from one's art usually has much to do with the standards of living, after necessary expenses, and in the art itself. Painting and sculpture, of course, are the most remunerative; acclaimed works, even by comparative unknowns, can command over a thousand dollars—the same fee usually extended to a composer to commission a piece that will take him at least a year to finish. Clive Barnes recently pointed out that neither Merce Cunningham nor Paul Taylor, two of the most acclaimed figures in contemporary choreography, earns as much as a bank clerk; and most of the eminent avant-garde composers, whether serial or chaotic, teach, conduct, lecture, and consult. Practitioners of intermedia are particularly indigent (unless, like the Joshua Light Show, the best of its kind, they are incorporated into a more lucrative setting, like Fillmore East), not only because the major foundations are still dealing in pre–60s categories but also because intermedia artists have yet to find their impresarios. On the first point, no known mixed-media practitioner has received a fellowship from the older foundations for this primary work, nor have any of that new breed of artistically polymathic critics (though one got a Guggenheim as a "historian"); for the establishments in America have not quite caught up to the avant-garde — nor, by definition, will they ever.

In addition to following the logic of its own history, art also responds to changes in the general historical situation. This explains why works (to say nothing of thoughts) formed after the rise of Sputnik; the decline of McCarthyism; the end of cultural censorship; the growth of mass television; the taste-leadership of John F. Kennedy; the increased affluence that has doubled nearly every middle-class income; the contraceptive pill and other new drugs; more widespread protests by minorities; Soviet-American detente; the dissemination of transistorized appliances and computers — after all that has happened in the past decade — will inevitably be different in form as well as content from those of ten years ago.

What characterizes the recent atmosphere in nearly all the arts is an unprecedented permissiveness, which encompasses a principled awareness of further possibilities, a tolerance of genuine originality, and an assumed freedom regarding both the artistic traditions and the available materials. This permissiveness also induces an enthusiasm for preposterous work and/or apparent dead ends (like silent pieces and blank canvases) that, in retrospect, seem more like ironically sensible explorations, if not indubitable breakthroughs. A related preoccupation of the time opens artists to materials not previously used for art — whether the noises of the environment, the sounds of nonmusical machines, the imagery of advertising, balls of string, crushed car parts, and so forth. An esthetic open to formal innovation also allows the inventive use of previously nonartistic matter, if not ultimately implying the extreme position that everything purposefully made by tasteful men may have the status of Art. For these and other reasons, the current moment in the arts is generally concerned with, as well as appreciative of, extrinsic exploration more than intrinsic achievement, creative process more than finished product, esthetic suggestiveness more than declarative statement, ontological questioning more than patent didacticism, in addition to unfamiliar visual, aural, and multisensory experiences.

Not only has the recent period been dominated by avant-garde art, which is to say, work ahead of the pack (and, thus, the time), but what is art-historically unprecedented has been the sheer number and stylistic diversity of genuine avant-gardes in every art. Perhaps the most radical movements, in fact, may not be art at all but something else, or perhaps miscegenated forms standing between art and philosophical discourse; for the gist of Inferential Art, as I call it, is that resonances of a work are far more interesting and important than its intrinsic achievement. For instance, when Claes Oldenburg, asked to sculpt a monument for New York City, hired gravediggers to excavate and refill a hole behind the Metropolitan Museum, the pile of churned dirt could, by inference, be considered an underground sculpture or an inverted monument. Perhaps the most extreme examples of Inferential Art are conceptual works, which can be outlined but not feasibly built, like Oldenburg's monstrous monuments for the world's cities, or essays about experiences in more than four dimensions. A converse variation is the record, usually in the form of an esthetically prosaic photograph, or work that no longer exists, such as furrows in the snow or holes and lines in the desert. Not only is this approach to artistic creation and experience distinctly new, but I doubt if such "artifacts" would have had much persuasive currency before the current time.

Similarly, the sometime painter Allan Kaprow moved logically from collage to assemblage (three-dimensional collage) into space-enclosing environments and then theatrical performances and finally into happenings, which broke down all restrictions upon space and materials, as well as turning the action of "action painting" into its own artistic medium. From this kind of career follows the strictly contemporary idea of the artist as ultimately not a painter or a sculptor but a man engaged in a creative adventure that will involve him with various media.

The fundamental difference between the two sets of avant-gardes in painting is that the first would isolate the processes and materials of the art — the application of paint to a plane of canvas — while the other direction would mix painting with procedures and materials from the other arts, such as making three-dimensional objects, and even using such decidedly nonpainterly materials as machines; and a similar difference between segregation and miscegenation separates the avant-gardes in the other arts.

This proliferation of miscegenated activity has created a number of new directions for art, if not entire new art forms that cut across the old arts. One is Environments, by which I mean an artistically enclosed space. Perhaps the most spectacular example was USCO's Meditation Room at the Riverside Museum three years ago, when the artists' collective (company of Us) pooled their talents for paintings, construction, audio collage, incense, and light to create a four-dimensional experience that affected the total sensorium. The trouble with Environments, from the classic point of view, is excess intimidation — by definition, they are so encasing that the spectator cannot escape their imposing stimuli unless he leaves the enclosure; however, one of the rationales for environmental creation is a dissatisfaction with the less involving communicative possibilities of the older media.

Another intermedium is mixed-means performance, which is to say theatrical events that emulate not from post–Renaissance literary drama but stand between the traditional arts. *Dionysus in '69* (1968), for instance, takes from both a classic script, freely interpreted, and dance choreography, while The Living Theatre's extraordinary *Paradise Now* (1968) fuses a Protestant revival freakout (with its passionate attempt to *convert* an audience by all available means) to traces of nonpitched music and choreography, in a theatrical presentation clearly like nothing one has seen before or since. John Cage and Merce Cunningham's aleatory spectacular, *Variations V* (1965), combines dance, music, film, slides, electronic apparatus, not so that one accompanies the other but so that all have more or less equal status in the mix. Larry Austin's *The Magicians*, shown this past Halloween at Hunter College, mixes music with dancing children, film, slides, closed-circuit television, props, black light, and a tape system designed to transform quickly the live sounds made on stage.

Yet another intermedium is Word-Imagery, or works of art where words are drawn or deployed to form images in a resonantly complementary way. This is not the same as "concrete poetry," which usually eschews recognizable words for an arrangement of linguistic signs. Instead, Word-Imagery is a more relevant communicative medium, concerned with the resonances of familiar words in unfamiliar formats (or vice versa), like Robert Indiana's well-known *Love*, John Furnival's *Le Tour Eiffel* (where words in several languages are deployed in the shape of the Eiffel Tower), and *Saga,* a 24-page fiction in Word-Imagery, by the Frenchman Jean-François Bory.

All metamorphoses in the arts bring not only a multiple reinterpretation of the arts' traditions but also a new society for art; and each radically different art usually creates a new audience for itself. In every art there is a new and an old, an avant-garde and a derrière-garde, or, more precisely, several strains of older styles and several streams of new, as well as numerous points among and between; yet the audience at, say, a Merce Cunningham concert overlaps scarcely a few percent with those attending the Joffrey Ballet or Balanchine's work at the State Theatre. The people at the Castelli Gallery on Saturday are not likely to stop at the Wildenstein too; and not too many regular spectators at Philharmonic Hall get to the superlative concerts of the Group for Contemporary Music at Columbia University. The major difference is more generational than not, for just as the spectators (and the admiring critics) of an Arthur Miller play presented on Broadway are, on the average, 45 or more years old, so the audience and critics for a mixed-media or Off Off Broadway performance is largely under 30. The same difference in average age separates the people flooding the Andrew Wyeth exhibition from those attending a show of new sculpture; for precisely because most disinterested people will admire the kinds of art they learned to appreciate in college for the rest of their lives, so it is a young audience that inevitably is more predisposed to the claims of avant-garde art. And so too it is the adventurous young artist who is apt to say, if not eventually demonstrate, that there is no end in contemporary art, but only an endless stream of new beginnings.

The Artistic Explosion (1980)

Revolution in art lies not in the will to destroy but in the revelation of what already is destroyed. Art kills only the dead. — Harold Rosenberg, "Revolution and the Concept of Beauty" (1959)

The future of the arts will be determined by two different kinds of developments—first, changes within the society of art, and second, new technological developments. It is common to speak of the former as "short-term" and the latter as "long-term," but an invention that is rapidly disseminated can have immediate effects upon an art. Consider what the typewriter did to literature or what cheap photocopying is doing to publishing or what acrylics have done to painting.

In every art, we are presently witnessing the hypercommercialization of the established art industry, because of both increased production expenses and absentee (conglomerate) ownership. The obverse of increased profits is a declining interest in new works that are perceived to be less immediately profitable. Thus, in every art, especially in America, we see the growth of alternative, less commercial enterprises, which produce and distribute art less for money than for love. In the theater, these enterprises have been called "Off Broadway" and, when Off Broadway became too commercialized, "Off Off Broadway." The analogue in literature is alternative publishing; in the visual arts, it is the network of publicly funded "alternative spaces" that have recently sprung up across the country.

One reason for this continuing shift is the increasing number of Americans who consider creative art to be their primary activity. In the past two decades, the number of serious poets in the United States has doubled, the number of painters has tripled, and the number of people seriously pursuing modern dance has quadrupled; and this artistic population will predictably increase. As long as the established art industries remain so closed to new work, the most talented young people are more likely to work in alternative institutions, and these will surely become the principal repositories of emerging excellence in every art.

In part because of this commercialism, poets and fiction writers, for instance, will be exploring alternative means of publication—of making their works publicly known. We have already seen the beginning of this development

266

in the popularization of the "poetry reading," in which a work is read aloud to an audience, often before it appears in print. There will be more interest in the broadcasting media, such as audio and video, not only for the transmission of such readings, but also as "paper" on which the literary artist may work directly, creating works of literature that will exist exclusively within the new media.

Technological inventions are easier to imagine than predict, in part because few of us are intimately aware of the procedures leading to their development. Will there be better paints than the new acrylics? Will there be a new sculptural material with the solidity of steel and the light weight of balsa wood? Could humanized anthropomorphic machines execute spectacular choreography better than live dancers? Could a single electronic instrument imitate the richly various sounds of a symphony orchestra? Could a typewriter be developed that would type out words as they are spoken? Could a television system reproduce images that are present only in one's head? Can psychotropic chemicals increase memory or other mental powers? Could computerized information retrieval give the writer of this essay immediate access to a far larger and more systemized library than he can keep in his office? Indeed, could an essay like this one be written by a machine that is far more intelligent, in the human sense, than any we have so far seen? My own prediction is that most, if not all, of these technologies will exist by my 90th birthday, which will occur in 2030.

Artists' Self-Books (1968)

Books, regarded as autonomous space-time sequences, offer an alternative to all existent literary genres. — Ulises Carrion, "What a Book Is" (1975)

Among the more valuable traditions established in the late sixties was the practice of consequential vanguard artists creating imaginatively designed books primarily about their own work and esthetic position — not only Allan Kaprow and Claes Oldenburg, but Andy Warhol's *Index* (1967), Iain Baxter's *A Portfolio of Piles* (1968), Dick Higgins' *foew&ombwhnw* (1969), and John Cage's *Notations* (1969), among others. (The last book, by accepting within its own frame everything offered by selected other composers, is perhaps esthetically more self-appropriate than Cage's two collections of essays, despite the patent compromise in *Notations* of such an unenhancing convention as presenting the contributions in alphabetical order.) Merce Cunningham's *Changes: Notes on Choreography* (1969) resembles its predecessors in the crucial aspect of being as much *like* as about Cunningham's dance.

The inside front cover has overlapping lines of crossing type on top of a photograph, a form reminiscent of the beams of light passing over dancers in *Winterbranch* (1964); a page in the middle has a column of type running down the center, superimposed over both a photograph and the program of *Variations V* (1965), very much like the disconnected simultaneity of the piece itself; and the structure of the entire book is as concentrated in discrete detail (the page) but as plotless and nonclimactic in overall form as Cunningham's choreography. While materials relevant to a particular piece are generally grouped together, the fragments are not presented in chronological order, the author avoiding one compromise of convenience; and need one say that this is not the sort of self-book that either George Balanchine or Martha Graham would publish.

Just as Cunningham's *Walkaround Time* (1968) freely mixes movement, sound, stillness, and lights and decor, so *Changes* mixes with similar freedom shrewdly chosen photographs, reproductions of performance programs and handwritten notes, rough sketches and diagrams, neatly typed remarks that were apparently transcribed recently (on the same multiple-font machine that Cage favors), letters written to friends, scribbled replies to a questionnaire, esthetic declarations, etc., etc. ("Dancing has a continuity of its own that need not be dependent on either the rise or fall of sound, or the pitch and cry of words. Its force of feeling lies in the physical image, fleeting or static.") Contained within this unpaginated potpourri are also some edifying descriptions of how chance procedures can be adapted to the gamut of choreographic variables.

In general, the pieces strike this nondancer (but sometime football player) as thoughtfully and thoroughly planned, even in their allowances for various degrees and kinds of indeterminacy (as in professional football — one hears, Cunningham's favorite spectator sport). Only an artist as unpretentious, unevasive, and succinct in his prose as Cunningham would admit, on one hand, that a 1944 dance, *Root of an Unfocus*, "was concerned with fear," or that in a more recent aleatory work "I find No. 9 and No. 10 were not used, did not come up as possibilities; and upon examining them carefully, I am relieved they did not." (The obvious point lost in the shuffling discussion is that while chance methods have the virtue of producing results beyond the conventions of premeditated choreography, not everything aleatory would be equally successful.)

"Dancing is movement in time and space," he announces early in *Changes* and a book, by analogy, is filled pages between the frame of covers. Populating this canvas is the achievement of the writer and designer Frances Starr, who brilliantly adapted Cunningham's compositional syntax to the bookish medium (that, need one add, more desperately requires stylistic resuscitation than, say, the ballet.) It is true that texts printed upside-down provide a bit of a nuisance, while in the middle of the book is reproduced a program whose year-date is perversely blocked out or omitted despite Cunningham's handwritten inscription, "I date my beginnings from this concert." Nonetheless, scattered between the covers is much genuine information and explanation unavailable elsewhere.

This book-composition is also a highly contemporary way for an artist-still-in-progress to forge a permanent but incomplete record of his or her own career. However, since this volume eschews an explanatory preface or recapitulatory afterword, the reader is left the task of interpreting significances from the evidence presented. Whoever does not comprehend Cunningham's choreographic imagination is not likely to understand his book, for *Changes* demands the sort of perceptual procedures honed on Cunningham's dance, not to speak of Cage's music and perhaps William Burroughs' fictions, too.

For these reasons, though almost every Cunningham work is displayed, the book simply cannot serve as an effective introduction for those millions who have heard (or read) but not seen — perhaps nothing performs this initiating role as successfully as Calvin Tomkins' chapters in the paperback edition of *The Bride and the Bachelors* (1968) — and *Changes* has considerably less academic information than the Cunningham issue of *Dance Perspectives* (Summer

1968), while the intrinsically justifiable lack of page numbers (and thus of an index) in *Changes* makes information-retrieval a bit arduous.

This book was first announced as a collection of the essays on dance matters that Cunningham has published over the years; and as someone who has gone to considerable effort to ferret several of them out of obscure and defunct journ ds, I was anticipating a more convenient form of storage. However, as much as those essays are too valuable to lie forgotten, here is a different book entirely, less a guide to individual Cunningham ideas or dances than a key to his characteristic imagination; and, as an artist's bookish essay on his own endeavors, *Changes* is a masterpiece of its particular kind.

P.S. On second thought, perhaps Cunningham's willingness to use the convention of bound, evenly cut, equi-sized pages parallels his current commitment to a permanent company; for both are archaic conventions that, in our times, are likely to induce historically conservative, if not esthetically constrained procedures. This observation inspires conjecture over what kind of book-about-himself a post–Cunningham dancer might want to produce — say, Yvonne Rainer, Meredith Monk, or Kenneth King?

"Artists' Books" (1976)

The media turn art into media — art retaliates by turning media products into art.
— Harold Rosenberg, "Art and Its Double" (1969)

As someone who made books before he made anything considered "art," I feel gratified, if not amused, by "artists" nowadays discovering the virtues of books — that they are cheap to make and distribute, that they are portable, that they are spatially economical (measured by extrinsic experience over intrinsic volume), and that they are infinitely replicable.

The economic difference between art-objects and book-objects is that the former need be purchased by only one person, while the latter needs many buyers to be financially viable. The trouble with commercial publishers is that they will not publish anything unless their salesmen can predict at least ten thousand purchasers. To commercial publishing, not even Robert Smithson's collected essays, say, are economically feasible. It is obvious that what is most necessary now, for those of us seriously interested in book-art, are book-publishing companies and distributing agencies that can issue in smaller numbers and still survive. Thus, the literary world has witnessed the emergence of small presses which are, by now, publishing a greater amount of consequential literature than large presses.

Whereas sometime visual artists seem most interested in fitting their visual ideas into the format of a standard rectangular book, I find myself more interested in expanding initially literary ideas into other media — ladder-books, oversized books, undersized books, newsprint books, card books, large prints, wall drawings, audiotape, videotape, film.

It is hard to know where "artists' books" begin and literary books end, and it would be self-defeating to draw definite lines, dividing territory, in advance of exploration and discovery.

My major quarrel with the category of "artists' books" is that it defines work by who did it, rather than the nature of the work itself. The term thus becomes an extension of the unfortunate custom of defining an "artist" by his or her initial professional ambitions or, even worse, his or her undergraduate major. Artistic categories should define work, rather than people, and the work at hand is *books* and book-related multiples, no matter who did them.

271

What would be most desirable now would be a situation where an artist-writer (or writer-artist) would feel equally comfortable about making an object, a performance, or a book, their choice of medium depending upon the perception of experience he or she wanted to communicate.

Books by "Artists" (1983)

When I thought of taking up painting seriously as I had once half-hoped to do before I went to college, the highest reward I imagined was a private reputation of the kind [Archile] Gorky and de Kooning then had, a reputation which did not seem to alleviate their poverty in the least. — Clement Greenberg, "The Late Thirties in New York" (1960)

"Artists' Books" is an epithet new to art discourse, and the question of what it means, or what it includes, is less evident than one might think. Tim Guest, a young Canadian who edited *Books by Artists* (1981) (bilingual in the Canadian way) and organized the exhibition accompanying it, writes that his subject is "artworks which exist within the formal structure of the book" and he later speaks of "books which are intended to be artworks in themselves." That seems definite and clear, until the reader discovers that this book, as well as the exhibition, is really about something else — not books as art objects, per se, but creative books made by people with acceptable visual arts reputations. Indicatively, after speaking intelligently about such issues as inventive page design, alternatives in the paginated presentation of information, and experiments in binding — after shrewdly asserting that the current "tendency towards cross-fertilization also allows an artist to belong to no explicit discipline while referring to many" — Guest switches track, without announcing that he is limiting his discussion and thus his exhibition only to those artistic books produced by a certain class of people.

This limitation explains not only his inclusions but the omissions. In fact, artists in many fields, not just visual arts, are making alternative books — books that are different in size, in shape, that are filled with materials other than evenly justified horizontal lines of type, punctuated by occasional illustrations. Some of the most artistic books known to me — "book-art books" I prefer to call them — are by Paul Zelevansky, Gerhard Rühm, Jose Luis Castillejo, David Arnold, Peter Barnett, Emmett Williams, Manfred Mohr, Jean-François Bory, Madeline Gins, Raymond Federman, Tom Ockerse, J. Marks, R. Murray Schafer, none of whom are included here, let alone mentioned, one supposes, because they do not have the acceptable visual arts credentials, they do not hustle the visual arts scene, they did not go to art college. For instance, Dick Higgins, an adventurous book-artist, is mentioned only for his collaboration with Wolf Vostell, a well-known Berlin visual artist, and not for his own extraordinary books.

This book closes with a longer essay by Germano Celant, a prolific Italian art critic, with a penchant for dropping strings of hot names in lieu of explanations or detailed evidence. Celant admits that the subject is not really the book as an artwork, or book-art, but something else—books made by prominent visual artists. Thus, in Celant's scheme, Andy Warhol is credited as the first "artist" to produce his own exhibition catalogue (at Stockholm's Moderna Musset, in 1968), as if that should be considered an important achievement, or as if there had not been a tradition of lesser-known creative figures producing books about their own work. Thus, this book/ exhibition is another example of the weak-minded fads of using the epithet "artist" to mean just visual artists and of talking about an emerging art not in terms of genuine critical categories, but in biographical terms. (What is important is not what you do, but where you came from or where you went to school; the result, if not the purpose, of this approach is nothing less than snobbery.) Biographical categories also have the merchandizing advantage of being more accessible to the buying public than art categories. ("New York school" was easier to sell than "abstract expressionism.") *Books by Artists* would have more integrity if its title identified its real subject—Books by Visual Artists—which is not at all identical with the far more interesting contemporary art of alternative, artistic books.

Book Art (1985)

The old art assumes that printed words are printed on an ideal space. The new art knows that books exist as objects in an exterior reality, subject to concrete conditions of perception, existence, exchange, consumption, use, etc. — Ulises Carrion, "What a Book Is" (1975)

The principal difference between the book hack and the book artist is that the former succumbs to the conventions of the medium, while the latter envisions what else "the book" might become. Whereas the hack writes prose that "reads easily" or designs pages that resemble one another and do not call attention to themselves, the book artist transcends those conventions.

The book hack is a housepainter, so to speak, filling the available walls in a familiar uniform fashion; the other is an artist, imagining unprecedented possibilities for bookish materials. The first aspires to coverage and acceptability; the second to invention and quality.

Common books look familiar; uncommon books do not. Book art is not synonymous with book design or literary art; it is something else.

There is a crucial difference between presenting an artist's work in book form — a retrospective collection of reproductions — and an artist making a book. The first is an *art book*. The honorific "book art" should be saved for books that are works of art, as well as books.

The book artist usually controls not just what will fill the pages but how they will be designed and produced and then bound and covered, and the book artist often becomes its publisher and distributor too, eliminating middle-men all along the line and perhaps creatively reconsidering their functions as well.

Three innate characteristics of the book are the cover, which both protects the contents and gives certain clues to its nature; the page, which is the discrete unit, and a structure of sequence; but perhaps neither cover nor pages nor sequence is a genuine prerequisite to a final definition of *a book*. The process indigenous to book-reading is the human act of shifting attention from one "page" to another, but perhaps this is not essential either.

One practice common to both books and paintings is that the ultimate repository of anything worth preserving is the archive — the art museum for the invaluable painting, and the research library for the essential book.

One trouble with the current term "artists' books" is that it defines a work of art by the initial profession (or education) of its author, rather than by qualities of the work itself. Since genuine critical categories are meant to define art of a particular kind, it is a false term. The art at hand is *books*, no matter who did them; and it is differences among them, rather than in their authorship, that should comprise the stuff of critical discourse.

Indeed, the term "artists' books" incorporates the suggestion that such work should be set aside in a space separate from writers' books — that, by implication, they constitute a minor league apart from the big league of real books. One thing I wish for my own books is that they not be considered minor league.

The squarest thing "an artist" can do nowadays is necessarily compress an imaginative idea into a rectangular format bound along its longest side. Some sequential ideas work best that way; others do not.

In theory, there are no limits upon the kinds of materials that can be put between two covers, or how those materials can be arranged.

This essential distinction separates imaginative books from conventional books. In the latter, syntactically familiar sentences are set in rectangular blocks of uniform type (resembling soldiers in a parade), and these are then "designed" into pages that look like one another (and like pages we have previously seen). An imaginative book, by definition, attempts to realize something else with syntax, with format, with pages, with covers, with size, with shapes, with sequence, with structure, with binding — with any or all of these elements, the decisions informing each of them ideally reflecting the needs and suggestions of the materials particular to this book.

Most books are primarily about something outside themselves; most book art books are primarily about themselves. Most books are read for information, either expository or dramatized; book art books are made to communicate imaginative phenonema and thus create a different kind of "reading" experience.

The attractions of the book as a communications medium are that individual objects can be relatively cheap to make and distribute, that it is customarily portable and easily stored, that its contents are conveniently accessible, that it can be experienced by oneself at one's own speed without a playback machine (unlike theater, video, audio or movies), and that it is more spatially economical (measured by extrinsic experience over intrinsic volume) than other non-electronic media. A book also allows its reader random access, in contrast to audiotape and videotape, whose programmed sequences permit only linear access; with a book you can go from one page to another, both forwards and backwards, as quickly as you can go from one page to the next.

Because a book's text is infinitely replicable, the number of copies that can be printed is theoretically limitless. By contrast, a traditional art object is unique while a multiple print appears in an edition whose number is intentionally limited at the point of production. It is possible to make a unique book, such as a handwritten journal or sketchbook, or to make an edition of books limited by number and autograph; but in the esthetic marketplace, the first is really a "book as art object," which becomes known only through public display, while the second is, so to speak, a "book as print" (that is destined less for exhibition than for specialized collections).

The economic difference between a standard book object and an art object is that the latter needs only a single purchaser, while the former needs many buyers to be financially feasible. Therefore, the art dealer is a retailer, in personal contact with his potential customers, while the book publisher is a wholesaler, distributing largely to retailers, rather than to the ultimate customers. The practical predicament of commercial publishers in the eighties is that they will not publish an "adult trade" book unless their salesmen can securely predict at least several thousand hardback purchasers or twice as many paperback purchasers within a few months. Since any proposed book that is unconventional in format could never be approved by editorial-industrial salesmen, commercial publishers are interested only in book hacks (and in "artists" posing as book hacks, such as Andy Warhol).

What is most necessary now, simply for the development of the book as an imaginative form, are publishers who can survive economically with less numerous editions at reasonable prices.

An innovative book is likely to strike the common reviewer as a "nonbook" or "antibook." The appearance of such terms in a review is, in practice, a sure measure of a book's originality. The novelist Flannery O'Conner once declared, "If it looks funny on the page, I won't read it." Joyce Carol Oates once reiterated this sentiment in a review of O'Connor. No, a "funny" appearance is really initial evidence of serious book artistry. Imaginative books usually depend as much on visual literacy as on verbal literacy; many "readers" literate in the second respect are illiterate in the first.

One purpose for the present is to see what alternative forms and materials "the book" can take: can it be a pack of shufflable cards? Can it be a long folded accordion strip? Can it have two front covers and be "read" in both directions? Can it be a single chart? An audiotape? A videotape? A film?

Is it "a book" if its maker says it is?

With these possibilities in mind, we can recognize and make a future for the book.

Richard Kostelanetz's Book-Art Bibliography

These titles satisfy three criteria: 1) They contain Kostelanetz's creative work, as distinct from his expository writing; 2) They were designed (and often drawn, typeset and/or produced) by him; 3) They are as books unusual in form. Many titles initially issued by other publishers have since been retrieved and are available only from him as RK Editions.

Visual Language (Assembling Press, 1970). Initial collection of his visual poetry. 64pp., 6 × 9, saddle-stitched, also signed & numbered one of 150 copies.

In the Beginning (Abyss, 1971), a visual novella based on the alphabet. 64pp., 5 × 8, perfectbound.

Ad Infinitum: A Fiction (International Artists Cooperation, n.d.), a second alphabetical novella. 16pp., 3 × 4¼.

Accounting (PN Books, 1973), the initial numerical book, in its revised edition. 14pp., 4¼ × 5½, side-stapled.

Obliterate (Ironwhosebook, 1974), a dissected fiction distributed over sixteen sheets. 2¾ × 2, in a folded case.

I Articulations/Short Fictions (Kulchur Foundation, 1974), initial collection of short fictions bound back to back with a second collection of visual poems, both preceded by prefatory "After Sentences" that were erroneously interchanged. 64pp. + 64pp., 7 × 10, perfectbound, also hardback, signed & lettered.

Recyclings (Assembling Press, 1974). Initial volume of a comprehensive nonsyntactic literary autobiography, this section recapitulating only 1959–67. 64pp., 5 × 8, saddle-stitched, also signed & lettered with red covers.

Openings & Closings (1975), over three hundred one-sentence fictions — alternately either the openings of hypothetical fictions or the closings. 96pp., 7 × 10, perfect-bound, signed & lettered, A–Z. Audiocassette edition (1975), 60 minutes, of the author reading parts of the text in inventively amplified stereo. A color videotape edition (1975), likewise 60 minutes.

Extrapolate (1975), an accordion of constructivist fiction, readable in either direction. 24pp., 3¾ × 90, also signed & numbered, 1–12.

Come Here (Assembling/Cookie, 1975), an erotic visual fiction that the U.S. copyright office refused to certify on the grounds that it "lacks copyrightable artistic expression." 20pp., 5 × 7, saddle-stitched, signed & lettered also.

Modulations (Assembling, 1975), another constructivist novella in the form of an accordion book that can likewise be read in either direction. 28pp., 3 × 84, on card stock, also signed & lettered.

Portraits from Memory (Ardis, 1975), a book-length visual poem of handwritten portraits of past loves. Hardbound, also paper, also signed & numbered to 10.

Constructs (WCPR, 1976), the initial collection of symmetrical line-drawings in systemic sequences. 112pp., 8¼ × 8⅛, also signed & lettered, with special black covers.

Rain Rains Rain (Assembling, 1976), a long poem whose twenty-three images can be read in any order, or mounted on a wall. Twenty-four unbound cards, 5 × 8, also individually signed & lettered.

Numbers: Poems & Stories (Assembling, 1976), the initial gathering of numerical work. 24pp., 11½ × 16, folded newsprint, also signed & lettered.

Prunings/Accruings (Ecart, 1977), nonsyntactic Biblical prose that can be read from front to back, or back to front. 24pp., 5¾ × 8¼, saddle-stitched, also signed & lettered.

Illuminations (Future/Laughing Bear, 1977), a third collection of visual poems. 48pp., 5½ × 8, saddle-stitched, also signed & lettered, with special red covers.

Numbers Two (Luna Bisonte/Future, 1977), visually organized numerical images. Seven cards, 8½ × 11, in an envelope, individually signed & lettered, A–Z.

One Night Stood (Future, 1977), a minimal fiction with no more than two words to a paragraph, published in two radically different formats. "I wanted to see whether the experience of reading the exact same words could be made radically different." 176pp., 5¼ × 4, perfectbound, also clothbound, clothbound signed & lettered. Also 24pp. newsprint, 11 × 17, also signed & lettered.

Constructs Two (Membrane, 1978), second collection of symmetrical line-drawings in systemic sequences. 80pp., 4¼ × 5½, also signed & lettered copies are available from the author.

Tabula Rasa (1978), a constructivist novel, approx. 1,000 pages, 8 × 8. Only twelve copies were signed and numbered by the author.

Inexistences (1978), constructivist stories, approx. 666pp., 4 × 4. Only twenty-six copies were signed & lettered by the author.

On Holography (1978), initial hologram of five syntactically circular, grammatically seamless statements about holography. 9½ × 14 (diameter), on a revolving stand.

Foreshortenings & Other Stories (Tuumba, 1978), which rearranges eighty-four module-sentences in systematically different ways. 28pp. Stereocassette (1977), with two completely different readings of the text, 60 minutes.

Exhaustive Parallel Intervals (Future, 1979), a book-length narrative, perhaps a novel, whose entire content is a diamond-shaped array of numbers whose positions change in systemic sequence, with an afterword by the author. 160pp., 6 × 9, perfectbound, also hardback, also signed & lettered by the author.

And So Forth (Future, 1979), over one hundred drawings of related geometric shapes that form modular narratives from page to page, published as loose sheets gathered into an envelope, with a preface by the author. 9 × 12. Ten complete sets were individually initialled and numbered by the artist.

More Short Fictions (Assembling, 1980), the most advanced collection of experimental stories, both verbal and visual, ever published in the United States — the harvest of the previous decade, with an afterword by the author. 224pp., 6 × 9, paper, also hardback, also signed & lettered.

Autobiographies (Future, 1981), a history of a life composed not as a continuous narrative but as an audacious multi-perspective collection of bits, written both recently and long ago (and at times by others). 284pp., 6 × 9, perfectbound, also clothbound, also signed & lettered.

Reincarnations (Future, 1981), a fiction composed entirely of recomposed photographs of the author in various incarnations, with a brief afterword. 64pp., saddle-stitched, 5 × 7.

Epiphanies (Literarisches Colloquium Berlin, 1983), the first gathering of his single-sentence stories that have been appearing in periodicals since 1979, translated collectively into German in an unusual way and imaginatively typeset. 48pp., 4¼ × 5¾. A video copy of a 20-minute film for German television.

Recyclings (Future, 1984), an extension and updating of the first volume, published a decade before, of this nonsyntactic literary autobiography. 320pp., 5 × 7, perfectbound, also hardbound, also signed and lettered.

ALSO OF RELEVANCE: *Wordsand* (1978), a catalogue of art-autobiographical essays, manifestoes and explanations, about art with words, numbers and lines, in several media, along with complete documentation, which was initially published to accompany an early retrospective exhibition, saddle-stitched, 92pp.

Audio Writing (1984), an introductory, comprehensive lecture-demonstration of his "publishing" with audiotape, with examples from over a dozen works. 91 minutes, stereocassette. (*Audio Art* [1978] is an earlier self-retrospective. 45 minutes, stereocassette.)

Time & Space Concepts (1977)

Stella's early work, and much of the Minimal sculpture that later affirmed it as a watershed, revised the Cartesian psychology behind Abstract Expressionism and behind the language of most critical responses to it. The emphatic objectivity of Stella's paintings implied a rethinking of the analogy between a painting's content and the "inner" capacities of its viewers. As more artists began to take clues from Stella's work, questions arose whether "deep" responses are incommunicable because they are profound or because "depth" is misunderstood and needs to be rethought or re-envisioned. — Kenneth Baker, *Minimalism* (1988)

Soon after Marilyn Belford asked me to participate in this symposium, I came across the following passage in Carla Gottlieb's new book, *Beyond Modern Art*, and the passage goes, "It would be difficult to name an artist or book on modern art that does not make free with the words *space, time, and motion.*" So with the weight of modern criticism and modern art behind me, I shall proceed to make free with these holy words, mostly by using them in several ways.

If we're talking about contemporary art, then we're necessarily talking about art since 1959, which I take as a turning point dividing what we customarily call contemporary art from modern art. And the first thing I notice in many of the more extreme, more innovative artistic developments of the past two decades is that both time and space are either much more, or much less, than they used to be. In the case of theater, say, I think of Robert Wilson's plays, which run far longer than previous plays, and yet are thought to be terribly slow because they present much less action within more time than previous theater.

The contrasting motif would be increasing the density of the amount of theatrical communication within less time; and we see that in Richard Foreman's recent theatrical pieces. I think we see it too in a dance of Merce Cunningham's called *Winterbranch*, that I like a lot, and in the Mabou Mines production of Samuel Beckett's *Play*.

Now, in nonliterary theater we've also witnessed a sharp expansion in the amount of space in which a performance can take place. John Cage, we remember, did the original presentation of *HPSCHD* in a 16,000-seat basketball arena in Urbana, Illinois, and he filled up that cavernous space with a multitude of visual and aural materials. And Alan Kaprow, the originator of so-called "happenings," once mounted a piece that took place in New York, Buenos Aires, and Berlin, simultaneously. Now that, surely, is a different kind of theatrical space from what went before.

In music, we hear "moreness" in the compositions of Milton Babbitt, where several distinct serial patterns are articulated in every single note and literally hundreds of discrete musical events are compressed into a few minutes. And we hear "lessness," by contrast, in La Monte Young's music, where a single chord is sounded for an interminable length.

Visual art, by contrast, deals less with time than with space, and here the apotheosis of lessness in both painting and sculpture has been mini-malism—that is, paintings of a single color, or sculpture of a single geometric shape and so forth. That is familiar to us all.

Similarly, one reason why we admire Joseph Cornell's work, or Nam June Paik's, is that, in this age of largely gigantic paintings, they have willfully chosen to work in smaller spaces—that is, Cornell with boxes, and Paik with a single video screen. Paik, however, sometimes reverses field, when he puts several video monitors into a single space, making our experience of televi-sion much, much more than it used to be.

To me at least, the exemplar of moreness in painting as painting is Willem de Kooning, especially in the incredibly complex visual fields of his Woman series, where a single image is viewed from a multitude of perspec-tives. In more recent years, let me suggest, the moreness impulse in visual arts gravitates away from canvas and into what we call artistic environments, or artistically defined spaces. I'm thinking of Lucas Samaras' *Mirrored Room*, Boyd Mefferd's *Strobe Lit Floor*, Stanley Landesman's *Walk-in Infinity Chamber*, which I saw in Milwaukee last week, or James Seawright's *Electronic Peristyle*. And all these surrounding, encasing pieces offer a greater abundance of visual stimuli than we found in previous art. (Some of these themes are elaborately developed in my comprehensive history of the non-literary arts in the sixties, *Metamorphosis in the Arts*.)

A second characteristic of the recent period, I think, has been the expan-sion of the professional space in which an individual artist may operate. By now, we all accept the truth that would have been forbidden to us two decades ago: that there's nothing to prevent a visual artist from making or even writing books. And similarly, nothing to prevent a sometime writer from making visual art for exhibition. John Cage has composed musical pieces, produced mixed-means theater events, published poetry, and made works of visual art. Although purists might object to such personal movement across the arts, no craft union is going to write John Cage off its rolls.

One reason why I've come to object to professional categories in describ-ing people—I have a bit about that in the new *Art-Rite*—why I object to such terms as "poet" or "critic" or even the holy term of "artist," is that they implicitly close off the space in which an individual can operate. If you're known as a "poet," for instance, it becomes a bit harder to do visual art seriously, or even worse, to get it accepted seriously. Secondly, when others define you as, say, a painter, then whatever writing you happen to do falls in the category of "painters' writing," or "artists' books." Both these terms suggest that such writings or such books should be set aside in a separate space—that they are separate from writers' or authors' books, or even worse, that they constitute a minor league, apart from the big league of real books. I don't object to categories defining work, but I think they're pernicious in defining people. They close off one's working situation.

In addition, the breaking down of professional barriers opens the spaces between the arts, creating a more fluid situation among them, or better yet, a single grand professional space in which all the arts collectively and simultaneously exist. Indeed, in Cage's work, as well as my own, and Paik's and Cunningham's, it's hard to know where one art ends and another art begins.

My final theme, which has something to do with space and time, is the grand expansion of the cultural space in which art takes place. This is most visible in modern dance, as Merce Cunningham can testify. When he began as a choreographer a little while ago, there were remarkably few showcases for dance even in New York City. Now there must be a dozen, if not two dozen, in New York alone, and many more around the countryside—spaces in which serious modern dance is regularly performed. One reason for this increase in professional space has been, of course, the precipitous increase in the sheer number of individuals working seriously, out of the most respected modernist traditions, in every art. There must be twice as many poets, three times as many painters, four times as many choreographers in comparison to only two decades ago. One necessary result of this sharp increase in the population of artistic professionals has been a similar if slower increase in the space or number of outlets for their artistic work. (So I've used the term "space" a fourth way now, right? That's playing very fast and loose.)

This expansion of professional space is a result of another theme which I take to be distinctly contemporary, and that is that artists, in all media, no longer feel obligated to wait around until the established institutions, the certifying agencies, "discover" them. Instead, dancers establish their own showcases, poets publish their little magazines, visual artists found co-op galleries, in part to say that they will not wait around, they will not take exclusion from the mainstream sitting down. The rise of alternative institutions in every art is thus of a piece, and together they constitute the most radical, most promising development in our professional lives.

The Opiate of the Artists (1979)

The attempt to define is like a game in which you cannot possibly reach the goal from the starting point but can only close in on it by picking up each time from where the last play landed. —Harold Rosenberg, "The American Action Painters" (1952)

A century ago Karl Marx characterized religion as "the opiate of the masses," a phrase that later Marxists changed to "the opiate of the intellectuals," which is to say that religion, more than anything else, distracted them from their proper work. Had Marx lived a century longer and visited America, he might have noticed that not religion but something else — sports, spectator sports — has become a principal opiate of the intellectuals. Nothing, but nothing, keeps many of us from our proper business of writing poems or stories, or composing music, or doing criticism, as much as spectator sports.

I know, alas. As a single gent who is not formally employed, I work nearly all the time at writing, art, reading, or related activities. I see less than one Hollywood film a year, I never watch TV game shows or sitcoms, I rarely read newspapers, I scarcely gamble. I bought my first television set when I was 27, only to watch sports; nine years later, I bought a color set, primarily because it presents sports so much better. I live with several thousand books, some thirty of which have my name on their spines, in SoHo, a Manhattan factory district where only professional artists can legally live. In truth, there is one and only one entertainment I share with everyone else — sports.

The paradox of my life is this: Whereas my art and writing are appreciated by an audience of at best a few hundred, who might think of themselves as an elite of sorts, there I sit several times a week, watching football, hockey, boxing, baseball, or soccer, along with millions of others who are an elite in other ways. When I hear the black radical lawyer Flo Kennedy speak contemptuously of the "jockocracy" that distracts America from social change, I wince, because I know damn well that she is speaking of me.

Why sports, rather than game shows, movies, or any of the other temptations that flood America? Well, obviously, I like them; I like them better than anything else. In general, I like them not as a partisan, although I do routinely root for certain local (New York) teams — the Jets (not the Giants), the Rangers (not the Islanders), the Yankees (not the Mets), and the Cosmos. However, I don't get upset for more than an hour if any of them lose, even in a playoff. Most of the time I can watch games between two non–New York teams, merely because I like to watch games. Once I start a game, I customarily watch it to the end, no matter who or what tries to interrupt me, not because I care who wins but because the pleasure of watching a sporting event includes seeing the entire show.

The sculptor Sol LeWitt, who recently had a retrospective at the Museum of Modern Art, told me he likewise always watches to the end because, "I get caught up in the drama of it. I don't care who's playing, if the balance is fairly close. The game goes to a certain climax and then changes completely, just like a drama. Baseball is particularly good for that, because the balances are so even. Any team can beat any other team at any time. As a structure, baseball is very well designed."

One characteristic of Art, we say, is that it is not useful — it offers no rewards other than the pleasures of appreciation; and with this definition in mind, it seems to me that I appreciate sports much as I appreciate Art and thus that my feelings toward sports are more esthetic, in a pure sense, than anything else. However, sports are a popular art, like rock 'n' roll and movies, but unlike poetry (especially of the more experimental sort that I do). In that case, it can be said that sports are the pop I like best.

Just as I am inclined to discriminate among works of art, so I routinely make distinctions among games — distinctions based not upon who wins or loses but upon how interesting, or excellent, one game is in comparison to others. A better football game, to me, is not one in which my team wins but one in which many good things happen — good things, such as spectacular individual plays, efficient team effort, close competition in the scoring, generally exciting play. A bad game is one in which nothing happens: the players are sluggish, the strategy uninspired, the competition lopsided. Bad games are the only ones I fail to watch to their ends. Playoff games are usually better than common ones, in part because they are played better. College games I find inferior simply because amateurs individually rarely play as well as professionals.

In certain games I enjoy the patterns of play — the arrangement of the players' energies on the field, especially as the vectors are recomposed from moment to moment. You can see this most clearly in soccer, as players move not to the ball but in response to its current location, each one covering a certain area of playing turf; and you can also see similarly changing patterns in hockey, although everything on ice happens so much faster. The patterns of play are different in style in football, though no less interesting, because of the singular role that conscious strategy plays in this game. In no other sport known to me does every player know in advance exactly what he is supposed to do on offense — *exactly* to the level of how many steps to take, which way to turn, which direction to block, etc.; so that quality of execution can have an esthetic value, apart from practical success. Raymond Federman, a Frenchman teaching in Buffalo, who writes extremely avant-garde novels in both English and French (he is a literary switch-hitter, so to speak), tells me, "Both football and hockey are extremely intellectual in terms of how the space and time are controlled. It's like playing chess or writing a novel."

My own taste extends to directly competitive sports, such as track (which was my principal recreation in high school) and, more recently, boxing, which I have discovered is more interesting than track, because two men are using not only their bodies but their heads in outwitting each other. One quality that makes Muhammed Ali such an interesting fighter is that he makes you wonder what he is thinking and, more recently, whether he can act on his thoughts. Walter Abish, an experimental American novelist who was born in Vienna and raised in Shanghai, likes tennis (which I scarcely watch) not only for strategies but for "how emotional responses affect those strategies, resulting in improvisation. I link this to my writing."

I personally like to watch games I do not normally see, such as rugby, lacrosse, Irish football, curling, all of which occasionally appear on my local public television station. (Otherwise, *never* do I watch that channel. Its artistic offerings are too middlebrow and insipid for my cultural tastes.) The one major sport I cannot watch, except perhaps around playoff time, is basketball, I think because so much depends on being outrageously tall and because the movements of the players are so limited. The only basketball team I would watch tomorrow is the Harlem Globetrotters, because they play the dull game creatively; and the one reason why all of us root for them to win their "exhibitions" is that esthetically they are so superior to their flat-footed opponents. Otherwise, to me, basketball flunks as art. The one television sport I cannot watch at all is golf; how even the announcer can avoid falling asleep I cannot comprehend.

Sports, I said, is the opiate of the intellectuals, not just *this* intellectual. Sometimes they watch for the same reasons everyone else has; other times, for different reasons. Because they are people who make it their business, if not their life, to be articulate, their reasons are usually interesting, if not generally relevant. The late Randall Jarrell once wrote a poem for the quarterback Johnny Unitas the day after they met; and his widow has written, "On Sunday we had pastries with Lowenbrau and watched the National Football League on television. Besides quarterbacking plays, Randall was continually appreciating scenes of the crowd, half in light and half in shadow, or half stadium and half turf with the athletes in combat on the bright limed lines of the grid."

The late historian Richard Hofstader saw in professional sports a quality of excellence that he did not see anywhere else in America. "Nothing in this country," he told me a dozen years ago, "is done as well as professional football. Compare it to our diplomacy." The literary critic Jerome Klinkowitz has a similar sense of sports as a kind of ideal activity. "Baseball is the ultimate elegant sport," he told me recently. "The movement of the ball is the only thing you need to watch. Football is too sloppy, too chaotic; it is too much like life. Baseball is also built upon the notion of possible (and sometimes attainable) *perfection*: perfect game, perfect day, each pitch a possible called strike or home run. Twenty-seven guys in a row can strike out, or they can get twenty-seven hits; each has happened." Klinkowitz is a Distinguished Professor of English at the University of Northern Iowa and the author of the most advanced books I know on contemporary fiction. On the side, he joins "several other local rummies," as he puts it, on the board of directors of the Waterloo (Iowa) Indians, a Cleveland farm team. To Klinkowitz, as consistent as a literary critic should be, the only football team worth watching is the Green Bay Packers "for the memory of that one great moment when they made the game into the art of baseball."

Nicholas Acocella, a political columnist for *Attenzione* and the editor of the *Diamondstein Book Digest*, was watching the television to the side of his writing desk when I called him to comment upon Klinkowitz's theme: "What makes perfection achievable in baseball is that it is such a statistically oriented game — everyone's play has numbers, carved indelibly in the record books. Every play is part of some statistic." Acocella echoes LeWitt in finding professional baseball more attractive than other sports precisely because it is more consistently competitive. "Remember that if the best team has a winning percentage of .667 and the worst team .333, then the weaker team has a one in three chance of beating the stronger team. In football, it's harder for a last-place team to beat a first-place team. That's why we don't have so-called 'upsets' in baseball." Come to think of it, LeWitt's comment that "any team can beat any other team at any time" echoes, in principle, Yogi Berra's classic contribution to the new 1980 edition of *Bartlett's Quotations*: "The game ain't over until it's over."

An artist and writer who also directs the Media Arts Program at the National Endowmen for the Arts, Brian O'Doherty, neatly refines this notion of sports as ideal activity. "There is a certain symmetry and a certain simplification of the complexities of life within a set of rules in which chance and skill still have a random dialogue." He declares himself "an absolute sports freak. One reason why I got cable television was that I could then watch ESPN — the sports network." However, as an Irishman educated in England before he came to America (and married the art historian Barbara Novak), O'Doherty is also a partisan. "I came from a small country that was totally oppressed, and one of our greatest moments came when our team beat the oppressors." He vividly remembers a rugby match in the early 1950s when Ireland beat England by a lopsided score (now, that sounds like a bad game to me), and he nowadays laments the sorry records of most New York teams.

To most artists and intellectuals, to repeat, a love for the game supercedes any partisan interests. "What do I watch?" the poet Donald Hall tells me. "Baseball, basketball, and football, in that order. When in England, I watch cricket. I love baseball the most. It seems the most interesting in character, and for characters. It is certainly the least twentieth-century. I like the game. I love minor league ball. I will stop by the side of the road to watch the married men play the single men, or, for a while, the eighth graders. I would see anybody play anywhere anytime. [Now that is *real* addiction.] I like the texture and the feel of it. I like all the intricacies. I don't even care so much about the outcome of the game, or staying to the last inning. There is no such thing as a bad game. People who don't care about baseball say that 'nothing happens.' I see things happen."

When I told Hall of my own frustrations with basketball, he replied, "The notion that 'the movements of the players seem so limited' is probably the most ludicrous observation yet made on basketball. [We also disagree vehemently about poetry.] The best athletes, in professional sports, are basketball players, and they have the *most* body control. Julius Erving makes Lynn Swann look like a quadriplegic. Basketball is a pattern-game that is best not seen on the tube but high in the balcony, that is as fast as hockey, but as precise as soccer." Making esthetic discriminations, he concludes, "It is best when it is played not by schoolyard types like Lloyd Free but by great passers, like the Boston Celtics.

"My ideal day begins at 4:30 or 5:00 in the morning, getting up and getting to work in the gorgeous early morning, and it ends with watching a game or part of a game on the television set. Everybody has to let the infant out, to talk, to air itself. Drinking is one way. Drugs obviously. T. S. Eliot read a murder mystery every night. I got sports." Hall's addiction to baseball even got him into writing a charming book, *Dock Ellis in the Country of Baseball* (1976). Hall recently wrote me, "I am about to become a baseball correspondent for the *Times Literary Supplement*," which is Great Britain's most august literary review. He will regularly cover not the game but books about the game. The latter, of course, provide their own kind of esthetic pleasure.

O'Doherty's double at the Literature Program of the National Endowment for the Arts is David Wilk, a poet who admits to being a baseball addict. "It is pure love. It is the perfect sport, because of its incredible complexity and various levels of activity. It is a pastoral game that combines periods of contemplation with activity of incredible intensity. Baseball is a personal game; the players have individual character. The identification factor is extremely large. In both football and basketball, the players look inhuman. Baseball is one of those incredibly rich activities that reflects human activity. It is a vast and complex machine that contains enough to be pretty comprehensive.

"The diamond itself you can turn on its side or stand on its end," he speculated. "It has a multitude of facets and characteristics. It is also prismatic, breaking light into its component parts that allow you to see it differently. I take baseball as a link to Jeffersonian democracy in the 19th Century and of the country to the city. We call it 'a park'; it is a meadow even in the middle of an industrial complex. There is a swatch in which time has stopped. Hugh Duffy, who played in the 1890s, could walk into a stadium today and would have no trouble playing the game." Wilk sounds like he could give a course in "Baseball Appreciation."

A different image of baseball comes to me from P. Adams Sitney, the codirector of the Anthology Film Archives, which is the principal New York and American showcase for avant-garde film in America. He also wrote the principal book on the subject, *Visionary Film* (1974), and teaches it at Princeton University. Notwithstanding the facts that he wears the same three-piece suit (or its duplicates) every day and lives alone in Manhattan's Chinatown without a television or even a telephone, he is a baseball maven who even brings his portable radio to summertime art functions. "Baseball, of all sports, alone thrills me," he told me in his Anthology office cluttered with bookshelves and film tins. "I mean daily professional baseball — not Opening Day, the All-Star Game, the Playoffs, the World Series, or the New York Yankees. They are inessential — for politicians and brokers.

"First of all, there is the field. Even glimpsed from the Evanston subway on an off-day, Wrigley Field is a hallowed sanctum. The sight of the manicured infield or a natural grass ballpark is the finest argument for city life. Then there is the rhythm of the game: the secret communications between the pitcher and the catcher, climaxed by the windup, sharpen the attention to the spectacular sounds when the ball is actually in play. I know no art or religion that so gracefully consecrates its repetitions of awareness." No question about it — this is an avant-garde art critic speaking.

"The temporality extends through and beyond the game. The greater the peg Dewey Evans or Dave Parker makes, the more vividly Clemente reappears in the mind. Every hit, play or error is triangulated with the history of the game as we have lived it. The individual stands before us in clarity and vigor. So many of the greatest days are wonderful because a minor player proves his worth. I will long remember Lenny Randle's first night as a Met; it was an allegory of redemption."

So why don't you have a television, I asked? "The strength of the imaginative function is so great for the baseballist," he replied without pause, "that radio retains its power only in the broadcasting of games." Now, I thought to myself, only a true addict, a true "baseballist," could come to that imaginative conclusion.

Not all of us artists and writers are baseball nuts. I can miss games without suffering and would never pause to watch amateurs and kiddies. So can the novelist Ralph Ellison, who prefers football and boxing. "I was a high school football player," he reminisced in his Manhattan apartment. "I like to observe the general development of skill and agility — to see one generation go beyond its predecessors. The grace and economy with which great athletes execute is esthetic. It is the difference between Willie Mays, the fast hands of Joe Louis and Sugar Ray Robinson and the people who depend upon courage and ruggedness. I think sports are an integral part of society. In the unruliness of modern life, sports teaches us how to win, how to lose, how to be graceful; all that is part of being civilized." Ellison was the first writer I ever knew to have a large-screen color television, and it wasn't for watching Shakespeare.

Ted Striggles has been, at various times, a high school letterman in running, swimming and football; a lawyer; a modern dancer; and executive director of the New York State Council on the Arts. He likewise prefers football and boxing. "Both are complex theatrical experiences; and like good theater, they give you moments of complicated action and then time to reflect about them. It is only on reflection that you can appreciate the complexity. Good sporting events must be paced, just like good theater.

"Football and boxing are the only sports in which form and function are appropriately correlated; you cannot separate one from the other. If you do unnecessary movements, someone will hit you, and you'll either stop or lose. A good crisp efficient punch is really the way to do it; the bolo punch doesn't work. It's inherent in the sport that the best way is the most efficient way. Football is an extension of the functionalism of boxing.

"Instant replays I don't mind at all, because they enrich your experience of what just went by. If you can look at it a second time and it looks the same, then you're watching a boring sport that doesn't interest me. That is baseball and chess. I also dislike all those sports in which judges give out numbered grades, like gymnastics and figureskating. All those invented sports, like target diving, are just silly—the equivalent of game shows."

The Conant Professor of Music at Princeton University, Milton Babbitt, composes music so complex and untraditional that it scarcely bothers him that only a few hundred people in the entire world fully understand it. Nonetheless, in the middle of his Princeton studio is not a piano or another musical instrument but a television set. "Baseball has become diluted with weaker players," he told me in the provocative style familiar to the musical world, "because other sports have become more remunerative, stealing many of the greatest athletes who might have otherwise gone into baseball. I can hardly look at baseball anymore; it is so inept. Soccer is too repetitious and improvisational. The football pros have basically only two plays: the run and the pass. They execute better than the collegians, but in my opinion, the best football, the game with the greatest variety of plays, is college football. It is better coached, better scouted; they take risks with their quarterbacks. The game is more strategic, more intricate and more truly cumulative—the momentary play can have its referent effect several plays later."

Always as much of a critic as an enthusiast, Babbitt would like to see TV coverage improved, "so that we could see the whole team. I would also like to see football become a possession game rather than a time game, to have, say, twelve possessions in a game. That would give you the kinds of options you have in cricket. Now most football games are over before they end in time. If you had possession, you could score and score before losing the ball, much as a baseball team does in the bottom of the ninth." (Then football would be a Yogi game that "ain't over until it's over.")

When do you watch television, I asked. "Not when I'm composing," he replied, scotching one professional rumor, "but when I'm copying or doing all that other dirty manual work that a composer needs to do. It provides me with the only real relaxation I get." A few years ago, he joined others at a university conference on the music of Arnold Schoenberg in postponing an afternoon session. It was Superbowl Sunday, you see, and Minnesota and Pittsburgh were playing. Once the game was over, the conferees resumed.

A high school guidance counselor by day, Irvin Faust authors remarkable New York City novels by night. In between he is a sports nut who can write fiction while listening to a radio game or watch one game on television while listening to another on radio. His favorite is indoor track, live, especially in Madison Square Garden. "It is very intimate, very personal," he testifies. "The pole vaulter appears to jump into your lap. I find it a cornucopia of color and action—not a three-ring circus but a six-ring circus. It's a fascinating kaleidoscope of bodies in motion and bodies in flight. I identify with the smart little New York kid who has to know how to elbow his way, how not to get pocketed, how to be tough or he'll be blasted off the track. I love indoor relay races. They are the epitome of intelligent New York know-how—not only of the runners but of the coaches in selecting the runners for each position."

Faust prefers college basketball to professional, not because it is more enthusiastic—the conventional reason for this preference—but because the absence of a 24-second rule allows more space for intelligence. Thus he likes the point guards who control the game and the coaches who get the most out of their players, such as Pete Carril of Princeton, whose players pass and pass until the opponents drop their guard. In Faust's most recent novel, *Newsreel* (1980), the trackmen Jim Ryun and Ron Delany appear; a new story, scheduled to appear in the *Atlantic Monthly*, is, he says, about a "sports-nut who is addicted to everything."

The choreographer Merce Cunningham would like people to think that the patterns of his dances are wholly abstract. However, sometimes their structures reveal the influence of a certain opiate. In *Field Dances* (1963), performers repeatedly come to the middle of the stage, make contact in various ways for several seconds, and then go off stage. When a British critic confronted Cunningham with the suspicion of a formal resemblance to American football, the choreographer acknowledged the truth.

In the writing not of a male writer but a female is an especially bizarre passage about American football. Though Gertrude Stein lived in Paris most of her adult life, she was not immune to its seductive powers:

There are two things about football that anybody can like. They live by numbers, numbers are everything to them and their preparation is like any savage dancing, they do what red Indians do when they are dancing and their movement is angular like the red Indians move. When they lean over and when they are on their hands and feet and when they are squatting they are like an Indian dance.

When I read this to Ted Striggles, he exclaimed, "That's marvelous, but she missed the ways in which the football players resemble dancing Indians the most — they put on costumes and wear war paint under their eyes."

Another woman who wrote appreciatively of American sports was Marianne Moore, a poet who lived most of her life in Brooklyn. Her "Hometown Piece for Messrs. Alston and Reese" lauds the entire team (later memorialized by Roger Kahn in *The Boys of Summer*, whose title, incidentally, comes from a poem by Dylan Thomas). Another poem of Marianne Moore's, "Baseball and Writing," opens with these lines:

Fanaticism? No. Writing is exciting
and baseball is like writing
          you can never tell with either
                how it will go
          and what you will do;

her lines echoing Walter Abish's point about the anxiety between intention and effect in both sport and imaginative writing.

It has been observed that for many writers alcohol is the opiate of choice and then for other, largely younger artists and intellectuals an opium of some kind was their favorite opiate. As far as I am concerned, the juicers can have their juice, the heads their dope, and the dopes their mysteries. For some of us there is no opium like sports — good sports — for reasons that I think are ultimately esthetic. If not for my love for sports I'd be writing and reading and perhaps making social change all the time — or perhaps finding another opiate.

Literary Video (1987)

Of course, in this electronic age of computers, radio and television, the writer can no longer be someone who sits up in his garret pounding a typewriter. —Marshall McLuhan (1966)

Literary video differs from other video art in its base of a text whose language is enhanced, rather than mundane—a text that is conceived within the traditions of modernist literature and a contemporary sense of verbal possibilities.

Literary video differs from video literary-reportage in which, typically, a poet is interviewed or is seen reading aloud; for in literary video, the author becomes an artist, exploiting the indigenous possibilities of the new medium—instant playback, overdubbing, selective vision, synthesis of both images or letters/words/sentences in live time, image distortion and so forth. In literary video, the screen is intelligently active, the author-artist visually enhancing his own language; in video reportage, by contrast, the camera's eye is visually dumb.

Literary video draws upon both literary materials and video possibilities, and integrates them, rather than keeping them separate; so that word complements image and vice versa.

The video medium is closer to books than to film, because the TV screen is small and perceptually partial, like the printed page, rather than large and enveloping, like the movie screen; and literary video is customarily "read" like a book, in small groups or alone. (Most of us feel no qualms about interrupting someone watching a videotape or reading a book; by contrast, people at a movie remain undisturbed.) Perhaps the most appropriate location for a home video monitor is in a bookshelf.

Because the video image is drastically less precise than a film image, and the former's light source is not in front of the screen but behind it, video is conducive not to realism but to anti-realism; video, unlike film, cannot produce a *trompe d'oeil*. Video instead offers an arsenal of techniques for producing image distortion less feasible in film (but comparable to the sound distortion capabilities of the machines that process recording tape). Such distortions generate a surrealism that, because of the size of the video screen, is perceptually more painterly, if not literary, than filmic. Looking at the source of light is a more hypnotic experience than the film viewer's looking with it, and the close physical proximity of the screen to the video viewer further encourages the experience of dreaminess.

Because the video screen is so much smaller than the movie screen, video is not effective in reproducing proscenium theater; even conventional films look ungainly within such a tiny frame (while subtitles are almost illegible). Video is more conducive to outlines than details; to individuals than choruses; to faces (and parts of faces) than milieus; to titles than subtitles; to one or two voices, rather than several.

The video image tends to be more flat (two-dimensional), more concisely structured, more sketchy, and less cluttered — it tends to be less like a film than a snapshot or a book. The visual imprecision of the video image, in comparison to film or photography, forces the viewer to fill in the picture, as he does in reading a comic strip; and this participational process can increase the degree of audience involvement.

Literary video should transcend both the familiar representationalism of conventional television and the conventional syntax of familiar literature; it should also transcend those constraints of subject, theme, and truth that imprison the story-telling of commercial television; it should present kinds of imagery and continuity, as well as visual-verbal perceptions, that are totally unavailable to every other medium.

An artist making a videotape may, unlike the filmmaker, examine his finished project immediately upon completing it, and may at that point decide to reshoot it in whole or in part; and this process of execution resembles, both temporally and perceptually, writing and rewriting at the typewriter.

The video medium leads itself to the presentation of continuous movement and, thus, not to poetry but to prose and to narrative.

Television is a mass medium; video, a private one. As television is treasured for its credibility, especially when bringing the day's news into our homes, video should be valued for its incredibility. Literary video is destined for an audience that is ideally both visually sensitive and literate; television for an audience that is neither.

As a veteran writer, I bring language, with which I am familiar, to video, which I have scarcely explored. Though I refuse to abandon one art to do another — that was a seventies fashion — I am, as a creative writer, presently experimenting not just vertically within literary arts but horizontally, with media other than the traditional small rectangular pages familiar to literature. Recently I have been casting language in silkscreened prints, offset posters, ladderbooks, collections of cards, audiotapes, and holograms as well as, now, videotapes.

Remarkably few "writers" have made creative video, though an army of poetic eminences have had their faces and voices memorialized on black-white videotape. It is surprising that no literary funding agency has ever, to my knowledge, supported literary video; for reportage about writers, that artistically lesser form, rips off all the available funds.

In my earliest videotapes, done in 1975, I was particularly concerned with relating language to synthesized abstractions, overdubbing, visual feedback, and image distortion, among other capabilities indigenous to video. For the text of "Plateaux," which relates stages in a love affair in one-word paragraphs (and was subsequently reprinted in my book *More Short Fictions* [1980]), I introduced an evolving moiré pattern whose languid circularity complements the unrelenting circularity of the original narrative. For "Excelsior," which switches rapidly between two voices seducing each other (and is also reprinted in *More Short Fictions*), I created two abstract designs and then swiftly alternated between them, eroticizing the text exclusively with rhythmic abstract imagery. (Recently, several years after he saw it, Nam June Paik told me that this he especially liked.) These two pieces were included in my first ¾″ videotape, *Three Prose Pieces* (1975), where the central work is "Recyclings." Here a sequence of nonsyntactic prose texts (drawn from a 1974 book of that title) is read by several nonsynchronous voices, all of which are mine. The color image consists only of pairs of lips (all mine), moving synchronously with audible speech. The first section has one voice and one pair of lips; the last (and sixth) section has six voices and six pairs of lips, each generation of lips-voices reading the same nonsyntactic text nonsynchronously.

My second videotape is based upon my book *Openings & Closings* (1975), a collection of single-sentence stories that are alternately the openings and the closings of hypothetically longer fictions. While each of these stories radiates outward (or forwards or backwards, to be specific), they have no intended relation to each other; and there are no intentional connections within the entire work, other than scrupulous discontinuity. Here I instructed the video engineers to alternate between color for the Openings and black-white for the Closings, and connected each system of hues to its own camera crew. My second instruction was that each crew make its next visual image of me (seated in a chair reading aloud) as different as possible from the one(s) before. My aim was to realize visually the enormous leaps of time and space that characterize the book's text. *Openings & Closings* is, incidentally, the only videotape I have made so far in which an image recognizable as me appears on the screen. (That fact alone is a measure of how far most of my work departed from the conventions of writing and writers on videotape.)

My next work, *Declaration of Independence* (1976), is based upon a text of that title that I published as early as 1975 (and reprinted in my book of *Prose Pieces* [1987]). Here the words of the original historic U.S. document are systematically reversed to appear backwards word by word, implicitly realizing within language my own declaration of independence from the conventions of normal syntax. (In that respect, my concerns here echo those of *Recyclings*.) On the screen are four pairs of superimposed bearded lips, each visibly different in size, reading this "Declaration of Independence" simultaneously (roughly), from beginning to end. Once the joke is caught, the tape can be very funny, with the kind of humor that thankfully does not diminish upon rehearing. Since I am as an artist not adverse to providing clues (or writing manifestoes), I added a continuous line of explanatory gloss that, in capital letters larger than those of televised movie subtitles, crawls from time to time along the bottom of the screen.

That last move represented my first discovery of the video character-generator — the machine mentioned before that electronically translates my typings into letters that appear on the screen. The text I chose was *Epiphanies* (in progress since 1979), which are single-sentence stories that, unlike those mentioned before, are not the openings or closings but the epiphany, which is to say the resonant moments that illuminate an entire fiction. I put the words of these Epiphanies (and only their words) on the video screen, one story at a time, in various typographical arrangements; and let them dominate the screen for durations roughly equal to the length of the stories. This videotape is very much about the experience of alternative reading — not only in concert with others (usually) but at a speed of presentation that cannot be controlled by the reader (unlike the conventional reading experience). Someone remembering silent movies has joked that this video *Epiphanies* is "all titles, no action," and that is true, as the visible words contain the entire action of each story. All these early works were put on a single VHS cassette titled *Early Literary Videotapes* (1987).

I planned my next video for character-generator, *Partitions*, in 1980, but didn't get to realize it until 1986. Acknowledging the limitations of the character-generator donated to me — one typeface, a memory able to retain eight pages in sequence — I wanted to reveal words within other words, to enhance language by revealing what is buried in it, within a sequence of eight images. In the title word, for instance are six words (pa, par, part, art, tit, it), each new word incorporating a letter of its predecessor, all of which could be shown before returning to the source word. As this machine offered the possibility of up to ten lines of horizontal type, I decided first to subject only one word to such eight-step partitioning, and then two words at a time, three words, up to ten words, all of which would metamorphose simultaneously, incidentally making the action on the screen ever more difficult to read as it became more populous. As a result, the exploration of the possibilities of language within a severe compositional constraint parallels the exploration of possibilities within the technological constraints of a severely limited letter-making machine.

The character-generator I used in these video *Epiphanies* and *Partitions* is rather primitive, compared to what is available. This machine could use, as noted before, only one style of lettering in one size; it was also limited to white letters on a black field, in a fixed grid of twenty-four characters across and ten lines high. By contrast, more sophisticated machines can use various typefaces, expandable to any size, available in a variety of colors, without any limitation on the number of lines. They can send words into the visual field from any place within the screen (in, say again, a steadily increasing visual crescendo) and then have words perform such acrobatic tricks as flipping over or turning inside out. I presently want to exploit such character-generators for video writing that will not supercede the printed page but become another medium for heightened, poetic language.

Language-Based Videotapes (1990)

In industrial society, the decorative crafts have been converted into mass media. Only the pressure of new creations against art as it has been defined keep art from merging with the media and allows works to survive for an interval as art. To maintain the pressure of de-definition has been the task of the avant-garde. — Harold Rosenberg, "Inquest into Modernism" (1978)

In an earlier memoir about my writing for/with videotape, I spoke of the standard small television screen as resembling the page of a book, in contrast to the larger, more enveloping visual field of the moviehouse, and suggested that the imagery most appropriate for such a small screen would be intimate and devoid of excessive detail. For my earliest video creations, collected as *Three Prose Pieces*, I favored simple screen-filling images similar to the essential page-filling images in the visual fictions I was also writing around that time (some of which were collected in *More Short Fictions* [1980]). In *Epiphanies* (1981) and *Partitions* (1986), I put on the screen only sequences of static arrays of words, fully realizing the resemblance to book pages. Two negative assumptions favored from the beginning were that the television box must be good at presenting images other than the solo talking heads that predominate in public transmissions and structures other than the collages favored by most "video artists." There was no need to duplicate what others were doing, no matter how opportunistic such aesthetic butt-kissing might be.

The next development began with a series of almost annual residencies at the Experimental TV Center in Owego, New York. Here, working with Hank Rudolph and Peer Bode, I had access first to slightly more sophisticated character-generators, or electronic letter-making machines. Instead of only one machine, I now had access to two, with different typefaces, each able (unlike before) to do smaller letters as well as full capitals; and these character-generators also possessed internal memories that allowed me to put a series of successive images, or pages, that could then be played back while the recording tape was running. Attached to this system was an external memory in a tape drive that can store on a single "data-cartridge" cassette as much as three hundred separate pages of text, any or all of which can be random-accessed. In addition, the ETC studio offered processing equipment that facilitated such kinetic moves as dividing the screen between two sets of images or adding color backgrounds that could be electronically changed as we recorded the images onto videotape. Thanks to rescanning, or the process of reshooting an image off a television screen, we could do yet more radical image-modification. I also used the so-called text programs of an Amiga 500 computer to "generate" letters that make words that move. As is my custom in guest residencies, I tried to exploit artistic possibilities within technological limitations, rather than entering a studio with detailed schemes designed to be realized at any cost.

With these technologies, I made a series of short pieces whose only content is language, some only a few seconds long, others perhaps a minute, and thought of these as *Kinetic Writings* (1988), to quote the title of a twenty-two-minute tape collecting, literally publishing, the best of them. But I also realized that the bulk of them could be divided into two categories — "Video Poems," which realize a conciseness of image and effect; and "Video Fictions," which imply movement from one place to another, which is to say narrative, even if abstract. However, since ETC's machines offer only synthesis, not editing, I must go elsewhere to produce a finished tape. That pair of hour-long tapes, when done, would represent, as far as I can tell, the first of their *literary* kinds.

Thanks to the data-cartridge technology, along with the character-generator's capacity to make letters "crawl" in an evenly paced horizontal line across the screen, I could cast on tape the "strings" I had written several years before. These lines of continuous letters contain overlapping words, each of which includes at least two or usually three letters from its predecessor (depending upon the rule made for each text). Most were in English, one was in German. Thus, Stringtwo, which has a two-letter overlap, opens with the following:

Stringtwomenteroticystitisolatenderotogenicheapplesbiannul. . . .

Once these extended strings of letters were entered into the data-cartridge, they could be continuously recorded in several ways: with just a single stream of letters running across the screen, at one of three available speeds, at times with colors changing in either the letters or the background; with an enlargement of the middle letters running as a counterpoint either above or below; with on-screen windows that contain changing fragments of the continous imagery. Some of the shorter strings were incorporated into a thirty-minute tape titled *Videostrings* (1989). The entire German text became *Stringsieben* (1989, twelve minutes), while *Stringtwo* (1990) alone runs well over thirty-five minutes. For the first, I added the music of Gordon Jillson, who had previously composed the sound track for *Partitions*; *Stringsieben* has harp music played by Nina Kellman. For the last I added a kind of continuous pseudo-speech composed by Joseph V. DiMeo.

I also used the character-generator and data-cartridge to put on screen the text of my second most difficult audio composition. The text of *Turfs/Arenas/Fields/Pitches* (1983) opens with those four words arrayed in the four corners of a single page, their bottoms toward the middle, and contains sixty more poems similarly structured. While in residence at Davis & Elkins College, I recruited four people to speak the words of each page in unison, as a kind of verbal chord, whose parts, I thought, should be individually comprehensible, much as the notes of a musical chord can be individually identified. Attractive though that perceptual purpose was in theory, it was more problematic in practice, especially on first hearing, and what was difficult with four-word poems became even less feasible with an octet of voices simultaneously articulating eight-word poems composed to a similar spatial principle (*Grounds/ Gridiron/Scrubs/Vocabularies/Tracks/Proscenia/Lists/Theaters*). So it seemed appropriate to put the verbal groups of all these poems on screen not in their original geometric forms, but as horizontal lines, for durations roughly corresponding to their appearance on tape. (The videotape concludes with silent arrays of sixteen-word poems, likewise similar in structure, silent because they have not yet been aurally recorded. Since this videotape has three sections, I decided to title it with an opening word from each section: *Turfs/ Grounds/Lawns* (1989, twenty-three minutes). As the sound track was processed at the Electronic Music Studio in Stockholm, where I have several times been artist-in-residence, it was transferred in stereo to the ¾" master videotape (and copied onto the hifi tracks of ½" VHS tape); its sound, apart from its picture, is thus best played back not through the single small speaker of a standard television monitor but a stereo system customarily used for records and compact discs. Because the audio track of such videotapes is as important as the pictures, I classify them, unlike the others, as *Audiovideotapes*. (I later used a more complicated video lettering to make visible the text of my audio *Onomatopoeia* [1988].)

I had previously explored the principle of composing videotapes to my audio compositions, starting with *Seductions* (1981) and *Relationships* (1983), two extended electronically enhanced readings of texts that resemble each other with explicit erotic content. For imagery I turned to the Amiga computer, which has an extraordinary capability for continuously generating richly colored kinetic pictures. Since my texts were already comprehensible, it seemed unnecessary to show what was said (as was done with *Turfs*); instead, we found in the Amiga an endless kinetic flow of lush shapes that had their own sensuous quality. Indeed, in many respects, the audiovideotapes *Seductions* (1988) and *Relationships* (1988) resemble the light show that I enjoyed at the best rock concerts two decades ago.

I realized that similar video syntheses might be effective with other audio compositions of mine. *Invocations* (1981, 1984), of and about the language of prayer, differs from *Seductions* and *Relationships* in having distinct sections, rather than continous sound, and so it seemed appropriate to make for each section a video synthesis as long as its sound. Thus, each section has its own visual "setting," to use a word that is customarily used to identify sound made to enhance language. Again, it seemed appropriate to use not representational pictures, remembering the commandment against graven images, but continuous kinetic abstractions. I extended this last principle to *The Gospels* (1982), a two-hour fugue of the initial four books of the New Testament; but rather than letting the audiovideotape go with only one video synthesis, we literally put a new one on top of an old one, making the tape denser and, as the emphasis between the new and the old shifted, more various. As four ministers are simultaneously reciting complimentary biblical texts, shapes flash across the screen. Some of them are circular, others rectangular, yet others stripes, their colors changing in stochastic ways, enhancing the acoustic experience without distracting from it (much like the light show at a rock concert).

Once I had these syntheses, I discovered what was not obvious at the beginning — that they were seen best not on standard small screens but on two-piece projection televisions that resemble film in having images that are looked at (not through, without fear of cathode-ray-tube-damage), but differ from film in having a blurred texture and rougher edges. Indeed, there is every reason to regard such projection television as a reproduction medium quite different from the book-like smallscreen television on one hand and film on the other.

For another audiocomposition, *Praying to the Lord* (1981), I made several Amiga syntheses that are similar in style but different in detail, hoping someday to broadcast them on several monitors, which is another medium for publishing background video, so that the images accompany not only the single sound track but one another.

In 1988, I finished an hour-long audiotape composition of and about the sound of baseball, *Americas' Game*, and wondered how to video it, so to speak. I didn't want live-action footage or other kinds of familiar illustrations. Preferring an image with its own power, I chose a single unmarked baseball, well-illuminated, that remains on screen, motionless, for the entire duration, sixty minutes, as a kind of Buddha that is worshipped, to be sure, as devoutly as other images of Buddha.

Only in this last piece do I deviate from my original assumption that my video art would be based on language or literature, for that assumption was the principle, as well as the signature, of my video art. I had noted before that few, if any, of my literary colleagues produced their own videotapes, as distinct from appearing as talking heads in videotapes made by others; and even though I have been making language-based videotapes for some fifteen years now, none of them of talking heads (though some with talking lips), my literary interest remains unique. There is more work to be done, by others as well as me, in discovering not only video possibilities for language but video contents different from the common run.

My Nonsync,
Two-Person Films (1988)

It is our task to achieve a true opto-acoustic synthesis in the sound film.... The "documentary sound film" and the "abstract sound film" will be reinforced by the "montage sound film," by which must be understood not merely montage of the optical and acoustic sections, but a mutually integrated montage of both. We ought to begin with a series of experiments in the sound element. — L. Moholy-Nagy, "Problems of the Modern Film" (1932)

I'm not a filmmaker in any academic sense. I never took a course, I've never shot a motion picture camera, and I can't operate an editing table. Nonetheless, I've been a collaborator, and then a sole producer. One truth I learned early from my principal artist hero, Moholy-Nagy, is never let a lack of education, let alone technical incompetence, prevent you from working in an art.

My first film, *Openings & Closings* (1976), drew upon the single-sentence stories published in a book of mine the year before. The governing ideas behind the text were that the story was either the opening sentence of an otherwise nonexistent fiction, or the closing sentence, and that there was no intentional connection between one sentence and another. In designing the book I alternated between openings set in roman type and then closings in italics. Working with Barton Weiss, then a filmmaking student at Columbia University, I decided, further to accentuate the profound differences between the two kinds of sentences, to film all the openings as black letters on a white background and then all the closings in negative, with white letters on a black background. We used a primitive animation stand. For acoustic background I chose a performance safely out of copyright—a piano recital of Modest Moussorgsky's *Pictures at an Exhibition*, as recorded in Bulgaria. There was no attempt to correlate the action of the music to what appeared on the screen.

The principal problem with this film, as I now see it, is that typefaces even smaller than the titles of silent films are simply too small for the movie screen; and, once I got into black and white reversals, there was no reason other than economy (or laziness) to keep one typeface for all the openings, and another typeface for all the closings. From the initial viewing of this film

302

came that gag, albeit true, that the content of my film was "all titles, no action." I still want to make a film whose screen would have only language, much as I've made videotapes whose only content was words; but there were other films to complete first.

Constructivist Fictions (1978) drew upon visual fictions of the same title, all drawn a few years before, when I was working with making successive pages of symmetrical line drawings that changed in systemic sequence. The systems informing these changes could be additive, reductive, permutational, or combinational, among other syntactic techniques. One recurring theme of this print-work is variation and development within a systemic constraint. Working on a primitive animation stand with Peter Longauer, then a graduate student at Columbia (and now a distinguished animator), I discovered that such drawings not only lent themselves to filming; they demanded filming. In book form, the images usually progress in only one direction at an indefinite speed, which depends ultimately upon decisions made by the individual viewer. In film, the rate of progression can be manipulated, so that the transitions occur at precisely determined speeds, which could be constantly slow, medium, or fast; or progressively accelerating or decelerating. The drawings can also be cycled — repeated at different rates of speed; they can progress or regress in wave-like patterns, among other possibilities. Film enables us to control not only the sequential ordering of the individual elements, but also the time allowed for their perception as well. As a result, the sequential imagery acquires a specific, fixed rhythm which would be impossible in print media. Such cinematic devices as fades and dissolves also served the ends of my abstract narratives, complementing the transitions; I felt that filming these stories widened the potentialities of my narrative structures and further enhanced the esthetic experience. For the sound track, we used Jon Gibson's marvelous *Visitations*, played not at its normal speed, but at a faster speed that gave his flute-playing a superhuman quality similar to the otherworldliness of both my imagery and the sequential manipulations; and although the visual track is divided into discrete stories, each with its own title, the sound track is continuous and thus as nonsynchronous as my later sound tracks would be.

Looking back on *Constructivist Fictions*, I find that computer animation has usurped my territory, able as it is to make perfectly symmetrical line-drawings almost automatically, whereas the cells for my film took hours and hours of painstaking work. At the time, a friend involved with experimental filmmaking told me that he could not tell how the films were made; now someone of his sophistication would think we had used computer animation, even though we hadn't! Back then, a pioneer in computer animation told me that I could better realize my ideas on a machine like his; and although I did not much like the quality of his imagery at the time, there is no doubt that now those reservations are obsolete. Because computer animation can also control sequence, it would probably be more effective than our hand-controlled animation stand, creating a precise linear rhythm comparable to music and thus more effective as well as helping us realize, as I wrote at the time, "a visual approximation of music." This film, unlike its predecessor, is still available for public screening. As recently as 1985, *Constructivist Fictions* won us honorable mention in the "Classe Independant" at the 25th Festival Mondial du Cinema de Courts Metrates.

II

> To use sound in this naturalistic way will destroy the culture of montage, for every adhesion of sound to a visual montage piece increases its inertia as a montage piece, and increases the independence of its meaning — and this will undoubtedly be to the detriment of montage, operating in the first place not on the montage pieces, but on their juxtaposition.
>
> Only a contrapuntal use of sound in relation to the visual montage piece will afford a new potentiality of montage development and perfection.
>
> The first experimental work with sound must be directed along the line of its distinct nonsynchronization with the visual images. And only such an attack will give the necessary palpability which will later lead to the creation of an orchestral counterpoint of visual and aural images. — Eisenstein, Pudovkin & Alexandrov, "A Statement" (1928)

My next major film, *Epiphanies*, begun in 1981, drew upon another set of single-sentence stories I had begun writing two years before and, indeed, continue to write. Whereas the earlier sentences were either openings or closings, these are epiphanies, in the James Joycean sense. In Joyce's theory of short fiction, we remember, the epiphany is the encompassing climactic moment that functions to illuminate the entire story. In my own *Epiphanies*, I have tried to suggest the same momentous quality within a single sentence, which is to say that each Epiphany is meant to be so evocatively sufficient that the remainder of the story need not be told. Collected together, these climactic moments (within otherwise nonexistent stories) provoke a fictional experience that is not linear, but spatial; not sequential, but thoroughly discontinuous; not nineteenth-century, but twentieth. No story in these fiction *Epiphanies* is more important than any other; no story is intentionally connected to another. None is, in context, merely transitional. One aim in my mind was to exploit the freedoms of its open-ended form to touch upon the fullest range of human experience — to write perhaps the most universal fiction ever written.

Wishing to extend this narrative principle into film, I decided that, instead of staging visually climactic moments, it would be better to find *Epiphanies* in outtakes gathered from other filmmakers. Had I shot my own footage, I figured, the style of a single cameraman or director would inevitably impose a consistency utterly contrary to my purpose of making each sequence a distinctly separate entity, as well as contrary to my desire for universality. So, I gathered thousands and thousands of feet of 16mm film, from the widest variety of sources both professional and amateur, in a diversity of formats and styles, in order to find moments, only in the visual track, that had this epiphanic quality. Often my viewing has been completely contrary to what the cameraman had in mind, but that is my prerogative as the filmmaker. For instance, one of my favorite sequences is simply of the film (or the cameraman behind it) trying to find the focus. Less than one-tenth of one percent of the film has been usable.

I took only the visual track, because the sound track of the film contains my stories, read by as many different voices as possible; some of the individual readings were electronically processed further to separate them from all others. And, of course, the compositional principle is that stories on the sound track should not relate to those immediately after and before, and not relate as well to those on the screen and then that the beginnings and ends of sound and sight not coincide. As a result, the sound track and visual track are esthetically similar, not only in unending climaxes but in utter discontinuity.

My wish is that the final film should be four hours long; but in the course of gathering footage, and recording audiotape, wholly without any outside funding, I have put together several versions literally of the work-in-progress. One film is about twenty-eight minutes long and silent; it was printed in Berlin in 1981. From time to time, I have screened it publicly in conjunction with an edited audiotape. Seeing this, the "Projektions" series of North German Television commissioned a twenty-minute version with a sound track of the stories read in German by sixteen readers; it was broadcast in 1983. Around the same time I edited a film perhaps seventy minutes long, but this has never been printed. Working with student interns, who relish hands-on activity, I've been assembling a sound track that is now two hours long, in addition to selecting more footage to mix with that already edited. I figure that, after several years of sporadic work, I am poised to complete it, once sufficient funding comes down (from Lord knows where).

The work is so various and abundant that people viewing it tend to come away with (1) a sense of the whole and (2) moments, either verbal or visual, that particularly appeal to them. In my experience, everyone has his or her favorites, usually for personal reasons (and whether these favorites are visual or verbal often indicates much about their perceptual outlook). In other words, the film *Epiphanies* is so expansively open that the only quality I as author/artist can expect viewers to perceive is its esthetic theme: the exhaustive experience of the experience of story. Anything else any viewer takes away is, literally, his or her own to possess. In truth, it is the favorite of my films, and the one I hope most likely to make a substantial contribution to film art.

As the film *Epiphanies* becomes longer and more various, it becomes in truth less appropriate for viewing in conventional ways. Several people who have seen the version-in-progress more than once have asked me if "the second film differed from the first." This indicates not trickery on my part but a quality peculiar to *Epiphanies*: a film so rich in discrete parts simply cannot be assimilated thoroughly in a single sitting. This perception suggests that it should be viewed in radically different ways. My initial feeling is that the film is best viewed in situations where members of the audience can enter and leave as they wish, confident that they could return at any point without difficulty. While they might have missed certain episodes, they would not, upon their return, feel in any sense lost. In that case it would be more appropriate to show the film continuously in public spaces where people could stay as long as they wish, perhaps because they had time on their hands. The possibilities that come immediately to mind would be waiting rooms at airports, hotel lobbies and other semipublic spaces (even movie houses) where moderately sophisticated people would be pleased to discover footage not just different in quality from what they normally see but also more interesting than musak and yet less demanding than a book. My suspicion is that once the film is completed, other projection alternatives will become apparent.

Another possibility would be dividing the 240-minute film into a large number of very short films—say fifty-two, between four and six minutes long, and running them in a sophisticated moviehouse, one each week for all the weeks of the year, as a kind of continuing discontinuous serial that would precede the regular feature (and thus allow lagging spectators a few extra minutes before the feature begins). One principle I should make clear is that I have no objection to individuals walking out on this film, because they aren't really "missing anything," except more of the same experience.

III

Perhaps the most engaging problem of cinema is the relationship that sound may have to visual image. — Paul Sharits, "Words Per Page" (1974)

In the course of living in Berlin, I came across an unusually evocative artifact—the great Jewish cemetery of Berlin-Weissensee. Founded in 1880, with over 110,000 graves, it more than anything else in Berlin today evoked pre–World War II culture, not only of Jews but of Berlin in general. My first thought was that this subject should become a book of photographs. Martin Koerber, a young Berlin filmmaker who helped me prepare *Epiphanies*, thought that it should be a film and became my partner in realizing it. We agreed that since the cemetery and its suggestive gravestones become an arch-aeological window into a Berlin that no longer exists, only it should appear on the screen. The sound track would be composed of recollections about the place gathered on audiotape from ex–Berliners. From such testimony, we would compose a sound track that could at times implicitly explain what was on the screen, and other times be a counterpoint. As the ex–Berliners spoke, it would become clear that they were real people, rather than actors, and that they were speaking from the authority of their own experience. With the help of a West Berlin grant, we made *Ein Verlorenes Berlin* (1983) that was subsequently screened at major international festivals in Berlin and Oberhausen, as well as the first Documentarfilmfestival in Munich in 1985.

Inter Nationes, the German translation agency, was predisposed to translating the film into other languages, adding subtitles to the original Ger-man print. However, since the gravestones already provided so much to read, we decided not to do that, or to allow the affectations of overdubbing. In-stead, we chose a more authentic documentary tactic of interviewing other Berlin refugees speaking those languages, and from their authentic testimony about their own experience—telling in their own voices different stories in an adopted tongue—to compose a wholly new sound track for each other language.

First we did Swedish, completing it in 1984; then we did English, which was completed in 1985, and then French, completed in 1986; and more re-cently Spanish and Hebrew—in sequence, *Ett Forlorat Berlin, A Berlin Lost, Berlin Perdu, El Berlin Perdido* and *Berlin Sche-Einena Jother*. As a result, there is no original version of which the others represent a translation; the only "original" is the visual track which could take a sound track in any language spoken by ex–Berliners.

This film too offers unusual opportunities for screening. Of course, it can be screened in a conventional way, all twenty minutes of it, and has been shown as such in festivals and over German television. In my personal tours as a filmmaker, I like to show it twice, first in English, say, and then in Ger-man, handing out an English translation for the latter, not only because the gravestone imagery begs to be reseen (and reread), but because that gives me a chance to expose an audience to our commitment to wholly original sound tracks in each language. In a museum, the visual track could be shown on a single screen while the audience has access to six different sets of head-phones, or radio receivers with six channels, each carrying one of the film's languages. A bilingual viewer could thus sit through the film twice, tuning into a different sound track each time; he or she could also switch among sound tracks in the course of a single viewing. Because the sound tracks do differ from each other, not only in content but tone, this would be the ultimate experience of our film.

IV

The idea of making films in conventional ways interests me not at all,
for a variety of reasons. First, they are too expensive; and unless you are rich
or have an immediate backer, you necessarily waste too much time trying to
raise money. A single patron is likely to want more control than you are willing to allow; and if you are a "nonprofit" operation, you will probably need
to solicit from more sources than you can remember. Either way the process
generates more human problems than I need just now, thank you. Secondly,
you are forced to work with too many people, too many of whom must be
pushed around, too many of whom have egos that must be assuaged. Serious
art is best made, in my experience, by one person working by himself or, at
most, with one associate or assistant. Other than the footage of Weissensee,
all my films have been made this way.

The writing of conventional film scripts would be tolerable, if I did not
need to take responsibility for realizing them; but that is not art-making, as
I understand it, as much as a kind of magazine-writing, which is to say
preparing texts for other people to package. The only film-writing I would
do on my own would be scripts comparable to Moholy-Nagy's fourteen-page
Dynamic of the Metropolis (1921–22), which appeared in his book *Painting
Photography Film* (1926). It consists of texts and pictures that are laid out on
two-page spreads in ways that would suggest a film, even though it would
never be realized as a film (and perhaps could not be). Indeed, I thought more
than once that I should like to do a whole book of such putative scenarios.

V

*When we say expanded cinema we actually mean expanded consciousness. Expanded
cinema does not mean computer films, video phosphors, atomic light, or spherical projections. Expanded cinema isn't a movie at all: like life it's a process of becoming, man's
ongoing historical drive to manifest his consciousness outside of his mind, in front of his
eyes. One no longer can specialize in a single discipline and hope truthfully to express
a clear picture of its relationship to the environment.* — Gene Youngblood. *Expanded
Cinema* (1970)

Now that I've made several films with nonsynchronous sound, I'm committed to the method; but in the future, rather than beginning with film, I
want to start with a sound track and then compose a film for it, in a reversal
of the common procedure. Of all my extended audio compositions, that
which lends itself most to film would be my *New York City* (1984), which was
first composed for the "Metropolis" series of Westdeutscher Rundfunk. An
extended audiotape of and about the sounds unique to my hometown, the work

currently exists in three different versions: (1) the original 90-minute, which I find the most satisfactory in overall structuring; (2) the 60-minute version prepared for WDR and subsequently included in its contribution to *Documenta VII* (1987); (3) the 140-minute tape, which I mean to be an American version, different from the others in containing more speech that, only to English-speaking ears, would sound typical of New York.

How to film it? If my theme is to be the variousness of the city, it should draw upon imagery from a variety of sources and thus have not one cameraman but many, most working with hand-held cameras, each in charge of gathering footage for one of the many audio sequences; and if only because I would rather not get involved with shooting the film (remember my bias against working with too many people), I would want this footage to come to me, editing it to my tape, much as we previously edited tape to our film. The result would, I hope, be like my audiotape — somewhere between a documentary and a composition, and in that way perhaps unique. One model in my mind is, of course, Walter Ruttmann's 1927 film about Berlin, *Symphony of a City*; and while I was living in Berlin, I thought more than once about composing for Ruttman's footage a contemporary electro-acoustic sound track of sounds unique to Berlin (beginning with the aggressive "pass control" of the East German border police), superceding the classical music that Ruttman himself had in mind. Someone else got that plum, to my regret; but now that my *New York City* exists on audiotape, I would like to film it myself, as long as I'm alive, rather than leave it, as Ruttmann necessarily did, for someone else.

On Not Reediting an Old Anthology, In Spite of Wanting to Do So (1989)

In sum, American art has been divided between copying and adapting European models, on the one hand, and sporadic efforts to break away from those models and derive sustenance from the new, on the other. — Harold Rosenberg, "Tradition — or Starting from Scratch," *Art and Other Serious Matters* (1985)

Over a decade ago I edited an anthology of esthetics that differed from others of its kind in focusing upon the uniqueness of post–1959 art. Entitled *Esthetics Contemporary* (Prometheus), it included essays so rich with illumination about contemporary arts in general that, in my judgment, they suggested philosophies of art for our time. With selections by both critics and philosophers, as well as artists, the book reflected a decade's reading; it was edited to emphasize encompassing ideas, touching upon everything important, and yet be free of fad and jargon (and devoid as well of opportunism and other departures from principle that were likely to become ever more glaring during the life of a book). As I wrote in the preface, "There is little in this book with which I totally disagree, and even less that I find totally incomprehensible."

Though *Esthetics Contemporary* was scarcely reviewed when it appeared in 1978, it sold sufficient copies in the past decade to warrant a second, tenth-anniversay edition, which I've just completed. Although I was prepared to revise everything from scratch (within the publishers's constraint of adding no more than fifty new pages) and thus read over fifty new books and countless articles, I wound up changing very little, for reasons that are not uninteresting.

The first problem was what to drop from the first edition. I asked colleagues to suggest excisions, especially if they were recommending something that they felt belonged instead; I also questioned those who used the book in their classes. However, only one colleague had persuasive suggestions; and when I offered others a few possibilities for cutting, especially in conversation with those who had taught the book, the reply was usually that omitting that particular essay would be a mistake. Sometimes I tried to substitute within a kind, such as replacing Robert Smithson's "A Sedimentation of the Mind" (1968) with Rosalind Krauss' "Sculpture in an Expanded Field" (1979); but that new piece did not seem as strong or work as well within the whole. Nothing by Donald Kuspit, among others, seems as weighty as Linda Nochlin's "Realism Now" (1968). Other possible additions disrupted the flow. (To my embarrassment now, I even solicited new permissions I did not use.) Making a new edition became a terribly perplexing business, as I was doing a helluva lot of work that was leading nowhere. I began to think that I had made an edifice so firm that no part could be replaced, although a few holes could be plugged in.

The key strength of the original edition, I now think, is that each selection is placed where it and only it can be; so that the flow from essay to essay proceeds unhindered, with new selections sometimes echoing themes in their predecessors. (Remember that the purpose of any anthology is to make a coherent book that does not, and would not, otherwise exist.) After my introduction, which is a critical history of American esthetic thought from Suzanne Langer to John Cage—from the 1940s to the 1960s—*Esthetics Contemporary* is divided into two major parts: essays on the arts in general, and those on specific arts. The first selection is Michael Kirby's "The Esthetics of the Avant-Garde," an inordinately illuminating essay that opens his book *The Art of Time* (1969), which has long been out of print. Then come two essays by L. Moholy-Nagy, whose last book, *Vision in Motion* (1946), survives for me as the single greatest compassing essay on artistic modernism. The remainder of my anthology's first part has the following:

> The Relation of Environment to Anti-Environment, by Marshall McLuhan
> Apropos of "Readymades," by Marcel Duchamp
> Art and Disorder, by Morse Peckham
> Chance-Imagery, by George Brecht
> Semi-Constructs of the Secretaire du Registre, by Carl D. Clark &
>   Loris Essary
> On Form, by Kenneth Burke
> Style and Representation of Historical Time, by George Kubler
> Art and Authenticity, by Nelson Goodman
> Systems Esthetics, by Jack Burnham
> Aesthetics and Contemporary Arts, by Arnold Berleant
> Art as Internal Technology: The Return of the Shaman—the Descent of
>   the Goddess, by José A. Argüelles
> Intermedia, by Dick Higgins
> Criticism and Its Premises, by Harold Rosenberg

Anyone familiar with even a few of these essays can recognize that this is a heady mix of ideas about contemporary art, touching on a variety of issues, including both radicals and conservatives, both philosophers and artists, contributors born in 1946 along with those born in 1906, 1897, and 1887.

In the second part of *Esthetics Contemporary* are essays on particular arts, and again the table of contents makes its own point:

In the second part of the book, to summarize, the discussion moves from painting to sculpture to artistic machines to architecture to music to dance to video to happenings theater to conceptual art to polyartistry, and as such the second part becomes a genre-centered survey that subsumes a more advanced esthetics.

For the new edition, I made three additions to the first part, all toward the end: one dealing in a comprehensive way with the new technology of the computer and its relation to art, the second dealing with art and radical politics:

To the second half of the book I added appropriately weighty statements about arts not covered before. Immediately after Robert Smithson's I put a Robert

Irwin elaboration of related themes about public art; behind Paul Sharits' essay on film, I put Peter Wollin's "Photography and Aesthetics" and A. D. Coleman's "The Image in Question." Immediately after Jerome Rothenberg's "Pre-face" went Ulises Carrión's "The New Art of Making Books," which is to say book-art, or the book as an art-object. In place of John Cage's 1974 statement about "The Future of Music," I put a collage of remarks that was drawn from a longer chapter on his esthetics in my book *Conversing with Cage* (1988). I replaced David Antin's 1972 essay on video with something more recent by Maureen Turim. Behind it now are new essays on radio and holography.

Since the contents of the new *Esthetics Contemporary* are not much different from the first, the only sign of all the fresh research and thinking I did is a longer bibliography! Damn, damn, damn; the book that defeated my attempt to revise it now makes me look much, much lazier than I was.

Kenneth Clark:
Truth in Titling? (1985)

If only it were possible to sell short on the art market! One would make a fortune betting against the judgment of certain critic-tipsters. — Harold Rosenberg, "The Cultural Situation Today" (1972)

A title as grand as *The Art of Humanism* evokes the image of a book equally grand, which this, alas, is not. *The Art of Humanism* is less about an artistic style or even an age than about five gentlemen named Alberti, Donatello, Uccello, Mantegna, and Botticelli. Indicatively, the book has only five chapters, one apiece on the five figures, since there is neither an introduction nor a conclusion that might support the title. Largely close analyses of visual details, these five chapters are best read in conjunction with the numerous, mostly full-page photographic illustrations. Internal evidence (such as "with which some of you may be familiar") suggests that the text began as scripts for Kenneth Clark's traveling slide shows, given Lord knows where or when (as no credits are provided), and then slapped together to make this book whose true title should incorporate an acronym of the subjects' names, "The Art of ADUMB." Much as we desire truth in advertising, so of book publishers, especially, we book-buyers have a right to demand truth in titling.

The assumption of the book's title is that these five fifteenth-century artists epitomize art we should call humanistic. However, neither Clark nor his publisher think this a thesis worth proving. Indeed, in the few times Clark uses the epithet or its variants, he usually refers to an intellectual attitude whose opposite is theist. However, Clark's subject is not belief but art; and for all of its usefulness as a platitude, *humanism* is no more of an esthetic (or art-historic) category than *animalism* or *vegetism*. Whether these five lectures have scholarly value with reference to earlier commentaries on these hot five, I cannot tell; as essays on art, they offer little.

If mislabeling is the first problem of the book, the second problem is Clark's style. In his fawning introduction, John Walker, director emeritus of the National Gallery, suggests that "the average reader" will be as "equally spellbound" as he the scholar-curator was. Not so. There is no way that an above-average reader, let alone a professional in areas other than art history, could get through this, among other passages (and then, as one test of comprehension, tell someone else about it):

> Once more we are aware of this conflict between a scientific and stylistic approach, a dilemma which does not seem to have troubled Alberti, but which underlies the whole of the *della Pittura* in the same way that a conflict between his realistic Tuscan business philosophy and the teachings of Plato underlies his moral writings. In that event it was the classicising and stylistic part of Alberti's writings, and not his scientific naturalism, which was realised in the painting of the next hundred years.

Indeed, the defect of Walker's collegial introduction is that instead of answering nagging questions about the provenance of these lectures, it is devoted to unctious promotional blather (that is no more acceptable now, after Clark's recent death, than it was before, when Walker wrote).

The truth is that Clark's writing is not merely witless and undistinguished; it is often inept. "This was perhaps the first time," he writes on page 48, "that the men of the Renaissance felt they had excelled that antique culture which both inspired and oppressed them." *Excelled*? I had to look twice to be sure. Is this a misprint for "exceeded"? That is possible, though perhaps "transcended" would be more appropriate. Other offensive sentences seem added as concessions to popularization: "Uccello was far from being the Noah's Ark and rocking-horse painter which the superficial have supposed him to be." Not only are Clark's adjectives flippant here but so is his escalation of "superficial," an adjective for a certain kind of intellectual inadequacy, into the putative name of an intellectual or social class (that, need we say, cannot be found on Earth).

What is the "average reader" to make of passing references such as this about Botticelli's illustrations to Dante? "Since the war the drawings have been in East Berlin (actually about a third of them are on loan in Dahlem)." Unless the reader knows already to what that last term refers, someone other than Clark must tell him or her that Dahlem is the name of a section of West Berlin in which, to extend the allusion, is located the Dahlem Museum. Since Clark does not even say "in the Dahlem," the suspicion is that here he is addressing an audience not of "average readers" but exclusively of professional colleagues who can grasp, without pause, not just the first level of his reference but the second!

Another problem is Clark's arrogance — such unwarranted confidence in oneself, as well as the immediate audience's acceptance of oneself, that controversial assertions need not be supported or qualified:

> Throughout history revolutions in art have taken the form of a return to nature against exhausted formulas of picture-making, or an excessive attachment to style for its own sake. All true revolutions are popular and anti-

hierarchic, and ultimately popular art is always realistic art. That modern
abstract art should be called "bolshevik" is a comical misnomer; far from being the art of the *bolshoi*, the many, it is the art of the very few, and in any
thorough-going revolution it would be swept away. It could be correctly described as anarchic, contrary to the old laws, and so entirely subjective.

What makes this passage arrogant is that not only obvious objections but
critical questions come to mind. If Clark's implicit point is that abstract
modernism is not really revolutionary, because it does not fit his putative
historical model for revolutionary art, then he should say so explicitly in his
next sentences which here, however, merely continue an earlier commentary
on Alberti. If this book were truly edited, rather than merely processed, a
statement like this would have been challenged and then either explained,
corrected, or deleted.

Why was this book published? Why do Kenneth Clark's scholarly,
detailed lectures on five fifteenth-century artists now appear as a trade book?
To go after an answer is to uncover a major intellectual scandal of our time —
a scandal everyone knows, but few acknowledge — which is, simply, that in
deciding which scholarly works to issue today, commercial publishers are less
concerned with intellectual value and even editorial accuracy than with the
fame of the author. The key that opens their coffers is *celebrity*, not insight or
reputation, which is to say, in this case, that once Clark became famous
through a television series, operations like Harper & Row were predisposed
to exhume his lecture notes. And naïve book reviewers were predisposed to
shower any new Kenneth Clark title with perfunctory praise. The cynical
assumption is that to be sold in sufficiently remunerative numbers a scholarly
book needs a familiar name, a pretentious title and then an introduction
assuring first the publishers, then the reviewers who read only introductions,
and finally the bookstore managers that this trade title ought to be accessible
to the general public. With so much deceit all along the line, everyone involved
should be ashamed.

(On the other hand, for all of the publisher's dream of dollar-signs, there
was not enough desire to make a book that agreed with the text. One reason
why *The Art of Humanism* is cheaper than other art books today is that the illustrations are all black and white. This limitation is scarcely noticed until a
particular painting is credited with "ravishingly beautiful colour," while the
illustration is only black-white, or Clark describes a certain sculpture as
"polychrome." In the latter case, the reader wants either to be told what colors
are there or to see them in an illustration. In this hasty transition from a slide
show to a book, we get neither. On the other hand, in the limitation of the
illustrations is perhaps an implicit slight — that Sir Kenneth, for all of his
celebrity, was not enough of a sure-fire star to justify the expense of color!
Only Norman Mailer or Marilyn Monroe would deserve that.)

The worst problem plaguing cultural communication today is that in choosing what intellectuals and ideas to push through their incomparable distribution systems, commercial book publishers appear to follow the new media more than lead them. As soon as a writer appears prominently on the tube, too many book publishers rush to scrape (and package) his lint off the screen. And most everyone else involved with the dissemination of culture, from book reviewers to teachers, appear predisposed to follow the wagging tail, exemplifying Harold Rosenberg's classic image of "the herd of independent minds." In my judgment, this abdication of cultural initiative, coupled with an inability to correct the corruptions of cultural communication, is, to be frank, the surest sign of the treason of the supposed intellectuals in our time.

Self-Sabotage: Donald Kuspit's Art Criticism (1989)

A mind is rarely as independent as it thinks it is. — Harold Rosenberg, "Artist of Our Time" (1975)

Donald Kuspit has emerged as the most visible art critic of the 1980s, contributing prolifically to all the art magazines (even those that normally exclude competitors' contributors from their own pages). Few of his contemporaries could collect recent journalism into a book as thick as *The New Subjectivism* (1988), which has over 530 pages of text, at five hundred words to a page, which is to say a quarter of a million words. Kuspit generally writes medium-length essays with authority, allusions and footnotes, letting his reader know that, at least for the duration of the essay, he is the real critic of a sort less common in art magazines than in literary. However, the making of a book provides a higher test for a journalistic critic, forcing him as it does to reveal assumptions and demonstrate coherence. Quite simply, writing that might seem persuasive in the context of an art magazine can, when launched on its own, seem considerably slighter, while a history of fashionably "solid" judgments can, if gathered together, reveal a pattern of opportunism, if not blatant contradictions.

A book-length collection also requires the critic to reveal "where he is coming from," as we say, and Kuspit, to his credit, doesn't shirk that responsibility. In the preface he acknowledges his subjectivism in the following forthright terms:

> I initially took a psychoanalytic stance in self-protective — self-perservative — response to the extreme narcissism of the many artists I know personally. Their self-centeredness — no doubt encouraged by their manic determination to be famous (with me as one instrument of that fame) — seemed to go beyond the "arrogance" Abraham Maslow notes as inseparable from creativeness.

What is odd here is the revelation, unknown to me from any other critic in any art, of initial negative motivations — he came to his approach not through love or esthetic discovery but personal distaste.

However, once you understand this peculiarity, the characteristic shape of Kuspit's evaluations become more apparent. His likes are inseparate from his dislikes, and behind all his advocacies stand, some more visible than others, certain denigrations. For his enthusiasm for German expression (and American imitators) there is a distaste for modern American abstraction; behind his love for painting is a distaste for conceptual art. And so forth. An essay titled "Beuys or Warhol?" is less a paean to the former than a hateful denigration of the latter. Dan Graham's work is praised not as multimedia minimal/conceptual art but for "its communalism or humanism [that "in fact contradicts"] the basic understandings of Minimalism and conceptualism [odd choices of capitalization his], which took the Modernist conception of art as a rigorously self-reflexive enterprise to its ultimate hermetic logic." Here, as elsewhere, the rhetoric of dump is stronger, filled as it is with jabbing asides, than that of puff.

This back-assed approach leads to riots of duplicity, where while appearing to confront one issue Kuspit is really attacking another. The best example of this is a 1984 essay, "The Emptiness of Pluralism, the End of the New," that begins as a critique of the current general acceptance of a diversity of artistic styles as equally valid. "It speaks not only against the emergence of any one art as authoritative in the present," Kuspit writes, "but against the authority of tradition, based on a supposed consensus of values which, while not predictive, stabilizes and unconsciously sets the limits for the scene of current production." However, a few paragraphs later, Kuspit is no longer attacking pluralism but the cults of youth and novelty. By his conclusion the initial subject was completely forgotten: "No critic worth that name can celebrate the new just because it is new — powered by immediacy — for pure novelty has a way of quickly aging. . . ." The deceit of Kuspit's argument is that the current acknowledgment of esthetic pluralism does *not* extend from or depend upon the tradition of the new at all, instead benefiting from its decline (and persistent attacks upon it), so that to equate the two, as Kuspit does, is at minimum duplicitous. What the current pluralism does allow is recognition of retrograde art, such as the expressionisms favored by Kuspit, along with genuine novelty; it also permits the acceptance of retrograde critics! What Kuspit is really advocating here, backing into his point, is anti–avant-garde, anti–Modernist painting whose canonization I take to be reactionary and grossly authoritarian.

In these negative respects, Kuspit resembles not Clement Greenberg and Harold Rosenberg, the two kings of post–World War II American criticism, both of whom were enthusiasts at the apex of their careers, but another figure whom Kuspit rarely mentions, perhaps out of embarrassment — Hilton Kramer, who remains the most promiscuous hater the art world has ever known. Not unlike Kuspit, Kramer cannot love without hating; and what they also share is subjective methodology — a desire to identify the culture and motives of an artist in his or her work, which is to say that both men let their sense of the creator, whether real or imagined, affect their evaluations of his or her creative career. The risk of this subjective approach is solipsism. (With this last thought in mind, anyone who has read both men can play the game of guessing who has committed the latter sin more often.)

Whereas Kuspit, as a self-styled intermediary between art and its public, wants to influence taste, much as Greenberg and Rosenberg did, his odd attitude, generously characterized as "ambivalence," courts the deficiency that has plagued Kramer's career — an inconsistent negativity that keeps him persistently inconsequential. (It is not for nothing that Kramer rarely collects his essays in his books; it is not for nothing that he moves from one editorial position to another, simply to ensure through the acquisition of such power a public presence that might otherwise disappear.)

Another fault distinguishing Kuspit from the masters is glibness. All too often at crucial points of his presentations are sentences like the following from page 180: "In the propane blow torch, Kounellis has a succinct metaphor for the entire process of passage from death to life, sickness to health. In this one object the entire process is stated and completed." (Only with a lot of imagination.) Or this from page 537: "The point of Postmodernism may be to remind us that there is no escape from the recognition of our own archaeological condition. Archaologism, at the least, is clearly a stock-taking." (Here, as elsewhere, the unironic shifting of diction becomes a sign of babbling.)

Hastiness also informs the process of putting this book together. Several footnotes refer to "current" exhibitions that are long gone (and won't return, alas). Whereas the appreciation of Eric Fischl includes an unnecessarily familiar illustration, that devoted to Victor Hugo's drawings desperately needs examples that no doubt appeared in the art magazine where the essay initially appeared but, alas, are not provided here.

Perhaps out of awareness of his lack of influence, Kuspit frequently adopts a bullying style, initially with psychoanalytic jargon (itself the lingo of oneupmanship):

> The prototaxic mode of experience is infantile. It is paradoxical that to establish an infantile mode of experience of the art object — immediate experience of it — requires such a heroic effort. But this is because only an infantile experience of the art object can disclose its extra-ordinary [sic] significance for us. Only the experience of it as "mothering" us with its "sensational" immediate givenness discloses the infantile character of our attachment to it. [Etc.]

Zowie, aren't you impressed? Don't you wonder who is?

For all the Greenberg- and Rosenberg-bashing prevalent today, a reading of this Kuspit book, especially in conjunction with the recent reissues of

Greenberg's early journalism (from Harvard Univ. Press) and Rosenberg's fugitive essays (from the Univ. of Chicago Press), confirms a point quite opposite perhaps from what Kuspit had in mind, which is that in their thrones the king and king, hand in hand, are safe for now.

The Perils of Preaching
to the Converted (1991)

A quarter-century ago, when I was living in a low-income project on the edge of Harlem (where our Congressman was Adam Clayton Powell, while the building across Amsterdam Avenue was represented by William Fitts Ryan), another Caucasian graduate student residing upstairs took me aside after I voted in a Democratic primary. "You should join the George Washington Carver Club," he told me. Why me? "I'm on the board of directors," he continued, "but since I'm going to teach at Vassar this year they'll put you on the board of directors." Huh? "They need a token white." Out of the Carver Club, remember, came David Dinkins and many of his loyal associates. I figure now that had I accepted this opportunity (and kept my nose clean) I might now be the New York City cultural czar. Another story from the time was Jackie Robinson's lament, after his son was arrested, that he was a better father to a universe of children than he was to his own son. True, I thought, and those children weren't only black.

What's missing from Lucy R. Lippard's *Mixed Blessings* (1990) is any sense of the realities behind either of these experiences — no sense of tokenism and no sense of the cultural interaction between minorities and majorities (which can at times include minorities). This unreality depends upon writing about the visual arts in isolation, for the "art world" is at once her subject and her blinder. With her protest in mind, one need only turn to sports or even to military politics for contrary insights. Remember, in the latter case, that the current chief of staff began with two strikes against him: The Bronx-born son of West Indian immigrants, he started his military career not in any of our august military academies but with ROTC at CCNY. Perhaps reverse discrimination, Crowjimism if you will, contributed to his ascendancy, as it might have contributed to mine, had I joined the Carver club; but reverse discrimination is very much a fact of American life in the late twentieth century. There is, to my recollection, no acknowledgment for it in *Mixed Blessings*.

Otherwise, her book consists of short sympathetic descriptive appreciations, none particularly longer than the others, of many artists "of color," which encompasses all peoples, or categories of peoples, that our government has come to define as "minorities." These individual artists are customarily introduced by their "color" affiliations: "African American," "Puerto Rican," "Seneca," "Colville/Okanogan," "Pinoy (Filipino)," etc. Not unlike the old-fashioned WASP, Lippard believes, you see, in the myth of privileged birth(s) and superior upbringing, tagging them onto her subjects just as the *New York Social Register* identifies its chosen few by favored prep schools and colleges—for much the same reason, to make them, by mere mention of an affiliation alone, acceptable to the cognoscenti. (Sometimes I think you must be a WASP to believe this myth. No Jewish male would, though some Jewish females reportedly do.)

The tags are necessary to Lippard's presentation because the illustrations are largely prosaic and academic in a variety of ways (mostly representational), which is to say that they wouldn't appear in a book without some privileged excuse. If any individual made sufficiently better art than the others, you'd think he or she would have gotten more of her critical attention. Admirers of Lippard's best polemical style, including myself, will find *Mixed Blessings* a tedious catalogue of too many names, portrayed within a limited set of critical terms, in sum reminding me of B. H. Haggin's characterization of Jacques Barzun's "lifetime of indiscriminate collecting of bits of material into files, then an equally indiscriminate emptying of the files into books." There is no persuasion here; only the marshalling of assent (and ascent). The publishing assumption must be that all the individuals named have enough relatives and, more important, teach enough courses to keep the book afloat. Remembering Lippard's earlier masters, it is not unreasonable to ask: What would Ad Reinhardt, were he still alive, think of this?

At one point Lippard acknowledges that one problem unique to the art biz is discriminations by taste—the pseudo-objective judgments by people educated to and experienced in making such judgments. Art admittedly isn't sports where someone can run measurably faster than his or her competitiors or box better, or steal more bases. Sports competition is a great leveler at which blacks have done quite well (though Asian-Americans haven't) without the need for "affirmative action" or reverse discrimination. African Americans have also demonstrated that pop music must be a fairly open domain, where sales into the millions are often achieved apart from corporate promotional efforts. However, popular discriminations by taste are realities, American realities, Lippard can't acknowledge. (I'm personally awaiting an exposé of insensitive discrimination against fat people, in art as well as life; everyone knows it exists, to minimal protest.)

Thanks to her blinders, the question Lippard won't address is why by 1990 "people of color" should have comparatively less upper-echelon presence in the visual arts than they do at comparable levels in sports, say, or pop music or even the military? Remember that the art world is just as competitive as sports or pop music or the military, which is to say that out of the

thousands who aspire only a few succeed. Lack of opportunity is not a sufficient explanation, as most of us with a thirty-year memory can recall artists
of color who received remunerative recognition early in their careers and yet
never rose to a higher level of professional success (perhaps because of the
perils of such early recognition). Lack of education is not a sufficient explanation either, as children of color are as likely as white to be exposed to art in
their schools and the more talented are likely to be encouraged. Lack of institutional support will not do either — not in an era of federally mandated affirmative action, where required percentages are more likely to be met through
arts departments than engineering, say, or slavic languages.

With her head buried in strange "of color" sand, Lippard also ignores the
issue of economic class within the art world, referring at one point to a nonex-
hibiting sculptor as "a well-traveled pan–Africanist who also spends time in
the Caribbean." Maybe one needs to be a poor unaffiliated artist to recognize
that this sculptor must be a beneficiary of academia, where table talk about
exotic travel represents the attainment of class (much as gossip about favorite
haberdashers and restaurants do for stockbrokers and lawyers). Perhaps her
own prominence accounts for why Lippard fails to identify artist-full professors, regardless of race, as a privileged or upper class within the art world
(if not an aristocracy, because their income comes not from selling art but
somewhere else). Similarly, few public institutions have been as effective as
academic hothouses in imposing quotas, whether against minorities until the
1960s or for them since the 1970s.

It seems to me that Lucy R. Lippard hasn't learned the lesson of her own
life. She was one of two young female independent art critics emerging in the
early 1960s, in a culture which, remember, never had such female art critics
(as distinct from newspaper reviewers). Lippard proved her mettle by doing
quality work — writing articles and books, creating taste, challenging her
readers with biases and specific judgments they had not considered before,
much as any ambitious male critic would, no doubt against gender
resistances. What she did not do was inferior work that would require extra-
esthetic, ideological rationalizations to become acceptable. In the 1970s,
however, she got religion, as we say — a kind of leftist feminism — and has
since devoted most of her energies to preaching to the converted, beginning
on the college campuses that are filled with those similarly religious.

Lippard now reminds me of no other "critic" as much as the Hilton
Kramer who writes for *New Criterion* (as distinct from the more challenging
contributor to the *New York Observer*). Her art criticism is based not upon
direct perception of anonymous work but initially upon the artist's biography.
As any commercial book publisher can tell you, nothing sells new work better
than personal images that can be made compelling (e.g., even Stephen
Hawking's). Lippard has become less a critic than a publicist, writing press
releases without receiving remuneration from her subjects, to be sure, but

situating herself to collect other rewards along the way, including contracts from a commercial publisher whose specialty has been selling books to the converted.

The question still to be asked is how Lucy R. Lippard the woman critic succeeded in spite of resistances? None of the intelligence gained from that real experience appears in this book, which creates an embarrassing spectacle of a major league player slumming through minor league ball. One peril of spending most of your energies preaching to the converted is that you can lose not just outside influence but your critical faculties without having anyone tell you.

Architectural Criticism? (1967)

The precondition for kitsch, a condition without which kitsch would be impossible, is the availability close at hand of a fully matured cultural tradition, whose discoveries, acquisitions, and perfected self-consciousness kitsch can take advantage of for its own ends. —Clement Greenberg, "Avant-Garde and Kitsch" (1939)

John Jacobus' survey of recent architecture is a terribly disturbing book, less because of the turgid quality of his commentary than the typical presuppositions informing his critical focus. Buildings, to Jacobus, are primarily exercises in style, creating three-dimensional images lying somewhere between sculpture and painting; and the vocabulary of his analysis echoes the clichés of art criticism: "Although the palpable, encompassing space of architecture is more immediate than the physically impenetrable world of a painting, it is no less mysterious in its total impact."

A professor at Indiana, Jacobus is as much a historian as a critic of artistic images, and nothing earns his chosen architects more credits than a resonantly visual stylistic contribution: "[Louis] Kahn's architecture possesses a distinctive kind of magic: an ability to shed *light* upon the work of his contemporaries, as well as to *illuminate*, by analogy, certain works of the past, both near and remote [italics mine]." What makes this lamp approach fallacious, if not pernicious, is Jacobus' neglect of a building's primary purpose — sheltering people and supporting particular kinds of functions.

Behind Jacobus' preoccupation with "an ideal of space and form" are, I suppose, the assumptions that a beautiful building enhances the lives of those who function within it and, conversely, that an ugly building has a pervasively depressing effect upon its inhabitants. For others I shall not vouch, but my own experience denies these generalizations. Just after graduating from college, I lived for several years in one of those low-rent New York City projects that architectural critics condemn as visual blight (and "not architecture"), and some nonresidents have even characterized, on esthetic grounds, as unfit for human habitation. However, seeing with only one sense cannot stand for believing with all five. As a place to live, my project apartment was far more comfortable and attractive than other houses I have inhabited, while its remarkably cheap rent only increased my pleasure.

Nor does Jacobus' assumption hold for some very beautiful buildings I have known. Three friends work in what he and other architectural pundits rank among the most important post–World War II structures — a research laboratory; and by common consent, they suffer its beauty. Glass walls on two sides of each lab create a stunning image to the outside world, but on the inside so much window front reduces the space available for shelving. The absence of shades permits sunlight to pour into those labs exposed to the south, making them so unbearably hot and glaring that, since curtains are forbidden by the architect, many researchers deface the top halves of the windows with tin foil and/or comic strips. The labs themselves are so needlessly small and the hallways so wide that large machines must be placed in the halls, creating a fire hazard. The architect's critically acclaimed decision to expose the pipes overhead makes every laboratory noisy and denies the researchers the aural privacy conducive to their work, etc. Although the architect himself suggested, in conversation with me, that his design aimed to fulfill the needs of functioning researchers, his principle-laden explanations revealed that he had hardly investigated the totality of their needs. What he had done, instead, was unwittingly impose his own definition upon their activity and then build to this image. The claims for functionalism made by and for International-Style architecture were, as even Jacobus admits, "largely fictitious," for such patter usually functions to veil a display-designer's mentality.

In discussing the later work of Le Corbusier, Walter Gropius, Mies van der Rohe, and Frank Lloyd Wright, as well as younger architects in their traditions, Jacobus emphasizes fine-art phenomena to the exclusion of such considerations as how much a building costs, whether it is mechanically efficient, how its designers integrated such new technologies as electrical air-conditioning, whether these buildings reduce internal accidents (or remain as dangerous to human life and limb as some automobile tail fins), and, most important, whether the forms are appropriate to the functions and the people inside. Quite simply, what distinguishes buildings from paintings and sculptures is that they cost more money to produce and that they encase people; and an architectural criticism that neglects these two realities deals solely in surfaces. Indicatively, Jacobus' opulently designed book is comparatively overpriced and so shabbily manufactured that, in the course of normal reading, the text of my own copy ripped away from one side of its binding.

It is not surprising that Jacobus' survey entirely omits those architects who regard their primary mission as the creation of human habitats, such as Constantinos Doxiadis and R. Buckminster Fuller, even though certain Fuller domes, like the recent one at Expo '67, also display esthetic virtues; for Jacobus concentrates too tenaciously on the fortunes of the International Style (in a period he characterizes as "derivative in style to a large extent") to consider other forms of radical stylistic innovation. Whereas Jacobus' exemplars presume that beauty enhances the spirit, the other stream regards constructive ingenuity, technical efficiency, and conditions conducive to creaturely comfort as establishing a quasi-esthetic integrity. Indeed, this preference for efficiency over conspicuous beauty, as well as an avowal of more concern for the pleasures of the many over the few, is historically such a deeply American bias — its exponents include Horatio Greenough, Ralph Waldo Emerson, and Thorstein Veblen — that I find it indicative that Jacobus' preface is dated in Paris and that this book was originally commissioned by a German publisher.

Any thorough historical survey of recent architecture, whether of forms or ideas, simply must include such recent advances as Fuller's geodesic domes, which may well be the primary structural achievement of the recent period. Technically, they constitute a real breakthrough, not only in enclosing huge volumes of space at less cost but also for constructing shelter so portable that helicopters can easily fly a frame from one place to another. In his *Architecture in Transition* (1963), Doxiadis remarks, "How dangerous it is that the whole attention of our present era should be directed toward the nonrepeated types of buildings, which usually tend to become monuments." In this respect, Jacobus' book reflects and sustains a malaise in Western culture; it compliments the general concern with how good an automobile looks instead of how efficiently it runs and how prone it might be to accidents. Precisely because buildings, like automobiles, are primarily habitats, rather than visual feasts, architecture needs a criticism and a history that regard certain values as more important than esthetic ones.

Waiting for Revisionism (1991)

Bids for validation often include an attempt for approval from at least one of the wings of academia, accompanied by vehement denials of academic contamination. — Karl Young, "Ways and Means" (1991)

Holography and videotape became public around the same time, a quarter century ago; and whereas the former attracted only a few people, most of them professional, the latter attracted millions, nearly all of them amateur. Video grew out of television much as holography grew out of photography, but both new media were profoundly different, not only from their predecessors but from each other. If holography was far less accessible than photography, video, by contrast, was more accessible to masses of people than television. It would be fair to say that as an easy-entry medium video has become the photography of our generation.

Nonetheless, the number of video artists who have received critical attention is remarkably few, if not suspiciously few, and the principal implicit function of this anthology of criticism, Doug Hall and Sally Jo Fifer's *Illuminating Video* (1991), is perpetuating the myth of a select few, most of whom also contribute their own prose to this book. To identify the canon, go first to the "Videography" and simply note which names are represented by more than two tapes: Vito Acconci, Dara Birnbaum, Judith Barry, Juan Downey, Harry Gamboa, Dan Graham, Doug Hall, Lynn Hershman, Gary Hill, Joan Jonas, Thiery Kuntzel, Tony Labat, Chip Lord, Mary Lucier, Antonio Muntadas, Tony Ousler, Nam June Paik, Martha Rosler, Ira Schneider, Steina Vasulka, Woody Vasulka, and Bill Viola. That's it.

For an art so new, as well as populous, that's patently too small a canon. On further thought, it is also limited verging on narrowness: too much collage (whose syntax of pointed juxtaposition is by now passé in all arts other than video), too much journalistic commentary disguised as leftish attitudinizing, too much literal representation, too much West Coast-style performance instead of other arts, too much willful obscurity, too much self in lieu of art, too many individuals whose skills at negotiating artistic politics exceed their mediumistic imaginations; but the principal collective fault of this canon, in my opinion, is a limited sense of what this new artistic medium is about or can do. To get a clearer sense of what's wrong, imagine a photographic canon stylistically so narrow. The contributors' writing reflects these limitations, being self-consciously modish, not only in the selection of subjects but in terminology and theoretical touchstones. The fact that most of the commentary comes from individuals who don't write criticism about anything else is at once a reflection of and essential to the limitations.

Indeed, it could be said that video criticism depended upon the critical-academic acceptance of photography and film only a few years before. Remember that in American universities only thirty years ago there were no courses in film history, let alone instruction in the writing of criticism of these newer arts. However, whereas writing about photography and film and even television depended upon years of scattered thinking about those media, video criticism emerged quickly, with individuals and publications filling another easy-entry vacuum opportunistically. Indicatively, there were no pervasively influential theoreticians comparable to Rosenberg and Greenberg in visual art or Rudolf Arnheim in film or Marshall McLuhan on television, and no video critics who had honed their skills in writing intelligently about other arts (as Rosenberg and Greenberg had about modern writing, Arnheim about radio and visual art, McLuhan about traditional literature); instead, there emerged a pseudo-critical consensus affirmed by both the new video writers and, more important, the magazines publishing their work.

Consider taking a larger and longer view in identifying video that reveals esthetic possibilties unique to the medium, which includes not only image processing and cameraless image generation on one hand but its incomparable portability on the other. Perhaps the epitome of the latter is Clayton Patterson's *The Tomkins Square Police Riot* (1988), acknowledged in this book's videography and once in the text. The parts that have appeared on American television, mostly in news shows, barely hint at the virtues of the entire work. By carrying his camera on his hip and turning off its telltale operating light, Patterson was able to shoot single-handedly a fierce social protest in the middle of a hot summer night; his camera's single eye and monophonic ear were able to become intimate with people, including squatters and policemen, who had no suspicion they were being documented in ways impossible with more cumbersome (and less stealthy) film. It is like a Frederick Wiseman film, but better than his work has been recently. *The Tomkins Square Police Riot* shows not a police riot, as its title claims, but New Yorkers repelling the befuddled (and visibly reluctant for the most part) police and retaking a slumland park. Having seen four hours of unedited rushes in 1988, I'm waiting for the finished work and even for the theatrical release that the work deserves, initially for its mediumistic revelations.

Among the other video artists mentioned only once in the videography are Paul Ryan, Frank Gillette, Shigeko Kubota, and John Sanborn; among the artists omitted completely are the late Ed Emshwiller, whose *Scapemates* (1972) redefined video's image scale as different from film's; Stephen Beck, whose *Video Weavings* (1975) revealed to me at least the possibilities of computer-generated, cameraless imagery; William Wegman and Davidson Gigliotti, who were once considered consequential; Buky Schwartz, who plays a video image off a solid object; Irit Batsry, who essays longer forms in the medium self-consciously dominated by short takes; James Seawright, whose *Capriccio for TV* was the best of the pioneering WGBH compilation *The Medium Is the Medium* (1969); Gerald Marks, whose specialty is 3-D imaging; Merce Cunningham-Charles Atlas and Amy Greenfield, who are separately redefining the possible representation of dance in video; and Reynold Weidenaar, whose tapes are represented in international festivals of both music and video, not only because his sound tracks are music compositions (that exploit the videotape medium's under-utilized capability for hi-fi stero sound) but because his screens have a painterly beauty.

Indeed, some of these works are better seen on a two-part projection system with a large screen, a medium different from the CRT monitor on one hand and a movie screen on the other. Even though this last opportunity has been around for nearly two decades, the contributors to *Illuminating Video* seem to know nothing about it. What most of my alternative canon display is a technological moxie and esthetic courage (in confronting possibilities as difficult as those posed by, say, holography) unavailable to the herd of putatively independent, easy-entry minds.

Both *Illuminating Video* and the criticism consensus behind it are so false to my sense of video art that I'm willing to wager dollars to donuts that, despite all this pandering for academic acceptability, we will witness within two decades the appearance of radically different versions of the early history of video, a new history that, not unlike other revisionist reinterpretations in art, will emphasize mediumistic discovery and intrinsic excellence over once-modish concerns and transient privileges. Such anthologies as *Illuminating Video* will then come to resemble a bush-league dated artifact. Anybody with donuts?

Artforum: Looking "Critically" (1988)

Many of the artists I knew did read the New York art magazines, but only out of the superstitious regard for print that they shared with most other people; they did not really take seriously what they read. Art publications from France, and Cahiers d'Art *above all, were another matter; these kept you posted on the latest developments in Paris, which was the only place that really mattered.* — Clement Greenberg, "The Late Thirties in New York" (1960)

Everyone familiar with the literature of contemporary art knows that *Artforum* has, since its inception in 1962, been the best of the five regular art magazines (the others being *Arts, Art in America, Art News,* and *The New Art Examiner). Artforum* prints more intelligent articles, panders less to its advertisers, and has a greater influence (of a particular kind) than its competitors. It is the only art magazine to which I've ever subscribed; and although I'm always letting my subscription lapse, out of disgust with its limitations and modishness, I find that back issues, which are worth keeping, consume at least three running feet on my shelves.

Its own anthology of articles from its first twenty-two years, *Looking Critically,* makes these modish limitations blatantly apparent. Perhaps because art critics worry more than literary critics about grossly mistaken judgments, the errors here are not of commission but omission. There is nothing in these pages about visual poetry or holography or computer art, remarkably little about artistic machines or book-art or experimental films (even though art museums have been far more receptive to the last subject than moviehouses). The only acknowledgment of black artists that I can find is a short review of a Langston Hughes-Roy de Carva book. Other readers can no doubt identify other neglects of art that has had presence over the past three decades, notwithstanding the absence of printed coverage. Given the modern truth, more true in visual art than elsewhere, that subsequent critics and scholars always discover and praise what was neglected in its own time, we can, by implication, use the omissions of an anthology like *Looking Critically* as a sure guide to the future.

Art magazines are not like literary journals. Most of the reviews in art magazines appear after the exhibition has closed, which is to say that they have little influence on the selling of art. Also, because visual art is a retail business whose products are so expensive, in contrast to literature which requires wholesale distribution of comparatively cheap items, consequential collectors are very sophisticated people who generally don't follow reviews. (I remember a former editor of the *New York Times Book Review* once telling me that his medium exists to review what's currently available in the bookstores, just as the *Times* theater critics review new shows, both of them advising on cultural merchandise that requires many customers to succeed.) Art magazines instead influence art discussion, which is to say table chatter, whether over coffee and drinks in artists' studios or over the lunchroom in art colleges. That accounts for why art magazines are read in art schools with a far greater seriousness than comparable literary programs would devote to literary journals.

This self-anthology calls itself "looking critically," but it should be understood that the second word is used in a sense unfamiliar to readers of literary journals. It does not mean "severely," as what is completely absent from *Artforum*'s pages is the kind of comprehensive deflation of reputation that might appear in a literary journal. (That's because negative art writing has no more impact on sales than rave reviews.) "Critically" here means appreciatively and theoretically (with reference to philosophy), and probably reaches its apex when theory and appreciation combine. In part because new visual art is generally more original/unusual/eccentric than literary art, it resists easy understanding, and that resistance in turn creates a demand for writing that would clarify mysteries. Given that most poets and fictioners nowadays strive not to transcend conventions but to fulfill them, there is not much need nowadays for such exploratory understanding in literary reviewing.

Notwithstanding its problems, *Looking Critically* is rich in a certain kind of art-chatter that I find "a good read," to use a British phrase that has no American equivalent; and I had no problem getting through more than three hundred pages of multicolumned prose about the major developments and individuals of the past three decades. (Out of a reluctance to make mistakes, the book is edited to be both modishly inclusive and persistently intelligent.) The contributors include artists as well as critics, all of them writing in a wider variety of styles than is common in most literary journals. Among my own favorite pieces are "John Cage in Los Angeles" (1965), Ad Reinhardt's "A Chronology" (1967), Brian O'Doherty's "Inside the White Cube" (1976), and Bazon Brock's "The End of the Avant-Garde? And So, the End of Tradition" (1981). Another reason why this book is such a good read is that collections of articles from magazines are invariably more interesting than journalism collections by a single pundit.

Art/Literature:
Wholesale/Retail (1988)

In these circumstances, criticism cannot divide itself into literary criticism, art criticism, social criticism, but must begin in establishing the terms of the conflict between the actual work or event and its illusory context. — Harold Rosenberg, *The Tradition of the New* (1959)

Both art and literature have no value at birth; they assume value only when they are sold, usually by someone other than the artist/author. There, however, the similarity ends, as they are sold in different ways. The principal merchandizing difference between literature and the visual arts is that literature is a wholesale biz and visual art retail. Editions of books are sold in quantities of thousands, paintings in quantities of one. What is the significance of this? It means, first of all, that when it is said a novelist "sells well," his publisher is selling not thousands of copies but tens, if not hundreds, of thousands of copies. When a painter "sells," so to speak, the number of items changing owners can be less than a hundred. In literature, it is possible to speak of popular, if not mass, response to new work; in visual art, really not. Also, a book is sold for only several times production costs, as are mens' shirts and other wholesaled items; a painting is sold for many times the cost of its materials, adding even the expense of labor.

An art dealer is a retailer, who knows most of his real customers, as distinct from those who just browse in his store. A book publisher doesn't know the end customer at all; he sells the titles on his new list only to bookstore managers, who are the retailers of literature. For this reason, when a painter brings slides of his work to an art dealer, the dealer should be thinking: Can I sell this work to my regular customers—to Jill and Joe, Sally and Bob? A book publisher, confronted with a similar opportunity for taking on new work, has no knowledge of ultimate customers. He necessarily asks whether a proposed manuscript resembles anything that he has recently wholesaled successfully, or perhaps a competitor has wholesaled successfully. That is why, in making publishing decisions, he is forced to base them not upon his sense of customers' tastes but upon numerical projections of sales estimates, which are usually based upon the actual sales of prior books similar in kind.

This difference between wholesale and retail also accounts for the different function of such devices as reviews and advertisements. Reviews are necessary in wholesaling, because press attention brings the new work to the attention of a larger audience of possible buyers. In Broadway theater, most notoriously, favorable reviews in the daily press are necessary for survival, because nothing else can reach thousands of potential ticket-buyers during the initial weeks of a theatrical run. In visual art, reviews appear in both newspapers and the trade press — the art magazines. As the latter customarily appear after a show has closed, they have little impact upon sales. (Their real function, it is joked, is certifying that an exhibition actually happened.)

Collectors of visual art don't follow newspaper reviews, which they know to be irrelevant. Such newspaper reviews are followed instead by (1) browsers who tour the galleries on weekends; and (2) curators who must justify their enthusiasms to someone else, and who thus need a favorable review to substantiate their purchase to, say, a board of directors. An example would be a director of a university museum. Every time I see Philip Pearlstein painting in a university museum, as I often do, I imagine that Hilton Kramer, who was Pearlstein's dogged supporter during Kramer's tenure at the *New York Times*, helped sell it to them.

Because visual art is retailing, most new art is sold in these three ways, in descending order of importance: (1) from dealer to collector, which is to say that a previously satisfied customer is sold something new; (2) from collector to collector, which is to say that one collector recommends an artist to another collector, as they might exchange hot stock tips, or the second collector admires an artist's work in the first collector's house; and (3) from artist to collector, which is to say that a collector asks an artist already in his collection whom else he should consider purchasing. Obviously, serious collectors are more likely to trust an artist than any reviewer, which is another way of explaining why in visual arts, unlike theater, a burgeoning reputation can survive negative reviews. A successful art dealer needs not good reviews but a good track record to succeed, just as a stockbroker must; and one element those two retailers have in common is that both persuade people to part with rather large amounts of money.

Visual art editions represent a promoter's attempt to wholesale what had previously been retail; and even though he is dealing in visual art, a print promoter is essentially a wholesaler, selling not to individual collectors but to local dealers, especially outside his immediate turf. Two differences between a book publisher and a print promoter are that the latter produces editions in smaller numbers and claims that his product will increase in value, which is to say that even in his wholesaling the art dealer is performing a most extraordinary magic, a legerdemain that I find insufficiently appreciated in the art world — of selling something for many times its production costs. Contrast him or her to the retailer who says, "Look, this cost me six; I'll sell it to you for eight," and you will realize how rare in even decadent capitalism is the art dealer's talent.

Trade publications have different functions in literature and the visual arts. The reason why most art gallery advertisements in magazines resemble the tombstones of stockbrokers is that such advertisements don't sell art, but are instead intended to establish "presence" (aka credibility) with artists, customers, and colleagues. One art dealer told me that an ad with a full color reproduction of an artist's work is actually aimed not at regular customers but at other dealers, ideally in other cities, who might judge the work reproduced attractive to the tastes of their own regular customers. Art magazines actually influence not art sales but art discussion, which is to say table chatter, whether over coffee or drinks in artists' studios, or over the lunchrooms in art schools, where magazines are read with far greater seriousness than literary magazines in the writing schools. Therefore, what is really reviewed in art magazines, especially in longer articles, is not art per se but terminologies of understanding.

Don't underestimate the power of newspaper publicity in merchandizing new book titles. The hoopla surrounding the discovery of Andrew Wyeth's "Helga" paintings indicated that what was ultimately for sale was not paintings for only a few million dollars but books for many more millions. Don't underestimate either the power of book reviewing in the mass-merchandizing of culture. It is commonly said that any new book reviewed on the front page of the *New York Times Book Review* will, regardless of whether the review is favorable or not, sell ten thousand more copies. (This was told to me by a former editor of the *Review* in the course of dismissing the art world as strictly business, but I had to remind him that if the new book retailed for $20, then two hundred grand changed hands. Few gallery shows are so successful.)

In a book of mine published over a decade ago, *The End of Intelligent Writing*, I showed how the *New York Review of Books*, co-founded and co-owned by a Random House vice-president, has consistently favored Random House produce, first in reviewing them, second in using Random House writers as reviewers, third in prepublishing excerpts from books on the Random House list; and one reason why Random House has been more successful at merchandizing certain kinds of political criticism and literature has been the collaboration of the *New York Review*. Not even the most ambitious art gallery, not even the most rapacious art collector, ever tried to do something similar in visual art, because it would, in truth, be unnecessary. For all of, say, Hilton Kramer's blathering to the contrary, art magazines are less vulnerable to corruptions than book reviews.

Nonetheless, precisely because visual art is retailing, its corruptions necessarily involve far fewer people. The principal accrediting agency in establishing reputation is the public museum which doesn't sell art as much as raise the prices for art that had previously been sold. (There is no comparable institution in literature.) That is why collectors like to sit on the boards of such museums, like to court staff curators, not only for advice on their own purchasing, but also to advocate shows that would draw upon their own collections, etc.

The principal problem of the visual arts world, as I see it, is that the number of galleries that actually sell work, rather than show it, are too few; the number that can influence museums is too few. That accounts for the current phenonemon, familiar to all, of insufficient disparity in institutional taste. It seems to be nothing short of scandalous that, in exhibiting recent art, the most prominent museums in New York City have essentially the same enthusiasms, confirm the same myths, etc. There isn't really a free market that allows the establishment of great reputations apart from those institutions, even though we know that in visual art, more than any other art, the top reputations of a certain time are likely to be forgotten at a later time. Don't forget that one of MOMA's favorite artists in the 1950s was Ben Shahn. In part because the art world is smaller than the literary world (and just as there are fewer art magazines than literary magazines, so there are fewer art critics than literary critics), reevaluations of, say, paintings' past, take place with far greater rapidity.

Autochronology

In the triviality, commonplaceness, and chaos which modern life cannot exclude, creating art is a force against dissolution. With de Kooning, painting is a total vocation, in that painting makes him what he is. — Harold Rosenberg, *Willem de Kooning* (1973)

1940 Richard Kostelanetz born New York, New York, 14 May.

1942 Identifies letters of the alphabet in the branch formations of the trees.

1944 Impresses adults with arithmetical tricks, mostly involving calendar dates and days of the week.

1951 Family moves to suburban Westchester — detached house with lawns on an approximate grid of streets.

1954 Decides writing should be his profession.

1956 Sings bass in All-State High School Choir, conducted by William Dawson of Tuskegee Institute.

1957 Sees first Mondrian paintings and is haunted by them.

1958 Matriculates at Brown University, eventually majoring in American Civilization.

1959 Decides not to take any further courses in art or music or "creative writing."

1960 Meets S. Foster Damon, Brown's noted Blakist, who teaches not how to write but how to be a productive, professional writer — there is a crucial difference.

1961 Coedits an off-campus literary magazine and is nearly expelled from college for publishing a colleague's putative pornography. Learns of Ad Reinhardt.

1962 Woodrow Wilson Fellowship for graduate work in American History at Columbia University.

1963 Discovers J. S. Bach through his "Passions" and then the music of Charles Ives and John Cage. Publishes critical prose in periodicals. Scores first book contracts.

1964 Fulbright scholarship, King's College, University of London. With little else to do away from home, briefly studies harmony and music composition.

1965 Hears Dom Sylvester Houédard lecture on "Machine Poetry and

Poetry Machines" at London's Institute of Contemporary Art. Returns to New York forever, resolving never to leave home again. Edits and coauthors *The New American Arts*. Meets Robert Indiana, Milton Babbitt and then John Cage.

1966   Reads Moholy-Nagy's *Vision in Motion* for the first time. Moves to East Village, forsaking academia for bohemia.

1967   Guggenheim Fellowship. Writes first poems worth preserving, discovering other uses for 8½" by 11" sheets of paper.

1968   Flunks preorals for Ph.D. and unequivocally retires from graduate school. Authors *The Theatre of Mixed Means*. Initial "illuminated demonstrations" of visual poetry, projected on slides with a voice-over narration, and initial publication, in both magazines and anthologies, of creative work. Begins verbally minimal fictions.

1969   Begins visual fiction and drafts, as an implicitly prophetic outline of future work, a much-reprinted manifesto of "Twenty-Five Fictional Hypotheses." Purchases John Furnival's six-panel masterpiece of visual poetry, "Tours de Babel Changées en Ponts."

1970   First book of creative work published. Edits documentary monographs on Moholy-Nagy and John Cage, as well as an anthology of *Imaged Words & Worded Images*. Cofounds *Assembling* and Assembling Press.

1971   Edits an anthology of *Future's Fictions*.

1972   Accepts first adult job, teaching arts one night a week to policemen. Begins numerical art.

1973   Edits *Breakthrough Fictioneers*, which remains unsurpassed as a gathering of radical fictional alternatives.

1974   Writes and narrates "Poetry to See & Poetry to Hear" for Camera Three, CBS television. Assimilates Theo van Doesburg. First silk-screened prints. Objects to precious obscurities in "Art." Drafts *Recyclings*, consciously regurgitating earlier writings for a different future. Moves to SoHo, shifting residency (and other allegiances) from Literature into Art.

1975   First one-man New York exhibition. Drafts *Constructivist Fictions*. Draws prolifically. Makes initial audiotapes and then videotapes, adding new arts without abandoning old ones. Appearance of several volumes of creative work to few reviews. Edits *Essaying Essays*, which likewise remains an unsurpassed graveyard of alternatives.

1976   Visits Mount Sinai, the beginnings of Western civilization, and then the Basel Art Fair, perhaps the end. Makes first films and photolinens. Establishes the Future Press. Stages sexti-media presentation of "Openings & Closings," 330 one-sentence stories. NEA-Visual Arts Services Grant.

1977   Visiting Professor of American Studies and English, University of Texas at Austin. Edits *Esthetics Contemporary*. Tours extensively around the United States, discovering the existence of "an audience" familiar with various works. Makes first photographs worth publishing. Founds RK Editions, initially to redistribute books that had flunked with their initial publishers. Objects to person-categories, such as "artist" or "writer," as needlessly self-restrictive; prefers "maker" or nothing.

1978   "Wordsand," a comprehensive retrospective of creative works with words, numbers and lines, on books, prints, drawings, audiotapes, videotapes, and films, begins a three-year tour, its catalogue containing, in lieu of illustrations, autobiographical-theoretical essays. Produces first hologram whose entire visual content is syntactically circular sentences about holography. Purchases four Ad Reinhardt prints.

1979   Organizes and later edits *American Writing Today* for "Voice of America." Finishes *Reincarnations*, a book-length sequence of self-photographs that appears as a book, and "Recall," another book-length sequence that appears only in parts, in magazines. Publishes *Exhaustive Parallel Intervals*, an extended fiction — a novel, if you wish — whose pages contain only numerals. NEA Planning Grant for Art in Public Spaces.

1980   First production of a theatrical text, "Epiphanies," during a literary festival at the University of North Dakota. Finishes *Autobiographies*, which is not a sustained self-portrait but a mosaic written in various formats, in various styles, at various times, even in part by other people, incidentally bringing together earlier training in historiography with later artistic preoccupations.

1981   Collects previous essays into *The Old Poetries and the New* for a "prestigious" university press series of Poets on Poetry, each of whom sell at least twice as many books. Receives an invitation and, more important, a stipend from the DAAD Berliner Kunstlerprogram, living in Europe for the first time in sixteen years, and discovers for himself the truth frequently heard for many years before — that many institutions in Europe are far more sympathetic to avant-garde proposals than those at home. Thanks to a commission from Sender Freies Berlin and an invitation from the Electronic Music Studio of Stockholm, completes first extended audiotape, *Invocations*. Unsuccessful finalist in a public art competition in Portland (OR).

1982   Returns to Europe to complete *Die Evangelien/The Gospels*, respectively one hour and two hours, for German Radio, and a film "Epiphanies" for German television. First of several foreign-language radio feature programs about "The Art of Radio in North America."

1983   Applies without success for a position running a writing program in an arts college, emphasizing criticism and experimental fiction — a job that remains conceptually more attractive than such conventional ones as teaching only "poetry" or "fiction."

1984   A book selection of "Epiphanies" appears in German only. A composition of and about the sound of New York City is premiered at Westdeutscher Rundfunk.

1985   Receives Senior Fellowship from NEA-Visual Arts for further work in Book Art. Second major hologram, "Antitheses." First of several residencies at the Experimental TV Center, Owego, NY, for video work initially with character-generator and later with Amiga synthesizer.

1986   Applications to NEA Music, Media and Literature do not succeed, illustrating, in our government's mind at least, that work in visual art must have measurably higher "quality." Drafts several manuscripts of minimal fiction that have so far appeared only in literary periodicals.

1987   Completes *The Old Fictions and the New* that collects critical essays on fiction. Completes, with Martin Koerber, the sixth sound track, each in a different language, with different authentic testimony, of a 21-minute film — "prize winning," thanks to one award — about the Great Jewish Cemetery of Berlin. Narrates Robert Boynton Weyr's videotape profile of the work and the studio in which it was produced. Discovers name in three different histories of contemporary music composition, as well as *Who's Who in American Art.*

1988   Rewrites *Literary Video* initially for publication, perhaps for exhibition. Drafts "Minimal Audio Plays." Completes hour-long audiotape of and about the sound of baseball, *Americas' Game.* Edits raw videotapes into several distinct extended works that comprise an oeuvre.

1989   Realizes a pluralistic professional situation where he can work at any time in any one or more of several areas, with roughly equal ease and ambition. Completes *Unfinished Business*, collecting a quarter century's worth of unfunded proposals, and *On Innovative Art(ist)s* which collects from the same period previously published essays on the expanded field of visual art.

Index of Proper Names

Someone once said that Cervantes managed to build into Don Quixote *all the possibilities that other novelists spent the next four centuries exploring. Similarly, Dr. Samuel Johnson used practically all the genres that later critics and scholars were to employ: the book review, the essay, the preface or introduction, the biographical-critical life of an author and judgment of his works, the editions, and the learned footnote.*
—Grant Webster, *The Republic of Letters* (1979)

343